New Perspectives on South-East Europe

South-East Europe presents a compelling agenda: a region that has challenged European identities, values and interests like no other at formative periods of modern history, and is now undergoing a set a complex transitions. It is a region made up of new and old European Union member states, as well as aspiring ones; early 'democratising' states and new post-communist regimes; states undergoing liberalising economic reforms, partially inspired by external forces, whilst coping with their own embedded nationalisms; and states obliged to respond to new and recurring issues of security, identity, well-being, social integration, faith and secularisation. This series examines issues of inheritance and adaptation. The disciplinary reach incorporates politics and international relations, modern history, economics and political economy and sociology. It links the study of South East-Europe across a number of social sciences to European issues of democratisation and economic reform in the post-transition age. It addresses ideas as well as institutions; policies as well as processes. It will include studies of the domestic and foreign policies of single states, relations between states and peoples in the region, and between the region and beyond. The EU is an obvious reference point for current research on South-East Europe, but this series also highlights the importance of South-East Europe in its eastern context; the Caucuses; the Black Sea and the Middle East.

More information about this series at
http://www.palgrave.com/gp/series/14733

Zdravko Petak
Kristijan Kotarski
Editors

Policy-Making at the European Periphery

The Case of Croatia

palgrave
macmillan

Editors
Zdravko Petak
Faculty of Political Science
University of Zagreb
Zagreb, Croatia

Kristijan Kotarski
Faculty of Political Science
University of Zagreb
Zagreb, Croatia

New Perspectives on South-East Europe
ISBN 978-3-030-08814-9 ISBN 978-3-319-73582-5 (eBook)
https://doi.org/10.1007/978-3-319-73582-5

Cover illustration: Amana Images Inc | Getty Images

Printed on acid-free paper

This Palgrave Macmillan imprint is published by the registered company Springer International Publishing AG part of Springer Nature.
The registered company address is: Gewerbestrasse 11, 6330 Cham, Switzerland

Contents

Contributors

Nikola Baketa Institute for Social Research, Zagreb, Croatia

Predrag Bejaković Institute of Public Finance, Zagreb, Croatia

Luka Brkić Faculty of Political Science, University of Zagreb, Zagreb, Croatia

Anita Čeh Časni Faculty of Economics and Business, University of Zagreb, Zagreb, Croatia

Milan Deskar-Škrbić Erste Bank, Zagreb, Croatia

Ivana Keser Institute for Development and International Relations, Zagreb, Croatia

Kristijan Kotarski Faculty of Political Science, University of Zagreb, Zagreb, Croatia

Sanja Maleković Institute for Development and International Relations, Zagreb, Croatia

Petra Palić The Institute of Economics, Zagreb, Croatia

Ivan Pepić Global Studies Institute, University of Geneva, Geneva, Switzerland

Zdravko Petak Faculty of Political Science, University of Zagreb, Zagreb, Croatia

Ana Petek Faculty of Political Science, University of Zagreb, Zagreb, Croatia

Jakša Puljiz Institute for Development and International Relations, Zagreb, Croatia

Dagmar Radin Faculty of Political Science, University of Zagreb, Zagreb, Croatia

Hrvoje Šimović Faculty of Economics and Business, University of Zagreb, Zagreb, Croatia

Daniela Širinić Faculty of Political Science, University of Zagreb, Zagreb, Croatia

Velimir Šonje Arhivanalitika Consulting, Zagreb, Croatia

Hrvoje Špehar Faculty of Political Science, University of Zagreb, Zagreb, Croatia

Marina Tkalec The Institute of Economics, Zagreb, Croatia

Igor Vidačak Faculty of Political Science, University of Zagreb, Zagreb, Croatia

Maruška Vizek The Institute of Economics, Zagreb, Croatia

Vuk Vuković Oraclum Intelligence Systems Ltd., Cambridge, UK

Tihomir Žiljak Faculty of Political Science, University of Zagreb, Zagreb, Croatia

List of Figures

List of Tables

CHAPTER 1

Croatia's Post-communist Transition Experience: The Paradox of Initial Advantage Turning into a Middle-Income Trap

Kristijan Kotarski and Zdravko Petak

1.1 Introduction

Understanding the political and economic development of Croatia after it gained independence and left the Yugoslav federation in 1991 requires an understanding of the dynamics of the political and economic development that preceded these events. At the peak of industrialization and the development of the capitalist system in Europe (which took place rather late in Croatian lands, in the late nineteenth century), Croatia—then part of Austria-Hungary—was a peripheral European country. Croatia, Slavonia and Dalmatia were among the most underdeveloped parts of the Austro-Hungarian Empire (Good 1994: 877). No essential change ensued after Croatia had joined the Kingdom of Serbs, Croats and Slovenes in 1918. On the eve of World War II, Yugoslavia was a backwater Balkan country, less developed than Czechoslovakia, Hungary and Poland of the day.[1] Although Croatia (together with Slovenia) was located in the western part

K. Kotarski (✉) • Z. Petak
Faculty of Political Science, University of Zagreb, Zagreb, Croatia
e-mail: kristijan.kotarski@fpzg.hr; zdravko.petak@fpzg.hr

Z. Petak, K. Kotarski (eds.), *Policy-Making at the European Periphery*, New Perspectives on South-East Europe,
https://doi.org/10.1007/978-3-319-73582-5_1

of the country, more developed than its remaining regions, it was nevertheless on the far periphery of Europe in terms of economy, with inadequate industry and a strikingly large share of rural population (Vinski 1970). Immediately after World War II, Croatia still lagged behind all of Central Europe and its GDP was even lower than in some Southeastern European countries. In 1945, Croatia became part of the Yugoslav federation and a socialist system was introduced. In the ensuing period Croatia saw an intensive economic development, together with the rest of Yugoslavia (Woodward 1995). Between 1952 and 1980, Yugoslavia's GDP grew by 4.72 times and Croatia's by 5.18 times (The Maddison Project 2013)—considerably more than the GDPs of the then socialist countries of Central Europe, all of which were more developed than Croatia at the outset. Of those former socialist countries, only Slovenia, as the most developed federal unit of Yugoslavia, was more developed than Croatia.[2] Up until that time, the country had undergone intensive industrialization and urbanization and the share of its rural population had been substantially reduced, gradually shifting Croatia (together with the rest of former Yugoslavia) from the very far periphery to the semi-periphery of Europe.

Croatia became a medium developed country, strongly oriented to the internal Yugoslav market, and was therefore badly affected by the subsequent disintegration of that market. The amount of Croatian export to third countries was approximately half the amount of its export to other republics of the then Yugoslav federation (Petak 2005).[3] However, in the early 1980s, a marked stagnation of the economic growth occurred (Dubravčić 1993: 266). Following the negative growth rates in 1982 and 1983, GDP grew insignificantly; it reached its high in 1986 but that peak was followed by another significant drop. In 1990, when the Croatian Democratic Union led by Franjo Tuđman scored a convincing victory in the first free multiparty election in Croatia, the country was already in a severe recession and had dropped back to the level of the late 1970s (Bartlett 2003: 89). In spite of this, at the beginning of the transformation of European post-communist countries into democratic systems with market economies, Croatia and other developed parts of former Yugoslavia constituted the most developed part of the socialist world, together with Czech Republic. In the following year (1991), Croatia and Slovenia opted for independence and departure from the federation they had belonged to. This triggered a brutal war in Croatia, with thousands of lives lost and with enormous destruction. However, after the end of the Homeland War and restoration of peace in 1995, Croatia never got back on track of the development it had seen in the 1960s and 1970s. The newly gained independence and disintegration of the Yugoslav single market, the economic and social costs of the Homeland War, and the emergence of a clientelistic system centred around various economic and social groups marked the descent of Croatia's economy into a sort of crony capitalism (Franičević and Bićanić 2007: 640–641). By not limiting its role on regulatory goals the state, fully under control of the ruling party, was left open to "numerous acts of clientelism, favouritism, nepotism, localism, informal dealings and outright corruption" (Franičević 1999: 38), which strongly affected the development of institutions and public policies, causing Croatia to lag behind the Central European post-communist countries more and more. Even after the centre-left coalition won the 2000 election, thus ending the absolute domination of the Croatian Democratic Union (HDZ), which had ruled the country on its own in the 1990s, things did not change substantially.

Reasons for this should be sought in the institutional arrangements that were established and the ways of policymaking that were introduced after the evident signs of stagnation of modernization efforts of socialist Yugoslavia in the 1980s (Rusinow 1988: 1–5).[4] These periods of stagnation were additionally intensified by the development of institutions and the ways of policymaking in the early and mid-1990s, which had all the typical features of crony capitalism (Franičević and Bićanić 2007). The previously mentioned processes riveted Croatia deeply into the European periphery and the country never managed to get back on track of the modernization and development it saw under socialism, particularly in 1960s and 1970s. The system of institutional arrangements established in the early 1990s debilitated the modernization and entrepreneurial potentials of the society, causing the country's gradual descent to the bottom of the list of the present-day post-communist member states of the European Union.

The central puzzle of Croatia's post-communist transition has been therefore the extent of economic and institutional divergence with new EU member states bound by common historical legacy and imperatives of institutional transformation, following a collapse of the old institutional order. Comparative historical analysis points out that there are two critical junctures in Croatia's growth trajectory that led to severe economic divergence with the European core, and later even with countries portrayed as a semi-periphery and periphery. The first one has already been mentioned and it refers to the period of socialist stagnation in the 1980s. The second

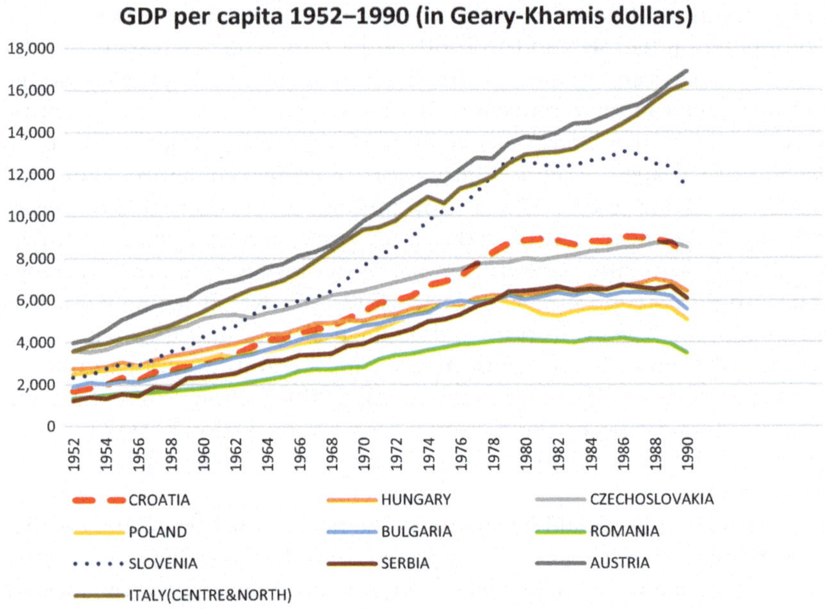

Fig. 1.1 GDP per capita 1952–1990 (in Geary-Khamis dollars) (Source: Maddison project (2013), author's own calculation)

one came on the wings of the global financial crisis (GFC), which ushered in the lost decade since 2008. Figure 1.1 shows that Croatia's GDP outperformed that of its socialist peers in the period from 1952 to 1980, although having more unfavourable initial position (Bolt and van Zanden 2013).

Despite authoritarian rule and socialist economy, the Yugoslav brand of socialism allowed at least some private initiative, unlike the more centralized approach taken by the rest of the Eastern bloc. By 1980, Croatia managed to close the gap with military dictatorships such as Portugal, Spain and Greece, even though it gradually diverged with the European core as exemplified by Austria and North/Central Italy. However, the latter trend was only reinforced due to the onset of socialist stagnation in the 1980s. On top of that came the economic devastation that arose from the Homeland War. However, until 1998 Croatia at least kept pace with the average GDP per capita of new member states (Central and Eastern Europe, CEE-10) as indicated by Palić et al. in Chap. 7 of this volume. Nevertheless, political choices made after gaining independence, such as partial reform equilibrium, the establishment of vast clientelistic networks and a captured state, are the major culprits of economic divergence with CEE-10 since 1999 (for a detailed discussion on 'captured state', see Chaps. 2 and 5, this volume). All of this came with even more vengeance when the GFC hit in 2008 and the captured state, deprived of essential steering capacity, collided with major external shock.

Wherein lies the rub for the emergence of inhibiting political economy structures that are likely to account for the potential continuation of divergence? This introductory chapter will firstly address the specific political economy of Croatia's transition and its impact on the current governance structure. Secondly, it will analyse the type of capitalism which emerged and consolidated in the years since Croatia's independence by using conceptualization first introduced by Bruno Amable (2003). Thirdly, we will address the governance capacity at work in Croatia, in order to show that difficulties are particularly striking in the very fragile system of the executive capacity of governance, where equally striking difficulties are caused by the problems related to steering capability and policy implementation.

1.2 The Political Economy of Croatia's Transition: The Case of Partial Reform Equilibrium

The violent dissolution of Socialist Yugoslavia represents a special political context in the overall comparison of Croatia's transition experience to the experience of other post-communist economies. In spite of this difference, the case of Croatia's transition reflected a similar dilemma facing other post-communist economies at the outset of this process. Namely, the political economy of double transition entails a difficult choice of choosing an appropriate reform strategy.[5] On the one hand, the J-curve model postulates that reform costs are narrowly concentrated in the short run and their benefits are widely dispersed in the long run. Hence, the central challenge of this model is the appropriate compensation of losers that may act as ex ante veto-players due to necessity of walking through the valley of painful transition, so that the higher hills of the reformed system can be reached (Przeworski 1991). The other model of political economy of reform posits that gains from engaging in the reform process are narrowly concentrated in the short run, and their costs are widely dispersed across the whole economy, especially in the long run (Hellman 1998). This model claims that the winners in economic reform represent the biggest threat to successful long-term transition due to their attempt at state capture. This step is deemed as essential in protecting rent streams generated by partial reform equilibrium. Hellman's pioneering study finishes with a conclusion that political systems more open to losers' participation weaken the potential for state capture by initial winners and that reforms pay off politically and economically, even though there exists higher government turnover and politicians are faced with shorter average tenure.

The historical experience of Croatia fits into the second narrative which identifies the main threat to deepening reforms in the rank of winners. Even though Croatia's experience provides us with frequent government turnovers (six governments in the course of 1990s) and relatively short average tenures (less than two years), these rotations did not alter the ultimate balance of power and the ruling party's firm grip on power (Vlada RH 2017).[6] Unlike the impact of similar government rotations in CEE-8 countries (CEE-10 less Bulgaria and Romania), consecutive Croatian governments did not lead to the emergence of new political coalitions which would pave the way for comprehensive economic and political reforms. The decade encompassing the Homeland War (1991–1995) and its immediate aftermath can be described as a decade of competitive authoritarianism (Levitsky and Way 2002). Hence, the partial reform equilibrium winners did not face a truly credible political threat which could have punished their decision to postpone reforms. What lies behind this historical trajectory?

The mounting challenge of extinguishing violence and establishing a stable social order in the midst of a violent state-formation was primarily addressed by forging a dominant coalition. This coalition was forged between the proponents of the old elite (ex-nomenklatura) and new aspirants in the ranks of social elites such as Croatian diaspora (Sekulic and Sporer 2002: 98). Hence, the newly established personal connections served as a basis for manipulating the economy through privileges, which was in turn facilitated by personalized institutions. The most important set of privileges generated at the very outset of the reform period was the decision to allocate ownership rights in former socialist enterprises before establishing transparent capital markets and erecting a well-honed regulatory framework. The dominant coalition was based on the partition of economic and political power, whereby the latter had been indispensable in obtaining the former. To sum up, Croatia's transition experience displays characteristics of a mature natural state (North et al. 2009).

One of the crucial aspects of the initial transition period in CEE-10 countries and Croatia was the challenge of building capitalism without capitalists and the need to avoid falling prey to crony capitalism. Nevertheless, not all post-communist countries possessed equal doorstep conditions. Croatian and Slovenian economic structures were more efficient as compared to economic structures in other post-communist countries, and social elites that had gradually emerged in the Yugoslav self-management system had an incentive to protect their existing rents. Economic structures of other CEE countries had simply imploded, which enabled a relatively clean slate for reform implementation and the emergence of a new social order (especially in Visegrad Group countries). Unlike in Slovenia, the state of war in Croatia enabled the centralization of overwhelming power in the hands of the executive. While Slovenian elites were held more in check by competitive elections and nascent institutions of liberal democracy, that was not the case with Croatia.

As already stated, the disbursement of privileges centered around a non-transparent privatization process was essential in cementing the tenets of dominant coalition. Instead of restructuring non-efficient socialist enterprises and putting them up for sale to the highest bidder, the Tuđman regime decided on another sequencing of reforms. The credo of privatization was the need to foster market economy, but that process ended in creating clientelistic networks and a quasi-private sector that heavily relies on transactions and horse trading with the state.[7] Unfortunately, Croatian-style privatization has generated neither efficiency nor dispersion of political power. Adding an insult to injury, the state took over the restructuring costs, primarily by accommodating unemployed workers and granting them premature pension rights (Cvijanović and Redžepagić 2011).

At every single point when the durability of the dominant coalition was under threat due to dissatisfaction of excluded interest groups, the dominant coalition reshuffled to stave off the transition from 'limited-access order' into 'open-access order' (Ivanković and Šonje 2011). Croatian dominant coalition also had two other options: to crush contenders or to open and depersonalize institutions such as media, corporations, judiciary and political parties. However, they opted for establishing and reinforcing existing clientelistic networks. This is clearly visible in the continuous government expenditures expansion since 1995. In 1995 government expenditures had accounted for 41% of GDP but they climbed to 48% of GDP by 1998 (IMF 2017). Afterwards, this ratio remained consistently bigger than the ratio for all remaining CEE-10 countries. Therefore, the Croatian dominant coalition decided to hold onto power by relying on the old and tried method: the usage of fiscal illusion (Tanzi 2011).[8]

Expenditures earmarked for sickness and disability, compensation of state employees, subsidies and intermediate consumption played the most important role in co-opting new members of the dominant coalition.

We decided to use the sum of three of the aforementioned expenditure categories to proxy clientelistic politics in Croatia, especially as compared to CEE-10 (see Fig. 1.2). We omitted sickness and disability expenditures from our calculation since those data are only available on a consistent level since 2009 (Eurostat 2017a). However, it is noteworthy to mention that as of 2015 Croatia had the largest chunk of GDP earmarked for this category of public expenditures among EU-28 member states (4.9% of GDP), while CEE-10 average amounted to only 2.11%. This category and war veterans' pensions had not been included in the budget immediately after the Homeland War. Nevertheless, they were included in the budget after pressures and protests from dissatisfied war veterans and laid-off employees of privatized enterprises threatened the stability of the dominant coalition.

During its slow and painful transition Croatia managed to emulate formal structures of democratic capitalism, such as private property, political parties, and regular elections. Nevertheless, the Croatian development trajectory can be labelled as a 'modernization without development' (Fukuyama 2014). At a more substantive level, the country still lacks depersonalized institutions aimed at holding the ruling elite in check and fostering merit-based elites. This conclusion rests on the following matrix

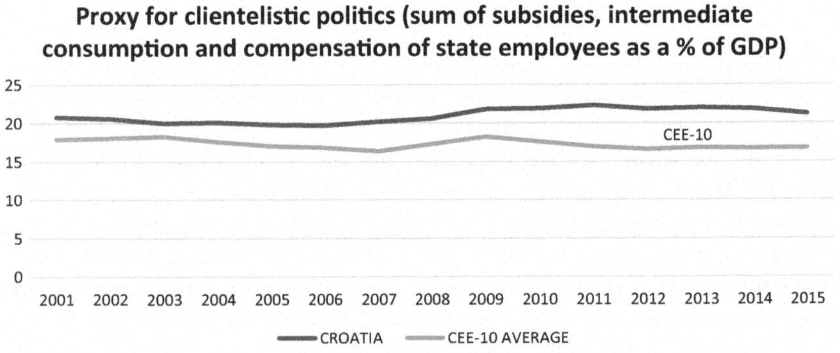

Fig. 1.2 Proxy for clientelistic politics (sum of subsidies, intermediate consumption and compensation of state employees as a % of GDP) (Source: Eurostat (2017a), authors' own calculation)

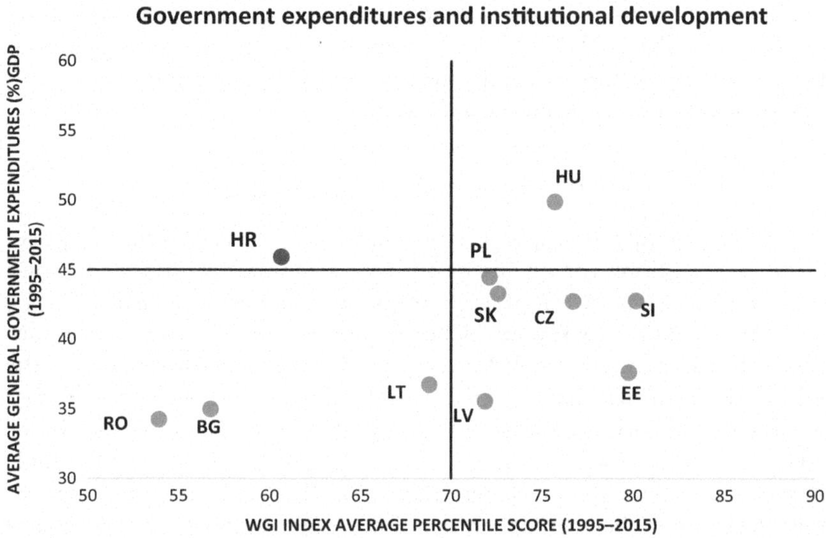

Fig. 1.3 Government expenditures and institutional development (Sources: World Bank 2017; IMF 2017, authors' own calculation)

which puts together our Worldwide Governance Indicators (WGI) index average percentile score and average government expenditures as a percentage of GDP for the period 1995–2015 (see Fig. 1.3).[9] The matrix shows a huge gap between Croatia's level of institutional development and average level of general government expenditures in the given period, the largest for the given sample of CEE-10. Unfortunately, the lack of institutional development paired with increased government expenditures makes an excellent breeding ground for clientelism and state capture.

1.3 Croatian Style Capitalism: Another Member in the Family of South European Capitalisms

Apart from shedding light on the role of political economy of partial reform equilibrium, explaining Croatia's sluggish performance as compared to its CEE peers requires a detailed account of Croatian capitalism which evolved since its independence. Having that in mind we will use Bruno Amable's conceptual framework which rests on the analysis of five key areas constituting organizational form of political economy. We argue that Croatia developed a typical South European variety of capitalism, according to the analysis of product market competition, wage-labour nexus, financial sector, social protection and education indicators; with only minor deviations from the ideal type.

1.3.1 Product Market Competition

The pattern of industrial specialization in Croatia remains primarily price-sensitive. Therefore, the quality of product, skill intensity and technological prowess seems to be out of reach for vast majority of Croatian producers, with the exception of several niche players like HS Produkt or Šestan-Busch. In the period from 1995 to 2014, Croatia and Slovenia were the only CEE countries that suffered a slight decrease in the level of their exports complexity, as measured by the Economic Complexity Index (ECI).[10,11] Other CEE countries such as Estonia, Poland and Romania overtook Croatia in the given period based to their ECI score and successfully leveraged their trade integration into regional supply chains (Hausmann et al. 2014).[12] In 2014, Croatian exports were still more complex than Bulgarian, Lithuanian and Latvian exports but this gap had been narrowing since 1995. Another important factor that points out the price sensitivity of Croatian exports refers to the real effective exchange rate (REER) trend and its impact upon balance of payments.

Prior to 2010, Croatian unit labour costs escalated rapidly and created massive current account deficit amounting to −8.8% of GDP in 2008. In the period from 2010 to 2016, Croatia suffered protracted internal devaluation, which led to REER depreciation, as measured against 37 trading partners (Eurostat 2017b).[13] This reversal contributed to the current account surplus of 2.7% GDP in 2016 (World Development Indicators 2017a). Furthermore, non-price coordination among Croatian producers is weak since not many of them are export-oriented and they compete against each other in a small domestic market. In a given case, the motivation to free-ride on jointly agreed deals like raising standards increases, since most of them perceive market competition as a zero-sum game.

State involvement in Croatia's economy is massive as evidenced by its 2013 Organization for Economic Co-operation and Development (OECD) Product Market Regulation index score, the highest among CEE-10 countries, with a final score of 2.08 (OECD 2017). The same can be said of the OECD state control index, which measures the presence of state-owned enterprises (SOEs) among 31 broad economic sectors. According to the ranking, only Poland, Bulgaria and Romania have slightly higher scores than Croatia (2.53) and more SOE involvement in the economy. When it comes to barriers to trade and investment Croatia keeps a moderate level of protection. The biggest progress has been achieved in easing cross-border trade since 2006. Croatia's *Doing Business* score, which measures business regulations across 190 economies, improved in the subcategory 'trading across borders' where its overall score jumped from 67.91 to 100, with successful EU negotiations taking the biggest credit for this improvement (Doing Business 2017). In the investment domain Croatia is open to foreign investment and preserves the right to equal treatment before the law for both residents and non-residents. Nevertheless, bureaucratic and political barriers remain and one of the greatest of these continues to be Croatia's inefficient and sometimes unpredictable legal system with a backlog of unresolved cases (U.S Department of State 2015).

Finally, Amable (2003) states that South European varieties of capitalism possess large dependence on SMEs as gross-value added creators and major employers. Unlike Greece, Italy, Portugal and Spain (GIPS), Croatian SMEs employ only 68% of the workforce, as compared to 78–81% range for the former group. They also generate only 54.8% of Gross Value Added (GVA), which is significantly less than the 68–70% range for the GIPS (Eurostat 2017c). Consequently, Croatian product market competition nexus exhibits strong similarity with South European capitalisms (price-sensitivity of exports, onerous state regulations, lack of non-price coordination). The only notable exception refers to the contribution of SMEs to economic aggregates. In that regard, Croatia differs in many respects from the predominant product market competition approach in CEE-10 countries, since they successfully developed their export sectors.

1.3.2 Collective Bargaining

Collective bargaining in Croatia currently takes place at industry and company/organization level. However, company-level bargaining is growing in importance. The comparison of collective-bargaining coverage between CEE-10 and Croatia shows that Croatia is much more similar in its structure to GIPS countries. Namely, all CEE-10 countries apart from Slovenia and Croatia have company-level collective bargaining schemes, while all GIPS countries put them at industry level. A case in point is that 61% of the Croatian workforce remains covered by collective bargaining and only Slovenia boasts a higher percentage (ETUI 2017). Among post-communist economies, Croatia enjoys the largest trade union density. Nevertheless,

Croatian labour market remains dual and large companies (primarily SOEs and state administration) grant higher labour protection in comparison to SMEs. Central government employees are 100% covered by collective bargaining, public administration employees 88.3%, public enterprises employees 74.8%, while only 36.2% of private sector employees can count on being covered by that arrangement (Eurofound 2015).

Tripartite partnership between government, trade unions and business associations remains elusive due to the fact that all three sides of the potential bargain face some structural limitations. The trade union scene is fragmented, which inhibits credible commitment because union leaders willing to compromise in negotiations might face the loss of membership and legitimacy. On the other hand, HUP (Croatian Employers' Association) as a central business association faces the difficulty of fostering internal consensus since the biggest members could easily undermine the common position and directly lobby government in a relatively small country like Croatia (Bagić 2013). Lastly, successive governments have lacked long-term vision for ensuring stable collective bargaining that would significantly improve the country's economic competitiveness.

Flexible work at the fringe gradually became more important and, in 2016, 20.8% of Croatian employees in the age group 15–64 were temporary employees, the third highest percentage among EU member states (Eurostat 2017d). This is a trait shared by almost all South European economies, and not something common among CEE countries. From time to time industrial relations can become conflictual and strikes occur but they are primarily located at the company level, when companies face the threat of insolvency or withhold wages. Periodic strikes or protests are sometimes seen among the ranks of public sector trade unions because of their ease of mobilization, as well as awareness of their political leverage.[14]

Finally, Croatia cannot claim active employment policy given its huge share of long-term unemployed among the active population (approximately 10%). In an EU-wide comparison, Croatia is in the group of lowest spenders on active measures, together with Slovakia, Bulgaria, Greece and Cyprus. The lack of active employment policy is not clear-cut, especially since Croatia does not spend much on passive measures, such as unemployment benefits, like Italy, Spain or Portugal does (European Semester Thematic Fiche 2016). After weighting all attributes in the wage-labour nexus we can conclude that on major counts Croatia resembles the GIPS countries' structures.

1.3.3 Financial Sector

Croatia's financial sector remains bank-based as proxied by the estimated ratio of fixed asset investments financed by bank loans relative to investments financed by equity or stock sales (GFDD 2017). There are no major differences between this feature among CEE countries and their GIPS peers. Large swaths of EU member states still remain dependent on bank-based financial sectors. Furthermore, banking concentration is high and the five biggest banks retain nearly three-quarters of Croatian market share, with 16 foreign-owned banks controlling 90% of bank assets (Hrvatska narodna banka 2016). Ownership concentration for foreign-owned banks goes beyond 90% threshold for a single foreign owner.

Nevertheless, judged by the trend of stock market capitalization of listed domestic companies relative to GDP, Croatia shares more similarity with GIPS countries than with CEE-10. In the years leading up to the GFC, Croatia saw one of the largest spikes in the ratio of stock market capitalization to GDP, with an increase from 26% in 2004 to 117% of GDP in 2007 (World Development Indicators 2017b). The sharp jump in Croatian stocks was followed by one of the biggest slumps in Europe (with similarity to patterns in Portugal, Spain and Greece). On the other hand, CEE-10 countries avoided a boom-and-bust cycle of the similar magnitude. In Croatia, the period before the GFC had been marked by a sharp increase in total economy leverage. Unlike the CEE-10 group, Croatia did not manage to successfully deleverage after the crisis. Private debt level to GDP has fallen but the leverage has been transmitted to the public sector balance sheet. Hence, Croatia's total debt (consolidated private sector debt + general government gross debt) remains without precedent in comparison to CEE-10 countries and Croatia is the most indebted EU member state from the Baltics all the way to Adria (see Fig. 1.4). More closely aligned with South European variety of capitalism than with export-led growth strategies of CEE-10, Croatia also relied on demand-led growth strategy, fuelled by an unprecedented credit binge. Furthermore, the aftermath of the GFC additionally increased the already high mutual dependence of banks and state sector in Croatia. Unlike Croatia, CEE-10 countries have successfully kept their credit to government/SOEs vs. GDP ratios remarkably stable.

Based on metrics provided by the World Economic Forum's 2015–2016 Competitiveness Ranking Croatia ranked 95th according to its financial market development component. It belongs in the cluster with GIPS

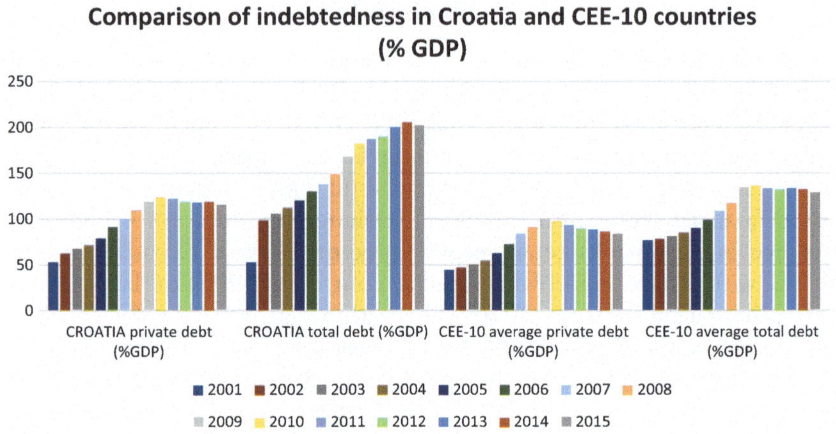

Fig. 1.4 Comparison of indebtedness in Croatia and CEE-10 (% GDP) (Source: Eurostat (2017e, f), authors' own calculation)

countries, which all rank lower than 75th place out of 140 countries, while on the other hand CEE-10 average score tallies at 4,1 (World Economic Forum 2016). That is significantly higher than Croatia's score of 3,6. Low sophistication of financial markets is visible in the absence of venture capital funds and there exists a generally low risk of corporate takeover. Mergers and acquisitions have mostly relied on government decision to privatize or sell-off government stakes in former majority SOEs, such as Hrvatski telekom or INA.

1.3.4 Social Protection

Croatia's expenditures on social protection benefits are moderate in EU-wide comparison and they represented 21.2% of GDP in 2015 (Eurostat 2017g). They are elevated as compared to the majority of CEE-10 countries but they are lower than in GIPS countries, let alone France and Scandinavian countries which are forerunners in that particular category of government outlays. However, one important feature of South European capitalism persists and that is unequal distribution of social benefits among end-users. A very wide range of problems and the state's limited capacity to address them has resulted in social policy fragmentation among particular interests (Dobrotić 2016). Some interest groups have been highly capable of mobilizing concentrated pressure on the state to redistribute resources (war veterans, pensioners) while the needs of unemployed and citizens at risk of poverty have been neglected.

Uncoordinated reforms have brought a myriad of parallel programmes and actors at multiple levels of government, which are responsible for different degrees of access to social protection (Stubbs and Zrinščak 2015). State-building, late Europeanization and dominant coalition formation produced vast clientelistic networks, especially in the category of sickness and disability, where the role of corrupt practices in distributing benefits has been rampant. As of 2015, Croatia had the largest chunk of GDP earmarked for this category of public expenditures among the EU-28 member states (4.9%), while the CEE-10 average amounted to only 2.11%. On the other hand, unemployment protection expenditures were one of the lowest in the EU (0.5% of GDP) and even lower than percentages for GIPS and majority of the CEE-10 (Eurostat 2017g), which is striking, given the fact that Croatia has the fourth highest unemployment rate in the EU.

To sum up, Croatia displays even more moderate level of social protection outlays as a percentage of GDP in comparison to South European economies and more generous outlays than the CEE-10 average. The case is not clear-cut in that regard. However, one common feature of South European capitalism prevails, the abundance of clientelistic networks and asymmetric access to social protection.

1.3.5 Education

Unlike the relatively low expenditures on education in GIPS countries (around 4% of GDP in 2015) and higher expenditures in the large majority of CEE-10, Croatia positions itself somewhere between, with an education budget that equals 4.7% of GDP (Eurostat 2017a). Amable's (2003) conceptualization rests on low enrolment rates in tertiary education as a common feature of South European capitalism. However, those features gradually eroded over time as more and more GIPS youngsters enrolled in tertiary education. Gross enrolment ratio analysis for both sexes put Croatia in a group of laggards, with one of the lowest enrolment ratios among GIPS and CEE-10 countries. Even though Croatian enrolment rates have significantly increased since 2000, other countries have made a bigger impact and Croatia satisfies Amable's criterion (World Development Indicators 2017c). Besides, higher education does not deliver cutting-edge results since Croatian universities are not among the top 500 in the world. The weakness of the Croatian vocational and higher education system is to be found in the third highest percentage of NEETs (young people neither in employment nor in education and training) in the EU, with Italy and Greece occupying top of the list (Eurostat 2017h). PISA (Programme for International Student Assessment) scores in 2015 revealed that Croatian pupils had fared rather worse in mathematics and science than all of their CEE-10 and GIPS peers, except for the Romanians, Bulgarians and Greeks (OECD 2015). The emphasis on lifelong learning is missing from the list of citizens' and policymakers' priorities since Croatia had the fourth lowest participation rate of population aged 25–64 in education and training, with Bulgaria, Romania and Slovakia occupying bottom of the list (Eurostat 2017i).

1.4 Croatian Capacity of Governance

When examining the factors that have turned Croatia into one of the lowest-ranking post-communist EU countries, the low level of governance quality is usually specified together with the above-mentioned shortcomings of the country's quality of institutions.[15] There is ample evidence that ranks Croatia at the lowest positions among the EU member states.[16] In Croatia's case, particularly questionable is the executive capacity of governance—a factor that reflects policymakers' capacity to formulate and implement policies (Petak and Petek 2009). There are numerous marked weaknesses in policy formulation in Croatia, arising from a very inadequate role of the analytics based on strategic planning and use of applied policy analyses in the formulation process (Koprić 2011; Sumpor 2013); numerous obstacles in policy coordination chains (Musa and Petak 2015); and a very limited use of evidence-based policy-making tools (Petak 2015); and a very limited inclusion of stakeholders and interested public in the policymaking process (Vidačak and Škrabalo 2014). It fares no better when it comes to policy implementation, especially when it comes to implementation of strategic development documents (Mirošević 2012).

In this respect, Croatia is a classical example of a weak state, used by Tanja Börzel (2011) as a common label for all Southeastern European countries. Weak states are those not capable of collecting taxes, organizing their land registers, controlling their borders and ensuring efficient monitoring of their policies. In such countries, the structures denoted by Page and Jenkins (2005) as *policy bureaucracy*—the rather autonomous structures that shape fundamental public policies together with incumbent politicians—are generally poorly developed. Instead, the public administration structures are very politicized; the hiring, promotion and rewarding of civil servants strongly depend on their loyalty to the ruling political elites (Koprić 2011). Paradoxically, all of this comes in spite of being the biggest spender on executive and legislative organs of the government among the EU-28 with a staggering 4.8% of GDP, while the CEE-10 averages only slightly below 3% of GDP (Eurostat 2017a).

1.5 Conclusion

The analysis conducted in the previous four sections places Croatian economy into the league of demand-led economies, which do not possess the institutional framework necessary for ensuring international competitiveness. Despite some progress in several aspects, such as REER depreciation since 2010, Croatia still lacks coordinated wage bargaining that can be used to hold down labour costs over the period of a whole business cycle. The same can be said about costs due to excessive product market regulation. On other hand, the Croatian education and vocational training system cannot support incremental innovation and ensure quality-based competitiveness. Finally, the Croatian financial sector lacks the flexibility needed for substituting capital for labour over time in order to boost quality of products and productivity of labour. In the absence of supportive institutions the Croatian economy has developed a high tolerance for debt-fuelled consumption, in a manner similar to its GIPS peers (Hall 2012).

In the nine years since the outburst of the GFC, Croatia's economy remains burdened by excessive macroeconomic imbalances. It has total debt level (public and private debt) larger than any other post-communist economy, which works in tandem with imminent demographic catastrophe due to high mortality and high youth emigration rates. Additionally, Croatia's median age of 42.7 (one of the highest in the world) directs Croatian politics in the status quo protection mode, which further saps its low long-term growth potential. Hence, the political economy of partial reform equilibrium combined with Croatia's adoption of key features present in South European variety of capitalism go a long way in explaining the paradox of initial advantage turning into a middle-income trap.

The circle was thus complete. The huge rent-seeking costs of institutionalized arrangements characteristic of a captured state, followed by the costs of maintenance of the social system, robust deindustrialization, and loss of traditional markets, has made it impossible for Croatia to keep the pace with other CEE countries. Instead, the country has strengthened its peripheral status even more strongly than it was a few decades ago, becoming a European super-periphery (Bartlett 2013; Bartlett and Prica 2013). This book is dedicated to the causes of this situation, but also to the prospects for development of the policies that could pull Croatia out of its peripheral status in the near future.

Notes

1. In 1952, Croatia's GDP was 1709 GK dollars and the Yugoslav average amounted to 1333 GK dollars. The socialist countries of Central Europe averaged 2960 GK dollars. As for Southeastern Europe, Croatia's GDP ranked second to Bulgaria's (1893 GK dollars) but was ahead of Romania's (1333 GK dollars) and Albania's (1046 GK dollars).
2. For a thorough understanding of the fact that Croatia acquired most of the characteristics of the unsuccessful Southeastern European economies during its transition, one should take into account the cost of dissolution of Yugoslavia and the former Yugoslav market.
3. Until 1990, Croatia was more dependent on the Yugoslav single market than on its exports to other countries, even though of all Yugoslav republics, it was second only to Slovenia in its exports to the countries of the then EEC. The importance of the then Yugoslav single market is reflected in the fact that the total sales of Croatian companies in other federal units in the mid-1980s was 3.19 times higher than its exports to third countries, mostly those of the then EEC (primarily Germany and Italy) and USSR. Croatia's import recorded a similar ratio (2.36). Slovenia was even less dependent on the single market (export—1.86, import—1.71). The ratios of other members of the former Yugoslav federation were much higher (Petak 2005: 60). The war, disintegration of the former federation and sudden loss of most of that market resulted in a collapse of a huge number of companies, the loss of hundreds of thousands of jobs and general economic breakdown. The proportions of this breakdown are clearly illustrated by the employee–pensioner ratio. In the late 1980s and early 1990s, this ratio was in Croatia still approx. 3:1 (it should be noted here that back in the early 1950s it was approx. 8:1). In the late 1990s, after many of those who had lost their jobs had been retired, the ratio was reduced almost to 1:1 (Vukorepa 2015).
4. The research carried out by Slovenian economist Aleksander Bajt showed that the investment efficiency of the socialist Yugoslavia was lower than that of the comparable countries of the then periphery of European capitalism—Ireland, Portugal, Spain, Greece and Turkey. Bajt showed that the highest GDP growth rate achieved by Yugoslavia in the period between

1960 and 1980 was characterized by a markedly large share of gross investments and a markedly small share of personal consumption of its population. The Yugoslav ratio of investments to GDP (0.17) was much lower than the average of the above-mentioned countries—0.265 (Turkey 0.31, Portugal 0.30, Greece 0.27, Spain 0.26, Ireland 0.185). However, Bajt's paper does not give details of the efficiency of investments in Croatia and Slovenia (Bajt 1988: 13).

5. Double transition refers to the transition from more or less non-market economic structures into full-fledged market economy and from one-party authoritarian political system into liberal democracy.
6. The ruling party at that time was conservative Croatian Democratic Union (HDZ).
7. A vivid example is the case of Agrokor, the largest national company led by the Balkan oligarch Ivica Todorić. The story of Agrokor's expansion to become the biggest national company can be roughly divided into two periods. The first period marks the expansion on the wings of insider-privatization in the 1990s (Šonje 2017). The second period starts after 2003 and is related to debt-fuelled expansion with the goal of achieving vertical integration through numerous and over-ambitious regional takeovers. From 2003 to 2016 Agrokor amassed 3.5 billion of EUR of debts to creditors and 2.2 billion of EUR debts to suppliers, totalling six times its equity (Buckley 2017). Over-expansion backed by high leverage, poor cost control and inadequate corporate governance structures were important triggers for Agrokor's collapse. For instance, its owner, Balkan oligarch Ivica Todorić had a 95% stake in the company and was not willing to surrender any control to new shareholders. However, this line of inquiry should not overshadow the political background of this story. Agrokor's expansion was politically sponsored either directly or indirectly over the last two decades. There are many instances of political sponsorship: insider privatization of Unikonzum and other companies in the 1990s; massive agricultural subsidies; lax enforcement of payments regulation; inadequate financial regulation of promissory notes issuance (CNB was not specially tasked for this job); tolerance for the conflict of interests in the ranks of private pension funds' managers who also sat in supervisory boards of Agrokor's companies and used insurees' payments for investing in Agrokor; lax enforcement of Competition Act; politically sponsored credit lines by the Croatian Bank for Reconstruction and Development (HBOR) and quasi-private Funds of Economic Cooperation. All of this was abetted by lax enforcement of campaign financing regulations and a revolving-door policy between Agrokor and both HDZ and SDP-led governments.

8. Fiscal illusion presupposes that citizens see things that do not exist (overestimation of fiscal multiplier from public expenditures) and do not see things that do exist (public debt burden and future inefficiency).
9. WGI index average percentile score represents a composite governance index calculated by multiplying each country's yearly score in every category with equal weight. This procedure is conducted across all six categories (rule of law, regulatory quality, control of corruption, government effectiveness, political stability and voice & accountability). We then added scores for every subcategory, for every given year and country, in order to produce a cumulative score which proxies the overall quality of governance. Finally, we calculated a mean score by using available data in the period from 1995 to 2015. We also calculated the mean for determining the average level of general government expenditures.
10. However, the value of Slovenian ECI (Economic Complexity Index) is double the size of Croatian ECI (1.466 vs. 0.773 in 2014).
11. The Economic Complexity Index measures ubiquity (the number of countries producing identical product) and diversity (the number of distinct products the country makes). More diversity and less ubiquity elevates a country in the rank of knowledge-based economies.
12. As of 2014, Croatia had the lowest export revenue per capita in constant dollars among CEE economies (Hausmann et al. 2014).
13. Only Ireland, Greece, Cyprus, Portugal and Hungary posted greater REER depreciations.
14. This leverage can be measured with the help of wage differential in the private and public sector. Employees in SOEs earn on average 40% more than employees in private sector companies (Trstenjak 2015).
15. Comparing Croatian capacity to governance with Bulgarian and Romanian, Bohle and Greskovits (2012) point out that, unlike those countries that were weak states in the socialist era, Croatia was initially a 'capable state', weakened during the transition period (Bohle and Greskovits 2012: 194).
16. Bertelsmann's SGI report for 2017 ranked Croatia at 40th place with respect to the quality of governance, within the list of 41 observed countries, EU and OECD members (Bertelsmann 2017: 17).

References

Amable, B. (2003). *The Diversity of Modern Capitalism*. Oxford: Oxford University Press.

Bagić, D. (2013). Neproduktivna ravnoteža moći: zašto nema kompromisa "socijalnih partnera" u Hrvatskoj i zašto je malo vjerojatno da će ga uskoro biti. In N. Vokić Pološki & A. Obadić (Eds.), *Zbornik radova okrugloga stola Uloga sindikata u suvremenome društvu* (pp. 15–35). Zagreb: Ekonomski fakultet.

Bajt, A. (1988). *Samoupravni oblik društvene svojine*. Zagreb: Globus.

Bartlett, W. (2003). *Croatia: Between Europe and the Balkans*. London: Routledge.

Bartlett, W. (2013, January–April). European Super-Periphery. *Academic Foresights, 7*. http://www.academic-foresights.com/European_Super-Periphery.html. Downloaded 7 July 2017.

Bartlett, W., & Prica, I. (2013). The Deepening Crisis in the European Super-Periphery. *Journal of Balkan and Near Eastern Studies, 15*(4), 367–382.

Bohle, D., & Greskovits, B. (2012). *Capitalist Diversity on Europe's Periphery*. Ithaca: Cornell University Press.

Bolt, J., & van Zanden, J. L. (2013). The First Update of the Maddison Project Re-Estimating Growth Before 1820, *Maddison-Project Working Paper WP-4*.

Börzel, T. (2011). When Europe Hits ... Beyond Its Borders: Europeanization and the Near Abroad. *Comparative European Politics, 9*(4–5), 394–413.

Buckley, N. (2017). Crisis at Croatia's Agrokor Poses Threat Beyond Creditors, *The Financial Times*, https://www.ft.com/content/ad8ecc4e-1edd-11e7-a454-ab04428977f9. Downloaded 13 April 2017.

Cvijanović, V., & Redžepagić, D. (2011). From Political Capitalism to Clientelism? The Case of Croatia. *Zbornik radova Ekonomskog fakulteta u Rijeci/Proceedings of Rijeka School of Economics, 29*(2), 355–372.

Dobrotić, I. (2016). Crisis and Croatian Welfare State: A New Opportunity for Welfare State Retrenchment? In K. Schubert, P. de Villota, & J. Kuhlmann (Eds.), *Challenges to European Welfare Systems* (pp. 301–324). Heidelberg: Springer.

Dubravčić, D. (1993). Economic Causes and Political Context of the Dissolution of a Multinational Federal State: The Case of Yugoslavia. *Communist Economies and Economic Transformation, 5*(3), 259–272.

ETUI (European Trade Union Institute), National Industrial Relations 2017. http://www.worker-participation.eu/National-Industrial-Relations/Countries. Downloaded 13 April 2017.

Eurofound. (2015). Croatia: Working Life Country Profile. https://www.eurofound.europa.eu/observatories/eurwork/comparative-information/national-contributions/croatia/croatia-working-life-country-profile. Downloaded 19 April 2017.

European Semester Thematic Fiche. (2016). Active Labour Market Policies. http://ec.europa.eu/europe2020/pdf/themes/2016/active_labour_market_policies_201605.pdf. Downloaded 14 April 2017.

Franičević, V. (1999). Privatization in Croatia. *Eastern European Economics, 37*(2), 5–54.

Franičević, V., & Bićanić, I. (2007). EU Accession and Croatia's Two Economic Goals: Modern Economic Growth and Modern Regulated Capitalism. *South East European and Black Sea Studies, 7*(4), 637–663.

Fukuyama, F. (2014). *Political Order and Political Decay: From the Industrial Revolution to the Globalization of Democracy*. New York: Farrar, Straus and Giroux.
Good, D. F. (1994). The Economic Lag of Central and Eastern Europe: Income Estimates for the Habsburg Successor States, 1870–1910. *Journal of Economic History, 54*(4), 869–891.
Hall, P. (2012). The Economics and Politics of the Euro Crisis. *German Politics, 21*(4), 355–371.
Hausmann, R., Hidalgo, C. A., et al. (2014). *The Atlas of Economic Complexity Mapping Paths to Prosperity*. http://atlas.cid.harvard.edu/media/atlas/pdf/HarvardMIT_AtlasOfEconomicComplexity_Part_I.pdf. Downloaded 18 May 2017.
Hellman, J. S. (1998). The Politics of Partial Reform in Postcommunist Transitions. *World Politics, 50*(2), 203–234.
Hrvatska narodna banka. (2016). Bilten o bankama 29. https://www.hnb.hr/documents/20182/950978/hbilten-o-bankama-29.pdf/f037d986-a62d-402a-bb32-9794e88a1a51. Downloaded 20 May 2017.
Ivanković, Ž., & Šonje, V. (2011). Nedemokratski kapitalizam i nova tranzicija. In *1. Zagrebački ekonomski forum* (pp. 5–21). Zagreb: Friedrich Ebert Stiftung.
Koprić, I. (2011). Contemporary Croatian Public Administration on the Reform Waves. *Godišnjak Akademije pravnih znanosti Hrvatske, 2*(1), 1–40.
Levitsky, S., & Way, L. A. (2002). The Rise of Competitive Authoritarianism. *Journal of Democracy, 13*(2), 51–66.
Mirošević, H. (2012, December). Analiza razvojnih dokumenata Republike Hrvatske. (EIZ Working Papers).
Musa, A., & Petak, Z. (2015). Coordination for Policy in Transition Countries: Case of Croatia. *Mednarodna revija za javno upravo/International Public Administration Review, 13*(3–4), 117–159.
North, D. C., Wallis, J. J., & Weingast, B. R. (2009). *Violence and Social Orders*. Cambridge: Cambridge University Press.
Page, E. C., & Jenkins, B. (2005). *Policy Bureaucracy: Government with a Cast of Thousands*. Oxford: Oxford University Press.
Petak, Z. (2005). Ekonomska pozadina raspada socijalističke Jugoslavije. In H.-G. Fleck & I. Graovac (Eds.), *Dijalog povjesničara-istoričara 9* (pp. 57–77). Zagreb: Friedrich Naumann Stiftung.
Petak, Z. (2015). Evidence-Based Policy Making and the Implementation of Regulatory Impact Assessment in Croatia. *Management and Business Administration. Central Europe, 23*(2), 147–162.
Petak, Z., & Petek, A. (2009). Policy Analysis and Croatian Public Administration: The Problem of Formulating Public Policy. *Politička misao/Croatian Political Science Review, 46*(5), 54–74.

Przeworski, A. (1991). *Democracy and the Market: Political and Economic Reforms in Eastern Europe and Latin America*. Cambridge: Cambridge University Press.

Rusinow, D. (1988). *Yugoslavia: A Fractured Federalism*. Washington, DC: The Wilson Center Press.

Sekulic, D., & Sporer, Z. (2002). Political Transformation and Elite Formation in Croatia. *European Sociological Review, 18*(1), 85–100.

Šonje, V. (2017). Agrokor treći dio: Plenkovićev zavjet. http://arhivanalitika.hr/blog/agrokor-treci-dio-plenkovicev-zavjet/. Downloaded 19 April 2017.

Stiftung, B. (2017). Policy Performance and Governance Capacities the and Sustainable Governance Indicators 2017. http://www.sgi-network.org/docs/2017/basics/SGI2017_Overview.pdf. Downloaded 16 September 2017.

Stubbs, P., & Zrinščak, S. (2015). Citizenship and Social Welfare in Croatia: Clientelism and the Limits of 'Europeanisation'. *European Politics and Society, 16*(3), 395–410.

Sumpor, M. (2013). Kako povezati kolektivne rocese participativnog strateškog planiranja I politiku (samo)volju vodstva? In A. Musa (Ed.), *4 Forum za javnu upravu* (pp. 27–45). Zagreb: Friedrich Ebert stiftung.

Tanzi, V. (2011). *Government Versus Markets: The Changing Economic Role of the State*. Cambridge: Cambridge University Press.

Trstenjak, J. (2015). Manje su efikasne, slabije likvidne ali s boljim plaćama od privatnih tvrtki, *Lider.* https://lider.media/aktualno/biznis-i-politika/hrvatska/manje-su-efikasne-slabije-likvidne-ali-s-boljim-placama-od-privatnih-tvrtki/. Downloaded 23 April 2017.

U.S. Department of State. (2015). Investment Climate Statement, Bureau of Economic and Business Affairs. https://www.state.gov/e/eb/rls/othr/ics/2015/241530.htm. Downloaded 30 April 2017.

Vidačak, I., & Škrabalo, M. (2014). Exploring the Effects of Europeanization on the Openness of Public Administration in Croatia. *Hrvatska i komparativna javna uprava/Croatian and Comparative Public Administration, 14*(1), 149–187.

Vinski, I. (1970). *Klasna podjela stanovništva i nacionalnog dohotka Jugoslavije u 1938. godini*. Zagreb: Ekonomski Institut.

Vlada, R. H. (2017). Prethodne Vlade. https://vlada.gov.hr/prethodne-vlade-11348/11348. Downloaded 25 April 2017.

Vukorepa, I. (2015). Lost Between Sustainability and Adequacy: Critical Analysis of the Croatian Pension System's Parametric Reform. *Revija za socijalnu politiku, 22*(3), 279–308.

Woodward, S. L. (1995). *Socialist Unemployment: The Political Economy of Yugoslavia 1945–1990*. Princeton: Princeton University Press.

Databases

Doing Business. (2017). Historical Data Sets and Trends Data. http://www.doingbusiness.org/Custom-Query. Downloaded 22 May 2017.

Eurostat. (2017a). Government Finance Statistics (EDP and ESA 2010). http://ec.europa.eu/eurostat/web/government-finance-statistics/data/database. Downloaded 24 May 2017.

Eurostat. (2017b). Industrial Countries Effective Exchange Rates Including New Member States-Annual Data. http://ec.europa.eu/eurostat/web/exchange-rates/data/database. Downloaded 18 May 2017.

Eurostat. (2017c). Statistics on Small and Medium-Sized Enterprises. http://ec.europa.eu/eurostat/statistics-explained/index.php/Statistics_on_small_and_medium-sized_enterprises. Downloaded 21 May 2017.

Eurostat. (2017d). Temporary Employees as a Percentage of the Total Number of Employees, by Sex and Age (%). http://ec.europa.eu/eurostat/web/lfs/data/database. Downloaded 18 May 2017.

Eurostat. (2017e). Private Sector Debt, Consolidated – % of GDP. http://ec.europa.eu/eurostat/web/products-datasets/-/tipspd20. Downloaded 19 May 2017.

Eurostat. (2017f). General Government Gross Debt. http://ec.europa.eu/eurostat/web/products-datasets/-/tsdde410. Downloaded 19 May 2017.

Eurostat. (2017g). Social Protection Expenditure. http://ec.europa.eu/eurostat/web/social-protection/data/database. Downloaded 18 May 2017.

Eurostat. (2017h). Young People Neither in Employment Nor in Education and Training by Sex, Age and Labour Status (NEET rates). http://appsso.eurostat.ec.europa.eu/nui/show.do?dataset=edat_lfse_20&lang=en. Downloaded 18 May 2017.

Eurostat. (2017i). Participation Rate in Education and Training (last 4 weeks) by Sex and Age. http://appsso.eurostat.ec.europa.eu/nui/show.do?dataset=trng_lfs_01&lang=en. Downloaded 19 May 2017.

Global Financial Development Database (GFDD). (2017). Global Financial Development. https://data.worldbank.org/data-catalog/global-financial-development. Downloaded 14 July 2017.

IMF. (2017). *World Economic Outlook*. https://www.imf.org/external/pubs/ft/weo/2017/02/weodata/download.aspx. Downloaded 10 October 2017.

OECD. (2015). Data. http://www.oecd.org/pisa/data/. Downloaded 27 May 2017.

OECD. (2017). Product Market Regulation 2013. https://stats.oecd.org/index.aspx?DataSetCode=PMR. Downloaded 23 May 2017.

The Maddison Project. (2013). Maddison Project Database. http://www.ggdc.net/maddison/maddison-project/data.htm. Downloaded 20 September 2017.

World Bank. (2017). *The Worldwide Governance Indicators (WGI) Project*. http://info.worldbank.org/governance/wgi/#home. Downloaded 23 October 2017.

World Development Indicators. (2017a). Current Account Balance (% of GDP). https://data.worldbank.org/indicator/BN.CAB.XOKA.GD.ZS?locations=HR. Downloaded 28 May 2017.

World Development Indicators. (2017b). Market Capitalization of Listed Domestic Companies (% of GDP). https://data.worldbank.org/indicator/CM.MKT.LCAP.GD.ZS. Downloaded 23 May 2017.

World Development Indicators. (2017c). Gross Enrolment Ratio, Tertiary, Both Sexes (%). https://data.worldbank.org/indicator/SE.TER.ENRR. Downloaded 24 May 2017.

World Economic Forum. (2016). Competitiveness Rankings. http://reports.weforum.org/global-competitiveness-report-2015-2016/competitiveness-rankings/. Downloaded 15 May 2017.

PART I

Policy-Making Process in the Newest EU Member State

CHAPTER 2

Policy-Making Context and Challenges of Governance in Croatia

Zdravko Petak

2.1 Understanding Croatian Policy-Making Context

To understand the Croatian policy-making context in the period after the country gained its independence and left the Yugoslav federation in 1991, three fundamental factors affecting the policy context in a community should be analyzed—institutions, actors and ideas (Howlett et al. 2009). The specific nature of the democratization and economic transformation processes in Croatia is primarily reflected in the fact that they were guided by the state-building idea (Bićanić 1994) and that they took place in the context of the war that broke out within a year upon the introduction of the democratic system in the country. These two factors had a triple effect on the subsequent policy development context in Croatia (Zakošek 2008). First, the all-out war that broke out a few months after the May 1991 referendum on independence substantially curtailed the development of democracy in Croatia (Dolenec 2013). The prerequisite for a reform of

Z. Petak (✉)
Faculty of Political Science, University of Zagreb, Zagreb, Croatia
e-mail: zdravko.petak@fpzg.hr

Z. Petak, K. Kotarski (eds.), *Policy-Making at the European Periphery*, New Perspectives on South-East Europe,
https://doi.org/10.1007/978-3-319-73582-5_2

political and economic institutions—establishing of a "national identity and territorial limits" (Schmitter and Santiso 1998: 79)—was not met in Croatia in the early 1990s (Kasapović 2001: 16). Second, the logic behind the way the state-building and war-waging efforts affect institutions and actors is usually not compatible with democratic development and transformation of economic institutions. That fact strongly influenced Western Balkans national economies (Farkas 2017; Franičević and Bićanić 2007). And third, a combination in which the state-building idea and a state of war are predominant is very favorable for "authoritarian centralization" processes (Zakošek 2008: 589) and the establishment of an authoritarian government (Bartlett 2003). These processes dominated the design of Croatia's political system during the rule of Franjo Tuđman and HDZ—the party he led until his death in 1999.

The above-described context had a pivotal impact on the development of the economic and political systems in Croatia in the 1990s (Fisher 2006). Although it had a rather sound starting position for economic development at the beginning of its transition period (just like other more developed parts of former Yugoslavia—for instance, Slovenia), the war led to an economic collapse of the country as early as in 1991, continuing throughout 1992 and 1993 (Vojnić 1995).[1] The first GDP growth was recorded only in 1994 and it was not before 2004 that Croatia managed to reach the highest GDP level achieved in socialism (The Madison-Project 2013). The extent of the economic collapse is perhaps best reflected in the *dependency rate* (the ratio of insured persons contributing to pension funds and the number of pensioners): it dropped from 3.0 in 1990 to 1.97 as early as in 1994 to an incredibly low 1.14 in 2014 (Vukorepa 2015). The war also had devastating effects on the Yugoslav single market (Dallago and Uvalić 1998; Gligorov 1993), where the purchase and sale volumes of the companies from all federal units of the socialist Yugoslavia had been substantially higher between other federal units than to external markets (primarily those of the then EEC, but also of other countries) (Petak 2005). The fact that Croatia's sales of goods in the single Yugoslav market were twice as high as its sales in the markets of other countries is a telling indication of the above.[2]

The second aspect was the marked centralization of government and setting up a political system with pronounced authoritarian characteristics. In the two final decades of socialist Yugoslavia—in the 1970s and 1980s—an intensive decentralization was implemented (Bogoev 1991; Petak 2012).[3] After independence, Croatia underwent a constitutional redesign by which almost 90% of the budget funds came within the competence of the central government. This ratio has practically remained the same to the present day (Jurlina Alibegović 2013). As a result, a very centralized system has been created in which almost all issues are decided upon by the central government. At the same time, there has been a fivefold increase in the number of local self-government units, leading to a marked fragmentation of that level of government and significantly reducing its policy capacities (Koprić 2010; Petak 2011). Subsequently, a meso-level (counties) was introduced into the system, without sufficient policy-making capacity.

2.2 Main Actors and Their Influence on Policy-Making

Led by Franjo Tuđman, Croatia's first president, HDZ assumed the crucial role in policy-making after the first parliamentary election of 1990. Constitutionally, a semi-presidential system was introduced, but the actual impact of the key political actors was much more important. Under Tuđman's leadership, HDZ functioned as "a charismatic party with strong clientelistic elements" (Kasapović 2001: 22), and the issue of "statehood and how to achieve it" dominated among the policy-related issues (Henjak et al. 2013: 449). Under Tuđman's rule, a markedly centralized system of governance was created, in which crucial decisions would be made at informal meetings and by the president's advisory bodies. This system of government was replaced after the parliamentary election in early 2000, when a center-left coalition led by the Social Democratic Party (SDP) won. With the 2000 and 2001 amendments to the constitution, the semi-presidential system was abolished and a parliamentary system was introduced, strengthening the role of the government (Zakošek 2008).

The center-left coalition parties led by the SDP, which ruled the country between 2000 and 2003, set as their priorities Croatia's accession to NATO and European Union. The subsequent HDZ governments, led by Ivo Sanader (2003–2009) and Jadranka Kosor (2009–2011), continued in the same direction. Although HDZ departed from Tuđman's original program and moved closer to European democratic standards under Sanader's leadership, the party nevertheless maintained its very strong clientelistic arrangements with a number of interest groups, including war victims and war veterans (Stubbs and Zrinščak 2015). The arrangements were based on the institutionalized generous supports of various interest groups in exchange for their political support to the ruling party, as a sort of clientelistic networking of various financial demands from the government (Cvijanović and Redžepagić 2011). Over time, these arrangements became so institutionalized that not even center-left governments led by SDP could challenge them without significant political backlash.

When it comes to the influence of other interest groups on policy-making, research has not yielded very exact results as yet. Research on non-governmental organizations' influence on policies (Bežovan and Zrinščak 2007; Đokić and Sumpor 2013; Petak and Vidačak 2015) has shown that NGOs' influence on the policy formulation process is still limited, albeit there are examples indicating a growth of their influence in certain domains of social policy, for example, in the disabled persons policy (Kekez Koštro et al. 2012; Petek 2010).

Although the research on trade unions' influence on the government policies is rather modest, some studies have shown that the radical downsizing of the unions' membership (which has more than halved since 1990) has substantially affected their power (Bagić 2010; Kokanović 1999). In addition, there are large differences between the influence of the unions representing workers in the economy and those representing public and civil servants. The power of the former is considerably weaker, as can be seen from the fact that a large number of those employed in the economy are not members of any union.

Perhaps the strongest influence on policies is the one exerted by the business sector. However, the employers' association is not the primary source of this influence—it is the hidden power of major entrepreneurs, arising from their direct contacts with the authorities and not from the tripartite social partnership system (Petak and Vidačak 2015). The social partnership system initiated by the center-left government in 2001 (bringing the government, employers' association and unions together in the Economic and Social Council) has failed to establish itself as a form of collective bargaining on policies, unlike in the numerous democracies of Northern and Western Europe (Wilensky 2002).

2.3 Steering Capacity of the Croatian System of Governance

The markedly centralized system of governance, introduced in the 1990s and containing numerous authoritarian features, has led to the distinctive weaknesses of governance in Croatia. This equally applies to the steering capacity, which is basically used as an indicator of the quality of the formulation of the policies intended to be implemented nationally, and to the process of implementation of these policies. Indeed, some authors note that the development of the democratic political system and market economy in Croatia has been accompanied by the state's decreased capacity to formulate and implement its policies (Bohle and Greskovits 2012).[4]

There are different ways of describing the steering capacity of governance (Pierre and Peters 2005), but they basically refer to the policy formulation phase. When reviewing the steering capacity of governance in Croatia, we will contain ourselves to four relevant factors: the role of strategic planning, policy coordination, the role of evidence-based policy-making in developing policies, and the role of societal consultation.[5]

The first element refers to the strategic planning. It is one of the fundamental tools of the new public management. This type of policy planning has been in place in Croatia as a normative framework but has had a very low level of efficiency. The results of the surveys on the quality of governance in Croatia can be seen as evidence of that. In one of the surveys, carried out among several dozens of leading scholars and practitioners of governance in Croatia (GONG 2013a), more than 85% of the respondents opined that the fundamental task of the state administration reform was to introduce strategic planning tools into the governance system in Croatia. Although some progress in the introduction of strategic planning tools into the Croatian governance system has been made during the Europeanization process, the level of their institutionalization is still very limited (Perko Šeparović 2006; Sumpor 2013).

The quality of strategic planning in Croatia is clearly indicated by the fact that most of the strategies and development plans adopted by the Croatian parliament, Government or ministries usually lack some of the implementing elements that such documents should include. Having analyzed 87 development documents from the period between 1990 and 2011, Mirošević (2012) found that only 11 of those documents included all four key elements that have a direct impact on their implementability (a proponent, implementation plan, financing plan and source of financing).[6] Taking into account the fact that the analyzed documents—one third of them entitled "strategies"—were the fundamental documents of Croatia's developmental policies, this finding threw into serious doubt the quality of the strategic framework of these policies. In most cases, these documents ended up filed in drawers, failing to become implementation programs constituting a strategic framework for taking action. This problem—the inability to determine a long-term development orientation—was also clearly observed in the works of the governance researchers in Croatia (Koprić 2011).[7] Although the Europeanization process has had a limited positive effect on the quality of the preparation of development documents (Liha Matejiček 2015), the problems remain considerable. Evidence of it can also be found in the European Commission's annual reports on Croatia, often pointing at the lack of strategic planning tools, which has a crucial effect on the steering capacity of the policies proposed by the Croatian government.[8]

The involvement of scientists—particularly social scientists such as public administration experts, macroeconomists, social welfare policy experts and experts in other domains of this sector—in the process of developing policies is also very limited, although not non-existent.[9] The problem, however, is that this involvement does not extend beyond the initial phases of policy formulation; it can rarely be found in the final phase of this part of policy process (Petak and Petek 2009).

The next dimension of the steering capacity is policy coordination—which is in Croatian case regularly one of the fundamental reasons for the inefficiency of the governance system. The studies that tackled the problem by investigating the functioning of the inter-ministerial coordination, coordination between the ministries and government and the way of functioning of the core executive (James and Staronova 2003; Musa and Petak 2015; Giljević 2015) indicated primarily that the core of the central government lacks an efficient, hierarchical strategic framework for directing the government's priorities. As a result, different strategies and fundamental development documents are interconnected. In addition, the arrangements of the horizontal coordination between ministries are very weak. Also, particularly inadequate are the arrangements for reconciling the differences between ministries before a policy proposal is submitted to the government. This is why uncoordinated materials from the ministries are often left to the committees of the government coordinating bodies and working groups that are, therefore, overloaded with details and cases that were supposed to be resolved by the lower levels of administration.

The next element of steering capacity problematic in Croatia is the usage of evidence-based policy-making tools. As part of the process of Europeanization and EU accession, the Office for Regulatory Impact Assessment was established in Croatia in 2007, only to be dissolved by a government decision as early as 2009. The office was dissolved so soon after its establishment because some media questioned its purpose and even claimed it was useless. Shortly afterwards, the European Commission warned that the office was required for ensuring a better regulation policy—one of the EU policies created by the OMC method (open method of coordination). Under such pressure, the office was reestablished within the Government Legislation Office as its separate department for regulatory impact assessment. A problem still persists; however, much legislation is still passed without being subjected to the regulatory impact assessment (RIA) procedure (Petak 2015).

The last steering-capacity element analyzed here is the societal consultation. In 2009, Croatian government adopted the Code of Practice on Consultation with the Interested Public in Procedures of Adopting Laws, Other Regulations and Acts, thus creating a basis for involvement of various interest groups in the policy development process. Nevertheless, studies on the involvement of various non-governmental stakeholders in policy-making in the Croatian case, particularly those belonging to civil society, showed a radically lower level of participation in comparison to developed democratic countries (Petak and Vidačak 2015).

2.4 Implementation Capacity of the Croatian System of Governance

For a long time, efficient policy implementation did not attract much attention from researchers and policy scientists. Research on the factors affecting policy implementation became one of the most important issues in policy process research (Sabatier 1991). The problem of implementation incorporates a series of elements, ranging from a government's general efficiency in policy implementation to the policy implementation monitoring capacity of ministries or agencies.

When the track record of successive Croatian governments in policy implementation is analyzed, preliminary indicators show that the country ranks at the lower end among the EU and OECD countries (Petak et al. 2017). It often happens that the government fails to implement numerous objectives of a policy or even to give up implementing the policies it has prepared for implementation for so long.[10] In the latter case, it is not just about giving up new policies; the legislative regulations within the policies that have been implemented for a while are also often changed without prior evaluation of the indicators of the progress made in attaining the objectives of a policy. The problems related to non-implementation of policies are too often solved "only by passing new laws and/or adopting new strategies, concomitantly with the neglect of the fact that they are useless if they are not implemented" (Bađun 2005: 296). Such evaluations of policy implementation indicate that Croatia has rather low government efficiency in the policy implementation phase. It turns out that the government is weak because it is not capable of implementing the policies it itself has proclaimed and designed.

An important problem here has to do with the capacity of monitoring the policies being implemented. The weaknesses in the monitoring of policies in Croatia constitute a serious structural problem due to the pronounced inefficiency present in this domain. The policies implemented by relevant ministries or various agencies must be monitored by central bodies of the Croatian government, but research has established that there is a fundamental problem here: the indicators required for monitoring policy implementation are usually very general and inaccurate, thus practically thwarting the systematic policy monitoring procedures (Koprić 2011: 21). Besides, the policy implementation-related reports are not being processed systematically. Clear evidence of this is the fact that, in 2012, only 54% of ministries and other administrative bodies submitted at least one or more reports on the implementation of individual policies and that only 15% of them submitted annual reports on their work (GONG 2013a).

This is why the fundamental priorities of public policies often fail to be realized in Croatia, even when the government manages to put them on the agenda, formulate them and legitimize them. This is why it is hard to precisely depict what measures set by the government were actually implemented in a particular period. Ministerial compliance also often becomes a problem in Croatia—in other words, are the policies implemented by the ministries fully coordinated with the government program? In cases where the level of "factionalism" is particularly high, ministers are much less motivated to implement government programs in particular sectoral domains (Koprić 2011). The issue of the monitoring of line ministries and monitoring of agencies is also connected with it. Studies of the core executive of the Croatian government showed that no effective mechanisms of monitoring or evaluation of the efficiency of the implementation of government decisions have been in place (James and Staronova 2003).

The effectiveness of public policy implementation appears, therefore, as one of the major problems in exercising governance in Croatia. The above-mentioned studies devoted to this issue showed that Croatian governments only partly implement the policies defined in their strategies, multiyear programs and action plans. An even bigger problem is their inability to set clear and measurable objectives for individual policies. This has become a growing problem in the communication with the European Commission: the Commission often returns to its Croatian counterparts the draft projects based on which the applications for EU funds are made—not just because the clear policy analysis terminology is not used in them, but also because they often do not specify efficient sustainable mechanisms for monitoring the implementation of the policies for which the EU funds are requested. This is why the European Commission's European Semester Country Report underlines once again that the implementation problem remains one of the major challenges of the Croatian governance system (European Commission 2017: 50).

2.5 Final Remarks

The policy context in which policies have been developed in Croatia since the 1990s are characterized by the overlapping political, economic, social and cultural factors that have led to the creation of institutional structures and interest arrangements best described as captured state. It is a policy context in which the state works directly on behalf of the elites that, at the moment of the transformation of the socialist economy into the capitalist one, used their political power to gain the decisive power in the economic regulation processes.[11] At the same time, such a context in policy formulation and implementation was followed by a strong clientelism in the distribution of various sorts of privileges to the social groups ready to give their political support to the authority organized in such way.

However, understanding the policy context that has largely determined the way of policy development in Croatia after independence also requires understanding the role of ideas in the whole process. The fundamental idea that guided actors in the policy development referred to the symbolical issues of Croatia's statehood and independence, not to the specific issues of economic, social and sectoral policies that would ensure the country's stronger development potential. The role of ideas in policy development should never be ignored as a factor influencing the policy context, as the ability of the elites to transfer some ideas to the policy-development arenas may even be the crucial element for understanding the policy context (Campbell 1998).

The researchers studying the role of parties in the policy development process in Croatia have shown that crucial for the political parties in Croatia was the extent to which they represented the expressive preferences of their voters, linked to such identity-related issues like independence, sex education, the roles of tradition, and the Catholic Church, not the issues related to the distinctive impacts of different strategies of economic, social and sectoral policies. Indeed, the parties never really developed competing strategies for such policies; instead, "a real policy would be substituted with a symbolical policy of staged differences" (Petković 2009: 95).

The influence of institutions, interests and ideas on the policy context developing in Croatia since its independence has ultimately led to what literature calls weak state capacity (Börzel 2011), indicating that the country has a poor capacity for policy management. In the European context, such an evaluation is usually reserved for the countries of the Western Balkans. In these countries, this fact has had a crucial effect on both the nature of the policy process and the level of involvement of particular actors in the process (Thomas and Bojicic-Dzelilovic 2015). In this context, it is not just a weak state problem, but also a problem of weak societies (Sissenich 2010): it turned out not only that the Western European countries have much more efficient states with higher policy-developing capacities, but also much stronger societies and higher levels of horizontal policy actors' involvement in the policy process. The former Yugoslav countries have turned out to be a particular problem here: with the exception of Slovenia, the civil society organizations' influence on the policy process is still inadequate in those countries (Fink Hafner 2015).

The problem weak states are facing is that their capacity for reforms is significantly lower than that of capable states. Such states cannot formulate and implement the reforms of fundamental policies, even when favorable conditions for such actions are created and when the states with an efficient governance system try to carry it out. Having examined the reform implementation timing, Alesina et al. (2006) showed that, in essence, there are four situations when governments undertake reforms: when facing serious crises, when assuming power, when they are strong and stable enough, and when the executive authority faces relatively small limitations (Alesina et al. 2006: 1). On the other hand, weak states carry out only partial reforms instead (Hellman 1998) or no reforms at all.

Such a conclusion can in large measure be applied to Croatia, where not one of the four above-mentioned situations has served as a basis for carrying out reforms. The basic reason for this lies in the embedded interests of the elites and of the vulnerable groups with whom the elites have established clientelistic arrangements to prevent any significant changes. In Chap. 5, Vidačak and Kotarski offer several very convincing examples of how embedded interests remain a fundamental hindrance to potential reform ambitions of the executive authority. The key issue, therefore, is the fact that low capacity of Croatian governments to formulate and implement public policies, which are put on the agenda, emerges from clientelistic arrangements that essentially determine the policy process in Croatia. If, additionally, we take into consideration the fact that corruption is still strongly present in numerous areas of public affairs it becomes clear why Croatia lags behind in economic, social and sectoral policies in comparison to other post-communist country members of the European Union.[12]

Notes

1. As early as in 1990—the year of the first multiparty elections and introduction of democracy—GDP already dropped by 9.9%. As it kept dropping in the years that followed (as much as by 21.1% in 1991, by 11.7% in 1992 and by 8.0% in 1993) (Franičević and Bićanić 2007: 643), in the first four years of the development of democracy and transformation of economy, GDP recorded a staggering drop of 50.7%.
2. Croatian companies' sales of goods to other Yugoslav republics (Bosnia-Herzegovina, Macedonia, Montenegro, Serbia and Slovenia) exceeded their exports to other countries (primarily to the then EEC member states) by 2.19 times. Also, the purchases from the companies from other Yugoslav republics exceeded the total import from other countries by 2.36 times. This illustrates the importance of the then Yugoslav single market, where the companies from all parts of Yugoslavia made significantly more of their total sales than in the markets of third countries. True, there were differences in the dependency on the said single market. While Slovenian companies' export to and import from this market was only 1.86 and 1.71 times, respectively, higher than their export to and import from other countries, the dependency on this market in the case of companies from other federal units was significantly higher. As regards exports, those made to the markets in other republics exceeded those made to other countries as follows: in Bosnia-Herzegovina by 3.15 times; in Macedonia by 4.91 times; in Montenegro by 5.35 times; and in Serbia by 4.20 times. As regards imports, those from the markets of other republics exceeded those from other countries as follows: in Bosnia-Herzegovina by 3.52 times; in Macedonia by 3.01 times; in Montenegro by 7.49 times; and in Serbia by 3.93 times. The ratios were calculated on the basis of the 1986 data published in Ekonomska politika, Belgrade, 1991. See Petak (2005: 60).

3. Decentralization reforms enacted in 1970s in the former Yugoslavia led to a situation where little more than approximately 20% of the budget funds was allocated to the federation. A total of 75% of the budget funds went to the sub-national units. In the 1980s, a decade before the disintegration of Yugoslavia, Croatia and other federal units had in place a markedly decentralized system in which more than 35% of public revenue went to local authorities—only a portion less than the share that went to the federal units (republics and autonomous provinces). The smallest of the shares went to the federation—somewhat more than 20% of public expenditure. See Bogoev (1991).
4. In their comparison of the development of capitalism in Romania, Bulgaria and Croatia, Bohle and Greskovits point out that between them—as the countries that neither have the democratic corporatist order in place (unlike, for example, Slovenia) nor have they developed a capable state—there is a substantial difference nevertheless. Unlike Romania and Bulgaria, which saw the introduction of the democratic order as weak states, Croatia saw the beginning of the transition period as a capable state. However, the political processes and the war of the 1990s "undermined an originally capable state" (Bohle and Greskovits 2012: 194).
5. Such a definition of governance steering capacity uses the same approach used in Bertelsmann's Sustainable Governance Indicators concept, where steering capability includes five dimensions: strategic capacity, interministerial coordination, evidence-based instruments, societal consultation and policy communication (Bertelsmann 2017).
6. The first development document adopted by the Croatian government was "The Basics of the 1991/1992 Economic Policy with a Program of Measures" (Mirošević 2012: 7) and the first document to contain the word "strategy" in its title was "The Development Strategy of Croatian Tourism" (Mirošević 2012: 17), adopted in 1993.
7. "Croatia is lacking proper strategic plans—in most cases the accepted strategies have technical shortcomings and serve mainly for excuse purpose." (Koprić 2011: 15).
8. In its 2017 European Semester: Country Report—Croatia, the European Commission expressly mentions in three places the need to eliminate the inadequacies in the implementation of the strategic planning tools as the crucial shortcoming in fundamental policy formulation. The report first assesses strategic planning as one of two crucial weaknesses in fiscal governance, then it points out that the absorption of EU funds remains hindered by the limited administrative capacity and strategic planning and, finally, that the supervisory boards controlling local public enterprises are not involved in the strategic planning system (European Commission 2017: 2, 10, 50).

9. For example, experts were rather intensively involved in the tax system reform of 2016, but that was one of a very few examples of their relevant involvement in policy formulation. The problem, however, is the fact that in only 24% of the cases when working groups were formed for drafting bills were scientists and other external experts invited to join them (GONG 2013b).
10. Croatian governments often take their time preparing policy proposals and allocate substantial funds for their formulation, only to give them up when they face a resistance to them in a form of petitions, protests or referendum threats. Recent examples include Zoran Milanović government's abandoning of its 2015 highway monetization program and Andrej Plenković government's abandoning of the introduction of real estate tax.
11. Cerami and Stubbs (2011) make a distinction between state-enabled market economies (in which they include Central European countries), state-influenced market economies (in which they include Croatia, other former Yugoslav countries except Slovenia, and Romania, Bulgaria and Albania), and state-interfered market economies (in which they include the countries emerged from the former USSR).
12. The researchers of the public sector in Croatia have several times reported on the problem of corruption as the key problem for Croatian governance reformers. The problem of tackling with corruption appears in their view an even bigger problem than coping with excessive public expenditure, because a weak government and a rather high level of corruption considerably impairs the efficiency of the public sector (Bađun et al. 2014).

References

Alesina, A., Ardagna, S., & Trebbi, F. (2006). Who Adjust and When?: The Political Economy of Reforms. *IMF Staff Papers, 53*(Special issue), 1–29.

Bađun, M. (2005). The Quality of Governance and Economic Growth in Croatia. *Financial Theory and Practice, 29*(4), 279–308.

Bađun, M., Deskar Škrbić, M., & Pribičević, V. (2014). Government Size and Efficiency as Constraints to Economic Growth: Comparing Croatia with Other European Countries. *Post-Communist Economies, 26*(3), 297–323.

Bagić, D. (2010). *Industrijski odnosi u Hrvatskoj: društvena integracija ili tržišni sukob*. Zagreb: TIM Press.

Bartlett, W. (2003). *Croatia: Between Europe and the Balkans*. London: Routledge.

Bertelsmann Stiftung. (2017). Policy Performance and Governance Capacities the and Sustainable Governance Indicators 2017. http://www.sgi-network.org/docs/2017/basics/SGI2017_Overview.pdf. Downloaded 16 September 2017.

Bežovan, G., & Zrinščak, S. (2007). *Civilno društvo u Hrvatskoj*. Zagreb: Jesenski i Turk.

Bićanić, I. (1994). The Economic Causes of New State Formation During Transition. *East European Politics and Societes, 9*(1), 2–21.
Bogoev, K. (1991). The Dangers of Decentralization: The Experience of Yugoslavia. In R. Prud'homme (Ed.), *Public Finance with Several Levels of Government* (pp. 99–112). The Haag: Foundation Journal Public Finance.
Bohle, D., & Greskovits, B. (2012). *Capitalist Diversity on Europe's Periphery.* Ithaca: Cornell University Press.
Börzel, T. (2011). When Europe Hits ... Beyond Its Borders: Europeanization and the Near Abroad. *Comparative European Politics, 9*(4–5), 394–413.
Campbell, J. L. (1998). Institutional Analysis and the Role of Ideas in Political Economy. *Theory and Society, 27*(3), 377–409.
Cerami, A., & Stubbs, P. (2011, December). Post-Communist Welfare Capitalisms: Bringing Institutions and Political Agency Back In, *EIZ Working Papers.*
Cvijanović, V., & Redžepagić, D. (2011). From Political Capitalism to Clientelism? The Case of Croatia. *Zbornik radova Ekonomskog fakulteta u Rijeci/Proceedings of Rijeka School of Economics, 29*(2), 355–372.
Dallago, B., & Uvalić, M. (1998). The Distributive Consequences of Nationalism: The Case of former Yugoslavia. *Europe-Asia Studies, 50*(1), 71–90.
Đokić, I., & Sumpor, M. (2013). *The Role of Croatian Civil Society Organisations in the European Union Accession Process.* Zagreb: TACSO.
Dolenec, D. (2013). *Democratic Institutions and Authoritarian Rule in South-East Europe.* Colchester: ECPR Press.
European Commission. (2017). Country Report Croatia 2017 Including an In-Depth Review on the Prevention and Correction of Macroeconomic Imbalances. https://ec.europa.eu/info/files/2017-european-semester-country-report-croatia_hr. Downloaded 20 September 2017.
Farkas, B. (2017). Market Economies of the Western Balkans Compared to the Central and Eastern European Model of Capitalism. *Croatian Economic Survey, 19*(1), 5–36.
Fink-Hafner, D. (Ed.). (2015). *The Development of Civil Society in the Countries on the Territory of the Former Yugoslavia Since the 1980s.* Ljubljana: Faculty of Social Sciences.
Fisher, S. (2006). *Political Change in Post-Communist Slovakia and Croatia: From Nationalist to Europeanist.* Basingstoke: Palgrave Macmillan.
Franičević, V., & Bićanić, I. (2007). EU Accession and Croatia's Two Economic Goals: Modern Economic Growth and Modern Regulated Capitalism. *South East European and Black Sea Studies, 7*(4), 637–663.
Giljević, T. (2015). Utjecaj okoline organizacije na upravnu koordinaciju: Ministarstvo uprave kao studija slučaja. *Hrvatska i komparativna javna uprava, 15*(4), 875–908.
Gligorov, V. (1993). Why do Countries Break Up? The Case of Yugoslavia. (Working paper No. 17). Department of Soviet and East European Studies, Uppsala University.

GONG. (2013a). *Pretpostavke uspješne provedbe reforme državne uprave u Hrvatskoj*. Zagreb: GONG.

GONG. (2013b). *Indeks dobrog upravljanja u Hrvatskoj 2012: rezultati istraživanja*. Zagreb: GONG.

Hellman, J. S. (1998). The Politics of Partial Reform in Postcommunist Transitions. *World Politics, 50*(2), 203–234.

Henjak, A., Zakošek, N., & Čular, G. (2013). Croatia. In S. Berglund et al. (Eds.), *The Handbook of Political Change in Eastern Europe* (pp. 443–480). Cheltenham: Edward Elgar.

Howlett, M., Ramesh, M., & Perl, A. (2009). *Studying Public Policy: Policy Cycles and Policy Subsystems*. Oxford: Oxford University Press.

James, S., & Staronova, K. (2003). Review of the Central Authorities for Policymaking and Coordination of the Republic of Croatia, Internal Report for the World Bank.

Jurlina Alibegović, D. (2013). Less is More: Decentralization in Croatia and Its Impact on Regional Development. In W. Bartlett, S. Malković, & V. Monastiriotis (Eds.), *Decentralization and Local Development in South East Europe* (pp. 51–66). Basingstoke: Palgrave Macmillan.

Kasapović, M. (2001). Demokratska konsolidacija i izborna politika u Hrvatskoj. In M. Kasapović (Ed.), *Hrvatska politika 1990–2000* (pp. 15–40). Zagreb: Fakultet političkih znanosti.

Kekez Koštro, A., Urbanc, K., & Salaj, I. (2012). Implementacija javnih politika kao operativno upravljanje: analiza transformacije hrvatske politike prema osobama s invaliditetom. *Anali Hrvatskog politološkog društva, 9*, 413–439.

Kokanović, M. (1999). Croatian Labour Realities, 1990–1999. *SEER South-East Europe Review for Labour and Social Affairs, 2*(3), 185–208.

Koprić, I. (2010). Prijedlozi za reformu lokalne i regionalne samouprave u Hrvatskoj. *Hrvatska javna uprava, 10*(4), 941–959.

Koprić, I. (2011). Contemporary Croatian Public Administration on the Reform Waves. *Godišnjak Akademije pravnih znanosti Hrvatske, 2*(1), 1–40.

Liha Matejiček, A. (2015). The Europeanisation of Regional Policy in Croatia: From Institutional Absorption to Transformation. In D. Lajh & Z. Petak (Eds.), *EU Public Policies Seen from a National Perspective: Slovenia and Croatia in the European Union* (pp. 167–180). Ljubljana: Faculty of Social Sciences.

Mirošević, H. (2012, December). Analiza razvojnih dokumenata Republike Hrvatske, *EIZ Working Papers*.

Musa, A., & Petak, Z. (2015). Coordination for Policy in Transition Countries: Case of Croatia. *Mednarodna revija za javno upravo/International Public Administration Review, 13*(3–4), 117–159.

Perko Šeparović, I. (2006). Strateško planiranje. In I. Perko Šeparović (Ed.), *Priručnik za dobro upravljanje* (pp. 11–31). Zagreb: Hrvatski pravni centar.

Petak, Z. (2005). Ekonomska pozadina raspada socijalističke Jugoslavije. In H.-G. Fleck & I. Graovac (Eds.), *Dijalog povjesničara-istoričara 9* (pp. 57–77). Zagreb: Friedrich Naumann Stiftung.

Petak, Z. (2011). Politics of Decentralization Policy: Explaining the Limited Success of the Croatian Case After 2001. *Politička misao: Croatian Political Science Review, 48*(5), 72–84.

Petak, Z. (2012). Ekonomski federalizam u socijalističkoj Jugoslaviji. *Politička misao, 49*(4), 212–227.

Petak, Z. (2015). Evidence-Based Policy Making and the Implementation of Regulatory Impact Assessment in Croatia. *Management and Business Administration. Central Europe, 23*(2), 147–162.

Petak, Z., & Petek, A. (2009). Policy Analysis and Croatian Public Administration: The Problem of Formulating Public Policy. *Politička misao/Croatian Political Science Review, 46*(5), 54–74.

Petak, Z., & Vidačak, I. (2015). The Political and Institutional Determinants of Civil Society Development in Croatia Since the 1980s. In D. Fink Hafner (Ed.), *The Development of Civil Society in the Countries on the Territory of the Former Yugoslavia Since the 1980s* (pp. 95–120). Ljubljana: Faculty of Social Sciences.

Petak, Z., Bartlett, W., & Bönker, F. (2017). *Sustainable Governance Indicators 2017: Croatia Report.* Gütersloh: Bertelsmann stiftung.

Petek, A. (2010). Transformacija politike prema osobama s invaliditetom u Hrvatskoj: analiza ciljeva. *Anali Hrvatskog politološkog društva, 7*, 101–121.

Petković, K. (2009). Simbolička nasuprot referencijskoj politici: neuspjeh javnih politika na parlamentarnim izborima 2007. In Z. Petak (Ed.), *Stranke i javne politike* (pp. 59–103). Zagreb: Fakultet političkih znanosti.

Pierre, J., & Peters, G. B. (2005). *Governing Complex Societies: Trajectories and Scenarios.* Basingstoke: Palgrave Macmillan.

Sabatier, P. A. (1991). Political Science and Public Policy. *PS: Political Science and Politics, 24*(2), 144–147.

Schmitter, P. C., & Santiso, J. (1998). Three Temporal Dimensions to the Consolidation of Democracy. *International Political Science Review, 19*(1), 69–92.

Sissenich, B. (2010). Weak States, Weak Societes: Europe's East-West Gap. *Acta Politica, 45*(1–2), 11–40.

Stubbs, P., & Zrinščak, S. (2015). Citizenship and Social Welfare in Croatia: Clientelism and the Limits of 'Europeanisation'. *European Politics and Society, 16*(3), 395–410.

Sumpor, M. (2013). Kako povezati kolektivne procese participativnog strateškog planiranja i politiku (samo)volju vodstva? In A. Musa (Ed.), *4. Forum za javnu upravu* (pp. 27–45). Zagreb: Friedrich Ebert stiftung.

The Madison-Project. (2013). The Maddison-Project. http://www.ggdc.net/maddison/maddison-project/home.htm, 2013 version. Downloaded 26 September 2017.

Thomas, M., & Bojicic-Dzelilovic, V. (2015). *Policy Making in the Western Balkans: Case Studies of Selected Economic and Social Policy Reforms*. Dordrecht: Springer.

Vojnić, D. (1995). Disparity and Disintegration: The Economic Dimension of Yugoslav's Demise. In P. Akhavan & R. Howse (Eds.), *Yugoslavia, the Former and the Future: Reflections by Scholars from the Region* (pp. 75–111). Washington, DC: The Brookings Institution.

Vukorepa, I. (2015). Lost Between Sustainability and Adequacy: Critical Analysis of the Croatian Pension System's Parametric Reform. *Revija za socijalnu politiku, 22*(3), 279–308.

Wilensky, H. (2002). *Rich Democracies: Political Economy, Public Policy, and Performance*. Berkeley: University of California Press.

Zakošek, N. (2008). Democratization, State-building and War: The Cases of Serbia and Croatia. *Democratization, 15*(3), 588–610.

CHAPTER 3

The Europeanization of the Croatian Political System

Hrvoje Špehar and Ivan Pepić

3.1 Introduction

The chapter analyzes the main institutional changes within the Croatian political system during the process of Croatia–European Union (EU) negotiations, focusing especially on some repercussions on domestic politics. The Europeanization within the framework of EU political studies is commonly understood as "domestic adaptation with national colors" (Risse et al. 2001: 1), which is the main research issue of this chapter regarding the Croatian case: (1) slow and special enlargement approach, from both the EU and Croatian side; and (2) unusual enlargement requirements with strong veto points and deeply connected with the past political environment of former Yugoslavia.

The Europeanization of the Croatian political system is deeply connected with the EU enlargement policy in the case of Eastern enlargement

H. Špehar (✉)
Faculty of Political Science, University of Zagreb, Zagreb, Croatia
e-mail: hrvoje.spehar@fpzg.hr

I. Pepić
Global Studies Institute, University of Geneva, Geneva, Switzerland

Z. Petak, K. Kotarski (eds.), *Policy-Making at the European Periphery*, New Perspectives on South-East Europe,
https://doi.org/10.1007/978-3-319-73582-5_3

(2004 and 2007), but with strong influence of the historical institutionalization of Croatian politics connected with different historical and political contexts. Moreover, scholars often perceive the Europeanization of Croatia through the lens of either Eastern enlargements or the new enlargement policies for Southeastern European states. However, this research shows that, because of different stages and dynamics, the Croatian case differs from both groups. Indeed, because of the late start of the EU enlargement process in Croatia (special political requirements within the framework of cooperation in the Balkans) it was rarely regarded within the EU institutions as a member of the Central Eastern European club. At the same time, Croatian economic and political development, confirmed by the official statements of the EU institutions since early 2000s, shows huge differences from the framework of the EU enlargement and Europeanization process in the Balkans. It makes the research of the Croatian case very sensitive compared to other cases of the Europeanization process.

The chapter will provide the periodization in three stages of the Croatian case: (1) the 1990s period before the negotiation process; (2) the 2000–2012 negotiation process and the fulfillment of the EU requirements; and (3) since 2013, EU membership. Within this periodization and considering Croatia's cooperation with the International Criminal Tribunal for the former Yugoslavia (ICTY), foreign policy towards Bosnia and Herzegovina (BiH), and the border dispute with Slovenia, the analysis will testify to the impact of Europeanization through hard conditionality. The main hypothesis is that the Europeanization, which affected national and geopolitical identities, has had strong repercussions on Croatian politics and the behavior of political parties even after the accession in 2013.

3.2 Europeanization Versus (Western-) Balkanization: Croatia–EU Relations in the 1990s

The relationship between the European Union (EU) and Croatia in the 1990s could be described as "complicated". On the one side, the Croatian political system had been designed to manage the crisis of the breakup of Yugoslavia and the Homeland War (1991–1995). This affected the behavior of the political parties and their elites, which were interested in all the help from the EU and, only then, in the Europeanization of Croatia. On the other side, at the very beginning of the breakup, the EU wished to solve the crisis by Europeanizing Croatia as part of Yugoslavia. This created some observable political impasses in the late 1990s, which was not the case in Central and Eastern European Countries (CEECs) affected by the enlargement.

The process of democratization in Croatia is unique in post-communist Europe because it involved the liberalization, democratization and the war all at the same time (Kasapović 1996: 84). This "triple transition" was not expected by the EU, which from the very beginning did not develop any strategy to Europeanize and alleviate the crisis as was the case with the CEECs. The first multi-party elections in 1990, the internal insurgency supported by the Serbian political parties, and the proclamation of independence in 1991 caught the EU without strategy. Indeed, in mid-1991 the main EU countries were against the Croatian independence and supportive of the survival of Yugoslavia and its democratization (Glaurdic 2011). Nevertheless, in 1992 all the EU members recognized Croatia as an independent and sovereign state.

Croatian public opinion and the elite regarded the EU institutions and countries as political partners who they could count on for the defense of the country (idem.). This was the case in particular in 1990 and 1991 at the beginning of the Homeland War and, moreover, following recognition in 1992. The idea of "partnership" between Croatia and the EU was used by, among others, the Croatian president Franjo Tuđman and his leading party, the Croatian Democratic Union (*Hrvatska demokratska zajednica*, HDZ). In fact, in 1991 in a televised speech Tuđman stated: "We hope that the European countries and the EU will understand that the Croatian struggle for its territorial integrity, its freedom and democracy is not only the fight of the Croatian nation, the fight against the restoration of socialist communism… but the fight for normal conditions when Croatia can join Europe, where it historically belongs" (quoted in Lindstrom 2003: 317). The idea of "return to Europe" was supported by liberal as well as conservative leaders of CEECs. In the mid-1990s, while Croatia was under military occupation, the EU started association and membership negotiations with some of the CEECs, including Slovenia, which resulted in the first gap between Croatia and other CEECs applying for EU membership. Despite this tactical position and constructivist rhetoric by the Croatian elite, the country was not involved in these negotiations.

Moreover, in March 1995 the EU extended its pre-accession financial program "Poland Hungary Aid for Restructure of the Economy" (PHARE) to Croatia, but because of the military offensive for the retake of territories under the self-proclaimed Serb Republic of Krajina, in August Croatia was suspended from the PHARE program (Bartlett 2008: 197).[1] This political decision was followed by the initiative of the European Commission in September when it started to promote the regional cooperation, which was a policy "to replace the previous bilateral approach toward each of the concerned states" (Grizo 2014: 141). The main idea was that the EU would push the countries of the former Yugoslavia towards "reinforcement of civil society, reconciliation and regional economic cooperation" (European Parliament 1996). Furthermore, the European Commission determined that the engagement of these states "in regional cooperation… and political reform will be determining factors in the future relations with the European Union" (European Commission 1995). For this purpose, the EU launched the Royaumont Process (1996), the Regional Approach (1997), the Stabilization and Association Process (SAP) (1999) and the Stability Pact for Southeastern Europe (1999). The main goals of these initiatives were to strengthen cooperation between non-governmental organizations, "reinforce the successful implementation of the peace agreements and the creation of an area of political stability and economic prosperity" (Schweiss and Jebb 2006: 106), and so on, with the difference that these initiatives depended on different European institutions. It became clear that one of the criteria for a successful process of Europeanization should have passed through the regional cooperation.

After the end of the Homeland War in 1995, the position of the Croatian government towards the EU was ambiguous because of EU's insistence on the regional approach: on the one hand, the Croatian government continued to support the membership and the cooperation with the EU and other international organizations, but it rejected the regional approach as one of the most important criteria, because it thought this meant Croatia would be isolated for a long time at the European periphery. The historical (path dependence) argument was used in order to persuade the European elite and to "show" how Croatia and the Others are culturally different, which has been one of the most used arguments of the Christian "New Europe" (see Risse 2010). Indeed, Tuđman (1998: 152, 171) stated: "we are for the normalization of relationships with all the countries in Yugoslavia and in this Balkan-South-Eastern European area. But only for membership and integration with Central Europe... On this issue of vital importance for the future of the Croatian people and the Croatian state" and "we do not accept such a regional approach … for a simple reason, and above all because Croatia, throughout its history, is an integral part of Western and European civilization". Moreover, in 1996 the Croatian parliament approved the constitutional law on the collaboration with the International Criminal Tribunal for former Yugoslavia (ICTY), but the commitment was weak, as it was the regional cooperation. Finally, in 1998 the Ministry of European Integration was formed within the Croatian government. Its goal was to accelerate the initiation of the adhesion process. Since the opposition parties were weak,[2] Tuđman's HDZ had strong supremacy over decisions concerning foreign policy.

The EU did not consider specific historical and geopolitical reasoning of the President and the Government of Croatia and their continued rejecting of the regional approach. In fact, the EU labeled this refusal as "nationalist policies", which prolonged the suspension from the PHARE program (Schweiss and Jebb 2006: 109). Furthermore, the EU stressed that problems existed considering the relations with neighbors, and concerning regional cooperation, there was "no progress in ensuring that Federation [of Bosnia and Herzegovina]/Croatia... relations were compatible with the peace agreements", even though it welcomed Croatia's "wish for integration into European structures" as it was "willing to resolve the outstanding questions by diplomatic means" (Council 1998).

During the 1990s the CEECs largely wanted to "return to Europe". On the other hand, the "triple transition"—liberalization, democratization and the Homeland War—distanced Croatia from former communist CEECs. Moreover, the EU did not completely accept the historical as well as geopolitical arguments by the Croatian government about a "fast" integration in the European family.

3.3 Convoy or Regatta? The Croatian Identity's Influence on the Start of Negotiations in 2000

Between 2000 and 2003, following the parliamentary election results of 3rd January, the coalition government was composed of social democrats and liberals.[3] The defeat of the HDZ led to a change of the system of government, from a semi-presidential to a parliamentary system. This change was welcomed by the European Commission (2000), which evaluated it as a democratic change. Moreover, the Commission announced the participation at the Zagreb Summit on 24th November 2000, launched by the French presidency of the EU. The Heads of State or Government of the Member States of the EU, Albania, the Former Yugoslav Republic of

Macedonia, BiH, Croatia, the Federal Republic of Yugoslavia (FRY), as well as the Foreign Minister of Slovenia, and the High Representative for the Common Foreign and Security Policy all participated in the summit.

Initially, the summit was thought to be "Balkan Summit", turning to the idea of "Western Balkan Summit" and finally fixed as the "Zagreb Summit". This semantic position was crucial for the relations between the EU and the Southeastern Europe: the first term opened the question about its participants, such as the possible inclusion of Turkey. The concept of "Western Balkans", however, was not welcomed by the Croatian public opinion or the center-right political parties, which had negatively perceived this geopolitical position because it did not take the Mediterranean and Central European identities of Croatia into consideration. In order to solve this impasse, the SDP tried to redefine Croatia"s geographical position, stating that: "Croatia is not solely a Middle European, but also a Mediterranean and a Balkan country" (Grubiša 2000: 118).

However, even though the new government redefined the state's position that the EU's regional approach towards the "Western Balkans" was acceptable, which had been denied for a long-time, the Croatian government continued to stress that the "return to Europe" would be accomplished only with the EU membership, equalizing Europe with the EU and, once again, forgetting about the "Western Balkans" neighbors. For instance, the social-democrat Prime Minister (PM) Ivica Račan stated: "The citizens of Croatia have expressed these choices in their wish for a 'return to Europe', with the strong belief that Croatia's belonging to a historical and contemporary European context is an unquestionable foundation for the right to make this dream come true… neither can the EU consider integration complete without a state stretching across the area where Mitteleuropa meets the Mediterranean" (quoted in Miošić-Lisjak 2006: 110). The 2000 Zagreb Summit was in the Commission's opinion an opportunity to "open the way for regional reconciliation and cooperation" facilitated by political changes in Croatia and continued "with the victory of democratic forces in the FRY in the elections of 24th of September," all of which were evaluated as "historic changes" (European Commission 2000). Furthermore, at the Zagreb Summit the Croatian government insisted on an "individualized approach to each of these countries" or, in Croatian president Mesić's words, "these countries are welcome to the Union – at the rate which they are capable of achieving, that is, individually, or in a regatta and not in a convoy" (Grubiša 2000:

118). The metaphor of "convoy" vs. "regatta" clearly shows that the choice of the government was the result of not only the determination to protect Croatia's territorial integrity, but also to fully collaborate with the European institutions in order to preserve the stability in Southeastern Europe (Grubiša 2000).

The individual approach, however, did not mean competition between countries. At the summit the governments accepted the fulfillment of the SAP criteria, which included trade relations, financial assistance, contractual relationships and regional cooperation as a factor of integration through the process of reconciliation, development of common infrastructures, and the establishment of trade areas between countries (European Commission 2000). Finally, unlike other former socialist countries, the regional cooperation became part of the EU's conditionality for Albania and former Yugoslavia's successor states, with the exception of Slovenia. This way, Croatia was excluded from the 2004 "Big Bang" enlargement, even though the political elite and public opinion perceived the position of Croatia as being more similar to Slovenia as both of them shared a similar political past, considering the 1990s' "return to Europe" and their position vis-à-vis the fall of socialist Yugoslavia. We recognize two types of conditionality: soft and hard. They are both applicable to the process of Europeanization of Croatia, which had a specific path towards the EU (Musladin 2012). In this chapter we consider only the hard conditionality.

3.4 Croatia's Europeanization Through Hard Conditionality Between 2000 and 2012

The logic of the EU hard conditionality lies in "bargaining strategy of reinforcement by reward, under which the EU provides external incentives for a target government to comply with its conditions" (Schimmelfennig and Sedelmeier 2004: 662). Moreover, the EU evaluates the candidate countries upon their compliance with the requirements, and whose costs should not exceed political benefits of a credible membership perspective (Freyburg and Richter 2010). The hard conditionality appears when the conditions of membership, which are often decided by the Commission, focus on sanction mechanisms if some conditions are not yet fulfilled, in accordance with the hierarchical idea of "carrot and stick". The pressures are mostly political and aim at meeting the criteria, often affecting the sovereignty of a state. Pressure is thus felt in the changes of the constitutions and political systems. We consider three hard conditions within the Croatian case: (1) the question of "full cooperation" with the ICTY, (2) relations with BiH, and (3) Croatian–Slovenian border dispute.

(1) The EU considered the ICTY as a fundamental actor in former Yugoslavia. The cooperation with this international court became a condition which is not directly linked to the *acquis communautaire*. In the opinion of the EU the ICTY had a crucial role of reconciliation between the states and peoples after the wars caused by the 1991–1995 military aggression of the FRY in BiH, Croatia and the 1998–1999 Kosovo war. Therefore, the EU took seriously all the statements by ICTY Chief Prosecutor, which became an EU membership criterion mentioned since the beginning in the European Commission's Progress Reports, even though certain analysis doubted the efficiency of the ICTY (see e.g. Robreno 2008).

In the opinion of the Chief Prosecutor, the "lack of cooperation" occurred twice, in 2005 and 2009. In the *first case*, after the signature of the Stabilization and Association Agreement in 2001, the formal application for membership in 2003 and the receipt of official status of candidate one year later, the Council announced the start of negotiation on 17th March 2005 after the Commission's positive opinion. Nevertheless, the Council postponed the negotiations, because the ICTY stated that Croatia had not fully cooperated. After the Council's decision in 2005 a fall in support for EU membership occurred, since both the "citizens and the political elite perceived the postponement as equalization with the aggressor" (Musladin 2012: 114). The "ICTY conditionality" was unpopular within the public opinion, because it challenged the question of national identity, but "domestic political elites still complied with it because the benefits of the European integration process were greater than its costs" (Ješe Perković 2013: 177). In fact, immediately after the Council's decision the government created a task force for the location and arrest of the former general of the Croatian Army Ante Gotovina, prosecuted by the ICTY Chief Prosecutor Carla del Ponte.[4] This was welcomed by her on 3rd October 2005, which was sufficient for the Council to start on the same day accession negotiations with Croatia. The *second case* occurred in September 2008 when the Chief Prosecutor Serge Brammertz said that the ICTY had problems accessing military documents concerning the

1995 Operation Storm by the Croatian Army. So, in February 2009, some EU members decided not to allow the opening of the negotiation Chapter 23 (Judiciary and Fundamental Rights) with Croatia, while the government formed, once again, a task force in order to find the missing artillery documents. Nevertheless, the majority of documents were never created or had not been located (Wikileaks 2009).

(2) The relations between Croatia and BiH were also considered by the EU, in particular by the European Commission. During the 1990s, Croatia had special ties with its ethnic kin in the neighboring BiH. The population of BiH is composed of Bosniak Muslims, Croats and Serbs who since the 1995 Dayton Agreement have been considered as constituent peoples with equal political rights. The wartime cooperation between Zagreb and BiH's Croats had created specific institutions within municipalities having Croatian majority, ruled by BiH's Croats. Since the Dayton Agreement, these institutions were integrated into the Bosniak-Croat entity of the Federation of BiH. Nevertheless, up until the end of the 1990s the HDZ government continued to support these institutions, which meant that BiH's Croats had parallel institutions within the Federation of BiH. Being supportive of the Dayton Agreement, the EU demanded "credible pressure on the Bosnian Croats to dissolve Herceg-Bosna structures and to cooperate in the establishment and functioning of the Federation" (Council 1997).

Since 2000, however, Croatian governments abandoned the politics of special ties with Croats in BiH, insisting on their cooperation with the ICTY. This turnaround was due to, first, the fact that the EU in the 1990s was against "parallel institutions" within the Federation of BiH and, second, the lack of support for Račan's government among Croats in BiH: the SDP-HSLS-HNS-IDS coalition got less than 5% of the votes from BiH's Croats, while HDZ was given more than 85% (DIP 2000). The European Commission evaluated this new trend as an improvement in relations between BiH and the Croatian government: "aiming at the strengthening of BiH central state institutions" (European Commission 2004). In addition, the European Commission (2005) stated that the "HDZ Government continues to pursue the policy of non-interference in Bosnia and Herzegovina's internal affairs, which was developed under the former Račan Government".

(3) The border dispute between Croatia and Slovenia started in 1993. The two states established a mixed diplomatic commission and solved, with bilateral agreements, a few problems. However, after 1995: "Slovenia further claims the right to territorial contact with the High Seas and the right to the integrity of the Bay of Piran (under its sovereignty), while Croatia claims a right to territorial contact with the territorial sea of Italy and requests an equidistant line to be applied for the maritime delimitation in the Bay of Piran" (Sancin 2010: 96–97). In order to solve the disputes, in 2001 the PMs signed an agreement, also known as the "Račan-Drnovšek Agreement". However, the Croatian parliament refused to ratify it, because in its opinion the agreement did not conform to national interests. The two sides tried to achieve an agreement in 2007, but unsuccessfully. A salient moment occurred in October 2008 when Slovenia blocked the accession negotiation of Croatia with the EU.

The conditions for resolving the dispute had been imposed by Slovenia as a Member State, but soon the EU engaged itself in the litigation. On 21st January 2009 the EU Commissioner for Enlargement Olli Rehn proposed to solve the dispute in front of a tripartite political commission, which was not accepted by the Croatian government. The second Rehn proposal on 23rd April, to submit the dispute to an ad hoc arbitration, was rejected by the Slovenian government. Finally, in June, Rehn submitted a third proposal, but it was rejected again. The solution arrived in summer 2009 following the meetings between the PMs Jadranka Kosor and Borut Pahor. The Arbitration Agreement between Croatia and Slovenia was signed on 4th November 2009, providing an arbitral tribunal composed of five judges, three of which were from countries nominated by the European Commission, one Croat and one Slovenian. Considering also that the United States had put considerable pressure upon the Slovenian side in order to unfreeze the negotiations, Slovenia removed the veto and permitted Croatia to open six and conclude 10 negotiation chapters (Wikileaks 2009; Sancin 2010). Finally, on 30th June 2011 the negotiations with Croatia were closed and the Accession Treaty was signed on 9th December 2011.

All the three aforementioned cases were part of Europeanization through hard political conditionality. Analyzing the Europeanization of Croatia, Freyburg and Richter (2010: 275) write: "national identity significantly influences the effectiveness of external democratization by political conditionality," adding that "identity conflict and partial identity change modified the scope of appropriate action such that the possibility arose of satisfying EU conditionality without infringing understandings of appropriate behavior." Indeed, Croatia was asked to deal with three hard questions, which have been the core of its identities. This was not possible without a partial redefinition of its national identity.

On the other hand, it seems that the theory does not follow Croatia's Europeanization praxis. According to one of the most cited definitions, Europeanization includes "processes of (a) construction (b) diffusion and (c) institutionalization of formal and informal rules, procedures, policy paradigms, styles, "ways of doing things" and shared beliefs and norms which are first defined and consolidated in the making of EU public policy and politics and then incorporated in the logic of domestic discourse, identities, political structures and public policies" (Radaelli 2003: 30).[5] Europeanization implies the incorporation of EU policies and its way of doing politics in domestic identities, policies and politics. It excludes, however, the imposition of unnecessary new identities (i.e. "Western Balkans") for the Europeanization of a country. Finally, the three hard conditions have remained a considerable challenge for the political system of Croatia, even after its EU membership in 2013, which raises the question about the success of Europeanization through hard conditionality that affects national identity.

3.5 The Heritage of Croatia's Europeanization After the 2013 Membership

The outcomes of the Europeanization through hard conditionality have had some repercussions on the political and party systems of Croatia after EU membership on 1st July 2013. First, the three abovementioned EU conditions (cooperation with the ICTY, relations with BiH, and the border dispute with Slovenia) have strongly influenced domestic politics and relations with the neighbors. Second, even though in some fields soft conditionality has been successful (i.e. transformation of political parties), the Europeanization through hard conditionality has created challenges which undermine the very essence of Europeanization.

The *first* repercussion of Croatia's Europeanization through hard conditionality concerns domestic politics and relations with neighbors. In 2005 the EU postponed the start of negotiations for half a year after ICTY

Chief Prosecutor's statement that the government was unsuccessful in arresting Ante Gotovina. This caused a fall in the support for EU membership, the rise of Euroscepticism and, moreover, continuing repercussions even after the accession to the EU, because Gotovina was acquitted of charges on 16th November 2012. This was evaluated by public opinion and the political elite as final proof that Croatia could not be equalized with the aggressor. On the other hand, Gotovina's acquittal provided the Serbian government with a "shield of rejectionism" (Subotić 2014) that contrasts the ICTY's position. Finally, the EU's decision to put transitional justice as a condition through the development of a common regional approach and a new identity of "Western Balkans", after the 2012 decision of the ICTY, paradoxically, has more divided than reconciled states and peoples. This has become clear from the reactions of Croatia's neighbor, Serbia.

Similarly, after Croatia was given a green light over the accession in 2011, Zagreb has been active in regional affairs switching from "abandonment of the so called 'escape from the region' policy with emphasizing the regional policy as one of the central issues of foreign policy" (Tatalović and Jakešević 2013: 238). Zagreb policy towards Sarajevo has changed as well: SDP representatives have insisted on equality between the three constituent peoples in BiH. Indeed, the former social democratic PM Zoran Milanović put relations with BiH social democrats on hiatus and opted for supporting the winning political party among Croats in BiH, the HDZ BiH. Since 2013, both the Croatian opposition and the government, consensually along with the collaboration of BiH's Croatian leaders, recognized the existence of a "Croatian question", which is perceived by Sarajevo as interfering with internal affairs.

The border litigation with Slovenia has continued since the 2009 Kosor–Pahor agreement on arbitration, as a modified European Commission's proposal. Both sides were committed to respect the arbitration agreement. However, in 2015 Croatia unilaterally quit the arbitration proceedings after audio recordings and transcripts revealed that the Slovenian agent and judge to the tribunal tried to develop "strategies to influence other members of the Tribunal and to manipulate with the file of the case" (Ministry of Foreign and European Affairs of the Republic of Croatia 2017). Moreover, notwithstanding the polarization of Croatian politics that has prevailed since the accession to the EU, members of the Croatian parliament approved unanimously a withdrawal from the arbitration process. The Slovenian judge resigned, followed by the Croatian judge, while the president of the tribunal appointed two others judges, a Swiss and a Norwegian one. Nevertheless, the arbitration continued and on 19th June 2017 the tribunal announced its decision that only Slovenia would implement (Ministry of Foreign Affairs of the Republic of Slovenia 2017). Moreover, after the tribunal's decision the First Vice-President of the European Commission Frans Timmermans stated that the Commission "expects both parties to implement it" and no unilateral steps would be taken (European Commission 2017). Zagreb perceived this message negatively, but remained convinced that the process was "contaminated", while Ljubljana insists again on its application using Timmermans's statement as proof. Since July, the two sides have had a few meetings in order to find a solution.

The *second* repercussion caused by the Europeanization through hard conditionality concerns its mitigation of the success of EU's soft conditionality, as the Europeanization of political parties through socialization. According to Mikucka-Wójtowicz, due to transnational political cooperation, Croatian political parties have adapted and standardized their programs, moving towards the center and the European mainstream. Moreover, at "the beginning of the new century the country underwent a marked ideological-cultural transformation" (2016: 251) under the influence of their European political groups that stimulated some organizational modifications, even though strategies among Croatian parties varied. For instance, HDZ used contacts with the European People's Party (EPP) during election campaigns, whereas Milanović's SDP refused the support of prominent politicians and activists of the German Social Democratic Party (idem.). Notwithstanding the successful Europeanization of the party system, according to the Economist Intelligence Unit's Democracy Index (2017), since 2009 Croatia's democracy has slightly dropped within few categories.[6] This could be attributed to the global democracy's backsliding and the polarization of domestic politics that exists because of the politicization of the history of the twentieth century.

Furthermore, Croatian political parties have changed their approach towards topics linked to national identity. Indeed, HDZ based its discourse on national history arguments, in particular invoking the Homeland War as a starting point for the construction of the national identity against, as the former HDZ leader Tomislav Karamarko said in 2013, "syntagm of the Western Balkans that we never belonged to" (Breglec 2015: 18). Other political parties were also prepared to "rediscover" the Homeland

War as part of the Croatian identity, partially abandoned because of hard conditionality. For instance, in 2015 Croatian liberal Member of the European Parliament (MEP) stated that "the ICTY has tried to balance the culpability of Serbia and Croatia" (Milošević 2017: 905). Considering relations with BiH, PM Milanović criticized the EU's disinterestedness over BiH, stating that he "will do everything to increase the interest of the EU leaders towards BiH" (Večernji.hr 2014). Moreover, since 2014 Croatian MEPs have regularly uploaded the discussion over political challenges for BiH, stating that BiH's Croats do not have equal political rights, as is the case for Serbs and Bosniaks. This way, BiH has seen the work of MEPs as interference with BiH's internal affairs, which have increased tensions between the two countries (Milošević 2017).

3.6 Conclusion

This chapter shows that the impact of Croatia's Europeanization through hard conditionality has opened new challenges which have influenced its politics since the 2013 EU membership. The analysis provides, first, Croatia's intention to "return to Europe" and pro-EU disposition in the 1990s which was, however, marked by strong opposition to the EU's regional approach and the identity construct of the "Western Balkans", perceived as a threat to national identity. Second, although it was not requested for post-socialist CEECs, between 2000 and 2013 Croatian governments accepted the EU's regional approach, which is confirmed by the examples of "full collaboration" with the ICTY, the change of foreign policy towards BiH and the resolution of the border dispute with Slovenia. However, the Croatian political elite continued to doubt the "Western Balkans" character of the country, which raised the question—both theoretically and practically—about the success of Europeanization through hard conditionality that shapes geopolitical and national identities. Third, despite the successful compliance, after the 2013 accession Croatia's politics has been challenged by the need for repositioning on identity and geopolitical issues. Thus, pre-accession conditions have mitigated the success of the Europeanization of political parties through soft conditionality. Indeed, the center-left as well as center-right political parties doubt EU decisions that shaped historical and geopolitical characteristics of Croatian politics, in particular through conditions related to neighbors, Slovenia and BiH, and transitional justice, which for a long time questioned the legitimacy of some of Croatia's operations during the Homeland War.

Notes

1. In fact, some international actors contested the offensive in August 1995 of the Croatian Army in order to retake the control over the occupied parts of the country by Serbian rebels, which led to the end of the war.
2. For example, at the parliamentary elections in 1996 the Social Democratic Party of Croatia (SDP) won 8%, the Croatian Social Liberal Party (HSLS) 9%, while the Croatian Democratic Union (HDZ) had 59% of seats.
3. The government was composed of SDP, HSLS, the Croatian Peasant Party (HSS), Croatian People's Party—Liberal Democrats (HNS) and the Istrian Democratic Assembly (IDS).
4. Actually, Ante Gotovina was arrested in Spain on 7th of December 2005 by the Spanish Police and immediately transferred to the ICTY in Hague.
5. Indeed, Claudio Radaelli's text containing his definition of Europeanization is the second most cited (1404 times) according to google.scholar research tool (12th of September 2017).
6. The Economist Intelligence Unit's Index of Democracy is based on five categories: electoral process and pluralism; civil liberties; functioning of government; political participation; and political culture. Since 2009, as well as many other Western and Eastern European countries, Croatia has fallen off in political participation, political culture and, since 2016, in civil liberties.

References

Bartlett, W. (2008). *Europe's Troubled Region: Economic Development, Institutional Reform and Social Welfare in the Western Balkans.* Abingdon: Routledge.

Breglec, Z. (2015). Balkan kao prazan ili lebdeći označitelj u hrvatskom javnom i političkom diskurzu. https://tinyurl.com/ycov3b5p. Downloaded 1 September 2017.

Council. (1997). 2003rd Council Meeting. http://europa.eu/rapid/press-release_PRES-97-129_en.pdf. Downloaded 10 March 2017.

Council. (1998). 2085th Council Meeting. http://europa.eu/rapid/press-release_PRES-98-109_en.htm. Downloaded 26 August 2017.

DIP. (2000). Izbor zastupnika u Zastupnički dom Hrvatskoga državnog sabora. http://www.izbori.hr/2000Sabor/index.htm. Downloaded 14 March 2017.

Economist Intelligence Unit's Democracy Index. (2017). Democracy Index 2016 Revenge of the "Deplorables". http://felipesahagun.es/wp-content/uploads/2017/01/Democracy-Index-2016.pdf. Downloaded 12 September 2017.

European Commission. (1995). Bulletin 10-1995 of the European Commission. http://aei.pitt.edu/65274/1/BUL380.pdf. Downloaded 29 August 2017.

European Commission. (2000). Zagreb Summit 24 November 2000 Final Declaration. www.esiweb.org/pdf/bridges/.../ZagrebSummit24Nov2000.pdf. Downloaded 26 April 2017.

European Commission. (2004). Communication from the Commission Opinion on Croatia's Application for Membership of the European Union. http://eur-lex.europa.eu/LexUriServ/LexUriServ.do?uri=COM:2004:0257:FIN:EN:PDF. Downloaded 12 March 2017.

European Commission. (2005). Croatia 2005 Progress Report. https://ec.europa.eu/neighbourhood-enlargement/sites/near/files/archives/pdf/key_documents/2005/package/sec_1424_final_progress_report_hr_en.pdf. Downloaded 12 March 2017.

European Commission. (2017). Statement by First Vice-President Timmermans. http://europa.eu/rapid/press-release_STATEMENT-17-1911_en.htm. Downloaded 29 August 2017.

European Parliament. (1996). Report on the Communication from the Commission on the Reconstruction in Former Yugoslavia: EU Aid Administration and Internal Aid Coordination. http://www.europarl.europa.eu/sides/getDoc.do?pubRef=-//EP//TEXT+REPORT+A4-1996-0178+0+DOC+XML+V0//EN#_part6_defl. Downloaded 29 August 2017.

Freyburg, T., & Richter, S. (2010). National Identity Matters: The Limited Impact of EU Political Conditionality in the Western Balkans. *Journal of European Public Policy, 17*(2), 263–281.

Glaurdic, J. (2011). *The Hour of Europe: Western Powers and the Breakup of Yugoslavia*. New Haven: Yale University Press.

Grizo, M. (2014). European Union's Policy of 'Regional Approach' 1996–1999: The Case of Macedonia. *Balkan Social Science Review, 3*, 157–177.

Grubiša, D. (2000). The Zagreb Summit and Croatian Foreign Policy. *Croatian International Relations Review, 20*(6), 117–121.

Ješe Perković, A. (2013). National Heroes vs. EU Benefits: Croatia and the EU Conditionality. *CEU Political Science Journal, 8*(2), 177–201.

Kasapović, M. (1996). Demokratska tranzicija i političke institucije u Hrvatskoj. *Politička misao, 33*(2–3), 84–99.

Lindstrom, N. (2003). Between Europe and the Balkans: Mapping Slovenia and Croatia's "Return to Europe" in the 1990s. *Dialectical Anthropology, 27*(3–4), 313–329.

Mikucka-Wójtowicz, D. (2016). Resilient or Resistant? The Impact of Transnational Party Cooperation on Croatian Political Parties. *East European Politics, 32*(2), 236–257.

Milošević, A. (2017). Back to the Future, Forward to the Past: Croatian Politics of Memory in the European Parliament. *Nationalities Papers, 45*(5), 893–909.

Ministry of Foreign Affairs of the Republic of Slovenia. (2017). Arbitration. http://www.vlada.si/en/projects/arbitration/. Downloaded 26 August 2017.

Ministry of Foreign and European Affairs of the Republic of Croatia. (2017). Termination of the Arbitration Process Between Croatia and Slovenia: Causes and Consequences. http://www.mvep.hr/en/other/termination-of-the-arbitration-process/. Downloaded 26 August 2017.

Miošić-Lisjak, N. (2006). Croatia and the European Union. *Policy Studies, 27*(2), 101–114.

Musladin, M. (2012). Europska politika proširenja i Republika Hrvatska: specifične okolnosti. *Društvo, 6*, 105–122.

Radaelli, C. M. (2003). The Europeanization of Public Policy. In K. Featherstone & C. M. Radaelli (Eds.), *The Politics of Europeanization* (pp. 27–56). Oxford: Oxford University Press.

Risse, T. (2010). *A Community of Europeans? Transnational Identities and Public Spheres*. London: Cornell University Press.

Risse, T., Green Cowles, M., & Caporaso, J. (2001). Europeanization and Domestic Change: Introduction. In M. Green Cowles, J. Caporaso, & T. Risse (Eds.), *Transforming Europe: Europeanization and Domestic Change* (pp. 1–20). London: Cornell University Press.

Robreno, K. I. (2008). The Right to a Fair Mistrial: A Criticism of the Procedures at the International Criminal Tribunal for the Former Yugoslavia. https://works.bepress.com/kelly_robreno/1/. Downloaded 16 March 2017.

Sancin, V. (2010). Slovenia-Croatia Border Dispute: From Drnovšek-Račan to Pahor-Kosor Agreement. *Journal on European Perspectives, 2*(2), 93–113.

Schimmelfennig, F., & Sedelmeier, U. (2004). Governance by Conditionality: EU Rule Transfer to the Candidate Countries of Central and Eastern Europe. *Journal of European Public Policy, 11*(4), 661–679.

Schweiss, J., & Jebb, C. R. (2006). The European Union in the Balkans: From Intervention to Accession. In J. Adamski, M. T. Johnson, & C. Schweiss (Eds.), *Old Europe, New Security; Evolution for a Complex World* (pp. 101–116). Farnham: Ashgate.

Subotić, J. (2014). Legitimacy, Scope, and Conflicting Claims on the ICTY: In the Aftermath of Gotovina, Haradinaj and Perišić. *Journal of Human Rights, 13*(2), 170–185.

Tatalović, S., & Jakešević, R. (2013). Europeizacija bilateralnog odnosa Hrvatske i Srbije: ograničenja i perspektive. In M. Podunavac & Ž. Paunović (Eds.), *Politika: nauka i profesija* (pp. 235–249). Belgrade: Faculty of Political Science.

Tuđman, F. (1998). *Zna se. HDZ u borbi za učvršćenje hrvatske državne suverenosti – knjiga 4*. Zagreb: Glavno tajništvo Središnjice HDZ.

Večernji.hr. (2014). Milanović u Mostaru o neredima: s BiH se šuta i napucava već 100 godina, Published on 9th February 2014, https://www.vecernji.hr/vijesti/milanovic-dosao-sam-u-mostar-smiriti-strasti-920059. Downloaded 19 April 2017.

Wikileaks. (2009). Pushing Croatia Forward on ICTY Cooperation and EU Accession. https://wikileaks.org/plusd/cables/09ZAGREB694_a.html. Downloaded 21 April 2016.

CHAPTER 4

Political Attention of Croatian Governments 1990–2015

Daniela Širinić

4.1 Introduction

In this chapter, we provide the first systematic examination of the macro-structure of government agenda in Croatia, in particular, its scope and long-term dynamics. To accomplish this we rely on the indicators of political attention obtained from the original data set of weekly government meetings containing over 40,000 agenda items. The data set contains an empirical measure of issue attention that captures how many times the government discussed and decided upon a particular issue as compared to all other issues on the agenda for the period between 1990 and 2015. Moreover, by following the policy dynamics approach we also ask whether the electoral turnover in governments induces variation in government agendas. In other words, we ask whether political parties have an impact on policy-making.

D. Širinić (✉)
Faculty of Political Science, University of Zagreb, Zagreb, Croatia
e-mail: daniela.sirinic@fpzg.hr

Z. Petak, K. Kotarski (eds.), *Policy-Making at the European Periphery*, New Perspectives on South-East Europe,
https://doi.org/10.1007/978-3-319-73582-5_4

4.2 Government Agenda Setting: Policy Dynamics Approach

Governments are central for the policy-making process (Laver and Shepsle 1996). From the fundamental activities of maintaining law and order, providing public services or negotiating trade relations with other countries, to handling school curriculums or staying on top of the weather emergency protocols—the government manages the national policy agenda. Ideally, a government agenda reflects the parties' strategic choices between policy alternatives that should be attended during the mandate; namely, it should include a list of previous commitments given to citizens through election manifestos, coalition agreements or government programmes (e.g. see McDonald and Budge 2005). Alignment between previous commitments and future policy-making is a key for democratic accountability. Citizens can only hold officials responsible if policy objectives, the benchmarks of success, are set *a priori*. Equally important, the overall distribution of political attention tells us not only whether the government fulfils its electoral promises, but reveals what policy-making *is about* and *who is included* in the process. Less diversity can bring about greater discrepancies in the representation of relevant social and political groups in the society.

Even with normative ideals aside, the careful prioritization of planned policy-making will not only make governance more effective but should also serve for re-election strategy (John et al. 2013). Parties have incentives to dedicate an uneven level of attention to policies preferred by their constituencies. They will give more priority to issues they traditionally 'own' to distinguish themselves from other parties (e.g. see Baumgartner et al. 2009). Consequently, the government agenda should reflect pre-commitments to ensure stable approval of the electorate when the end of the term in office is closing in. Nonetheless, it is also entirely possible that the translation of policy preferences into policy outputs is constrained by the inability or reluctance of political parties to formulate clear objectives and follow through on their promises. This scenario is most likely in clientelistic systems where the logics of party competition differ from Western party systems. If clientelism is present, political parties dedicate their attention to those issues that maximize instrumental outcomes. Policies target their own clientelistic bases in order to ensure electoral support regardless of the promises made during electoral campaigns (Roberts 2009).

Since the late 1970s there have been a number of empirical studies trying to assess the partisan influence on various stages of policy-making. The studies have so far generated ambiguous findings. Proponents of partisan differentiation maintain that the change in the composition of government has some bearing on differing policy outcomes. As an illustration, some studies have shown that party manifestos can be a good predictor of spending priorities (Budge and Hofferbert 1990; Hofferbert and Budge 1992). However, evidence coming from the camp of proponents of 'party neutrality' thesis, argue that agenda setting bears the characteristics of a zero-sum game. Governments do not operate in a vacuum and their time and resources are scarce (John et al. 2013). The space of decision-making is limited and the ability of governments to translate their policy preferences into policy outputs is constrained by many factors that in terms of influence on agenda setting outperform partisan change in government (e.g. Baumgartner and Jones 2010; Jones and Baumgartner 2005, 2012). Two most prominent limitations are *organizational-cognitive capacity* and *institutional constraints*.

Only small segments of government activities include planning, as their time is limited by the need to react to outside events that often cannot be anticipated even in the most stable and coordinated systems and under optimal conditions. This reactive role of governments includes screening, processing, summarizing information and considering relevant alternatives to the problem at hand. Such activities sometimes overlap with some other issues that the government is already attending to; however, multitasking and juggling between specialized and often unconnected policy topics is the general rule rather than the exception in day-to-day governing. Even if we consider that governments do not operate in a vacuum, as they have the support of a number of civil servants and experts who prepare relevant information, the attention of executives is still limited by the *organizational and cognitive capacity* to aggregate and process such large amounts of limited information that they receive at their end of the process (e.g. see Jones 2001).

Also, government activities depend on various *institutional constraints*, most notably mandate length, coalition bargaining, public discussions with relevant veto players, legislative timetable, financial resources or multilevel governance structures, such as the European Union (e.g. see Chaqués Bonafont et al. 2015). Governments often need to prioritize between a set of issues because there is no more time to process new legislation, because limitations in the budget do not allow the simultaneous corrections in several prioritized domains, or because the European Commission has recommended focus on some areas that governments did not plan to attend to in the given period. It is also important to note another limitation to agenda space: some issues governments attend to are always more important and prominent than others. Those issues correspond to the core functions of government and include the economy, defence, international affairs, government operations and the rule of law (Jennings et al. 2011). When highly salient, these five core issues dominate most modern government agendas, squeeze out agenda-setting space for other relevant policy topics and reduce overall agenda diversity (Jennings et al. 2011).

Research on agenda setting, and government agendas in particular, has contributed to understanding the patterns of attention allocation and the determinants of agendas in the US and in Western European democracies. However, agenda-setting research in the new democracies' settings, especially in post-communist countries, is still not available. To ask *what governments have been up to, how their attention is distributed across policy topics and what the possible factors attributing to attention allocation besides party preferences are* is relevant in any political system. By the same token it is essential in countries with a short history of democratic experience that are still going through rapid social, economic and political transitions where both citizens and political elites are still catching up with day-to-day democratic policy-making. Furthermore, while we know a lot about these countries' party systems, voting behaviour, state-building and institutional frameworks, there is a significant gap in understanding the everyday governance. This is due to the fact that research was focused on the most crucial areas at the time, namely, processes and actors related to democracy building and consolidation, but also because of a pronounced lack of transparency of government daily policy-making. Studies of government agendas are usually restricted because of the lack of publicly available records; however, in countries where policy-making, and policy-implementation in particular, are covered by the veil of clientelism and patronage, the black box of government has, until recently, often been impenetrable for researchers. Motivated by these gaps and borrowing from the literature on agenda setting, we first present a short overview of the institutional-political context surrounding government activities in Croatia, in order to formulate hypotheses on the expected macro-structure of government attention allocation and expectations on the role of political parties on agenda change in Croatia.

4.3 Croatian Governments in Institutional-Political Context

Croatia's path to democracy, similar to other post-communist countries, was characterized by rapid social, economic and political changes. The first stage of transformation began with the breakaway election in 1990 that produced a two-party system with the winning Croatian Democratic Party (HDZ) versus the left block consisting of a four-party coalition of the Democrats (HDS), the Christian Democrats (HKDS), the Social Liberals (HSLS) and the Social Democrats (SDH, now SDP) in the opposition (Henjak et al. 2013). Croatian Parliament quickly adopted a new constitution and established a strong semi-presidential system. However, while the initial stage of transformation looked promising, conflict with Belgrade soon escalated into open aggression and war (Henjak et al. 2013), and the new president Tuđman had a mandate to respond to the ongoing crisis (Zakošek 2008). So, unlike fast transitions in other post-communist regime changes, Croatian democratization was protracted because the war has prevented full-scale progress to democracy and a market economy (Zakošek 2008). The HDZ and, most of all, Tuđman, seized the moment and mobilized the electorate around the ideas of national unity and state-building as key political priorities.

As a result, the new Croatian democracy in the 1990s exhibited all features of defective and illiberal democracies, with the concentration of powers in the hands of a president with authoritarian tendencies (Dolenec 2013). The president appointed and dismissed the prime minister and had the complete power over the executive (Boban 2007). He convened government sessions and presided over them. Furthermore, the president had the monopoly on deciding what issues appeared on the government weekly agenda, and de facto full control of the executive. During the HDZ predominant party rule and Tuđman's monopoly over executive powers, prime ministers and cabinet members were changed according to his arbitrary decisions. Before Croatia officially declared independence, Stjepan Mesić (HDZ) and Josip Manolić (HDZ) led the government as presidents of the executive council. Members of the cabinet during the terms of first two governments, with the exception of one HDZ minister in each government, were nonpartisan (Kasapović 2005). As a response to the escalation of conflicts during the second half of 1991, Tuđman established a 'government of democratic unity' led by Franjo Gregurić (HDZ) that included representatives from the majority of parties (Zakošek 2008).

However, Greguric's government slowly dissipated as a new election was announced and ministers from other parties gradually left the government. They were replaced by HDZ ministers. After the 1992 parliamentary election mandate was given to Hrvoje Šarinić, who was replaced by Nikica Valentić in 1993. His term ended after the 1995 parliamentary election, when Zlatko Mateša was appointed prime minister.

Tuđman died while in office in 1999 and the new centre-left coalition led by the Social Democratic Party (SDP) gained electoral victory—marking the beginning of the second stage of transition. The new coalition government led by Ivica Račan first implemented comprehensive constitutional reforms towards the establishment of a parliamentary system. Constitutional reforms increased the role of the executive, and subdued the functions of the president to mostly symbolic and ceremonial roles. The executive power was placed in the hands of the government, with the prime minister as the head of the executive branch. Parallel to the far-reaching constitutional reforms, the new oversized coalition was also determined to end the period of international isolation—a result of Tuđman's uncooperative foreign policies—as Croatia joined NATO's Partnership for Peace program and signed the Stabilisation and Association Agreement with the EU. However, faced with right-wing protests organized by war veterans over the cooperation with the Hague Tribunal, the government was destabilized and the pressure resulted in government split. Račan formed a new cabinet, which was in office until parliamentary election in 2003.

During Račan's mandate, HDZ was transforming. Ivo Sanader, a new HDZ president, repackaged HDZ into a moderate pro-European conservative party and managed to win the 2003 parliamentary election (Nikić Čakar 2013). The new government, supported in parliament by several smaller parties, had continued the previous government's foreign policy agenda and accelerated the accession process by emphasizing a policy of anti-discrimination against ethnic minorities. At the same time, however, this reformist programmatic turn did not imply the abandonment of the established patterns of clientelistic links, as HDZ continued to exploit state resources by designing policies for their constituencies, in particular to war veterans and their families (Stubbs and Zrinščak 2009), which helped them win the second consecutive term in office after the 2007 parliamentary election. However, Sanader suddenly resigned from office in 2009 and was replaced by Jadranka Kosor. Prior to the 2011 election,

Croatia faced record unemployment rates, a negative GDP rate and a web of corruption practices. The Social Democratic Party (SDP), the Peoples Party-Liberal Democrats (HNS), the Istrian Democratic Assembly (IDS) and the Croatian Party of Pensioners (HSU) formed the so-called 'Kukuriku' coalition and won the 2011 parliamentary election, and the new government, led by Prime Minister Zoran Milanović, was formed.

In contrast to the weak single-party governments under the auspices of Tuđman during the first decade of Croatian transition, the second decade is characterized by coalition governments. From 2000 to the end of 2015, the period analysed in this chapter, Croatia saw the formation and termination of six governments. Not all changes stemmed from parliamentary elections, as the first, Račan, government ended because of a conflict within the coalition and the second, Sanader, government because of his resignation. However, this separation of government mandates is consistent with the widely accepted Grofman and Roozendaal's (1997) markers of government termination. After the constitutional changes in 2000, governments assumed their full executive powers and independence. While the executive is now responsible to the parliament, as in other parliamentary democracies, the government has control over legislative activities as it proposes more than 90% of all laws in parliament. At least in formal terms, institutional constraints set by the semi-presidential system from the 1990s were lifted and governments took over the role of dominant executive power. In this regard we expect to find significant differences in the overall distribution of policy attention before and after 2000. Moreover, the shift from a transitional to consolidated democracy that occurred in 2000–2001 certainty qualifies as a major institutional change that should result in a large shift in overall agenda attention and content.

However, for more than two decades Croatian elites have competed on a set of symbolic and cultural values that were very effective in polarizing the electorate (e.g. see Henjak et al. 2013). Strong identity-based divisions grounded in competing interpretations of history and transition have guided political competition and dominated political space since the beginning of democratic transition in the 1990s (Henjak et al. 2013). However, while the persistence of these divisions has played a crucial role in party system stabilization, the majority of citizens are not satisfied with the way democracy works in the country; they are becoming more inclined to stay home on election day or show their anti-party sentiment by voting for new political parties. While there have been some changes in party programmes' differentiation, whereby parties have tried to move away from the cultural dimension of competition and emphasize socio-economic issues, these differences are still not well pronounced and are often presented in an inconsistent way (Dolenec 2009; Petković 2009).

This limited policy space and inability of political parties to clearly convey their socio-economic differences to the electorate blurs the necessary lines of accountability because vague policy promises cannot constrain future governments' activities. What is more, weak programmatic differentiation is confirmed by the practice of governing coalitions to start their mandates with policy-blind agreements (Kasapović 2005) or to present very vague and general policy objectives in coalition manifestos (e.g. see Petković 2009). More importantly, such symbolic and non-substantive expressions of party policy preferences continue to weigh on long-term challenges and underlying structural instabilities such as the sustainability of the pension system, rampant corruption, rising unemployment or lack of regulatory infrastructure. Important issues are often swept under the carpet and raised only when they could benefit electioneering strategies. Because of these observations *we do not expect to see significant differences in political attention distribution between right and left coalition governments.*

4.4 Issue Attention: Approach and Methodology

Early on, policy agenda research examined how issues come to government attention, who and by what mechanisms defines issue alternatives or how political attention changes and under what conditions (e.g. see Kingdon 1984). Pioneers of this research were Baumgartner and Jones (2010). With the goal of analysing the dynamics of political attention in a systematic way by quantitatively capturing issue attention, they collected all hearings and laws of the American Congress from the entire post-war period and devised a codebook of policy topics and subtopics that covers the universe of public actions. Because they had information on the entire universe of public actions they were able to measure how many times the government discussed and decided upon a particular issue compared to all other issues on the agenda. This enabled them to examine the entire policy agenda and provide a broader and more general perspective on the temporal dynamics of issue attention. Baumgartner and Jones methodology was soon after 'syndicated' to other Western democracies through the Comparative Agendas Project (CAP). CAP was initiated to develop a baseline infrastructure for the systematic comparison of political attention across countries, but also to test theories developed in the United States on a wider set of cases. A result of this international network is the CAP codebook, which defines universal standards for classifying the topics of public policy activity. Designed in an effort to capture every issue attention regardless of the historical or institutional settings, the Codebook lists all core policy sectors and policy issues within each sector and travels well both across countries and across time (Bevan 2014).

Following the standards set by the CAP codebook, we have initiated the Croatian Policy Agendas project. The major source of data on government agendas were the archives of the government weekly meetings from the 1990 to 2011, which have undergone the procedure of official declassification solely for the purposes of the project. The agendas of the meetings held from the end of 2011 until the end of 2015 were downloaded from the central government portal. The source data set, of over 40,000 items, was coded according to the methodology of the CAP. Each item appearing in the government weekly meetings, which included various types of government decisions such as legislative proposals, programmes, strategies or decisions on nominations, was classified according to the CAP codebook. The Codebook is organized into 21 major policy topics covering general national policy sectors such as 'Domestic Macroeconomics', 'Social Welfare' or 'Defence' (see Table 4.1.). Major topics consist of 214 policy subtopics that include specific issue areas within each major topic.[1] Topic categories are mutually exclusive and exhaustive, which implies that each issue on a government agenda can only be assigned to one category and that each agenda item should fit into one of the categories. Whenever a legislative proposal, strategy or government decision proposal covered more than one topic, it was coded under the predominant topic or under the general subcategory of the major topic. Moreover, classification implies that the document is coded according to the predominant policy area, and not by specific targets or policy instruments. For instance, the decision to change the VAT rate for books and newspapers should be coded as the regulation of media industry and media policy, and not as general taxation policy, since the change in tax rates is a policy instrument (Bevan 2014).

The main limitation of policy agenda studies, and similar content analysis-based research, is the amount of documents required to create functional data sets. This is why we decided to code source data sets by combining manual and automated topic classification by means of machine learning techniques. Our approach to automated topic classification is based on supervised learning models, whereby an algorithm 'learns' about the common features of set categories from a manually coded sample data

Table 4.1 Summary statistics of weekly government meetings' topic attention by year, 1990–2015

Topic	*Name*	*N*	*Mean (%)*	*SD (%)*	*Min (%)*	*Max (%)*
1	Domestic macroeconomic issues	3053	6.6	1.7	3.8	9.8
2	Civil rights and minority issues	1067	2.1	1.1	0.4	5.0
3	Health	1117	2.2	1.0	0.5	4.5
4	Agriculture	1230	2.7	0.9	1.2	5.1
5	Labour and employment	598	1.4	0.7	0.4	3.9
6	Education	823	1.7	0.6	0.7	3.0
7	Environment	971	2.0	0.8	0.7	3.9
8	Energy	1057	2.2	0.6	1.4	3.6
9	Immigration and refugee issues	50	0.1	0.3	0.0	1.6
10	Transportation	2019	4.3	0.8	2.9	6.2
11	Law, crime, and family issues	2053	4.3	1.4	1.6	8.1
12	Social welfare	1148	2.5	0.6	1.6	4.6
13	Community dev. and housing issues	1729	3.6	1.2	2.0	8.0
14	Banking, finance, and dom. commerce	3511	7.4	1.1	5.8	9.5
15	Defence	2263	4.9	1.2	2.5	8.1
16	Science, technology, and communication	928	2.0	0.6	0.9	3.9
17	Foreign trade	1388	3.0	1.4	0.9	5.9
18	International affairs	7125	14.5	4.2	7.7	22.3
19	Government operations	12424	26.9	5.0	19.5	35.5
20	Public lands, water, and territory	2671	5.4	2.8	1.0	11.3
21	Cultural policy issue	210	0.4	0.2	0.1	1.1

set and uses that information to predict policy topic membership for other, still not classified, items. Since the success of automated coding is entirely based on the quality of the manually coded data set, we introduced multiple checkpoints during the manual coding procedure to ensure that our human 'gold standard' is as accurate and reliable as possible. We hope that lessons learned from these experiments will be useful to others working on the same or similar task for other languages; a detailed description on the ATC and the procedures conducted to ensure that data is classified with a high degree of reliability can be found in Karan et al. (2016).

4.5 General Patterns of Governmental Issue Attention

We start our analysis by examining the content of government issue attention during the entire period from 1990 to 2015. Table 4.1. provides a summary of our findings. It shows the list of major CAP topics, the

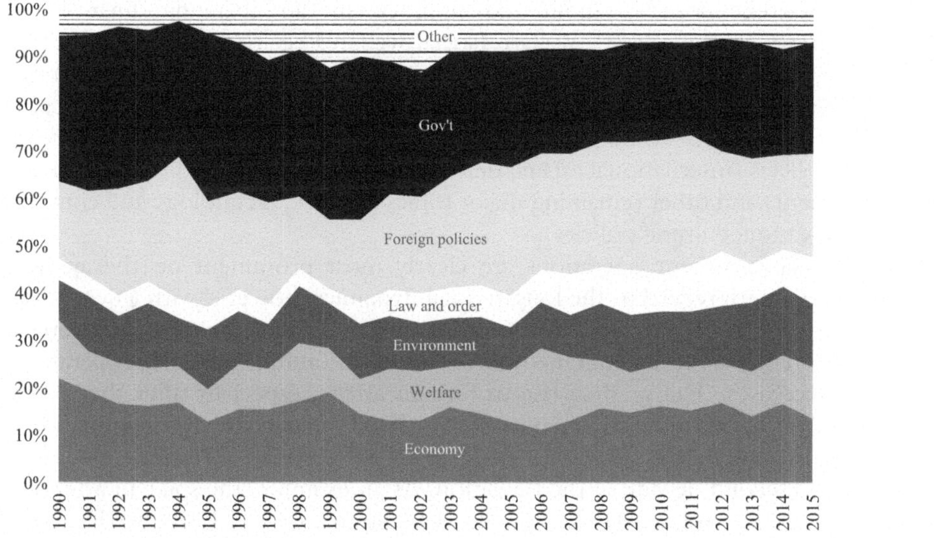

Fig. 4.1 Variation in issue attention over time

number of agenda items per topic and the average percentage share of each major topic over the period under examination. The largest major topic on the Croatian government agenda is government operations as they account for more than a quarter of total government attention. Government operations include activities related to the civil service, local governments, budgeting, regulation of political parties, questions on nominations and appointments, government procurement procedures and, most relevantly for Croatia, the management of public property and privatization. The second major topic is international affairs, which includes issues concerning EU accession and membership and issues regarding relations with neighbouring countries. Foreign relations are followed by banking, finance and domestic commerce, macroeconomic issues and decisions related to public lands, water, and territory management. Taken together, these topics account for more than 60% of the whole attention of the governments over the entire period.

Figure 4.1 shows the distribution of major topics over time, thus enabling a more detailed interpretation. Issue attention is calculated on a yearly basis. For the purpose of this chapter, and borrowing from Breunig (2014), major topics were aggregated into seven macro categories: economy (macroeconomics; labour and employment; and banking, finance and domestic commerce), welfare (social welfare; health; housing and urban development; and education), environment (environment; energy; transportation; and agriculture), law and order (law, crime and family; civil rights and minority issues; and immigration), government operations, foreign policies (international affairs; defence and public lands and water management) and other remaining major topics (science, technology and communication; cultural policies).

Government operations are clearly most prominent on the agenda, even with regard to the longitudinal dynamics, however with a decreasing trend after the democratic consolidation in 2000. Foreign policies attention rises almost simultaneously as the attention to government operations decreases. The gradual rise in foreign affairs, especially after the formal application to the EU membership in 2003, reflects the new dominance of EU accession as a political priority for all Croatian governments during the second decade of the transition. As an example, the spike in attention to foreign relations in 2011 reflects a culmination of EU entry talks, especially regarding the last chapters on judiciary and competition policy. In a similar vein, attention to economic issues rises and falls as a response to economic hard times, especially at the onset of the transition to open markets in early 1990, during the late 1990s, and during the global economic crisis that started in 2008.

Other topics, such as environmental issues, agriculture and transport, or welfare, including a set of general social policies, seem to be more erratic and do not respond to any major changes in the political and economic environment. However, a more detailed and specified analysis is needed to confirm these observed patterns. But it is evident, as suggested by earlier research, that attention to core topics reduced the space for other policy areas. For instance, sudden increases in attention to welfare were possible only when there was a general reduction in attention to government operations and foreign policies, as was the case in 2006. Similarly, the largest increase in remaining major categories was recorded in 2002 when there was a decrease in attention to government operation, and foreign policy attention had not yet reached its peak.

However, it is remarkable how little the shift to consolidation has changed the overall distribution of the agenda topics. To confirm this finding, it is necessary to calculate a measure of the relative concentration or dispersion of attention. The most commonly used indicator is Shannon's

H, a probabilistic measure of the spread of observations across a number of nominal categories (Jennings et al. 2011).[2] If all issues appear equally in the agenda, maximum entropy score for the 21 major topics would be 3.04 and if a single major topic dominates the entire agenda, entropy score would be 0. Overall agenda diversity is 1.91 during the first decade of transition and is 1.98 during the second period from 2000 to 2015. This relatively small difference shows that, contrary to expectations, the shift from transitional to consolidated democracy, did not result in major structural shifts in agenda diversity.

4.6 Government Partisanship and Agenda Change

The first part of this chapter looked into the general, macro patterns of governmental agenda across issues and across time. In this second part of the analysis we ask whether there are any differences in issue attention stemming from changes in government. Since the constitutional changes in 2000 the government formally received full executive powers, the focus of this part of the analysis is on the period starting with the mandate of Ivica Račan and ending with the mandate of Zoran Milanović. For ease of interpretation we first look at the differences in issue attention across topics by governments aggregated into two camps—left and right. Left governments include two Račan and one Milanović mandate, and right governments include HDZ coalitions under Sanader and Kosor (see Table 4.2).

At first glance, the table does not reveal any large differences in attention allocation. Relative to their prominence in the agenda, the largest differences are present in the areas of international affairs and public property management. When it comes to international relations, it is clear that differences cannot be attributed to government partisanship but rather to the timing of EU accession. As an additional test we have generated correlation coefficients for each of the succeeding pairs of cabinets. As an illustration, Račan cabinet's issue attention distribution across major policy topics (all 21 topics) was correlated with that of Mateša's cabinet, the last of Tuđman's prime ministers. The same calculation was applied to all successive governments. To ensure that our results are not biased by a high level of aggregation to major policy topics, we have applied the same measure to study correspondence between

Table 4.2 Differences in government attention across topics, by government prevailing ideology

Major topic	*Left governments' attention share (%)*	*Right governments' attention share (%)*	*DIFF (%)*
Domestic macroeconomic issues	5.6	6.8	−1.2
Civil rights, minority issues, and civil liberties	2.2	2.3	0.0
Health	2.4	2.3	0.1
Agriculture	2.5	2.6	-0.2
Labour and employment	1.3	1.2	0.1
Education	1.8	1.7	0.1
Environment	2.3	1.9	0.4
Energy	2.6	2.1	0.5
Immigration and refugee issues	0.2	0.0	0.2
Transportation	4.8	4.0	0.8
Law, crime, and family issues	5.1	4.0	1.1
Social welfare	2.3	2.5	-0.2
Community development and housing issues	3.1	3.9	-0.7
Banking, finance, and dom. commerce	7.7	7.3	0.4
Defence	4.5	4.9	−0.4
Science, technology, and communication	2.0	1.9	0.1
Foreign trade	2.9	2.9	0.0
International affairs	13.6	15.7	-2.1
Government operations	26.0	26.3	-0.2
Public lands, water, and territorial issues	6.5	5.2	1.3
Cultural policy issue	0.4	0.5	-0.1

cabinets given agenda subtopics, 214 of them. Results are shown in Fig. 4.2, all correlations are statistically significant at the 0.05 level.

Correspondence between agendas at the level of major topics is staggering. With the lowest correlation of 0.83 between Mateša and Račan, there is a strong indication that the relative distributions of all governments since 2000 can hardly be differentiated from their predecessors. This confirms the general impression from Fig. 4.1. A closer look at agenda distribution across subtopics gives us a more nuanced picture. The largest shift in agenda

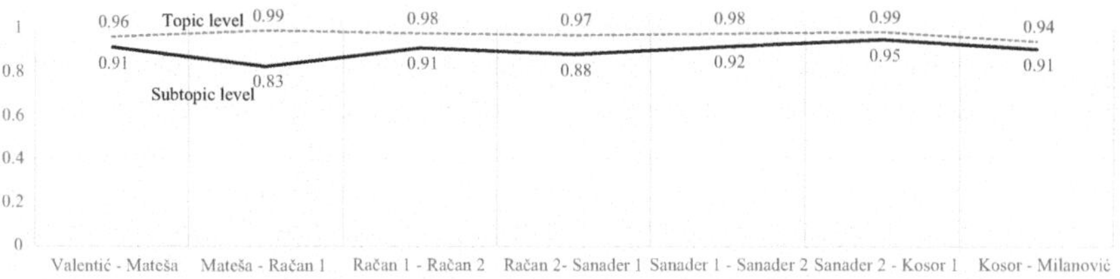

Fig. 4.2 Correlation coefficient of issue attention by topic areas from one government to the next

distribution, with still relatively high correspondence between Račan and Mateša, occurred in 2000. The second notable shift was in 2003, when Sanader's government replaced the centre-left coalition. Interestingly, there is a stronger resemblance between the Kosor and the second Sanader government, than Sanader's two consecutive terms.

4.7 Discussion and Conclusion

This chapter has provided only a short glance at the dynamics of government attention distribution in Croatia. Our first analysis showed that the majority of government decisions, over 60% of them, relate to government operations, international affairs, commerce and banking, domestic macroeconomic issues and issues related to lands, water and territory management. By looking at the dynamics of issue attention during the period from 1990 to 2015, we were also able to discern the trade-off between government operations and international relations, as the spike in one core area appears to reduce the space for attention in the other. Aside from the smaller increase in attention to categories related to law and crime, and the observed increase in the importance of EU-related decisions, there were no significant changes in attention diversity when comparing the two distinctive Croatian transitions. Similarly, an analysis of the differences in policy attention given government turnovers revealed expected findings. Apart from a change in agenda allocation that occurred after 2000, which can mainly be attributed to greater attention to government property management issues during the Račan government, there are no great differences in agenda setting between Croatian governments after the year 2000.

One explanation for this finding is already discussed in the introduction, whereby a lack of initial programme differences between party options simply transfers into agenda setting. If parties cannot be distinguished based on their policy positions and their coalition agreements do not state clear policy objectives, their attention allocation will not be guided by party preferences but will mostly be a reaction to outside events. The second explanation relates to the previous findings concerning the core concerns of the government. Every government, regardless of its partisan composition, has to deal with routine activities. Predominance of government operations is one example of such core area. More importantly, the 'innovation' potential of new governments in new democracies might be lower than expected because the core functions of the government are still in flux. From market reforms, privatization, the building of social welfare nets and the restructuring of public services, new governments might not have time to deal with contemporary challenges such as environment or education reforms. And thirdly, international pressures, especially those stemming from EU membership, might actually be a reductive factor in agenda diversity.

Notes

1. For example, major topic 'Defence' has 18 additional subcategories such as: 'General Defence', 'Defence Alliances and Security Assistance', 'Military Intelligence and Espionage', 'Military Aid and Weapons Sales to Other Countries' or 'Oversight of Defence Contracts and Contractors'.
2. Shannon H is calculated according to the following formula: $H = (-1) \sum p(xi) \ln(p(xi))$, where H is the negative sum of the likelihood p(x) for all topics, that a unit of analysis (x) belongs to a particular topic (i), multiplied by the natural log of that likelihood (Jennings et al. 2011).

References

Baumgartner, F. R., & Jones, B. D. (2010). *Agendas and Instability in American Politics*. Chicago: University of Chicago Press.

Baumgartner, F., Brouard, S., & Grossman, E. (2009). Agenda-Setting Dynamics in France: Revisiting the 'Partisan Hypothesis'. *French Politics, 7*(2), 75–95.

Bevan, S. (2014). Gone Fishing: The Creation of the Comparative Agendas Project Master Codebook. In *Technical Report*. Mannheim: MZES.

Boban, D. (2007). Abandoning of Semi-Presidentialism in Central Europe? Cases of Croatia and Poland. Presented at *21st World Congress of the International Political Science Association*, Santiago de Chile, Chile, July (1–22).

Bonafont, L. C., Palau, A., & Baumgartner, F. R. (2015). *Agenda Dynamics in Spain*. Basingstoke: Palgrave Macmillan.

Breunig, C. (2014). Content and Dynamics of Legislative Agendas in Germany. In C. Green-Pedersen & S. Walgrave (Eds.), *Agenda Setting, Policies, and Political Systems* (pp. 125–144). Chicago: University of Chicago Press.

Budge, I., & Hofferbert, R. I. (1990). Mandates and Policy Outputs: US Party Platforms and Federal Expenditures. *American Political Science Review, 84*(1), 111–131.

Dolenec, D. (2009). Demokratizacija stranačkog sustava u Hrvatskoj: ponuda i potražnja javnih politika. In Z. Petak (Ed.), *Stranke i javne politike – Izbori u Hrvatskoj 2007* (pp. 27–57). Zagreb: Biblioteka Politička misao.

Dolenec, D. (2013). *Democratic Institutions and Authoritarian Rule in Southeast Europe*. Colchester: ECPR Press.

Grofman, B., & Van Roozendaal, P. (1997). Modelling Cabinet Durability and Termination. *British Journal of Political Science, 27*(3), 419–451.

Henjak, A., Zakošek, N., & Čular, G. (2013). Croatia. In S. Bergund, J. Erman, K. Deegan Krause, & T. Knutsen (Eds.), *Handbook of Political Change in Eastern Europe* (pp. 443–480). Cheltenham: Edward Elgar Publishing.

Hofferbert, R. I., & Budge, I. (1992). The Party Mandate and the Westminster Model: Election Programmes and Government Spending in Britain 1948–85. *British Journal of Political Science, 22*(2), 151–182.

Jennings, W., Bevan, S., Timmermans, A., Breeman, G., Brouard, S., Chaqués-Bonafont, L., & Palau, A. M. (2011). Effects of the Core Functions of Government on the Diversity of Executive Agendas. *Comparative Political Studies, 44*(8), 1001–1030.

John, P., Bertelli, A., Jennings, W., & Bevan, S. (2013). *Policy Agendas in British Politics*. Basingstoke: Palgrave Macmillan.

Jones, B. D. (2001). *Politics and the Architecture of Choice: Bounded Rationality and Governance*. Chicago: University of Chicago Press.

Jones, B. D., & Baumgartner, F. R. (2005). *The Politics of Attention: How Government Prioritizes Problems*. Chicago: University of Chicago Press.

Jones, B. D., & Baumgartner, F. R. (2012). From There to Here: Punctuated Equilibrium to the General Punctuation Thesis to a Theory of Government Information Processing. *Policy Studies Journal, 40*(1), 1–20.

Karan, M., Šnajder, J., Širinić, D., & Glavaš, G. (2016). Analysis of Policy Agendas: Lessons Learned from Automatic Topic Classification of Croatian Political Texts, *Proceedings of the 10th Workshop on Language Technology for Cultural Heritage, Social Sciences, and Humanities (LaTeCH 2016)*, ACL 2016, Berlin.

Kasapović, M. (2005). Koalicijske vlade u Hrvatskoj: prva iskustva u komparativnoj perspektivi. In G. Čular (Ed.), *Izbori i konsolidacija demokracije u Hrvatskoj* (pp. 181–212). Zagreb: Biblioteka Politička misao.

Kingdon, J. W. (1984). *Agendas, Alternatives and Public policies*, (2011 reprint). Essex: Pearson Education Limited.

Laver, M., & Shepsle, K. A. (1996). *Making and Breaking Governments: Cabinets and Legislatures in Parliamentary Democracies*. Cambridge: Cambridge University Press.

McDonald, M. D., & Budge, I. (2005). *Elections, Parties, Democracy: Conferring the Median Mandate*. Oxford: Oxford University Press.

Nikić Čakar, D. (2013). *Prezidencijalizacija političkih stranaka: komparativna analiza britanske Laburističke stranke, Španjolske socijalističke radničke stranke i Hrvatske demokratske zajednice*. Zagreb: Fakultet političkih znanosti.

Petković, K. (2009). Simbolička nasuprot referencijskoj politici: neuspjeh javnih politika na parlamentarnim izborima 2007. In Z. Petak (Ed.), *Stranke i javne politike – Izbori u Hrvatskoj 2007* (pp. 59–103). Zagreb: Biblioteka Politička misao.

Roberts, A. (2009). *The Quality of Democracy in Eastern Europe: Public Preferences and Policy Reforms*. Cambridge: Cambridge University Press.

Stubbs, P., & Zrinščak, S. (2009). Croatian Social Policy: The Legacies of War, State-Building and Late Europeanization. *Social Policy & Administration, 43*(2), 121–135.

Zakošek, N. (2008). Democratization, State-Building and War: The Cases of Serbia and Croatia. *Democratization, 15*(3), 588–610.

CHAPTER 5

Interest Groups in the Policy-Making Process in Croatia

Igor Vidačak and Kristijan Kotarski

5.1 Introduction

This chapter seeks to explore the development of the contemporary scene of organized interests in Croatia and the strategies they use to gain access and exert influence in national policy-making venues. For the purpose of this chapter, we will be using a broader definition of interest group as a formally organized association that seeks to influence public policy (Thomas 1993, 2017), which goes beyond the traditional narrow approach of including only private associations that have a distinct, formal organization. Our definition encompasses also various entities of government: national, regional, and local government agencies or state-owned enterprises (SOEs), as important lobbying forces in Croatian society. Along with the term 'interest group', we will be using occasionally the term 'interests', to denote broad or less-formalized political constituencies, such as disability benefit users or religious organizations. Similarly, we will also opt for the term 'interest' when considering government entities working to influence other government bodies (e.g. local and regional

I. Vidačak (✉) • K. Kotarski
Faculty of Political Science, University of Zagreb, Zagreb, Croatia
e-mail: igor.vidacak@fpzg.hr; kristijan.kotarski@fpzg.hr

Z. Petak, K. Kotarski (eds.), *Policy-Making at the European Periphery*, New Perspectives on South-East Europe,
https://doi.org/10.1007/978-3-319-73582-5_5

self-government units lobbying for increased funding from the national government) or powerful informal groups of political and professional elites that may not be recognized as formal groups but have undeniable informal influence on shaping public policy. For the purpose of explaining reasons for the underdevelopment of evidence-based policy-making in Croatia, as well as of influence of certain interest groups on the overall economic development of the country, we also make use of Olson's concept of distributional coalitions (Olson 1982).

5.2 Emergence of the Contemporary Landscape of Croatian Interest Groups

The growth and operation of interest groups in Croatia has been influenced by a number of factors which are mostly related to the specific legacy of the communist era, consequences of the Homeland War (1991–1995), and an almost two-decades-long electoral domination by the conservative party (HDZ), as well as the predominant role of the executive over legislative power in the policy-making process. Compared to other countries in Central and Eastern Europe, some authors argue that the self-management socialism of the Socialist Federal Republic of Yugoslavia (SFRY) was less monolithic and allowed for a moderate political space for the development of several semi-autonomous and some autonomous interest groups in policy-making (Mirić 1971; Rusinow 1988), as well as certain forms of interest group pluralism,[1] especially in the last decade of communist era (Zakošek 1995). Fink-Hafner considers that the socialist system of self-management in Yugoslavia was founded, among other things, on neo-corporatist ideas, which is relevant for the analysis of post-1990 evolution of trade unions, neo-corporatism and social partnership (Fink-Hafner 2015). Other authors emphasize that, despite its specific features, the socialist regime did not leave room for different needs and positions in the society and economy to emerge as interests (Dvornik 2009). This has had a major impact on the low-level of civic engagement and predominant public attitude that the state is responsible for solving all social and economic problems, which still continues to exist in contemporary Croatia (Bežovan 2004).

The rise of new environmental, political and cultural movements in Croatia by the beginning of the 1980s contributed to the eventual breakdown of the communist political system and the country's independence from Yugoslavia in 1991. However, further development of interest groups was hindered by the consequences of the Homeland War, which not only caused significant economic decline, but also promoted ethnonationalist ideological homogenization of society, thus reducing the space for public articulation and recognition of pluralism of interests throughout the 1990s. Bearing that in mind, Croatia has remained deeply split due to the experience of war trauma, despite the fact that it is more than 90% ethnically homogenous and that conflict ended 20 years ago (Glaurdić and Vuković 2016). Therefore, exactly this cleavage disproportionately impacts mobilization of organized interest, unlike traditional cleavages such as capital–labour or rural–urban cleavage. A very specific phenomenon of the war-affected scene of organized interests was the proliferation of the war veteran groups, which established a strong clientelistic relationship with the government and demanded a comprehensive set of benefits and privileges for all categories of war veterans' associations and members of their families.[2] In contrast to Olson's argument that war breaks up 'distributional coalitions' (Olson 1982), the example of Croatian war veterans' associations shows that it can actually strengthen them and make them more comprehensive.

Unlike these groups, which became natural allies of governments run by conservative HDZ, most prominent civic activists and watchdog organizations were exposed to a very negative campaign led by leading politicians until the late 1990s. At the same time, with the support of the international community, an increasing number of humanitarian and human rights NGOs started to develop, with the goal of democratization and post-conflict stabilization. In the 1990s trade unions had to fight to retain their positions and pursue their claims. Despite being constantly marginalized in policy-making, Grdešić argues that trade unions held up and continued fighting for their demands by organizing massive strikes and demonstrations during the whole decade. They resisted direct attempts by the ruling regime to curb their activities and weaken organized labour by encouraging its fragmentation (Grdešić 2006).[3]

Due to a number of constraints, lack of institutionalized and meaningful structures of dialogue, interest group activities were predominantly conducted through informal avenues at both central and local levels of policy-making, along with various interest groups closely connected with the ruling party. Nevertheless, after a landmark election in 2000, the new legislative and political framework gradually allowed for a number of social organizations in the field of sports, culture, disabled persons and citizens' associations to proliferate. In the context of gradual institutionalization of relations with the EU, the new centre-left government established a number of new ways to facilitate dialogue between the Government and interest groups. As the social dialogue became subject of the regular monitoring activities of the European Commission Progress Reports, gradual democratization of the political environment enabled tripartite dialogue through national and local, economic and social councils, but also through other institutional structures and advisory bodies dealing with economic and social policies (Stambolieva 2016). In addition, with increasing international attention on creating a more enabling environment for civil society development, liberalization of the legal framework for exercising freedom of association, as well as promotion of inclusive styles of governance and participatory decision-making throughout the 2000s, there has been a continuous trend of the pluralization of organized interests (Petak and Vidačak 2015). For instance, as of 2016, 29% of Croatia's citizens were active members of civil society organizations, which represents the second-highest share among 17 Central and Eastern European countries (Bertelsmann Stiftung 2016).[4]

As opposed to the experience of the 1990s, the period since the 2000s provides a completely different picture in terms of visibility and numerousness of interest groups. In the period since 2000 Croatian governments were mostly fragmented due to the introduction in 2000 of a proportional representation system with multi-membered districts (Vučković and Basarac Sertić 2013). The nature of coalition government formation increased the number of institutional access points for interest groups in the policy-making process.[5] At the same time, the government has continued to be the major political force in most phases of policy formulation and implementation. Both the predominant strength of the executive branch and the still highly centralized government structure have substantially influenced strategies and tactics of interest groups and shaped their access to the policy-making arena. Informal avenues of influence are still strongly present as is the direct political lobbying of traditional power groups.

Despite the aforementioned spike in pluralism since 2000, the political salience of interest groups continues to be very uneven. The character of a captured state from the early 1990s changed through the inclusion of new organized interests (distributional coalitions) in the dominant coalition, but the policy-making process continues to be hijacked by their agency. The major difference makes up both the size and composition of the dominant coalition, which increased in order to defuse mounting social pressures.[6] In the following sections we will give a brief overview of several distributional coalitions in Croatia that have a disproportionate impact on policy-making. Some of them derive and retain their power status from actively pursuing their interests through lobbying or staging protests (war veterans' associations), while others are more fond of relying on structural and productive power (local and regional self-government and SOEs).[7]

5.3 Clientelism and Distributional Coalitions as Foundations of the Captured State

When analysing Croatia as a captured state we can avail ourselves of two important concepts comprising organized interest. The first one refers to clientelism and the second one to distributional coalition. We kick off our analysis with clientelism, which can be defined as the selective distribution of rents and divisible benefits in exchange for granting political support (Piattoni 2001). Those rents take various forms such as public sector employment, direct cash payments, political favours, and contracts specially tailored for selected companies, as well as selective provision of public services (health and education). Structural power often comes into play as a part of this non-market-based exchange. Namely, the stabilization of institutional order confers structural power to those that hold key positions within clientelistic arrangements, since it limits the range of available options to outsiders.

However, in modern and plural societies formal monitoring mechanisms for ensuring clientelistic bargains do not suffice, especially since they entail relatively high costs. Therefore, the advocates of clientelistic arrangements also reach for a two-pronged strategy of norm internalization and fearmongering, which constitute an example of productive power. Identity-based politics and simplified narratives reduce transaction costs of political patronage by means of easily recognizable attributes of belonging to a given 'political tribe'. In Croatia, the aforementioned way of upholding a reciprocal relationship between political sponsors (patrons) and their clients is far from unfamiliar. On the contrary, it has great potential for political mobilization. Perversely, this supplements formal monitoring (by elections) and ensures the return on political investment.

This argument is further strengthened by the European Bank for Reconstruction and Development (EBRD) Life in Transition Survey (LITS), which analyses the voting motives in local and parliamentary elections in 2016. In this part of the survey respondents were offered several voting motives and they needed to pick only one which they deemed as the most important for influencing their vote in the last elections. The modalities on offer were: candidate/party programme and promises, political affiliation of the candidate, good manager/competent, candidate's reputation for honesty, and the religion or ethnic origin of the candidate/party. After combining both 'political affiliation of the candidate' and 'the religion or ethnic origin of the candidate/party' modalities and dividing this figure with the total sample size, we get a good proxy for the presence of clientelistic arrangements (EBRD 2017a). Among the group of 17 post-communist countries Croatia ranks very high on both levels of voting. In terms of local elections Croatia ranked 3rd with more than 25% of respondents identifying 'political affiliation of the candidate' and 'the religion or ethnic origin of the candidate/party' as the most important motive for influencing their vote. On the other hand, 28.7% of respondents espoused the very same motives when it came to influencing their voting behaviour in parliamentary elections, which puts Croatia in 5th place (idem). Unfortunately, competence and honesty of candidates is still not prioritized enough in the eyes of a great number of Croatian voters and the structure of voting offers an important answer to the question of why evidence-based policy-making remains underdeveloped.

The second concept in our story on organized interests in Croatia is the notion of distributional coalition. Olson (1982) defined it as a group with exclusive orientation towards the redistribution of income and wealth, enjoyed by their members, instead of a wealth-maximizing agency for the benefit of majority. This view is similar to Lowi's notion of 'interest group liberalism', which according to him degenerates at times into an effective instrument for seizing bureaucratic power (Lowi 1979). Unlike Robert Dahl's (1967) optimistic view of interest groups as agents of political competition with great potential for establishing democratic accountability, this line of argumentation claims that democracies constantly face the threat that interest groups will turn into distributional coalitions.

The danger that their power becomes assessed through the prism of political resources, as opposed to the rationality and moral imperative of their argument, is all the more present in weak democracies, such as that of Croatia. Distributional coalitions slow down society's capacity to innovate and reallocate resources according to political and not economic imperatives. Hence, Croatia represents an 'exhibit A' for harmful effects of Olson's logic of collective action, especially with regard to economic malperformance and impaired institutional development. In the next section we identify several especially important distributional coalitions: SOEs, and war veterans' associations, disability benefit users in the domain of social policy with clientelistic features, as well as local and regional self-government units. We estimate that those distributional coalitions directly encompass 400,000 members.[8] Therefore, the next three sections will delve into those issues.

5.4 SOEs as a Distributional Coalition

In societies deeply immersed in clientelistic arrangements, the reliance on political connections and the possibility of manipulating state institutions represents the most secure channel of achieving economic security and wealth, especially when compared with more risky options of relying on entrepreneurship and education (Fukuyama 2014). Furthermore, this is also evidenced by the EBRD LITS data from 2010 (data from 2016 are not available), which show the state of employment preferences among the sample of 17 post-communist countries (EBRD 2017b). Respondents were offered five modalities: government employee, employee in a state-owned enterprise, employee in a large private enterprise, employee in a small private enterprise and self-employed. The ratio of respondents opting for public sector employment vis-à-vis those preferring private sector employment amounts to 2.26 in favour of public sector employment. The given ratio puts Croatia in the very high 3rd place, only behind Bosnia & Herzegovina and Serbia (idem).

The very high preference for public sector employment would not make a great difference if Croatia's public sector had some semblance of efficiency and transparent management. However, recruitment of state and SOE employees has not been based on fair and meritocratic principles. EBRD LITS also shows that a very large percentage of respondents think that to get a good job in the government sector, it is essential or very important to rely on people who can influence decisions in their favour. The ratio of respondents in the 'essential/very important' vis-à-vis the 'somewhat important/not important at all' camp amounted to 4.24 in 2010, which put Croatia in the 3rd place among the sample of 17 post-socialist countries (EBRD 2017b). In 2016, Croatia managed to decrease this ratio to 3.02, ranking 7th (EBRD 2017a). A deeper political economy analysis illustrates the extent to which Croatian SOEs represent a significant distributional coalition. There are several data sets which portray them as especially inefficient and problematic.

First, the share of SOE employment as a percentage of total employment remains one of the highest among the EU member states. The ILO (2017) data set reveals that Croatia has the second highest share of SOE employees, only surpassed by Greece. In the period between 2010 and 2014 (when data are accessible in a consistent and comparable manner) Croatian SOEs generated on average 12.5% of total employment (Fig. 5.1). In absolute numbers this amounts to an average of 220,000 SOE employees in the period from 2004 to 2014.

Those employees are almost 75% unionized (Kotarski and Petak 2018) and they display immense structural power, which at times they can effectively combine with productive or discursive power. The latter often takes the form of 'we won't let foreigners take over or privatize our national wealth' public campaigns (e.g. the campaign against the monetization of Croatian Motorways).

Second, the privileged position of SOE employees can be inferred from their average nominal wage in the decade from 2004 to 2014. On average, SOE employees had an 18% bigger take-home pay than the employees in the private sector (EIZG 2014). This would be justifiable if the latter

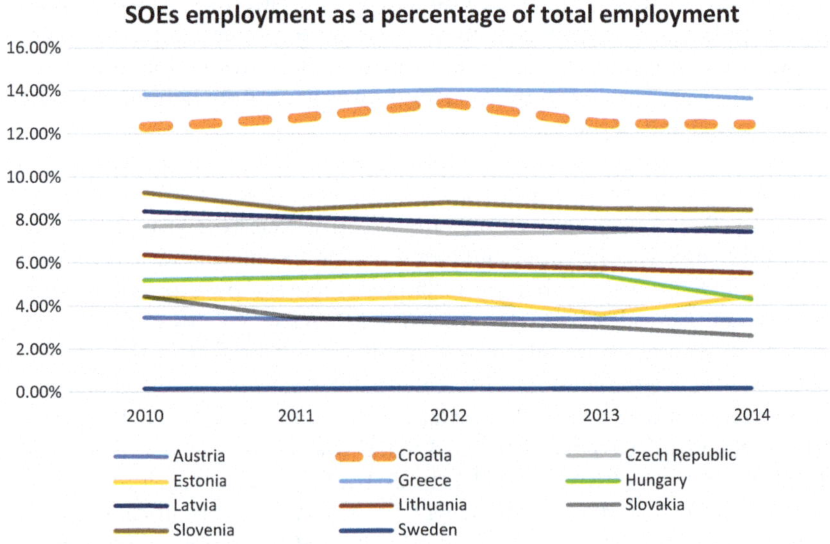

Fig. 5.1 SOEs employment as percentage of total employment (Source: ILO 2017)

category of employees were less productive as compared to their SOE peers. Nevertheless, this is far from reality since SOEs display low level of efficiency and the wage premium can be only explained by greater potential for political mobilization on the part of SOE employees. In Chap. 11 of this volume Velimir Šonje (2018) showed that among 1000 biggest Croatian companies, private companies had a 35% share in the total sample equity, while at the same time they generated 72% of total revenues. His empirical analysis shows that 100% state-owned and mixed SOEs are generally inefficient. In spite of this inefficiency, in the period from 2004 to 2014 SOEs received on average 42% of budget subsidies that amounted to HRK 2.5 billion (Godišnjaci Ministarstva financija 2017).

Third, a high degree of dependence of Croatian economy on SOEs is additionally illustrated by the Deloitte report on the 500 biggest companies in Central and Eastern Europe (Deloitte 2016). Croatia participates with 13 companies on the aforementioned list and its structure is the following. Four companies are majority-owned by the state, two of them are less than 50% owned by the state, and one formerly private company (Agrokor, the biggest company in Croatia) was put under government receivership in 2017. Upon dividing the number of enterprises majority-owned by the government with the total number of national companies represented on the Deloitte 500 list, it is clear that Croatia boasts the biggest quotient among CEE-10 group. To conclude, SOEs represent an extremely powerful political block. A very high concentration of revenues, assets and employment in the ranks of SOEs hamper professionalization of their management and sap the potential for boosting overall factor productivity. This is a testimony to the power of SOEs as one of the strongest distributional coalition in Croatia. We do not claim that employees of various SOEs have convergent goals all the time. Our claim is that when it comes to make or break for a major overhaul of SOEs' practices, the structural power of affected parties guarantees serious political backlash.

5.5 Social Clientelism and Distributional Coalitions

Croatia clearly represents the case of 'institutional particularism' which is characterized by manipulation of social rights and their extremely asymmetric distribution (Stubbs and Zrinščak 2015). This notion was introduced by M. Ferrera in denoting the proliferation of disability benefits in

Southern Italy during the 1970s, as well as unemployment benefits for the agricultural unemployed in Spain in the 1980s (Ferrera 1996). There are many similarities between Croatia and previously mentioned cases. For instance, WHO (2017) reveals that Croatia has the largest number of people receiving social/disability benefits per 100,000 among the EU-28 member states.

The biggest increase occurred in the period between 2003 and 2009 when corrupt and clientelistic practices in obtaining benefits abounded. A good example represents the number of war veterans receiving pensions, which more than doubled from 34,323 in 2004 to 72,472 in 2009, almost a full decade after the Homeland War ended in 1995 (HZMO 2017). The timing of this upward trend in benefits proliferation is of utmost significance.[9] It happened after pressures and public protests threatened the stability of the existing dominant coalition at the end of 1990s (see Kotarski and Petak 2018). This group with a potential for organized violence became part of the Croatian dominant coalition. The strength of this particular distributional coalition is discernible in budget figures. In the period from 2005 to 2014 the total expenditure on war veterans was bigger than the combined expenditures on unemployment benefits, child benefits and social aid (Godišnjaci 2017; HZMO 2017). However, EBRD's LITS shows that Croatian respondents overwhelmingly identified war veterans as the least marginalized social group that needs to be prioritized by government spending (EBRD 2017a, b).[10] Their influence on agenda setting is enormous and on numerous occasions they organized public rallies and protests.

On the other hand, a large chunk of disability benefit users without a war track-record represent a heterogeneous group which emerged spontaneously due to badly conducted corporate restructuring in the 1990s, followed by the widespread practice of early retirement. Outright corruption practices were also rampant (Škiljić Ravenšćak 2012). Nevertheless, the political significance of this group has been more latent, as opposed to a more overt attempt at agenda setting by war veterans' associations (Bertelsmann Stiftung 2016). Namely, every determined attempt by the party in power at stamping out deceitful disability benefit users would be met with stiff and significant electoral opposition (Fig. 5.2).

Ferrera (1996) offers several important answers to the question of why clientelism and the emergence of distributional coalitions became so entrenched in countries characterized by a South European variety of capitalism, as well as a corresponding type of social protection. First, the expansion of social programmes had occurred in the context of weak state

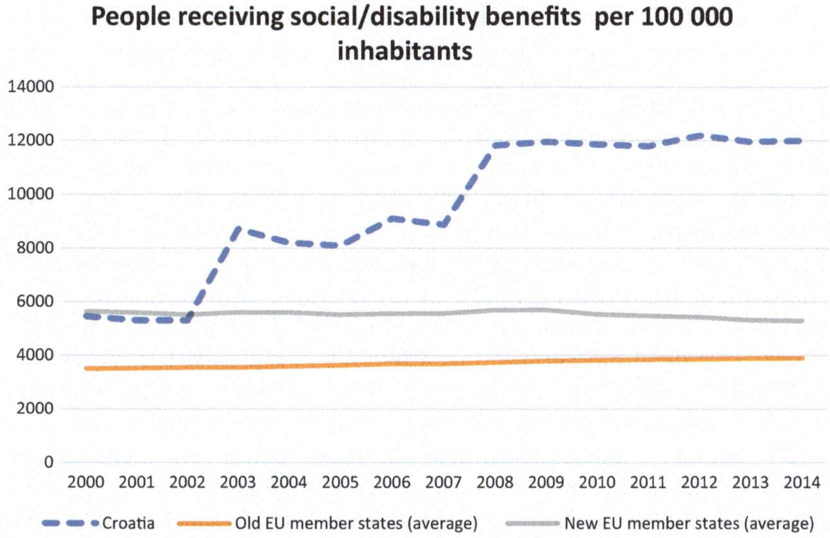

Fig. 5.2 People receiving social/disability benefits per 100,000 inhabitants (Source: WHO 2017)

institutions (deprived of professional and autonomous bureaucracy), which enticed and consolidated clientelistic bargains. Second, the domination of political parties as leading protagonists in aggregating and articulating societal interests has remained a mirror image of relatively underdeveloped civil society and of unfavourable circumstances for democratization in a post-authoritarian political context. Third, strong ideological polarization increased the viability of strategic orientation towards building homogenous political constituency as compared to the value of depersonalized approach in disbursing social benefits. In the process of creating state institutions Croatia faced all three of the abovementioned challenges. Despite gradual development of organized interests in the domain of civil society and a progress towards moderate political polarization, many features of socialist legacy and wartime rule have been transferred into subsequent years (Bertelsmann Stiftung 2016). Unfortunately, Croatian social policy has been captured by well organized and numerous distributional coalitions whose lobbying and protest activities prove to be effective.

5.6 Croatian Local and Regional Self-Government as a Distributional Coalition

In the period from 1997 to 2008 the number of employed in local and regional self-government bodies and utilities increased by staggering 80% (Bajo 2009). This amounted to more than 66,000 employees and could be only partly explained by decentralization efforts since the 2000 elections. The biggest percentage of employed in local and regional self-government bodies and utilities as a percentage of total employment has been prevalent in areas where war devastation took place, where one can also find predominantly HDZ local strongholds.[11] In spite of a deep recession induced by GFC, Franić (2012) shows that local and regional self-government level (without public utilities) increased employment from 35,311 in 2007 to 40,661 in 2011 (a 15.2% increase), and expenditures for those employees increased by HRK 1 billion (a 26% increase). In contrast, to illustrate the strength of this distributional coalition, the number of people working in crafts, trades and as freelancers diminished from 261,547 to 212,848 during the same period (DZS 2008; DZS 2011).

Additional suspicion that local governments have often turned into significant rent-seeking machines comes from the study by Ott and Bronić (2016). They show that in the period from 2002 to 2014 total debt by local and regional self-government spiked from HRK 2 billion to HRK 4.5 billion. A mirror image of this trend has been increased siphoning off of public funds by dubious procurement contracts, as illustrated by Vuk Vuković in Chap. 6 of this volume. It is beyond the scope of this chapter to give a more nuanced account of local and regional self-government as distributional coalition. However, the essence of keeping the existing functional fragmentation of the Croatian system of local and regional self-government (through 127 cities and 428 municipalities) has been to perpetuate its dependence on central government funds, in exchange for collecting votes for the party in power at the national level. Central governments' inertia and increased lobbying effort against reduction in the number of administrative units by Association of Municipalities of the Republic of Croatia, as well as Association of Cities in the Republic of Croatia, cements the status quo, to the detriment of quality of local services provision.

5.7 Key Access Points and Channels of Influence of Interest Groups on Policy-Making

As pointed out by many authors, location of political power in the political system has the most direct impact on determining the access points and methods of influence used by interest groups (Baumgartner and Mahoney 2008; Thomas 2017). As in other parliamentary systems where the executive is chosen from the legislature, and due to very strict party discipline, the power in Croatia is concentrated in the executive, which is therefore the main focus of lobbying. The government is by far the predominant sponsor of laws adopted in the parliament, although there is a growing number of cases where amendments of laws were adopted based on proposals from other authorized sponsors of laws; namely, parliamentary working bodies, political groups or individual members of the Parliament.[12]

Mazey and Richardson (2006) assume that bureaucracies have a tendency to construct stable and manageable relationships with interest groups in each policy domain as a means of securing some kind of 'negotiated order' or stable environment. This seems to be largely confirmed in the Croatian case. Over the years, the Government of Croatia has established more than 100 advisory/cross-sector bodies (committees, councils, standing working groups, etc.) involving more than 800 representatives of various organized interests in policy-making from various sectors (CERANEO 2013). In addition to the Economic and Social Committee (ESC) as a central tripartite forum of social dialogue of trade unions, employers' associations and government representatives, one of the most active advisory bodies with long continuity of work is the Council for Civil Society Development. It was established in 2002 as a government advisory body composed of representatives of NGOs from 16 fields of activity (chosen by the NGOs themselves, following a public call and a transparent and democratic procedure). Furthermore, it also includes similar number of representatives from ministries/government agencies and corresponding policy fields. In addition, parliamentary working committees include more than 100 representatives of interest groups, selected on the basis of open public call for expression of interest, serving as permanent committee members, and therefore enjoying regular access to decision-makers in parliament. These widespread neo-corporatist structures are significantly exploited by various interest groups as a venue for informing themselves, but also for influencing agenda setting and to a certain extent formulation of public policies, to the advantage of interest or constituencies they represent.

Largely due to the influence of the EU accession process and stronger emphasis on access to information and transparency standards, the policy-making procedures have become more formalized, predictable and accessible for organized interests. The adoption of the Code of Public Consultations in Procedures of Adopting New Laws, Other Acts and Regulations adopted in 2009, but also the enactment of amendments to the Law on Access to Information and amendments to government and parliamentary Rules of Procedures in 2013, raised the expectations of citizens and interest groups on minimum standards of responsiveness of government bodies to their contributions to draft policies. Besides, the launch and ever-increasing use of the central online platform for public consultations (esavjetovanja.gov.hr) enabled open monitoring of inputs of all interested stakeholders to open consultations on policy proposals in all sectors. It also enables access to government responses pertaining to contributions from an increasingly diversified spectrum of interests using this platform. In the first two years of the platform's existence (as of April 2017), more than 20,700 comments on 1143 draft laws, by-laws, strategic policy documents and other acts were received from more than 11,000 registered users, out of which there were 9000 individual citizens, 849 companies, 460 associations, 168 institutes, 167 crafts, and a number of other legal entities. In addition to allowing the wider public and the media to be regularly informed on all draft acts prepared by ministries/government agencies, an important added value of the online platform is in encouraging regular formal written contributions to policy consultations from the strongest economic interest groups and power players which have traditionally relied only on informal channels of influence. This increasingly visible online platform for policy dialogue, combined with increasing attention to the standards of access to information and proactive transparency (monitored by a newly established independent Commissioner for Information), has undoubtedly given an impetus to new trends for more open and inclusive policy-making.

Regardless of the growing number of institutionalized channels of influence, informal avenues of access and lobbying continue to be widely used, mostly by the biggest corporations and employers' associations, but also by NGOs, as confirmed by respondents of interviews of top government officials and leaders of various interest groups conducted in the spring of 2015. The nature of the group and its resources seem to be among the major factors explaining the choice of informal or formal lobbying strategies and tactics within a political system. This has been also pointed out by Thomas who makes a clear distinction between 'insider' and 'outsider' groups in policy-making processes, where 'insiders' would obviously have many more strategic influence options available to them than 'outsider' groups (Thomas 2017). In general, it requires precise and empirically-based evidence on the insider and outsider status of different groups. In the Croatian context, 'insider' groups would be traditional business, labour and professional groups with extensive resources (including money), as well as established platforms such as the Croatian Employers' Association, Croatian Chamber of Commerce, Croatian Banking Association, Croatian Bar Association, Croatian Medical Chamber, and the Coordination of Croatian Trade Unions. They are usually more able to pursue informal, insider lobbying tactics and rely on their close friends and associates in government to pursue their goals. The Catholic Church is also routinely considered as an important insider actor with undeniable structural power. Also, a number of government agencies and local governments often act as important insider lobbyists with a high power in an executive dominated political system. On the other hand, outsider groups tend to include new associations that usually lack key contacts with policy-makers and major financial resources, thus opting for indirect methods of gaining media coverage. In addition to the group's financial resources and networks of personal contacts, it is also specific communication strategy, managerial and political skills of its leaders, the size and cohesiveness of its membership, political timing, the extent to which government officials need the group, and the relative level of organized opposition to a group regarding a certain policy issue, that can determine the success or failure of certain interests in the policy-making arena. Political timing and internal cohesion, but also advanced PR and media relations, have proved to be crucial factors for the successful influence of several NGO coalitions during the EU accession, related to the strict monitoring of Croatia's performance. For example, in the case of the adoption of anti-discrimination law, as well as the adoption and implementation of advanced standards of access to information, protection of minority rights, prevention of conflict of interest and more transparent financing of political parties.

The success of a recent referendum on the constitutional definition of marriage launched by a conservative NGO, *In the Name of Family*, highlighted the importance of a strong membership base as well as logistic and infrastructure support for communicating key messages to ordinary citizens. Despite an intense opposition to this initiative's cause by a large coalition of human rights NGOs and a largely supportive media, it was extremely difficult to compete with the public and well-organized support of the Catholic Church for this referendum initiative. Another example of the use of a referendum as a method of influencing policy-making was the 'We are not giving away our motorways' initiative against the monetization of highways. Started in 2014 by a broad coalition of trade unions and civil society activists, the initiative was aimed at stopping the government's plan to lease the motorways, which are public property, to private concessioners. The successful collection of more than 460,000 signatures (more than needed) for a referendum on this issue eventually resulted in the government's decision to back down from monetizing of highways, and brought to the surface new, non-traditional lobbying coalitions among trade unions, NGOs and different civic activists. It opened the way for more advanced and potentially more influential transversal lobbying coalitions in Croatia (CCRC 2015).

However, the power to exploit referenda by various organized interests remains limited. The prohibitive stipulation that organizers need to collect signatures by 10% of the electorate in less than two weeks, rendered many referendum initiatives unsuccessful. Out of 11 attempts at organizing nationwide referenda in Croatia's recent history, six were unable to collect signatures, four were hampered by an activist constitutional court, and only one was successful. At the local government level only two out of nine local referenda managed to achieve obligatory voter turnout of more than 50% to be valid (Butković 2017).

5.8 Impact of the EU Accession on Interest Groups' Strategies and Influence-Seeking Behaviour

In many ways, Croatia's accession to the EU has had an impact on the relationships between state bodies and interest groups, but also on the strategic orientation and influence-seeking behaviour of interest groups in the national policy making arena. As has been the case both in new and old EU member states, the process of European integration further strengthened the national executive in relation to interest groups and national parliaments (Fink-Hafner 2014). In the pre-accession phase, due to highly accelerated legislative dynamics and the adoption of the EU acquis-related laws through urgent procedure in the parliament, there was domestic information deficit about EU matters both among parliament members and the wider public. Urgent procedure was applied in 80% of the cases, rising from 67% in the period 2000–2003, prior to negotiations, to 87% in the peak negotiation period 2007–2011, during which almost a third of laws and regulations, mostly acquis-related, was adopted unanimously (Vidačak and Škrabalo 2014). The overall 'hurry-up' atmosphere of the entire EU accession negotiations process substantially restricted the space for a meaningful access for the majority of interest groups to policy formulation until the end of negotiations in 2011. However, the structural power and political significance of traditional power players could be seen from the content of the Croatian government's negotiating position on special tax exemptions for the benefit of Catholic Church, tobacco industry and war veterans, that was leaked in July 2007. This event provided the incentive for an ad hoc civil society initiative that demanded public disclosure of all negotiation positions, with the argumentation that the case had shed serious doubt about the public interest being safeguarded in the EU accession negotiations.

In the absence of direct access points for influence on formulation of policies, the majority of capacities and efforts of interest groups, especially the leading 'watchdogs', were focused on indirect lobbying strategies. This created incentives for key government officials, acting as gatekeepers, to open up through numerous demonstrations and public campaigns, often with strong support from the media and European networks. As explained in the previous section, these efforts, combined with strict EU conditionality, led to formalizing standards of open and inclusive public consultations and introducing innovative online tools for stakeholders' engagement in policy-making in the post-accession phase.

Additional impetus for strengthening the role and visibility of interest groups was provided through networking with their EU-based counterparts and receiving strategic support from European networks in influencing domestic policy-making processes at various stages. In addition to increasing European networking and participating in various EU policy debates, stronger interest groups engaged in direct lobbying with EU institutions and opened representative offices in Brussels. This Europeanization of interest groups strategies and behaviour is still used by some organizations as an instrument for strengthening their own position and impact in national policy-making. Access to the use of EU pre-accession and later structural funds has also provided an opportunity for different groups to increase their managerial and communication skills, strengthen their public visibility, multiply opportunities for direct access to decision-makers at national and local levels, and diversify lobbying strategies. On the other hand, extremely complex procedures of preparation and implementation of EU funded projects had a very strong impact on the professionalization or bureaucratization of the work of some organizations, also reducing their capacities to respond to increasing needs for multilevel lobbying strategies in the post-EU accession phase.

5.9 Conclusion

This chapter shows that the Croatian landscape of organized interest has significantly evolved since Croatia's independence. It reflects on specific political and social circumstances that affected the development of the scene of organized interests since the early 1990s. We also provide insights into the main factors that determine interest groups' influence and choice of lobbying strategies, prior to and following accession to the EU. Moreover, the central part of this chapter explores different forms of organization and articulation of interests that have become entrenched in policy-making processes in Croatia. In that regard, we put great emphasis on the still widespread clientelistic arrangements that encompass some of the most powerful distributional coalitions (interest groups). Therefore, we elaborate on the main features of three especially important distributional coalitions: SOEs, war veterans' associations and disability benefit users in the domain of social policy with clientelistic features, as well as local and regional self-government. Our goal has been to show how those distributional coalitions led to a captured state and impaired evidence-based policy-making. Unlike the experience in the 1990s, the period since the 2000 elections has been marked by increased pluralism. However, the skewed distribution of political power still hampers the creation of a level playing field which would be conducive for new interest groups entering the political scene, and which would work towards diminishing the power of the existing distributional coalitions. This situation continues to burden Croatia's institutional and economic development, in spite of Croatia's accession to the EU.

Notes

1. Partly as a consequence of the Act on Social Organisations and Associations of Citizens adopted in 1982 by the Croatian parliament, which provided a legal framework regulating the right to free association, in 1985, six years before the dissolution of the Socialist Yugoslavia, there were 10,844 social organizations and 547 citizens' associations registered in Croatia (Bežovan 2004).
2. Similar to strong identity-based divisions structuring party competition, interest groups' differentiation is strongly influenced by various identity divisions. Communities that experienced war trauma tend to overwhelmingly vote for the conservative HDZ (party which led the country through the war). Hence, interest groups such as war veterans associations continue to exert a large influence on Croatian politics.
3. See section on collective bargaining by Kotarski and Petak in Chap. 1 of this volume.
4. In 2014, there were 51,837 citizens' associations registered in Croatia, 137 foreign associations, 207 foundations, 13 funds, 650 trade unions, 63 employers' associations, 452 private institutes, 52 religious communities, 377 organizational forms of religious communities and 2038 legal entities of the Catholic Church (Petak and Vidačak 2015).
5. Increased frequency of coalition governments accentuated the common-pool problem between ruling parties where each of them will try to benefit their own constituencies through higher government expenditures. This has had a deleterious impact on Croatia's economic performance.
6. Dominant coalition represents an amalgamation of various distributional coalitions.
7. We use Strange's (1988: 31) definition of structural power as a capacity *to change the range of choices open to others without apparently putting pressure directly on them to take one decision or to make one choice rather than another.* On the other hand, we claim that productive power operates by shaping the actors' self-understanding and interests (Woll 2014).
8. We arrive at this figure by crudely adding 220,000 SOEs' employees, 80,000 war veterans receiving pensions, part of the disability benefit users who receive it under false pretences, almost 70,000 of employees in local government bodies (which receive more than 50% of financing from the local budget) and local utilities. This is more than 10% of the electorate without members of their families and war veterans' associations already mentioned above.
9. It occurred under both governments led by prosecuted former Prime Minister Ivo Sanader (HDZ).

10. Furthermore, this should be put in the context of Croatia having the fourth largest unemployment rate among EU member states during the same period (Eurostat 2017).
11. The other main party SDP (Social Democratic Party of Croatia) has been also engaged in this patronage, but to a smaller extent.
12. See Official Statistics of Croatian Parliament, www.sabor.hr

References

Bajo, A. (2009). Struktura zaposlenih u lokalnim jedinicama, *Institut za javne financije*. http://www.ijf.hr/newsletter/43.pdf. Downloaded 29 September 2017.

Baumgartner, F. R., & Mahoney, C. (2008). Forum Section: The Two Faces of Framing Individual-Level Framing and Collective Issue Definition in the European Union. *European Union Politics, 9*(3), 435–449.

Bertelsmann Stiftung. (2016). Croatia Country Report, *BTI 2016*. https://www.bti-project.org/fileadmin/files/BTI/Downloads/Reports/2016/pdf/BTI_2016_Croatia.pdf. Downloaded 30 September 2017.

Bežovan, G. (2004). *Civilno društvo*. Zagreb: Globus.

Butković, H. (2017). The Rise of Direct Democracy in Croatia: Balancing or Challenging Parliamentary Representation? *Croatian International Relations Review, 23*(77), 39–80.

CERANEO. (2013). Indeks održivosti organizacija civilnog društva u Hrvatskoj u 2012. https://udruge.gov.hr/UserDocsImages/userfiles/file/Ceraneo%20-%20Indeks%20održivosti%20OCD-a.pdf. Downloaded 26 September 2017.

Constitutional Court of the Republic of Croatia (CCRC). (2015). Decision No. U-VIIR-1158/2015. http://narodne-novine.nn.hr/clanci/sluzbeni/2015_04_46_919.html. Downloaded 4 October 2017.

Dahl, R. A. (1967). *Pluralist Democracy in the United States: Conflict and Consent*. Chicago: Rand McNally.

Deloitte. (2016). Central Europe Top 500: An Era of Digital Transformation. https://www2.deloitte.com/global/en/pages/about-deloitte/articles/central-europe-top500.html. Downloaded 25 July 2017.

Dvornik, S. (2009). *Actors Without Society – The Role of Civil Actors in the Post-Communist Transformation*. Berlin: Heinrich Böll Stiftung.

DZS (Državni zavod za statistiku). (2008). *Persons in paid employment, by activities*. Priopćenje. https://www.dzs.hr/hrv/publication/2008/9-2-1_12h2008.htm. Downloaded 2 October 2017.

DZS (Državni zavod za statistiku). (2011). Persons in paid employment, by activities. Priopćenje, https://www.dzs.hr/Hrv_Eng/publication/2011/09-02-01_12_2011.htm. Downloaded 2 October 2017.

EBRD. (2017a). Life in Transition Survey III: A decade of Measuring Transition. http://www.ebrd.com/cs/Satellite?c=Content&cid=1395236498263&d=Mobile&pagename=EBRD%2FContent%2FContentLayout. Downloaded 24 June 2017.

EBRD. (2017b). Life in Transition Survey II: After the Crisis. http://www.ebrd.com/cs/Satellite?c=Content&cid=1395236498263&d=Mobile&pagename=EBRD%2FContent%2FContentLayout. Downloaded 24 June 2017.

Ekonomski institut Zagreb (EIZG). (2014). Analiza plaća u javnom i privatnom sektoru. http://www.eizg.hr/hr-HR/Analiza-placa-u-javnom-i-privatnom-sektoru-u-Hrvatskoj-1353.aspxb. Downloaded 20 August 2017.

Eurostat. (2017). Employment and Activity by Sex and Age – Annual Data. http://ec.europa.eu/eurostat/web/lfs/data/database. Downloaded 18 August 2017.

Ferrera, M. (1996). 'The "Southern Model" of Welfare in Social Europe. *Journal of European Social Policy, 6*(17), 17–37.

Fink-Hafner, D. (2014). Towards the Dominance of the Executive. *Anali Hrvatskog politološkog društva : časopis za politologiju, 10*(1), 71–90.

Fink-Hafner, D. (2015). A Framework for Studying the Development of Civil Society on the Territory of the Former Yugoslavia Since 1980s. In D. Fink-Hafner (Ed.), *The Development of Civil Society in the Countries on the Territory of the Former Yugoslavia Since the 1980s* (pp. 1–22). Ljubljana: Založba FDV.

Franić, J. (2012). Zapošljavanje na lokalnoj razini u Republici Hrvatskoj tijekom gospodarske krize. Institut za javne financije. http://www.ijf.hr/upload/files/file/newsletter/71.pdf. Downloaded 2 October 2017.

Fukuyama, F. (2014). *Political Order and Political Decay: From the Industrial Revolution to the Globalization of Democracy.* New York: Farrar, Straus and Giroux.

Glaurdić, J., & Vuković, V. (2016). Voting After War: Legacy of Conflict and the Economy as Determinants of Electoral Support in Croatia. *Electoral Studies, 49*, 135–145.

Godišnjaci Ministarstva financija. (2017). http://www.mfin.hr/hr/godisnjaci-ministarstva. Downloaded 11 August 2017.

Grdešić, M. (2006). Tranzicija, sindikati i političke elite u Sloveniji i Hrvatskoj. *Politička misao, 43*(4), 121–141.

HZMO. (2017). Statističke informacije Hrvatskog zavoda za mirovinsko osiguranje. http://www.mirovinsko.hr/default.aspx?id=723. Downloaded 6 September 2017.

ILO. (2017). Public Employment by Sectors and Sub-Sectors of National Accounts. http://www.ilo.org/ilostat/faces/oracle/webcenter/portalapp/pagehierarchy/Page27.jspx?subject=EMP&indicator=PSE_TPSE_GOV_NB&datasetCode=A&collectionCode=YI&_afrLoop=433817398088831&_afrWindowMode=0&_afrWindowId=1a7ljmael_1#!%40%40%3Findicator%3DPSE_TPSE_GOV_NB%26_afrWindowId%3D1a7ljmael_1%26subject%

3DEMP%26_afrLoop%3D433817398088331%26datasetCode%3DA%26collectionCode%3DYI%26_afrWindowMode%3D0%26_adf.ctrl-state%3D1a7ljmael_54. Downloaded 8 September 2017.

Kotarski, K., & Petak, Z. (2018). Croatia's Post-communist Transition Experience: The Paradox of Initial Advantage Turning into a Middle-Income Trap (this Volume).

Lowi, T. J. (1979). *The End of Liberalism: The Second Republic of the United States* (2nd ed.). New York: W. W. Norton & Co.

Mazey, S., & Richardson, J. (2006). Interest Groups and EU Policy Making: Organisational Logic and Venue Shopping. In J. Richardson (Ed.), *European Union: Power and Policy Making* (pp. 247–268). New York: Routledge.

Mirić, J. (1971). Interest Groups in the Political System of Yugoslavia. *Revija za sociologiju, 1*(1), 56–72.

Olson, M. (1982). *Rise and Decline of Nations – Economic Growth, Stagflation, and Social Rigidities*. New Haven: Yale University Press.

Ott, K., & Bronić, M. (2016). Zaduženost županija, gradova i općina od 2002.–2014., Institut za javne financije, http://www.ijf.hr/upload/files/103.pdf. Downloaded 6 October 2017.

Petak, Z., & Vidačak, I. (2015). The Political and Institutional Determinants of Civil Society Development in Croatia Since the 1980s. In D. Fink Hafner (Ed.), *The Development of Civil Society in the Countries on the Territory of the Former Yugoslavia since the 1980s* (pp. 95–120). Ljubljana: Založba FDV.

Piattoni, S. (2001). Clientelism in Historical and Comparative Perspective. In S. Piattoni (Ed.), *Clientelism, Interests and Democratic Representation* (pp. 1–30). Cambridge: Cambridge University Press.

Rusinow, D. (Ed.). (1988). *Yugoslavia: A Fractured Federalism*. Washington, D.C.: Wilson Center Press.

Škiljić Ravenščak, A. (2012). USKOK podnio optužnicu protiv Rubale i još 68 osoba, *Večernji list*. https://www.vecernji.hr/vijesti/uskok-podnio-optuznicu-protiv-rubale-i-jos-68-osoba-419624. Downloaded 30 September 2017.

Šonje, V. (2018). The Competitiveness of Croatian Economy: The Comparison of Private and Public Sector Enterprises, (this Volume).

Stambolieva, M. (2016). *Welfare State Transformation in the Yugoslav Successor States-From Social to Unequal*. Abingdon: Routledge.

Strange, S. (1988). *States and Markets: An Introduction to International Political Economy*. London: Pinter.

Stubbs, P., & Zrinščak, S. (2015). Citizenship and Social Welfare in Croatia: Clientelism and the Limits of 'Europeanisation'. *European Politics and Society, 16*(3), 395–410.

Thomas, C. S. (Ed.). (1993). *First World Interest Groups – A Comparative Perspective*. Westport: Greenwood Press.

Thomas, C. S. (2017). Interest Groups, *Encyclopaedia Britannica*. https://www.britannica.com/topic/interest-group#toc257764. Downloaded 7 June 2017.

Vidačak, I., & Škrabalo, M. (2014). Exploring the Effects of Europeanization on the Openness of Public Administration in Croatia. *Hrvatska i komparativna javna uprava – Croatian and Comparative Public Administration, 14*(1), 149–187.

Vučković, V., & Basarac Sertić, M. (2013). The Effect of Political Institutions on the Size of Government Spending in European Union Member States and Croatia. *Financial Theory and Practice, 37*(2), 161–179.

WHO. (2017). People Receiving Social/Disability Benefits per 100,000. https://gateway.euro.who.int/en/visualizations/bar-charts/hfa_414-people-receiving-socialdisability-benefits-per-100-000/. Downloaded 10 September 2017.

Woll, C. (2014). *The Power of Inaction: Bank Bailouts in Comparison*. Ithaca: Cornell University Press.

Zakošek, N. (1995). Organizirani interesi u Hrvatskoj. *Erasmus, 3*(11), 28–32.

CHAPTER 6

Political Economy of Corruption, Clientelism and Vote-Buying in Croatian Local Government

Vuk Vuković

All politics is local
Thomas "Tip" O'Neill, Speaker of the US House of Representatives, 1977–1987.

6.1 Introduction

Local politics in Croatia is no different than any other political environment throughout the transitional world. The system is riven with endemic corruption, serving simultaneously the interests of the politicians (the patrons) and either the rent-seeking private sector, politically connected voters, or any other vested interest (the clients). In such a system the best response function of each agent is to be connected and be part of the appropriate clique, the goal of which is to act upon common interests of all those included. The clients get their exclusive deals with the govern-

V. Vuković (✉)
Pembroke College, University of Oxford, Oxford, UK
e-mail: vuk.vukovic@pmb.ox.ac.uk

Z. Petak, K. Kotarski (eds.), *Policy-Making at the European Periphery*, New Perspectives on South-East Europe,
https://doi.org/10.1007/978-3-319-73582-5_6

ment, while the patrons get re-elected and keep holding power, virtually unconstrained.

Consider the following few examples that testify to this infamous practice. The mayor of Zagreb was arrested in 2014 on several charges of corruption, during his fifth consecutive term in power. He was soon released after paying the biggest bail thus far in Croatia of 15 million kunas, but was caught breaking his probation and sent back to jail a few weeks later. He spent six months in jail, and after he got out—thanks to a surprisingly quick constitutional court decision in his favor (Jutarnji list 2015)—he was elected as a member of parliament twice in parliamentary elections in 2015 and 2016, and has even won re-election as mayor for a sixth consecutive term in 2017. His trials are still ongoing but this has not prevented the voters for entrusting him with one more term. The mayor of Varaždin is a similar story. He stepped down as mayor after his arrest and corruption trials, only to come back six years later to win the election and become mayor again. The mayor of Dubrovnik is arguably the most perplexing case. Whereas the first two are still in trial, the mayor of Dubrovnik was actually sentenced for corruption in 2013, served his six-month sentence, and then came back to win a local by-election in 2015 (Novi List 2015). Many other local cases of corruption have been uncovered with the protagonists sent to trial, but only in a rare few cases did it actually harm the politicians. They seem to be immune to punishment for corruption.

Why do these scenarios keep happening? What prevents Croatian voters from punishing their politicians for corruption, who in turn are able to stay in power uninterrupted for more than 20 years? Do they suffer from some type of Stockholm syndrome or is the story more complex in which Croatian politicians build quid-pro-quo relationships with their voters where votes are traded for various concessions? This chapter attempts to provide an answer to some of these questions by looking into the political economy of local governance in Croatia. It summarizes the empirical findings of three research papers on local political economy in Croatia, two of which (Vuković 2017a, b) directly apply the logic of the Bueno De Mesquita et al. (2005) selectorate theory, and the third (Glaurdić and Vuković 2017) that looks at the practice of vote-buying in Croatian local government. The chapter uses both empirical and theoretical findings of each of these papers in addition to many others that explain the persistence of negative outcomes in democratic systems, to paint a full picture of why Croatia is captured by crony political elites and how the system is skewed to their benefit.

Lack of proper accountability and scrutiny enables local political elites to subvert democratic procedure and fully promote their own interest and the interests of their cronies rather than the public interest. In local politics, where oversight does not exist at the same level as in national politics, every politician will benefit if they adhere to the rules of the logic of political survival, rather than the rules of democracy. This way it is possible for politicians at a local level to increase their re-election chances if they engage in more corruption; it is possible to build small powerful coalitions of interests to keep a politician in office for long periods of time, to keep local taxes high and avoid any punishment for doing so, and finally it is even possible for national politicians to help local ones retain office and buy votes through biased grant distribution.

The following section presents the underlying logic of the selectorate theory according to which political survival depends on operating within a small willing coalition of key supporters. It will also make a case in point of why Croatia fits perfectly within this theory. The next three sections each focus on one particular case of showing the selectorate theory in practice in Croatia. Section 6.3 will examine the impact of corruption on mayors' re-election chances by using fraudulent public procurements as a proxy measure for corruption. Section 6.4 will look into how mayors build coalitions of vested interests, directly implicating the selectorate theory where small winning coalitions increase the scope for corruption, and offer a greater incentive to manipulate public finances (keeping both taxes and budget deficits high). Finally, Sect. 6.5 will provide a quick insight into vote-buying in Croatian local politics; namely, how central governments use intergovernmental grants to reward their local co-partisan mayors as well as showing how mayors can act as local political brokers for their national parties. The final section concludes by offering a brief outline for potential reform of local government.

6.2 Selectorate Theory in the Croatian Context

The logic of political survival revolves around two main goals: staying in power and extracting rents. This is a standard finding of political agency research (see e.g. Brennan and Buchanan 1980; Ferejohn 1986; Persson and Tabellini 2000; Besley 2006), which has been further theoretically and empirically synthesized by the so-called *selectorate theory* in Bueno De Mesquita et al. (2002, 2005). The idea is that politicians build a powerful coalition of supporters with key players in the electorate that keeps them in office for long periods of time, while the supporters receive their own benefits in terms of fraudulent procurement contracts, favorable legislation or regulation, or various monetary and non-monetary concessions. The coalition is referred to as a *winning coalition* (W), and it represents a small group within a large subset of all voters called the *selectorate* (S). The smaller the ratio of the winning coalition to the entire selectorate, the greater the chances for political survival. How so? One advantage is smaller size of the coalition, which immediately implies that politicians in power have a smaller group of people they are accountable to and need to satisfy. In a dictatorship these are usually military leaders and chief police officials who need to be paid well to support the dictator. In a democracy the winning coalition consists of key members of influential interest groups, such as union and religious leaders or even from selected entrepreneurs and businessmen who depend on government contracts and are thus highly invested into who holds power in their national or local community.

A small winning coalition environment (a small W/S ratio) implies a lower level of accountability towards the voters since politicians only need to satisfy their key supporters to gain enough votes to stay in power. This as a consequence results in poor governance, less transparency, the personalization of governing institutions, and the creation of clientelistic networks of interest. In each case political elites create mutually beneficial relationships with a number of actors they find crucial to help them hold on to power, who in return get rewarded with either direct monetary concessions, favorable legislation and regulation, fixed procurement contracts, or nepotistic allocation of jobs. It is in the best interest of every actor within this network to keep the corrupt politician in power, regardless of what the voters want.

North, Wallis, and Weingast (2009) developed a similar framework to the selectorate theory where they define two institutional frameworks that both differ in the level of personalization of political institutions. If political institutions are personalized by well-organized ruling elites, then they are free to manipulate economic outcomes to their benefit. This is an example of a *limited access order* that does not need a legal contract to achieve trust—it depends only on loyalty between connected powerful individuals. If, however, institutions are depersonalized it makes it much more difficult to set up and maintain clientelistic relationship. This is called an *open access order*, in which the legal system works well in delivering fair outcomes and does not depend on politics. A political system will thus always deliver negative economic outcomes as long as its institutions are subdued to the interest of the ruling elites. This, too, can help explain the persistence of corrupt politicians in power and their successful rent extraction.

Given the aforementioned examples of endemic corruption in which corrupt politicians avoid any punishment from the voters for years, Croatia is a useful case study to be analyzed under either one of the two frameworks. There has been ample research showing the extent to which corruption poses a serious problem in the country. In addition to official measures from Transparency International, which ranks Croatia as a "mostly corrupt country" (TI 2016), or the European Commission (2014) ranking it in the bottom five member states, particularly when it comes to corruption in procurement contracts, Bićanić (1997), Franičević (1997), Madžarević-Šujster and Mikulić (2002), Bejaković (2002), and Ott (2002) have all tried to capture the extent of Croatia's systemic corruption. The overreaching conclusion is that Croatia's economic development is significantly constrained by its political system that seems to generate and feed itself of rent-seeking, clientelism and nepotism. Ivanković and Šonje (2011) use the framework from North et al. (2009) to coin the phrase 'undemocratic capitalism' that can best explain Croatia's failed transition. They claim that the personalization of institutions has yielded a particularly worrisome political economic outcome where major economic winners are all selected by politics. This further depletes both social capital (Štulhofer 2004), and the trust in domestic institutions (Budak and Rajh 2012).

Moving this further into the realm of local politics, Mačkić (2014) finds support for the political business cycle theory in Croatian cities and shows that opportunistic and rent-seeking behavior is the main modus operandi of local politicians. This is further confirmed in Vukovic (2017a) who measures corruption of local officials using public procurement data, following the findings from Ateljević and Budak (2010), who uncover the various ways corruption is to be found in procurement tenders, and Bađun (2011), who finds that the easiest way for corruption to arise is through public investment spending. However, there still lacks an overreaching theory to explain the systemic failure of domestic institutions, the existence of endemic corruption in general, and the reason why voters fail to punish corruption in particular. In two recent research efforts Vukovic (2017a, b) attempts to connect the dots in order to provide a theoretically and empirically consistent picture of the political institutional environment that tends to generate negative socio-economic outcomes, either in terms of high corruption, bad governance, poor institutional performance, or lack of transparency and accountability. This chapter will summarize some of these findings in order to paint the entire picture of Croatia as a case-study exemplifying the logic of political survival.

6.3 Corrupt Mayors Are More Likely to Be Re-elected

The first major finding links corruption to chances of political re-election. Does corruption help or hinder chances of political survival? According to Vukovic (2017a) corruption does help re-election chances but this relationship is non-linear: there is an upper limit to how much politicians can steal. To construct a valid proxy for local corruption Vukovic (2017a) uses local procurement contracts for all Croatian cities and municipalities during a single mayoral term in office, from 2009 to 2013. A procurement contract is defined as suspicious based on several factors. The first are cases in which firms without employees (also called 'fake firms') compete as the only bidder on the tender and receive contracts worth millions. The second are cases in which firms get contracts several times higher than their own revenues (also a signal of 'fake firms' that engage in money laundering). And finally, cases where the local government indirectly subsidizes firms with large losses by giving them exclusive contracts (which constitutes bad practice and is always a result of a political connection). In each case, corruption is defined as a ratio of contract value from a suspicious tender to the contract value of all tenders in a given city or municipality, administered during a single mayoral term. Defining corruption this way is more accurate than by using survey perception indices, as it provides a direct insight into the operations of local government and its political connections.

There are several factors that have been recognized as potential motivators of corruption in Croatian local government. Vukovic (2017a) shows a positive link between the length of a local mayor's term and the total level of corruption in a municipality. This can be seen by comparing local mayors who are serving their first term in office to those serving two or more terms. Mayors with two or more terms have on average 54% higher corruption indices than mayors in their first term, as shown in Table 6.1. The difference in corruption between first-term and higher-term mayors shows statistical significance at a 5% level for each given approximation of corruption.

Table 6.1 Corruption for single-term and multiple-term mayors

	Number of mayors	*Total corruption (% of suspicious procurements)*	*Corruption (contract larger than revenues)*	*Corruption (zero employees)*
Mayor with one term	167	6.7%	9.1%	4.5%
Mayor with two or more terms	379	9.1%	15.7%	7.1%
Difference in corruption between first term and multiple term mayors (*p*-value)		−2.3% (0.04)**	−6.7% (0.015)**	−2.6% (0.02)**

Note: Average corruption is measured in three different ways comparing mayors in their first term to mayors in their second or higher term. Each measure of corruption measures the share of suspicious public procurement in total procurement for a particular city or municipality.

Source: Vukovic (2017a)

Furthermore, corruption tends to increase with the number of years a politician is in office. This confirms the hypothesis that politicians need time to build their own coalitions of interests, and that they tend to reap rewards with a certain time lag. Another important finding is that the level of corruption increases with greater levels of political homogeneity in a city or municipality. If one political party stays in power in a given municipality for a long period of time, regardless of its ideological inclination, the level of corruption for that city or municipality is higher. Voters therefore tolerate corruption as long as they perceive the mayor as 'one of them'. In addition, corruption is higher in wealthier areas, and in municipalities where a larger coalition of parties is necessary to support the mayor in the local assembly. In homogenous areas, non-transparency encourages corruption, while in areas with higher assembly size (mostly cities) corruption is motivated by the purchase of councillors.

How does this affect re-election? The main finding of the Vukovic (2017a) paper is that corruption increases the probability of re-election but only until a certain cutoff point after which further corruption does get punished and reduces the probability of re-election (see Fig. 6.1). The cut-off point is about 20% of suspiciously allocated procurements – this is the level of corruption which maximizes the probability of re-election. A mayor loses elections with certainty when he or she allocates at least half of all public procurements in a potentially fraudulent way. Even though corruption does get punished at the polls when mayors go too far, a

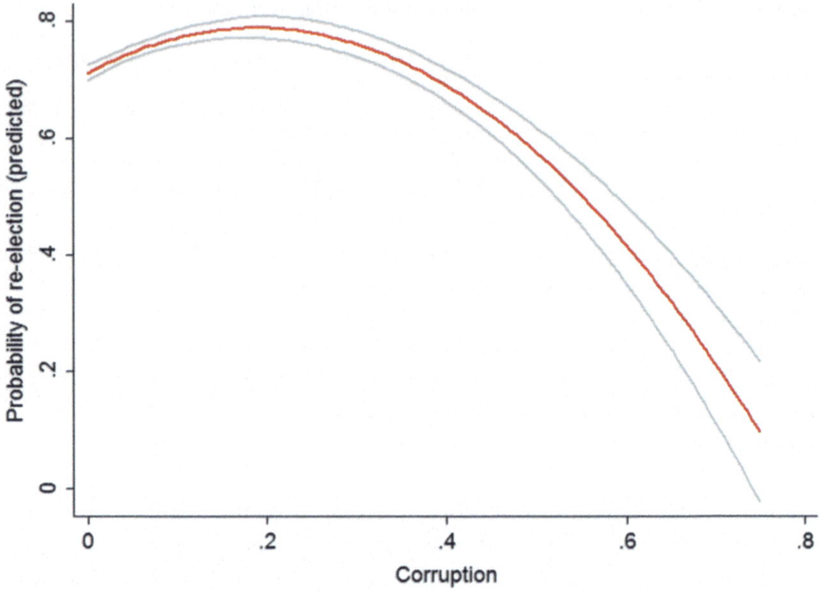

Fig. 6.1 The concave relationship between corruption and the probability of re-election in Croatian local government (Source: Vukovic 2017a)

re-election probability maximizing 20% of corruption is too high. This implies that Croatian voters do find corruption acceptable and even permissible to some extent. The question remains as to why this is so—is it because they choose to be rationally ignorant, or because they pragmatically accept corruption as long as the mayors deliver some of the concessions to the voters as well?

Finally, there is an interesting difference in how the voters react to corruption in the first and second-round electoral races. Mayors who win directly in the first round (i.e. get more than 50% of votes immediately) on average have double the size of corruption as mayors who lost immediately in the first round (see Table 6.2 below). However, if they compete in the second round, more corrupt mayors have lower chances of victory. Mayors who limit corruption to a voter-acceptable level have greater chances for re-election in the second round. The t-test for the differences in corruption is statistically significant at a 1% level for first-round races and at a 5% level for second-round races. The estimates control for

Table 6.2 Average levels of corruption (% suspicious purchases) in both election rounds for winners and losers

	Election first round (%)	*No of mayors*	*Election second round (%)*	*No of mayors*
Win	7.1	269	9.4	127
Loss	4.2	31	10.9	118
Difference in corruption (*p*-value)	−2.8 (0.007)***		1.5 (0.039)**	

Source: Vukovic (2017a)

municipality size given that larger cities usually have more candidates and it is thus more difficult for them to win outright in the first round.

This finding adds to the concave relationship described above, as the positive effect of corruption on re-election exists only for first-round races where it rewards entrenched mayors. If the voters want to punish their mayor they are more likely to do so in the second round.

6.4 Mayors Build Coalitions of Vested Interests and Manipulate Public Finances

The aforementioned findings fit well within the scope of the selectorate theory so the next research effort was to show that the selectorate theory holds in practice in Croatia. A paper by Vukovic (2017b) tests this by explicitly calculating the aforementioned W/S ratio; winning coalition divided by the size of the total electorate. The paper uses an approximation similar to the original Bueno De Mesquita et al. (2005) measure where it looks at the number of votes for the incumbent mayor divided by the total number of eligible voters in a municipality (the W/S ratio ranges from 0.034 to 0.68, with the mean of 0.27 and standard deviation of 0.102). This albeit imperfect approximation of the W/S ratio suggests that in certain local environments the lower the required number of voters for the mayor, the easier it is for him or her to shun accountability and get away with corruption.

The findings perfectly align with the theoretical implications of the selectorate theory. Vukovic (2017b) uses a matching approach to estimate the impact of coalition size on three factors: political longevity in office, total corruption, and local tax rates (income tax surcharge rate, *prirez*).

The paper confirms that a small winning coalition environment increases total time in power by on average one and a half years. When looking across three terms, a mayor coming from a low winning coalition environment is likely to have one more term on average in power than a mayor coming from a more accountable and transparent political environment. Mayors with longer political tenure almost exclusively operate within low winning coalition environments where accountability is low and their coalitions of vested interests can keep them in power for as long as 30 years.

In addition to maintaining uninterrupted rule, small winning coalition environments, because of their lack of transparency and accountability, offer fruitful ground for corruption. Figure 6.2 plots this relationship for a sample of all 556 Croatian cities and municipalities over a single term in local office, from 2009 to 2013. The size of the effect is also quite large. Moving from a municipality with a high W/S ratio to a municipality with a low W/S ratio increases corruption by an average 6 percentage points, where corruption is defined the same way as before: share of suspicious procurements. Given that average levels of corruption in the sample were 8.3% with a standard deviation of 12.7%, this too constitutes a large effect.

Finally, the size of the winning coalition also affects local taxes. Mayors in small winning coalition environments set higher tax rates than mayors coming from large winning coalition environments. This effect is also large in magnitude as a switch from a high W/S municipality to a low W/S municipality increases local tax rates by 1.2 percentage points (the average is 4.3%, with a standard deviation of 4%). The right panel of Fig. 6.2 depicts a similar relationship as before.

To summarize, a mayor that built himself a small coalition of vested interests is more likely to stay in power for longer, be more corrupt, and even set higher tax rates. Such environments, characterized by lower levels of transparency and political accountability, enable the mayors to govern poorly, extract resources, and alleviate any punishment for such behavior. Their tenure, and hence their corrupt activities, depend not on satisfying all voters and the public interest, but rather on satisfying a small clique of their own key supporters which deliver votes and get various concessions in return. Accordingly voters in Croatia do not punish their politicians because they rationally chose to be beneficiaries of a politically biased allocation of resources.

This can be seen in yet another artifact of domestic politics—how voters respond to electorally motivated deficit spending. In a paper by Glaurdić and Vuković (2016) Croatian voters are portrayed as 'fiscal

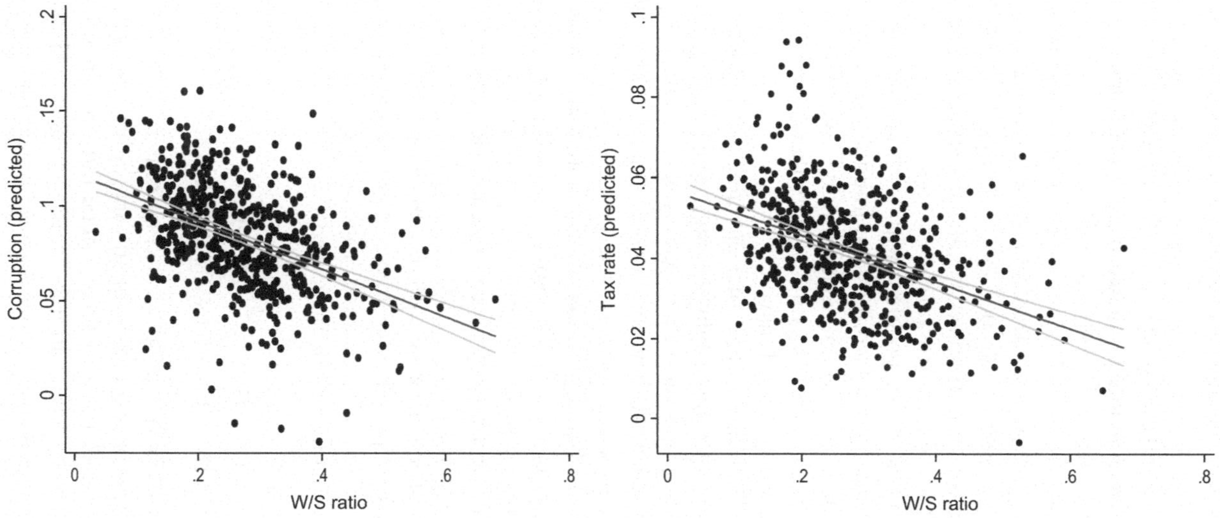

Fig. 6.2 A lower winning coalition environment (a lower W/S ratio) suggests greater scope for corruption (left) and higher local taxes (right) (Source: Vukovic 2017b)

liberals' (an inverse of Peltzman's (1992) US voters as 'fiscal conservatives'). Croatian voters tend to reward mayors who increase public spending ahead of elections and even tend to punish the fiscally more conservative ones. The higher the local budget deficit in election years, the greater the chance of a mayor to get more votes. Furthermore, Croatian voters particularly favor 'bridges to nowhere', as one particular category of the budget tends to be highly sensitive to electoral wins and losses: net non-financial assets. Non-financial assets are defined as any construction or repair work that needs to be done, from road repairs and construction, to local parks and buildings, and social infrastructure spending, such as on schools, kindergartens or hospitals. A big problem with such capital expenditures is that they are most susceptible to bribes and fraudulent procurement contracts. However, the voters do not seem to mind. Whenever there is any construction work being done in a municipality this is very likely to boost the re-election chances of a local mayor.

This striking set of findings, that voters are able to overlook corruption, higher taxes, and fiscal irresponsibility as long as something is being built, creates a paternalistic impression that politicians are somehow promoting the public interest, whereas they only serve to further their own survival goals. Having only to satisfy their internal group of vested interests, they need not worry about being punished by the voters as long as they keep building 'bridges to nowhere'. The voters are left with ever-increasing debts that consequently push domestic interest rates up, which discourages spending and investment; whereas a nepotistic system keeps unemployment high and forces unconnected individuals to flee the country. As long as the voters collectively keep suffering from a cognitive fiscal illusion where public goods are perceived as free and politicians that deliver them even in haphazard ways as benefactors, the status quo of the selectorate model of local governance will be preserved.

6.5 Vote-Buying: The Biased Nature of Intergovernmental Grants

Mayors in Croatia therefore build local coalitions to keep themselves in power, and use this to be more corrupt and set higher tax rates. They face almost no accountability towards their voters, but there is someone they are accountable to—their national party leaders. However, this accountability comes at a cost as it yields another significant distortionary effect of Croatian local politics.

The most important link between the national government and local governments are intergovernmental grants—monetary transfers given to municipalities with the aim of alleviating fiscal inequalities between them. Municipalities differ in their levels of development and consequentially in their fiscal capacity to collect enough tax revenue to finance the necessary public goods and services. The central government steps in and helps the less developed areas so that its citizens are not deprived of the basic public goods. However, such intergovernmental transfers are usually subject to political bias driven by partisan interest rather than developmental goals. Parties that hold power nationally help their local co-partisans win elections and can count on their support in fundraising and delivering votes during national election campaigns.

A paper by Glaurdić and Vuković (2017) measures the size of the political distortion in the allocation of such grants for Croatian local government. It finds that the size of this distortion is 32% (similar to Argentina, Russia or Brazil where it is around 40%, but much higher than in the US, Germany, or Sweden where it is around 4–5%; see Larcinese et al. 2006; Berry et al. 2010; Brollo and Nannicini 2012; and Sole-Olle and Sorribas-Navarro 2008). This means that if a mayor comes from the same party that holds power at the national level, he can expect on average 32% more money from the central government than if he comes from opposition parties. In Croatia this constitutes around 1.3 million kunas on average per municipality every year, which are allocated based on political criteria rather than any developmental factor. On average intergovernmental grants constitute between one fifth and one third of all local government revenue, meaning that 1.3 million kunas allocated in a politically biased way is a very large number. Extrapolating this further, this means that around half of all intergovernmental grants (700 million out of 1.5 billion kunas that gets distributed) are allocated on political rather than developmental criteria.

National-level parties also follow their own interests in the allocation of these grants. They worry about increasing their electoral chances during national elections. The Glaurdić and Vuković (2017) paper finds that the party holding national power tends to allocate more money to municipalities where its support is increasing over time. They do not necessarily reward areas where they win, but only those where they gain vote share from one election to another. For example, a city or municipality where the current ruling party won more votes in the last national elections will receive about 5.8% more money than the local unit where the support to the ruling party has not increased. Timing is another interesting issue—when is the money being allocated to local governments? As expected when it is most needed—in election years. Both in the months before the election, to help a mayor win office, and in the months after the election to reward the local co-partisans. In the year of national elections, we can expect as much as 26% more money to be allocated to the local government, while in the year of local elections this effect is half or 12.6%.

This relationship is perhaps best described by the broker-mediated model of redistribution as defined by Stokes et al. (2013). Local brokers can be defined as agents that design and control 'dense social networks and who provide the local knowledge that is required for conditioning distribution on voter preferences or behavior' (Stokes et al. 2013). Local brokers tend to leverage this influence when they 'sell' supporters to party leaders, and given the informational asymmetry in the knowledge between brokers and parties, the brokers take advantage of this in terms of more rents for themselves. In particular they are more likely to target loyal voters instead of swing voters, as this is a fairly cheap strategy to get the rents from the party, which in turn can explain the empirical fact of why national governments tend to target loyal voters more than swing voters (shown by Stokes et al. 2013 in the cases of Argentina, Mexico, Venezuela, and India).

In Croatian local politics brokers are defined a bit differently from the developing world setting identified by Stokes et al. (2013). They tend to be local party leaders (local mayors) who push loyal voters to turn out during national elections and vote for their national party. Glaurdić and Vuković (2017) have shown that this type of behavior, where local partisan mayors increase turnout in their municipalities in national elections, leads to more rewards to such mayors through greater intergovernmental grants after the national election. In other words, national level grantors reward their co-partisan mayors (brokers) for greater turnout of loyal supporters. The brokers have successfully done their job. This can in turn explain the success of local mayors across all parties in preventing any attempt of local government reform. They possess a credible mechanism to leverage the national party leadership not to engage in reform, as they will stop delivering the votes in national elections.

The voters once again do not perceive this as anything wrong. Similar to the aforementioned approvals of deficit spending and even corruption to a certain extent, voters reward the politically biased allocation of resources as long as they themselves are on the 'right side' of the distribution. However these distortions do not necessarily coincide with actual public interest with an aim to reduce regional inequality. For example, even though more money does go to war-affected areas, islands, and rural areas (areas of special state concern), when looking at the rest of the sample, cities and municipalities with higher fiscal capacity, namely, the richer ones, get more money from the central budget, not less. Even more bizarre, cities and municipalities in which income per capita increases over time get more money, while cities and municipalities where unemployment increases over time get less money. It is obvious that the politically biased allocation of grants is inefficient and unsuccessful in achieving its main goal of alleviating regional inequalities.

6.6 Conclusion

This chapter has provided a brief overview of the corruption, clientelism, and vote-buying practices in Croatian local politics. It has shown that corruption helps mayors stay in power, a finding that was reinforced by confirming the logic of the selectorate theory where mayors build small powerful coalitions of interests with rent-seeking entrepreneurs that keep them in office for long periods of time. This coalition reduces any accountability of the mayors towards the voters and the taxpayers meaning that mayors can easily get away with manipulating local public finances and by engaging in direct vote-buying with money from the central government.

The final question of why voters put up with this is open for discussion. Small winning coalitions that mayors tend to build are strong enough to persuade enough voters to support the mayor no matter what. In addition, vote-buying prior to election time directly helps the mayors get re-elected as the voters get a short-term gain, whereas their fiscal illusion prevents them from fully realizing the long-term loss. Three options remain as an explanation of the voters' behavior. The first is lack of proper information—voters are simply not aware that their leader is corrupt, and any discovery of corruption is dismissed as an attack coming from the 'biased media'. The second hypothesis is that Croatians have a culture/mentality issue, where voters cynically accept that politicians are corrupt, but they tend to justify their corruption as long as some resources are returned to the voters (there is a famous Robin-Hood-esque saying in Croatia—"he steals, but he also gives back"). Finally, perhaps the local networks of interests are preferable to any disruptive politician primarily because they offer protection from risk and uncertainty to a large group of voters.

In the context of Croatia all three hypotheses are probably true. One thing binds them together—ideology. Croatian voters tend to punish a politician only if he or she is of the 'wrong' ideological spectrum. Corruption by the ideologically close candidate is, albeit unconvincingly, justified but any sign of corruption from the ideologically distant candidate is strongly objected to. This would imply that Croatian voters, in addition to having a mentality issue and an informational asymmetry problem, also tend to suffer from deep hypocrisy. However, these character traits are hardly limited only to Croatian voters, so they cannot explain the reasons of institutional failures of Croatian democracy. The problem therefore is not in the voters per se, the problem is in the effectiveness of the country's institutions, particularly judicial, to truly punish corruption and clientelism. Unfortunately, breaking up such a system can only occur by chance; if a group of people willing and committed to reforming the country's legal institutions are elected into office. Given that Croatia ranks among the worst brain drain countries (WEF 2016), chances for this are very slim.

References

Ateljević, J., & Budak, J. (2010). Corruption and Public Procurement: Example from Croatia. *Journal of Balkan and Near Eastern Studies, 12*(4), 375–379.

Builder Bađun, M. (2011). Odnos političke korupcije i javnih investicija – slučaj Hrvatske. *Društvena istraživanja, 20*(2), 295–316.

Bejaković, P. (2002). Corruption in Croatia: Institutional Settings and Practical Experiences. *Politička misao, 39*(5), 128–155.

Berry, C. R., Burden, B. C., & Howell, W. G. (2010). The President and the Distribution of Federal Spending. *American Political Science Review, 104*(4), 783–799.

Besley, T. (2006). *Principled Agents? The Political Economy of Good Government.* New York: Oxford University Press.

Bićanić, I. (1997). Mjerenje veličine i promjena neslužbenog gospodarstva. *Financijska praksa, 21*(1–2), 15–28.

Brennan, G., & Buchanan, J. (1980). *The Power to Tax: Analytical Foundations of a Fiscal Constitution.* Cambridge: Cambridge University Press.

Brollo, F., & Nannicini, T. (2012). Tying Your Enemy's Hands in Close Races: The Politics of Federal Transfers in Brazil. *American Political Science Review, 106*(4), 742–761.

Budak, J., & Rajh, E. (2012). Corruption Survey in Croatia: Survey Confidentiality and Trust in Institutions. *Društvena istraživanja, 21*(2), 291–313.

Bueno de Mesquita, B., Smith, A., Siverson, R., & Morrow, J. (2002). Political Institutions, Policy Choices and the Survival of Leaders. *British Journal of Political Science, 32*(4), 559–590.

Bueno de Mesquita, B., Smith, A., Siverson, R., & Morrow, J. (2005). *The Logic of Political Survival.* Cambridge: MIT Press.

European Commission. (2014). EU Anti-Corruption Report. http://ec.europa.eu/dgs/home-affairs/e-library/documents/policies/organized-crime-and-human-trafficking/corruption/docs/acr_2014_en.pdf. Downloaded 1 March 2014.

Ferejohn, J. (1986). Incumbent Performance and Electoral Control. *Public Choice, 50*(1/3), 5–25.

Franičević, V. (1997). Temeljne značajke neslužbenog gospodarstva. *Financijska praksa, 21*(1–2), 45–70.

Glaurdić, J., & Vuković, V. (2016). Post-War Voters as Fiscal Liberals: Local Elections, Spending, and War Trauma in Contemporary Croatia. *Under Review.*

Glaurdić, J., & Vuković, V. (2017). Granting Votes: Exposing the Political Bias of Intergovernmental Grants Using the Within-Between Specification for Panel Data. *Public Choice, 171*(1), 223–241.

Ivanković, Ž., & Šonje, V. (2011). Nedemokratski kapitalizam i nova tranzicija, Prvi zagrebački ekonomski forum, *Friedrich Ebert Stiftung*, 5–21.

Jutarnji list. (2015). Ustavni sud uvažio tužbu. Bandić je na slobodi, vraća se 15 milijuna kuna jamčevine! Željko Petrušić, Jutarnji list, published on 9th April 2015. http://www.jutarnji.hr/vijesti/hrvatska/ustavni-sud-uvazio-tuzbu-bandic-je-na-slobodi-vraca-se-15-milijuna-kuna-jamcevine/374065/. Downloaded 8 April 2017.

Larcinese, V., Rizzo, L., & Testa, C. (2006). Allocating the U.S. Federal Budget to the States: The Impact of the President. *Journal of Politics, 68*(2), 447–456.

Mačkić, V. (2014). Political Budget Cycles at the Municipal Level in Croatia. *Financial Theory and Practice, 38*(1), 1–35.

Madžarević-Šujster, S., & Mikulić, D. (2002). Procjena neslužbenog gospodarstva sustavom nacionalnih računa. *Financijska teorija i praksa, 26*(1), 31–56.

North, D. C., Wallis, J. J., & Weingast, B. R. (2009). *Violence and Social Orders. A Conceptual Framework for Interpreting Recorded Human History.* Cambridge: Cambridge University Press.

Novi list. (2015). Biračima korupcija ne smeta: Zašto nikoga ne brinu pravomoćne presude kandidatima? Ladislav Tomičić, Novi list, published 15th March 2015. http://www.novilist.hr/Vijesti/Hrvatska/Biracima-korupcija-ne-smeta-Zasto-nikoga-ne-brinu-pravomocne-presude-kandidatima. Downloaded 8 April 2017.

Ott, K. (2002). Neslužbeno gospodarstvo u Republici Hrvatskoj 1990–2000. *Financijska teorija i praksa, 26*(1), 1–30.
Peltzman, S. (1992). Voters as Fiscal Conservatives. *Quarterly Journal of Economics, 107*(2), 327–361.
Persson, T., & Tabellini, G. (2000). *Political Economics. Explaining Economic Policy.* Cambridge: MIT Press.
Sole-Olle, A., & Sorribas-Navarro, P. (2008). The Effects of Partisan Alignment on the Allocation of Intergovernmental Transfers: Differences-in-Differences Estimates for Spain. *Journal of Public Economics, 92*(12), 2302–2319.
Stokes, S. C., Dunning, T., Nazareno, M., & Brusco, V. (2013). *Brokers, Voters, and Clientelism. The Puzzle of Distributive Politics.* Cambridge: Cambridge University Press.
Štulhofer, A. (2004). Percepcija korupcije i erozija društvenog kapitala u Hrvatskoj 1995–2003. *Politička misao, 41*(3), 156–169.
Transparency International. (2016). Corruption by Country: Croatia. www.transparency.org/country#HRV_PublicOpinion. Downloaded 18 February 2015.
Vuković, V. (2017a). Corruption and Re-election: How Much Can Politicians Steal Without Getting Punished? *Doctoral Dissertation.* First Paper, DPIR, University of Oxford.
Vuković, V. (2017b). The political economy of local government in Croatia: winning coalitions, corruption, and taxes. *Public Sector Economics, 41*(4), 387–420.
World Economic Forum. (2016). *Global Competitiveness Report 2015–2016. Country capacity to retain talent.* http://reports.weforum.org/global-competitiveness-report-2015-2016/. Downloaded 5 August 2017.

PART II

Croatia's Political Economy

CHAPTER 7

Long-Term Trends in Croatian GDP Growth

Anita Čeh Časni, Petra Palić, and Maruška Vizek

7.1 Introduction

The economic divergence of the Croatian economy has a long history that predates the collapse of socialism and transition to a free market system. Longer GDP per capita series available from the Maddison database (The Maddison-Project 2013) suggest Croatian GDP per capita had been converging in absolute terms from 1952 to the beginning of the 1980s with regards to GDP per capita of Old Member States of the European Union (OMS). In the early 1980s the divergence of Croatian Gross Domestic Product (GDP) per capita from that of the OMS had started and by the end of the decade it had become apparent. After Croatia declared independence in 1990, the income divergence continued, spurred by a deep transition recession.

A. Č. Časni (✉)
Faculty of Economics and Business, University of Zagreb, Zagreb, Croatia
e-mail: aceh@efzg.hr

P. Palić
The Institute of Economics, Zagreb, Croatia
e-mail: ppalic@eizg.hr

M. Vizek
The Institute of Economics, Zagreb, Croatia
e-mail: mvizek@eizg.hr

Z. Petak, K. Kotarski (eds.), *Policy-Making at the European Periphery*, New Perspectives on South-East Europe,
https://doi.org/10.1007/978-3-319-73582-5_7

After a successful stabilization program in late 1993, Croatian GDP per capita had started to grow again until the financial crisis of 2008 (with a small receding period in 1998, due to the banking crisis). The Great Recession of 2008 had an adverse effect on Croatian economy, which ended up in a six-year-long recession that has widened further the income gap with respect to OMS as well as to the New Member States of the European Union (NMS).

In this chapter we will take a deeper perspective on the reasons for the relatively weak performance of the Croatian economy in the post-transition period, compared to its peer countries and the OMS. With that aim, this chapter is divided into six parts. After a brief introduction, in the second part we survey the existing literature on growth and convergence trends as well as characteristics of new EU member states. We also discuss major features of development patterns of NMS and Croatia with the aim of providing the frame for our empirical analysis. Also, in the third part we give some stylized facts about long-term growth performance of the Croatian economy, comparing it to that of its regional peers and NMS, thus detecting potential reasons for the relatively weak economic performance of the Croatian economy. In the fourth part of this chapter we present the formal results of β- and δ- convergence, which allowed us to assess the state of convergence of Croatian income with regards to its peers. In Sect. 7.5, we describe how Croatian sectoral structure shifted over the last two decades and how these shifts may have affected the economic growth. Finally, Sect. 7.6 concludes the chapter.

7.2 Literature Review

According to a comprehensive review of Podkaminer (2013), the studies of transition in Central and East European countries (CEEC) can be broadly grouped into the early studies of transition (which led to inconclusive results) and recent econometric studies that deal with the impact of global financial crisis. Among the early studies of transition that deal with aspects of changes in the CEEC since 1990, there are studies by Kornai (1998, 2000, 2006a, b), Kolodko (2000) and Nuti and Portes (1993). The pioneering work by Barro (1991) develops an empirical model with the aim of explaining the performance of transition countries depending on various factors. Campos and Coricelli (2002) are concerned with the data problems in studies of transition. Namely, the availability and reliability of data in econometric studies that pool together very diverse countries like, for instance, in de Melo et al. (2001), may have serious consequences on the appropriateness of the conclusions drawn about analyzed CEEC countries. For example, in Eichler and Schreiber (2010) there is a scatter plot showing the relation between structural policy index and GDP per capita for 26 transition countries, suggesting strong positive relationship between analyzed items. However, a closer look at the scatter plot reveals that for the small sample of those 26 CEEC countries, that relationship is not positive but a negative one. Moreover, cross-country or dynamic-panel econometrics studies of transition are in many cases inconclusive. Anyway, the growing realization of data problems (like endogeneity of explanatory variables) and more sophisticated econometric techniques applied in the analysis, along with the rising popularity of new institutionalism, led to studies like Hall and Jones (1999), Roland (2000) or Rodrik et al. (2004), to name a few.

In their study published in 1996, Fisher et al. concluded that countries that achieved macroeconomic stability and undertook deeper reforms grew faster. They have also pointed out the importance of initial conditions. Along with that, Havrylyshyn and Rooden (1998) and Berg et al. (1999) also confirm that adverse initial conditions hurt growth. However, de Melo et al. (1996) find that initial conditions and economic policy jointly determine the difference in economic performance. Falcetti et al. (2002) state that, over the period from 1989 to 1999, the initial conditions dominate the impact of reforms on growth. However, in their 2006 study, Falcetti et al. conclude that initial conditions importance actually declined over time as a growth determinant.

The recent econometric studies of transition changed their focus. Namely, they started to analyze the determinants of specific policies like, for instance, in the study of Bennett et al. (2007) the relationship between privatization methods and growth performance. Institutional changes and their determinants were observed by Cheptea (2007). Other studies, like for example Eicher and Schreiber (2010), Hall and Jones (1999) and Acemoglu et al. (2004) deal with econometric evidence on the role of institutional improvements. Studies like Böwer and Turrini (2010) or Schweickert et al. (2011) deal with EU accession or NATO membership as determinants of institutional changes.

Also, recent econometrics studies of transition underline that the global financial crisis of 2008 spilled over into the CEEC in 2009, resulting in the weak growth and questionable validity of econometric estimations of potential drivers of long-term economic growth in CEEC countries. That is obvious in the study by Darvas (2010) where the break in the data series caused by financial crisis had great consequences on parameter estimates. Accordingly, in the existing literature there is no consensus on the econometric model that could describe CEEC economic performance.

Considering the literature that deals with economic growth in Croatia, there are studies that deal with aspects of changes in Croatia since 1990, which use a mostly comparative approach and descriptive statistics (e.g. see Franičević and Kraft 1997) and there are studies which use econometric models analyzing various aspects of economic growth in Croatia as well as sectoral dynamics. In the group of studies that analyze various aspects of economic growth in Croatia, there are for instance Bađun et al. (2014) and Drezgić (2011). Bađun et al. (2014) analyze binding constraints to economic growth in Croatia, which is according to their findings a weak government plagued by corruption. They also analyze the average optimal size of government in old EU member states and in new EU member states by applying data envelopment analysis and Tobit regression models. Drezgić (2011) deals with regional income convergence of Croatian regions and different growth rates of capital accumulation, which results in different growth rates across the regions by using static and dynamic measures of income inequality. Sectoral dynamic in Croatia is analyzed in studies like Tkalec and Vizek (2014), Stojčić et al. (2012) and Tkalec and Vizek (2009), to name a few.

7.3 Stylized Facts on Croatian GDP Growth

As can be seen in Fig. 7.1, Croatian GDP per capita mainly followed New Member States (NMS) GDP per capita, from 1992 until 1998, with divergence in 1993 (stabilization program) and especially 1998 when the banking crisis took place. From 1999 until the financial crisis of 2008, a divergence of Croatian GDP per capita with regards to NMS GDP per capita is evident. However, it has become even more noticeable from 2009 onwards, as Croatia entered a protracted six-year recession. On the other hand, NMS GDP per capita mainly follows the Old Member states (OMS) GDP per capita trend. For instance, if we compare the GDP per capita in Croatia and OMS in 1993, we can conclude that Croatian GDP per capita was 18.31% of OMS GDP per capita. However, in 2016, Croatian GDP per capita was 27.47% of OMS GDP per capita. In addition, when we compare Croatian GDP per capita to that of NMS, in 1993, Croatian GDP per capita was 90.53% of NMS GDP per capita. On the other hand, in 2016,

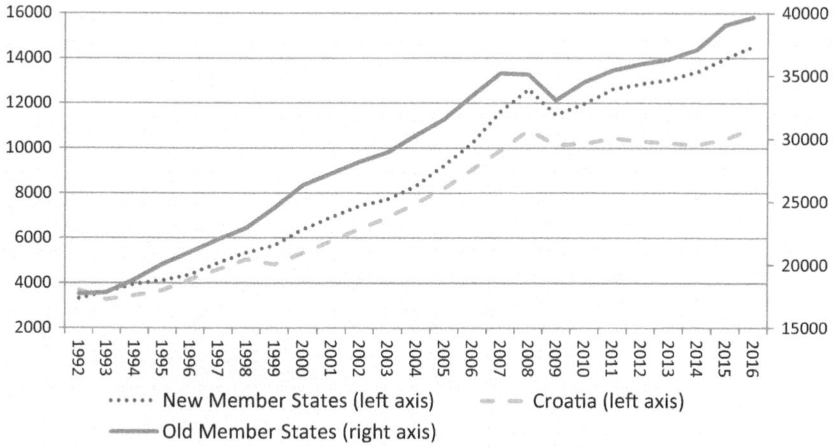

Fig. 7.1 GDP per capita in OMS, NMS and Croatia, in euros (Source: authors' calculations based on Vienna Institute for International Economics data)

Croatian GDP per capita was only 75.04% of NMS GDP per capita, confirming the increasing income gap in Croatia with respect to NMS.

Additionally, we calculated contribution points to GDP and gross value added growth in the 2000–2016 period in order to investigate similarities and differences in growth sources between Croatia and its peers. In an upper left panel of Fig. 7.2, GDP contributions per component and contributions of GDP components in OMS, NMS and Croatia are presented. In the lower left panel of the Fig. 7.2, the relative importance of each component is calculated by dividing the individual contribution of each component with total GDP growth achieved in the analyzed period. One can notice that the overall contribution of all demand components in Croatia was lower when compared to NMS, which is not surprising given the fact that the overall growth of Croatian GDP was lower when compared to average NMS growth. However, when one considers the relative importance of each component, it turns out that in Croatia investments and government consumption had a much more important role in driving the overall GDP growth when compared to its peer countries. Personal consumption and international trade were in that context of lesser importance when compared to NMS.

As far as gross value added (GVA) contributions per component in OMS, NMS and Croatia are concerned, by observing the right-hand side

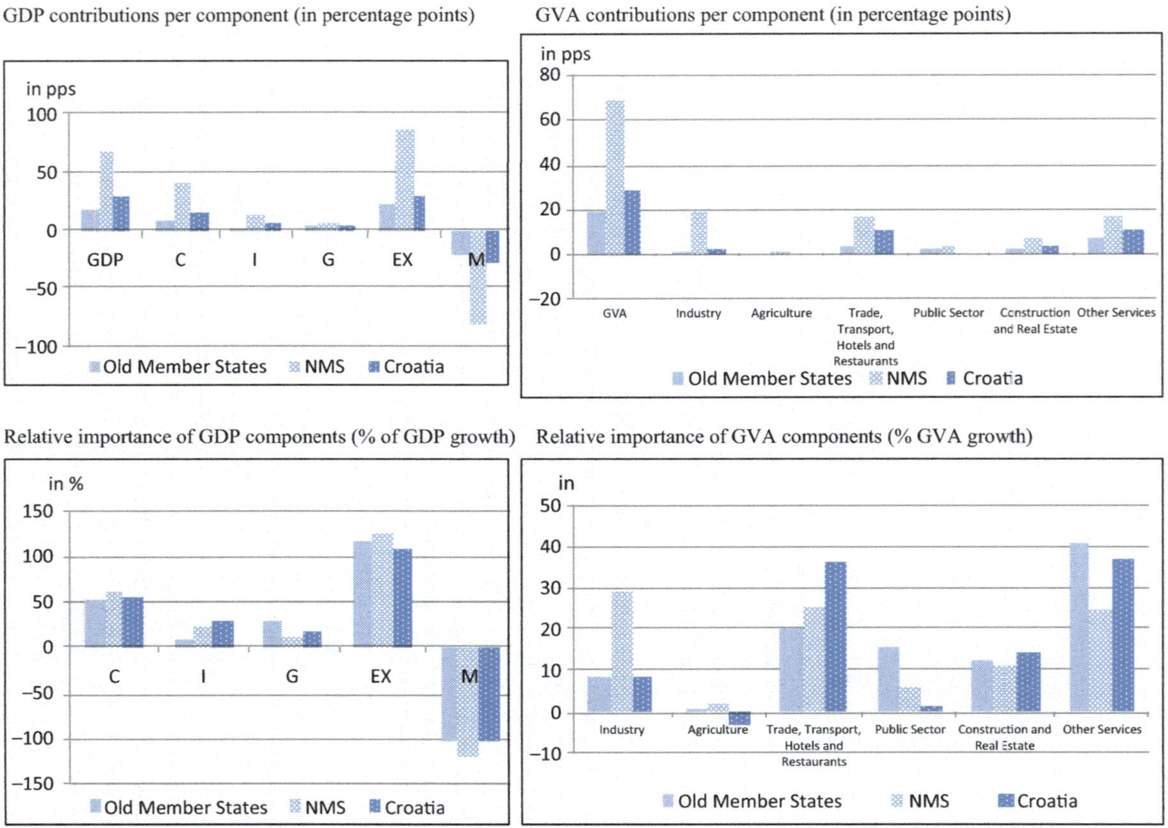

Fig. 7.2 GDP and GVA growth and relative importance of their component contributions in OMS, NMS and Croatia (Source: authors' calculations)

panel of Fig. 7.2, the following conclusions can be drawn. Distinctive differences in absolute GVA growth and its components contributions are noticeable in Croatia and NMS. Namely, total GVA growth in Croatia is roughly 40% less than in its peer countries (27.9% vs. 67.9%, upper right panel). Considering contributions of GVA components to overall GVA growth (bottom right panel), the most relevant determinant of GVA growth in Croatia is trade, transport, hotels and restaurants, construction and real estate and other services. In NMS countries the most relevant sector is industry. Industry and the public sector have lower contributions to total GVA growth in Croatia when compared to NMS. The contribution of agriculture to GVA growth in Croatia is negative, while in NMS and OMS it is positive. An interesting finding emerges when one analyzes the relative importance of contribution of government consumption and public sector to GDP and GVA respectively. Namely, government consumption contribution to overall GDP formation in relative terms is more important for Croatia when compared to NMS. However, the Croatian public sector contributes less to GVA formation when compared to average NMS public sector. This suggests that intermediate consumption of the public sector (which forms the final consumption of the government, but it is not counted in GVA) is driving government consumption and overall GDP growth.

This in turn means that the public sector is probably experiencing both underinvestment and lower-than-average increase of public sector salaries when compared to peer countries, which may decrease the overall quality of public services. On the other hand, the greater role of intermediate consumption in the formation of government consumption opens the space for various forms of rent-seeking behaviors within the country. It also creates strong and relatively lucrative domestic demand for goods and services, thus motivating the entrepreneurs to focus on satisfying this demand (although competing on this quasi-market often involves corruptive practices) instead of focusing on meeting demand for exports.

7.4 Long-Term Convergence Trends of Croatian GDP Per Capita

In this segment we focus on trends in income convergence process of Croatian economy with regards to both OMS and NMS. We test for β- and δ-convergence of Croatian economy employing simple cross-section procedures suggested by Baumol (1986) and Hossain (2000). β-convergence takes place due to the assumption of diminishing returns. Namely, as marginal productivity of capital is expected to be higher in a capital-poor country, poorer economies should, therefore, grow faster. This in turn suggests GDP per capita increases faster in countries with lower initial GDP per capita when compared to countries with higher GDP per capita. Regressions testing β-convergence are thus often referred to as growth-initial level regression, where the coefficient of the initial income variable in these regressions is supposed to pick up the negative correlation (Islam 2003). σ-convergence is present when the dispersion of the GDP per capita decreases across countries over time. This concept arose because negative growth-initial level regression does not necessarily imply a reduction in this dispersion (Quah 1993).

We test β-convergence and estimate the following growth-initial level equation for all 28 EU member states:

$$\ln\left(\frac{y_{it}}{y_{i,t-\tau}}\right) = \alpha + \beta ln\left(y_{i,t-\tau}\right) + \mathrm{u}_{it} \tag{7.1}$$

where y_i is per capita GDP in a given country, subscript t denotes end of the time period under examination, and $t - \tau$ is the beginning of the time period. The equation is estimated for 1992–2016 period, and for two subperiods within that period: 1992–2000 and 2000–2016.

The results presented in Table 7.1 suggest that average β-convergence in per capita income levels for individual 28 EU member states towards the EU28 club is indeed present, as the β coefficient is negative and statistically significant in the observed 1992–2016 period. When we split the estimation in two subperiods, it appears that β-convergence had speeded up during 2000–2016, when compared to 1992–2000 period.

This exercise, however, does not indicate how successful Croatian economy was in achieving β-convergence in per capita income with regards to the club of EU member states. Thus, in order to assess how individual countries fared in β-convergence process, we present the scatter plot diagram of GDP per capita levels in 1992 and cumulative GDP per capita growth in 2016 when compared to 1992 for individual EU member states, and draw a regression line in order to graphically recreate the result of the growth-initial level equation for 1992–2016 period presented in the first row of Table 7.1 (Fig. 7.3). Countries that are placed above the regression

Table 7.1 β and σ-convergence results in Croatia and EU member states

Regression period	*β coefficient*	*Standard error*	*t-statistics*	*p-value*	*R^2*
***β-convergence regression:** Croatia and all EU member states*					
1992–2016	−0.561	0.055	−10.1	0.00	0.82
1992–2000	−0.292	0.049	−5.93	0.00	0.60
2000–2016	−0.343	0.042	−8.09	0.00	0.74

Variable	*Coefficient*	*Standard error*	*t-statistics*	*p-value*
***σ-convergence:** Croatia and all EU member states*				
C	9.167	0.019	482.0	0.000
T	0.074	0.0034	22.1	0.000
T^2	0.00014	0.0001	−10.4	0.000
RSS = 0.0291	R^2 = 0.992	LL = 54.5		
***σ-convergence:** Croatia and new EU member states*				
C	7.181	0.024	302.0	0.000
T	0.099	0.0042	23.5	0.000
T^2	−0.0024	0.00015	−15.3	0.0000
RSS = 0.0293	R^2 = 0.985	LL = 48.8		
***σ-convergence:** Croatia and old EU member states*				
C	8.814	0.026	338.0	0.000
T	0.0479	0.0046	10.4	0.000
T^2	−0.0003	0.0001	−1.46	0.158
RSS = 0.035	R^2 = 0.984	LL = 46.5		

Source: authors' calculations

line performed above average when β-convergence is concerned, countries near or on the regression line performed in line with the average EU performance, while countries below the line performed worse than the EU average.

When observing the figure, one clearly notices that three Baltic countries experienced faster β-convergence when compared to average club EU β-convergence. Slovakia, Czech Republic and Slovenia performed in line with the average β-convergence, while all other countries, including Croatia, experienced slower β-convergence when compared to average convergence speed suggested by the size of the β coefficient. One must, however, note that the largest relative discrepancy between observed GDP per capita growth rate in the 1992–2016 period and the expected cumulative GDP per capita rate is warranted by the average EU β-convergence speed and is recorded for Croatia and Greece. This suggests that the Croatian economy was the worst performing economy among new EU

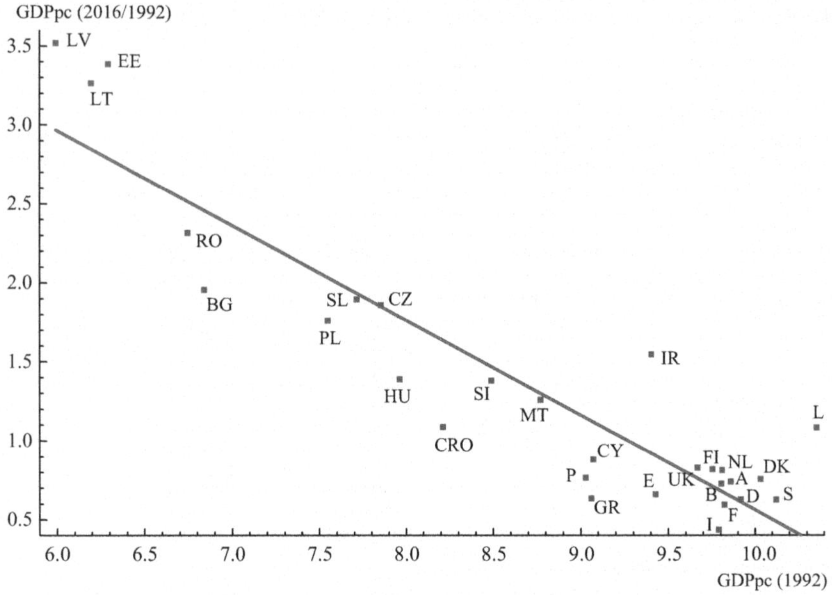

Fig. 7.3 β-convergence in 1992–2016 period: Croatia and all EU member states (Source: authors' calculations)

member states when it comes to β-convergence of its income level. The only EU economy that fared even worse was Greece, for the reasons that are by now quite well known. The sources of the lagging performance of the Croatian economy, however, have yet to be established, and in this chapter we offer several potential explanations for this occurrence.

In order to test for σ-convergence, we calculate the dispersion (that is the standard deviation—σ) of logarithm of per capita GDP for 28 EU member states for each year in 1992–2016 period. We then regress a constant (C), linear and quadratic time trend (T and T^2) on standard deviation of GDP per capita:

$$\sigma_t = C_t + \alpha_1 T + \alpha_2 T^2 + u_t \tag{7.2}$$

If linear time trend from this equation is statistically significant and negative, we conclude that σ –convergence is present as the dispersion of income levels is decreasing over time (Hossain 2000). The lower part of

Table 7.1 gives the results of such exercise for all EU member states, for Croatia and NMS, and for Croatia and OMS. In all three cases we can witness increasing income dispersion (as indicated by the positive and statistically significant *T* coefficient), thus suggesting the absence of σ-convergence in all three definitions of EU clubs. The dispersion increases the most within NMS, which once again indicates that (although we do not formally test for this) the performance of Croatian economy exhibits diverging properties.

7.5 The Influence of Supply-Side Factors and Technology on Economic Growth in Croatia

In this segment we use the database of financial reports of the population of Croatian enterprises for the period from 2000 to 2015 to analyze how the sectoral structure had shifted over last 15 years and how these shifts may have had affected the creation of gross value added. Table 7.2 presents the shares of individual corporate sectors in corporate sector aggregates for 2000, 2005, 2010 and 2015. In addition, Table 7.3 presents the shares of manufacturing sectors classified according to technological intensity in total (corporate) manufacturing sector aggregates. In order to do that, we used aggregation of manufacturing based on NACE Rev. 2 derived from Eurostats' indicators on high-tech industry and knowledge-intensive services. This methodology classifies sector according to the levels of intensity of usage of technology and knowledge in production of goods and services. Manufacturing is thereby divided into four groups: high-technology, medium-high-technology, medium-low-technology and low-technology.

According to absolute values of total assets and revenues, the size of the Croatian corporate sector has doubled in the last two decades, drawing from the growth of the service sector and construction. Namely, shares of GVA, total assets, exports, investments and employment in agriculture, forestry and fisheries sector and manufacturing sector significantly declined. More specifically, for agriculture, forestry and fisheries sectors, the share of total assets declined from 8.05% in 2000 to 0.72% in 2015. On the other side, accommodation and food service activities, financial and insurance services, real estate, professional, scientific, technical and support service activities showed robust growth in total assets and GVA share. Moreover, employment in accommodation, food service activities,

Table 7.2 Relative importance of economic sectors (in % of total corporate sector)

		Total assets (in %)	*Total revenues (in %)*	*GVA (in %)*	*Exports (in %)*	*Investments (in %)*	*Employment (in %)*	*Labour productivity (in 000 KN)*
Agriculture, forestry and fisheries	2000	8.05	1.51	1.34	0.59	0.48	3.86	41.28
	2005	1.61	1.02	1.18	0.48	0.39	3.23	65.40
	2010	0.54	0.90	1.00	0.46	0.65	2.63	79.00
	2015	0.72	1.06	1.50	0.53	1.04	2.39	133.90
Mining and quarrying	2000	0.74	1.07	0.12	2.14	2.14	0.72	19.21
	2005	0.91	1.42	0.14	4.08	2.03	1.13	22.50
	2010	0.77	1.06	1.70	3.89	1.91	0.96	370.38
	2015	0.68	0.87	1.20	2.20	1.95	0.71	363.22
Manufacturing	2000	15.70	28.26	33.38	61.15	22.24	23.16	171.84
	2005	14.67	21.11	20.52	52.80	15.18	19.00	193.99
	2010	12.99	20.02	22.05	51.08	18.59	16.64	276.60
	2015	11.01	18.94	19.11	43.75	16.06	17.34	235.36
Water collection, treatment and supply of electricity, gas, steam and air conditioning supply	2000	8.79	5.12	6.50	0.56	20.00	5.91	262.18
	2005	13.26	7.41	8.68	4.21	9.49	6.25	458.58
	2010	10.43	8.47	8.91	4.19	7.88	4.44	646.95
	2015	13.39	9.32	9.49	6.10	16.68	4.27	767.44
Construction	2000	33.08	6.50	3.70	1.73	7.32	8.48	52.00
	2005	27.58	7.96	9.02	1.94	21.24	9.77	165.81
	2010	26.50	6.40	7.86	1.95	17.20	8.77	186.83
	2015	24.83	5.13	6.46	2.38	11.06	6.34	217.82
Wholesale and retail trade; repair of motor vehicles and motorcycles	2000	9.44	29.35	12.61	8.19	8.56	17.11	87.86
	2005	13.74	36.32	18.17	14.14	12.92	23.61	138.24
	2010	17.13	39.55	16.89	17.20	18.37	26.82	131.44
	2015	13.79	40.37	17.46	23.72	16.59	25.54	145.96
Transportation and storage	2000	3.45	3.39	6.68	6.88	1.99	6.57	121.28
	2005	5.71	4.62	9.96	8.34	7.10	11.86	150.80
	2010	5.08	4.19	6.73	7.01	10.68	9.10	154.46
	2015	5.21	4.15	6.99	6.42	12.78	8.49	175.62

(*continued*)

Table 7.2 (continued)

		Total assets (in %)	*Total revenues (in %)*	*GVA (in %)*	*Exports (in %)*	*Investments (in %)*	*Employment (in %)*	*Labour productivity (in 000 KN)*
Accommodation and food service activities	2000	0.73	0.55	0.70	0.22	0.43	1.40	60.10
	2005	0.91	0.64	1.03	0.35	0.83	1.95	94.72
	2010	1.16	0.73	1.09	0.25	0.63	2.56	89.12
	2015	1.50	1.20	1.79	0.30	1.07	4.43	86.32
Information and communication	2000	5.16	8.92	15.88	7.25	21.94	7.29	259.72
	2005	6.36	8.52	15.85	6.66	10.59	6.92	411.34
	2010	4.89	7.93	14.20	5.47	10.13	7.13	415.64
	2015	5.01	7.44	13.39	5.60	15.53	6.86	416.98
Financial and insurance services	2000	2.15	0.92	1.60	0.19	2.38	0.41	470.44
	2005	5.33	2.88	4.51	0.25	10.66	2.15	376.22
	2010	4.73	1.15	1.89	0.13	0.38	1.42	277.91
	2015	6.87	1.22	2.46	0.10	0.60	1.72	304.49
Real estate, professional, scientific, technical, administrative and support service activities	2000	3.44	5.36	6.29	3.86	5.29	6.31	298.82
	2005	9.13	6.74	8.42	6.55	8.69	10.82	487.22
	2010	14.93	8.27	15.27	8.05	12.46	15.12	638.24
	2015	15.63	8.47	17.28	8.15	5.55	17.37	735.96
Public administration, education and health care	2000	0.09	0.15	0.31	0.01	0.04	0.71	581.97
	2005	0.21	0.30	0.81	0.11	0.12	0.94	822.35
	2010	0.30	0.48	0.83	0.02	0.32	1.42	409.22
	2015	0.33	0.57	1.10	0.06	0.27	1.75	406.07
Arts, entertainment, recreation and other services	2000	0.52	0.88	1.28	0.56	0.56	1.42	216.87
	2005	0.58	1.06	1.71	0.09	0.77	2.37	238.79
	2010	0.56	0.87	1.57	0.29	0.80	3.00	207.70
	2015	0.97	1.24	1.68	0.69	0.75	2.78	248.27

Source: authors' calculations

Table 7.3 Relative importance of manufacturing sectors classified according to technological intensity (in % of total manufacturing)

		Total assets (in %)	*Total revenues (in %)*	*GVA (in %)*	*Exports (in %)*	*Investments (in %)*	*Employment (in %)*	*Labour productivity (in 000 KN)*
High technology	2000	19.37	15.68	24.16	30.01	33.08	10.60	391.54
	2005	26.50	14.72	17.77	23.82	6.23	9.18	375.40
	2010	18.52	12.53	14.59	17.16	6.89	9.69	416.52
	2015	16.43	16.40	17.01	24.08	14.60	11.25	355.75
Medium-high technology	2000	17.33	16.17	11.48	21.63	6.57	20.35	96.93
	2005	16.17	18.08	15.62	26.57	8.43	23.64	128.22
	2010	16.19	17.53	14.33	26.38	8.53	21.76	182.20
	2015	16.97	14.75	14.05	20.93	6.03	15.48	213.66
Medium-low technology	2000	37.19	41.43	35.21	38.87	39.28	31.12	194.43
	2005	34.79	42.89	35.24	38.12	70.52	28.93	236.30
	2010	43.90	46.03	46.14	45.88	72.52	30.39	419.96
	2015	35.85	38.68	37.32	37.37	54.90	26.28	334.26
Low technology	2000	26.11	26.72	29.15	9.48	21.07	37.93	132.08
	2005	22.54	24.31	31.36	11.49	14.82	38.25	159.07
	2010	21.39	23.91	24.94	10.58	12.05	38.16	180.74
	2015	30.75	30.17	28.79	17.62	24.48	46.99	144.21

Source: authors' calculations

real estate, and professional scientific and technical activities noted strong employment growth, while in the remaining sectors employment share declined.

As far as GVA is concerned, secondary sector (mining, manufacturing and construction) generated 37.2% of total GVA of the corporate sector in 2000, which is substantially less than GVA recorded in 2015 (26. 77%). The primary sector (agriculture, forestry and fishing) accounted for only 1.5% of GVA in 2015. The share of GVA for services sector increased from 35.7 in 2000 to 44.7% in 2015. Labor productivity increased for all economic sectors except financial and insurance services, public administration, education and health care. In 2015, mining, quarrying and construction stood out with the highest productivity growth rates compared to 2000.

As one can notice from Table 7.3, structural shifts related to technological development were quite unfavorable for Croatian manufacturing. Manufacturing sectors characterized by high technological intensity lost share in total assets, GVA, investments and exports, while revenues and employment were stagnant. However, probably the most worrisome development in these sectors is related to labor productivity, measured as GVA per employee. Namely, labor productivity shows a downward trend probably related to the underinvestment in new capacity, which is also reflected by the data in Table 7.3. On the other side, industries characterized by low technological intensity gained prominence and increased its share in all aggregates. Particularly striking is the increase in share of employees in these industries which shot up from 38% to 47% of total employment in manufacturing in 15 years. These sectors also almost doubled their share in total manufacturing exports in the observed period.

Manufacturing sectors characterized by medium-high intensity of utilizing technology and knowledge also decreased their share in the overall exports and employment of manufacturing sector, but increased somewhat GVA and investment shares. Further on, these sectors are the only sectors with substantial increase in labor productivity in the observed period. Thus, even though the medium-high technology sector exhibited more favorable trends, the overall picture remains quite bleak. It suggests deterioration in the production structure and increasing dependence on industries characterized by smaller value added and mark-up per product unit. These changes may in turn lead to slower productivity growth and might drive the income divergence observed in Croatia.

7.6 Concluding Remarks

When one summarizes all the findings presented in this chapter, one can conclude that long-run trends in Croatian GDP growth are very unfavorable. GDP per capita in absolute terms has been diverging both with respect to the club of NMS and OMS countries, with this income gap becoming even wider from 2008 onwards, as Croatia entered a protracted six-year recession. Formal income convergence tests also corroborate income divergence hypothesis. In terms of β-convergence Croatia is the worst performer among NMS countries and the second worst among EU countries (with Greece being the worst performer). In other words, Croatia exhibits the second largest gap between recorded GDP per capita growth rate in the 1992–2016 period and the expected cumulative GDP per capita growth rate warranted by the average EU β-convergence speed. Our findings also suggest that the dispersion of income levels across all EU countries and across all NMS (including Croatia in both cases) has actually increased over time, thereby confirming diverging properties within these income convergence clubs that include Croatia as a member.

In order to understand the factors driving these adverse trends we looked into the structure of GDP and GVA growth in the last 15 years and concluded that the sectoral growth pattern followed by the Croatian economy differentiates substantially from that of NMS. Namely, in Croatia investments and government consumption had a much more important role in driving the overall GDP growth, while personal consumption, and especially international trade, appear to be much more important for GDP growth in NMS. At the same time, the public sector and industry in particular are much less important for GVA formation growth in Croatia when compared to NMS, while the services sector is much more important. In addition, the contribution of agriculture to GVA growth in Croatia is negative, while in NMS and OMS it is positive. We can thus conclude that choosing services-led growth fueled by investments (mostly in real estate and large public infrastructure projects) and government consumption was in comparative terms a suboptimal strategy for achieving income convergence.

The analysis of sectoral developments also revealed concerning trends related to deindustrialization and technological degradation. Therefore, it is not so important that tradable sectors (agriculture and manufacturing) are becoming less pertinent for GVA creation. What is of most concern is a structural shift from manufacturing sectors, with higher intensity of using technology and knowledge, towards sectors with low required usage of technology and knowledge. Such a shift might have dampened productivity growth and decreased potential growth, thus contributing to a widening income gap between Croatia on the one side and NMS and OMS countries on the other.

Finally, one also has to take into account that income divergence in Croatia did not coincide with the transition period. On the contrary it can be traced back at least to the beginning of 1980s. Thus, income divergence is not specific to the transition period. Purely economic reasons for such developments in the transition period are addressed in this chapter: from excessive focus on services-led growth fueled by investments in non-tradable sectors, from government consumption to deindustrialization and failing to keep up with technological upgrading of tradable sectors. However, there are other reasons that also need to be examined in order to obtain a complete overview of reasons for income divergence, such as the quality of institutions, the definition and implementation of specific policies, the quality of market mechanisms, and the role of the public sector in economic outcomes.

References

Acemoglu, D., Johnson, S., & Robinson, J. A. (2004). Institutions as the Fundamental Cause of Long-Run, *NBER Working Paper No. 10481*. http://www.nber.org/papers/w10481. Downloaded 2 May 2017.

Bađun, M., Pribičević, V., & Deskar-Škrbić, M. (2014). Government Size and Efficiency as Constraints to Economic Growth: Comparing Croatia with Other European Countries. *Post-Communist Economies, 26*(3), 297–323.

Barro, R. J. (1991). Economic Growth in a Cross Section of Countries. *The Quarterly Journal of Economics, 106*(2), 407–443.

Baumol, W. J. (1986). Productivity, Growth, Convergence, and Welfare: What the Long-Run Data Show. *American Economic Review, 76*, 1072–1085.

Bennett, J., Estrin, S., & Urga, G. (2007). Methods of Privatization and Economic Growth in Transition Economies. *Economics of Transition, 15*(4), 661–683.

Berg, A., Borensztein, E., Sahay, R., & Zettlemeyer, J. (1999). The Evolution of Output in Transition Economies: Explaining the Differences, *International Monetary Fund Working Paper No. 99/73.*

Böwer, U., & Turrini, A. (2010). EU Accession: A Road to Fast-Track Convergence? *Comparative Economic Studies, 52*(2), 181–205.

Campos, N. F., & Coricelli, A. (2002). Growth in Transition: What we Know, What we Don't, and What we Should. *Journal of Economic Literature, 40*(3), 793–836.

Cheptea, A. (2007). Trade Liberalization and Institutional Reforms. *Economics of Transition, 15*(2), 211–255.
Darvas, Z. (2010). Beyond the Crisis: Prospects for Emerging Europe, *Bruegel Working Paper 2010/06*. http://aei.pitt.edu/15444/. Downloaded 2 May 2017.
De Melo, M., Denizer, C., & Gelb, A. (1996). From Plan to Market: Patterns of Transition, The World Bank, *Policy Research Working Paper* No. 1564.
De Melo, M., Denizer, C., Gelb, A., & Tenev, S. (2001). Circumstance and Choice: The Role of Initial Conditions and Policies in Transition Economies. *The World Bank Economic Review, 15*(1), 1–31.
Drezgić, S. (2011). Public Investments and Regional Income Convergence: Empirical Analysis of Croatian Regions. *Social Research, 3*(24), 43–55.
Eicher, T. S., & Schreiber, T. (2010). Structural Policies and Growth: Time Series Evidence from a Natural Experiment. *Journal of Development Economics, 91*(1), 169–179.
Falcetti, E., Raiser, M., & Sanfey, P. (2002). Defying the Odds: Initial Conditions, Reforms, and Growth in the First Decade of Transition. *Journal of Comparative Economics, 30*(2), 229–250.
Franičević, V., & Kraft, E. (1997). Croatia's Economy After Stabilisation. *Europe-Asia Studies, 49*(4), 669–691.
Hall, R. E., & Jones, C. I. (1999). Why do Some Countries Produce so Much More Output Per Worker Than Others? *The Quarterly Journal of Economics, 114*(1), 83–116.
Havrylyshyn, O., & Van Rooden, R. (1998). Recovery and Growth in Transition Economies 1990–97: A Stylized Regression Analysis, *IMF Working Paper No. 98/141*.
Hossain, A. (2000). Convergence of Per Capita Output Levels Across Regions of Bangladesh, 1982–97, *IMF Working Paper 2000/121*.
Islam, N. (2003). What Have we Learnt from the Convergence Debate? *Journal of Economic Surveys, 17*(3), 309–362.
Kolodko, G. W. (2000). *From Shock to Therapy: The Political Economy of Postsocialist Transformation*. Oxford: Oxford University Press.
Kornai, J. (1998). *From Socialism to Capitalism: What Is Meant by the Change of System?* London: Social Market Foundation.
Kornai, J. (2000). Ten Years After 'The Road to a Free Economy': The Author's Self-Evaluation. *Annual Bank Conference on Development Economics, 2000*, 49–66.
Kornai, J. (2006a). The Great Transformation of Central Eastern Europe. Success and Disappointment. *Economics of Transition, 14*(2), 207–244.
Kornai, J. (2006b). The Great Transformation of Central Eastern Europe: Success and Disappointment-First Published. *Montenegrin Journal of Economics, 2*(4), 11–38.

Nuti, D. M., & Portes, R. (1993). Central Europe: The Way Forward. *Economic Transformation in Central Europe: A Progress Report*, 1–20.

Podkaminer, L. (2013). *Development Patterns of Central and East European Countries (in the Course of Transition and Following EU Accession)*. Vienna: Verein Wiener Inst. für Internat. Wirtschaftsvergleiche (WIIW).

Quah, D. (1993). Galton's Fallacy and Tests of the Convergence Hypothesis. *The Scandinavian Journal of Economics, 95*(4), 427–443.

Rodrik, D., Subramanian, A., & Trebbi, F. (2004). Institutions Rule: The Primacy of Institutions Over Geography and Integration in Economic Development. *Journal of Economic Growth, 9*(2), 131–165.

Roland, G. (2000). *Transition and Economics: Politics, Markets, and Firms*. Cambridge: MIT Press.

Schweickert, R., Melnykovska, I., Belke, A., & Bordon, I. (2011). Prospective NATO or EU Membership and Institutional Change in Transition Countries. *Economics of Transition, 19*(4), 667–692.

Stojčić, N., Benić, Đ., & Karanikić, P. (2012). Regional Determinants of Export Competitiveness in Croatian Manufacturing Industry. *Proceedings of Rijeka Faculty of Economics: Journal of Economics and Business, 32*(2), 193–212.

Tkalec, M., & Vizek, M. (2009). The Impact of Macroeconomic Policies on Manufacturing Production in Croatia. *Economic Trends and Economic Policy, 121*, 61–92.

Tkalec, M., & Vizek, M. (2014). Real Estate Boom and Export Performance Bust in Croatia. *Proceedings of Rijeka Faculty of Economics: Journal of Economics and Business, 32*(1), 11–34.

Databases

Eurostat database, GDP per capita. http://ec.europa.eu/eurostat/data/database. Downloaded 24 April 2017.

FINA database. (2000–2015). agregati po djelatnostima.

Maddison database. (2013). The Maddison-Project. http://www.ggdc.net/maddison/maddison-project/data.htm. Downloaded 24 April 2017.

Wiiw, GDP. https://data.wiiw.ac.at/. Downloaded 25 April 2017.

Wiiw, Wages. https://data.wiiw.ac.at/. Downloaded 25 April 2017.

CHAPTER 8

Monetary Policy in a Highly Euroized Economy

Kristijan Kotarski and Marina Tkalec

8.1 Croatian Monetary Policy in Historical Context: From the Breakup of Yugoslavia Until Financial Opening in the Early 2000s

The implementation of monetary policy in former Yugoslavia and independent Croatia is marked by significant differences in terms of politics and policy instruments. The Yugoslav political economy was primarily characterized by an emphasis on boosting nominal GDP growth and employment, while price stability came only second. These policy priorities reflected the imperative of keeping political stability in a highly fragmented and multiethnic federation, especially after Tito's death in 1980. The attainment of this goal was achieved by a combination of external borrowing and arbitrary money printing. The logical corollary had been

K. Kotarski (✉)
Faculty of Political Science, University of Zagreb, Zagreb, Croatia
e-mail: kristijan.kotarski@fpzg.hr

M. Tkalec
The Institute of Economics, Zagreb, Croatia
e-mail: mtkalec@eizg.hr

Z. Petak, K. Kotarski (eds.), *Policy-Making at the European Periphery*, New Perspectives on South-East Europe,
https://doi.org/10.1007/978-3-319-73582-5_8

double-digit inflation in the 1970s and 1980s, which slipped out of control in 1989 with an inflation rate approaching 1199% (Tica 2009).

The transition from a socialist to a market economy and hyperinflation mark the first phase of monetary policy in Croatia. The breakup of Yugoslavia coincided with 'monetary intrusion' of Serbian banks into the Yugoslav monetary system and the loss of access of Croatian banks to common foreign exchange (FX) reserves held by the Yugoslav central bank (NBJ).[1] Soon afterwards, at the very beginning of the Homeland War in 1991, the Croatian National Bank (CNB) was putting a lot of effort into acquisition of FX reserves, desperately needed to finance imports and war-related expenses. This resulted in excessive printing of Croatian dinar in order to buy foreign currency from citizens, followed by an inflationary spike in 1993.[2]

At that moment stabilization of inflationary expectations became indispensible for the survival of a new state. The CNB managed to communicate to the highest levels of state authority the priority of ensuring stable prices. A stabilization program had been initiated in 1993 to tackle rampant hyperinflation, which served as a milestone in establishing the CNB's image of credibility. The coordination of monetary and fiscal policy achieved rapid disinflation and the inflation rate fell down to 3% in 1994. This kind of intervention established a quasi-currency board as a monetary regime (Vujčić 2003). According to this regime, the volume of monetary aggregate M1 is always smaller than the amount of FX reserves and domestic money is primarily created through foreign exchange interventions.[3] At the same time, the exchange rate peg of Croatian kuna (HRK) against the German mark (DEM) was chosen as a nominal anchor of monetary policy for stabilizing inflationary expectations.

The decision to opt for the exchange rate instead of the interest rate or the level of particular monetary aggregate was based on (a) a very high initial level of euroization, (b) the openness of the Croatian economy, and (c) foreign indebtedness denominated in foreign currency. Nevertheless, the most important factor that contributed to choosing the exchange rate was the inherited level of euroization. As compared to other postsocialist countries, Croatia had had the highest level of deposit euroization at the beginning of 1994, which was only surpassed by Serbia in 2005. This came as a consequence of several interwoven trends such as past financial crises (hyperinflation and bank failures in 1990s), monetary expectations (exchange rate depreciation and subsequent inflation), large FX inflows from tourism, and socioeconomic characteristics (significant diaspora remittances). All of this may explain the initial proneness of Croatian citizens and enterprises to adopting the German mark in their economic transactions (replaced by the euro in 2002), which was further reinforced by network externalities (Brown and Stix 2014).

After the successful stabilization in 1993, monetary policy focused on gradual capital account liberalization and dealt with capital inflows that were becoming abundant towards 2008. This second phase of monetary policy starts with the successful Paris and London club agreements in 1995–1996 on the issue of unallocated Yugoslav foreign debt, and ends in the early 2000s. The series of events was followed by obtaining an investment grade credit rating in 1997.

The aforementioned step opened the door for the arrival of foreign banks willing to exploit the difference between lower international and higher domestic interest rates. All of this was facilitated by dual stability centered on the price level and the exchange rate. This had been conducive to the emergence of a serious currency mismatch, which ushered in the second banking crisis of 1998–1999. Unlike the first banking crisis in 1996, which had been related to the large old state-owned banks and their nonperforming loans (NPLs), the second banking crisis was caused by the rapid inflow of foreign exchange willing to profit from aggressive strategies of expansion by several mid-sized banks (Vujčić 2003).

This came in spite of the CNB's imposition of Chilean-style capital controls, such as the requirement for commercial banks to put aside 30% of short-term credit in the form of deposits at the CNB. The costs of the first banking crisis are estimated at 22% of GDP while the second banking crisis cost 5% of GDP (Šonje and Vujčić 2000). Despite the lower economic costs of the second banking crisis and CNB's warnings prior to its outburst, some of the public, several politicians and bankers tried to blame the central bank. Nevertheless, the CNB managed to shrug the pressure off its shoulders and paved the way for gradual development of macroprudential tools. This policy change was facilitated by the Croatian Parliament passing the Act on the CNB in 2001. According to Garriga (2016), in 2000 the independence score of the CNB was only 0.44 on the 0–1 scale, significantly below the CEE average score.[4] A year later, in 2001, the CNB's score jumped to impressive 0.89.

In spite of the CNB's success in taming inflation, its work has been steadily criticized. The main line of criticism in the 1990s came from uncompetitive sectors of the economy that had been accustomed to soft budgetary constraints. They were invoking pro-inflationary monetary policy, which would have led to significant transfer of wealth from savers to debtors, one of the basic tenets of the Yugoslav political economy during the 1980s. The postponement of necessary restructuring in the corporate sector provoked renewed pressures on the CNB's independence (Faulend et al. 2000). Some economists also criticized the low ratio of money supply to GDP and saw the solution to liquidity and solvency problems in monetary expansion rather than in structural reforms (Baletić and Zdunić 1999). Fortunately, the trend towards more central bank independence has not been reversed and the CNB upheld its track record of credibility.

8.2 Monetary Policy at the Dawn of the Global Financial Crisis (GFC)

The third phase of monetary policy starts with the 2003 Foreign Exchange Law, which allowed foreigners to participate in most capital markets, with the primary market for short-term government debt as a sole exception. This move was followed by removing prohibition on Croatian residents giving loans to nonresidents and removing the ban on opening bank accounts abroad in 2010, as a part of preparation for EU membership (Kraft and Galac 2011). According to the Chinn-Ito index of capital account openness, Croatia boasts a constant score of 1.082 on a scale from −2.5 to 2.5 (more vs. less restrictiveness), after the introduction of liberalization measures in 2003.[5] The comparison of Croatia with other postsocialist economies leads to the conclusion that Croatia kept more restrictions on capital inflows than the CEE-10 average, especially after 2003.[6]

Croatia was an example of a country with an intensive reliance on countercyclical macroprudential policy measures in order to sap rapid credit growth prior to 2008. This stems from the Tošovsky dilemma, which postulates that in the context of high capital inflows raising interest rates only stimulates additional flows (Brkić and Kotarski 2009). Although the CNB only became officially responsible for ensuring financial stability with the amendment of the Act on the CNB in 2013, the CNB had already started with the implementation of those measures in 2003.

- Unlike the attempt to dampen capital inflows with an interest-based sterilization policy, the CNB introduced a panoply of measures, such as quantitative restrictions on lending (annual credit growth ceiling of 16% from 2003 to 2007 and 12% from 2007 to 2009), the introduction of marginal reserve requirements of up to 55% to reduce the incentive for banks to engage in foreign borrowing (from 2004 to 2009), foreign currency interventions to combat HRK appreciation, the maintenance of minimum required foreign currency claims to ensure liquidity buffers against potential deposit withdrawal (32% in 2003 down to 17% at the moment of writing), higher risk-weights on loans indexed to foreign currency, and the increase in capital adequacy standards from 10% to 12% of risk-weighted assets (RWA) (Kraft and Galac 2011; Vujčić and Dumičić 2016).

This largely anticipated the spirit of the Basel III framework agreed upon in 2011. Nevertheless, the CNB's persistence in securing financial stability with attendant speed limits to credit growth did not manage to satisfactorily slow down rising private debt. There were several evasion channels for willing domestic borrowers, such as direct foreign borrowing from parent banks abroad and borrowing through leasing companies. Closing loopholes in this cat-and-mouse game between regulators and financial market participants was extremely difficult to achieve.[7] All of this enabled a threefold increase in Croatia's foreign debt from 2001 until 2008, and a staggering current account deficit, which averaged 6% of GDP from 2001 to 2008 (The World Bank 2017b).

8.3 Monetary Policy Since 2008

GFC hit in 2008 and took a heavy toll on the Croatian economy. This marks the fourth phase of monetary policy in Croatia. A major drop was primarily recorded in personal consumption, exports and imports, since Croatia represents a very open economy. Those aggregate demand components turned out to be very procyclical and externally driven, while investments displayed the biggest volatility as measured by their standard deviation (Družić et al. 2016). At this stage the Croatian economy faced a sudden stop of capital inflows, which was threatening exchange rate stability. The CNB reacted by relying on large foreign currency interventions and mandated that a certain portion of reserve requirement on foreign exchange deposits must be held at the central bank in the form of domestic currency. One additional feature of Croatia's financial system helped in stabilizing the HRK-EUR exchange rate in 2008 and 2009—'lukewarm capital' (Vujčić 2003). Unlike hot money represented by hedge funds and investment banks that rushes to the exit immediately after perceived bad news, 'lukewarm capital' represents domestic residents that are less sensitive to slight exchange rate volatility. Luckily, those structural characteristics and the CNB's policy choices staved off the emergence of a twin crisis.

The banking sector felt the burden of the crisis mostly through an increase in the NPL ratio from 4.88% in 2008 to a 16.70% peak in 2014 (The World Bank 2017a). However, Croatia has not experienced bank failures since 2008 because the CNB insisted on high liquidity and capital requirements prior to 2008. As opposed to 2003–2008 macroprudential tightening, the CNB significantly relaxed credit growth restrictions in 2009 in an attempt to jumpstart fallen financial intermediation. Therefore, the following seven years before the economy started to recover in 2015 were characteristic for the struggle to obtain dual goals of both exchange rate stability and expansionary monetary policy. This opened up intense debate on the role of monetary policy in boosting exports through nominal exchange rate depreciation, as well as other aggregate demand components through lowering interest rates. Yet, those debates were not fiercely embraced by leading political parties but rather by the economics profession.[8]

The CNB's critics claim that monetary policy was not sufficiently expansionary in averting the private sector's deleveraging (Radošević 2011). They also claim that the CNB did not use the possibility of relying on unconventional monetary instruments such as securities purchases in the secondary market to reduce debt-servicing costs by the state and to stimulate private sector lending (Ivanov 2014). Those views echo the 'money view' of monetary policy whose main goal is to restore total money supply, with the associated focus on banks' liabilities (Brunnermeier and Sannikov 2016). Other authors contrast those claims and point out that by 2012 the CNB released 6.1 billion EUR or more than 14% of GDP through reduced general reserve requirements, as well as through the removal of marginal and special reserve requirements. This improved liquidity of the banking sector enabled regular servicing of the government's liabilities (Vujčić and Dumičić 2016). Nevertheless, liquidity was not transmitted into rising credit portfolio since there had been a lack of healthy credit opportunities. This view is closer to the 'credit view' of monetary policy with associated focus on banks' assets side. Hence, the challenge primarily lies in the existing levels of indebtedness; institutional uncertainty, such as a weak legal system; irresponsible fiscal policy and accompanying low credit rating; lack of credit culture; and weak domestic demand.

Empirical evidence in this debate is weighted more on the side of the CNB's monetary policy defenders. A study of the relationship between interest rates and GDP in Croatia shows that interest rates do not represent an effective transmission mechanism of monetary policy and only few industries react to changes in interest rates as compared to fiscal policy changes (Tkalec and Vizek 2009). Another study posits the insensitivity of the unemployment rate in Croatia to the change in the level of monetary aggregate M1 both in the short and long run, mustering support in favor of the long-run neutrality of money concept (Benazić and Rami 2016). On the issue of depreciation, the Eurochambres Economic Survey 2017 offers a clear insight that entrepreneurs perceive exchange rate as the least important barrier to doing business.[9] Furthermore, a detailed analysis of improvement in Croatian exports since 2008 shows the centrality of the real effective exchange rate (REER).

Over the last two decades, the HRK-EUR nominal exchange rate was very stable but REER was skyrocketing (appreciating) prior to the GFC, with Croatia posting one of the largest divergences in labor productivity and salaries among EU countries (Globan 2017). Afterwards, a significant REER depreciation worked in tandem with Croatia's accession to the Single Market in 2013. To conclude, key barriers to financially sound domestic- and foreign-oriented companies are not to be found in the change of monetary regime or the attempt at lowering costs of financing by expansionary monetary policy. They are first and foremost fiscal and structural.

We finish this historical overview with the ongoing final phase, in which Croatia is determined to introduce the euro, especially in light of the joint accord by the Croatian Government and the CNB in 2017 to move in this direction. Weighing the pros and cons of euro adoption points to an overall balance that is more in favor of EMU membership than standing at its doorstep. In terms of pros, due to bulk of trade with the euro area, the introduction of the euro would lead to lower transaction costs. It would also signal lower risk premia to public debt holders due to potential recourse to the EMU's stabilization mechanisms introduced following the last crisis. This would also lower financing costs for other sectors of the economy. Definitely the largest benefit amounts to the elimination of foreign currency-induced risk where each economic sector (households, public sector and private nonfinancial sector) carries more than 60% of debt indexed to the HRK-EUR exchange rate (Deskar Škrbić 2017).

In terms of the major cost of euro adoption and the subsequent loss of monetary sovereignty, Croatia would not suffer significant downsides. As already mentioned, expansionary monetary policy in a highly euroized economy has been impaired by the ineffectiveness of monetary policy transmission mechanism. The CNB's limited lender-of-last-resort (LORL) role and constraints upon exchange rate and interest rate transmission channels give an incentive for formal euroization. Furthermore, the synchronization of the Croatian business cycle with that of the euro area gives an additional impetus for EMU membership. It is to be seen whether actors responsible for fiscal policy will be committed enough to fulfilling fiscal criteria (reducing chronic public debt) for euro adoption in the coming years. This remains the central puzzle of Croatia's path towards the EMU.

8.4 Key Monetary Policy Instruments in Croatia

Foreign exchange interventions are probably the most important monetary policy instrument in Croatia. This is, of course, no surprise as inflexible regimes such as exchange rate pegs and different sorts of intermediate regimes normally use indirect instruments to keep exchange rate expectations anchored. In Croatia, occasional and typically unannounced interventions react to larger movements in the nominal HRK-EUR exchange rate, to keep expectations anchored or simply to sterilize an abundant supply of euro (for example in the tourist season or after public borrowing abroad) or kuna (in the case of capital outflows). The CNB never committed to a target band but tight management suggests the level of 7.50 kuna for one euro is somewhere within the CNB comfort zone.

Foreign exchange interventions affect the money market immediately as lack of or abundance of kuna affect short-term interest rates. A typical CNB intervention in 2009 in the midst of capital outflows was to sell euro (deplete foreign exchange reserves) and buy kuna from banks (see Fig. 8.1). These interventions tightened monetary policy which somewhat slowed down capital outflows and reduced depreciatory pressures. High interest rates on the downside worsened the ongoing recession, as fiscal policy at the time did not have space for expansion and it failed to support aggregate demand. On the other hand, during summer months, when a lot of foreign currency enters the economy through tourism, CNB buys euro to prevent kuna appreciation.

Figure 8.1 shows that in the mature recessionary phase (2011–2015) kuna managed to keep a stable level of 7.55 HRK for one euro. At the time, the CNB intervened exclusively (except one small intervention in September 2012) by selling foreign currency to the banks and depleting

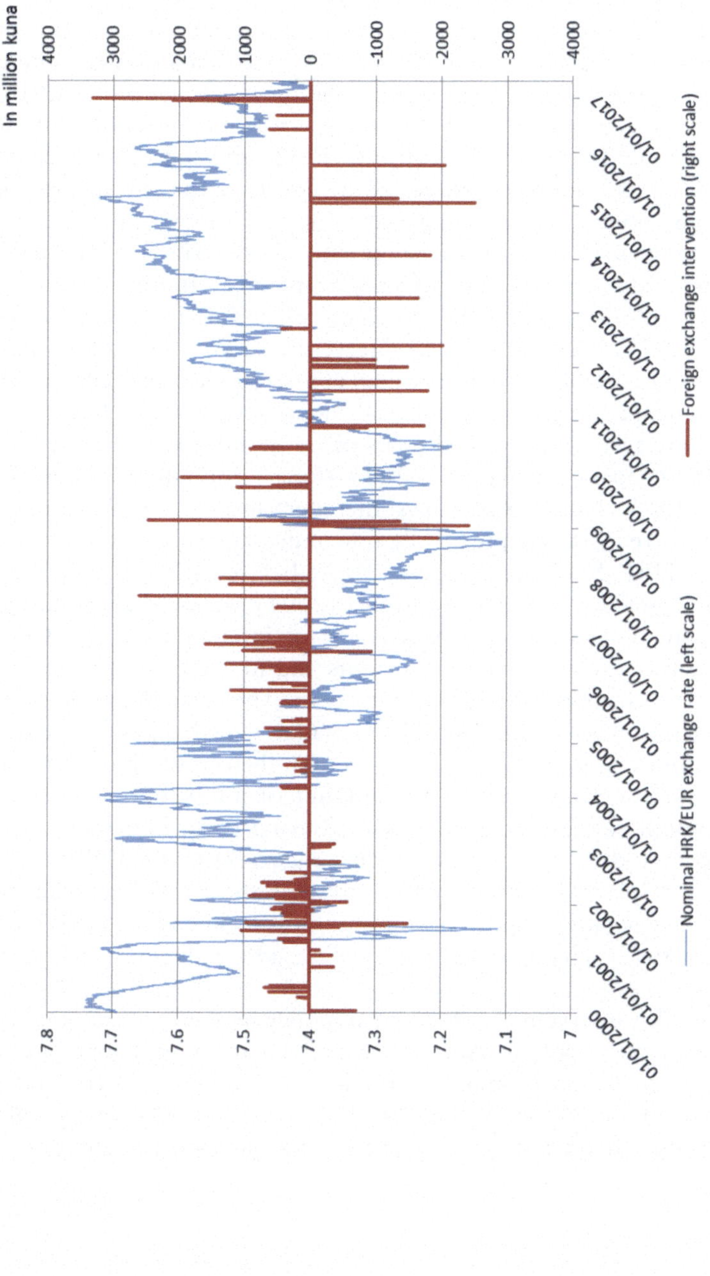

Fig. 8.1 Foreign exchange intervention and the nominal exchange rate (Note: A negative amount of foreign exchange intervention assumes the central bank is selling foreign exchange to banks in order to suspend depreciatory pressures) (Source: Croatian National Bank)

its reserves in order to suspend depreciatory pressures and keep the HRK from sliding even further. The tight management at the time was necessary, as with exchange rate depreciation all loans in euro and those indexed to the HRK-EUR exchange rate go up in kuna value and the annuities for households and enterprises start rising. As soon as Croatia started recording positive GDP growth rates and when public finance stabilized in 2016, kuna appreciated and even went below the psychological level of 7.50. At that time, the CNB intervened by buying euro from banks, thus keeping exchange rate expectations anchored. To demonstrate the effectiveness of this policy instrument, we do a simple econometric analysis of the sensitivity of the nominal HRK-EUR exchange rate, short-term and long-term interest rates and loans to foreign exchange rate intervention.

We collect the data on all FX interventions in Croatia from January 2000 to April 2017; altogether 120 interventions. We were able to pair these daily data together with money market interest rates and data on the nominal exchange rate, as these are available on a daily basis. Regarding loans and long-term rates we had to focus on monthly data from either January 2000 (loans) or January 2004 (long-term interest rates) to December 2016. Figure 8.2 shows the mechanism of CNB foreign exchange intervention. We present by how much and in which direction the nominal HRK-EUR exchange rate moves before the CNB is inclined to intervene. Similarly to Lang and Krznar (2004), we use the measure of exchange rate movements five days ahead of intervention. The CNB closely monitors exchange rate movements and in the case of large and uncomfortable changes it decides to intervene. The vertical axis presents by how much the nominal HRK-EUR exchange rate changes on the day of intervention compared to the level five days before the intervention, while the horizontal axis depicts the amount of intervention. Again, a positive amount suggests that the CNB is buying euro, thus preventing further appreciation, and a negative amount suggests that the CNB is selling euro to suspend depreciatory pressures. As shown in Fig. 8.2a we would expect a negative slope in the linear regression line as the CNB buys euro when the exchange rate appreciates, and sells euro when it depreciates.

Before CNB's intervention, short-term money market rates respond to the change in the supply of kuna and euro. When the exchange rate is appreciating, the supply of kuna is shrinking, thus bringing interest rates up. The intervention in which the CNB buys euro and sells kuna should help bring interest rates down. We present the data on the amount of

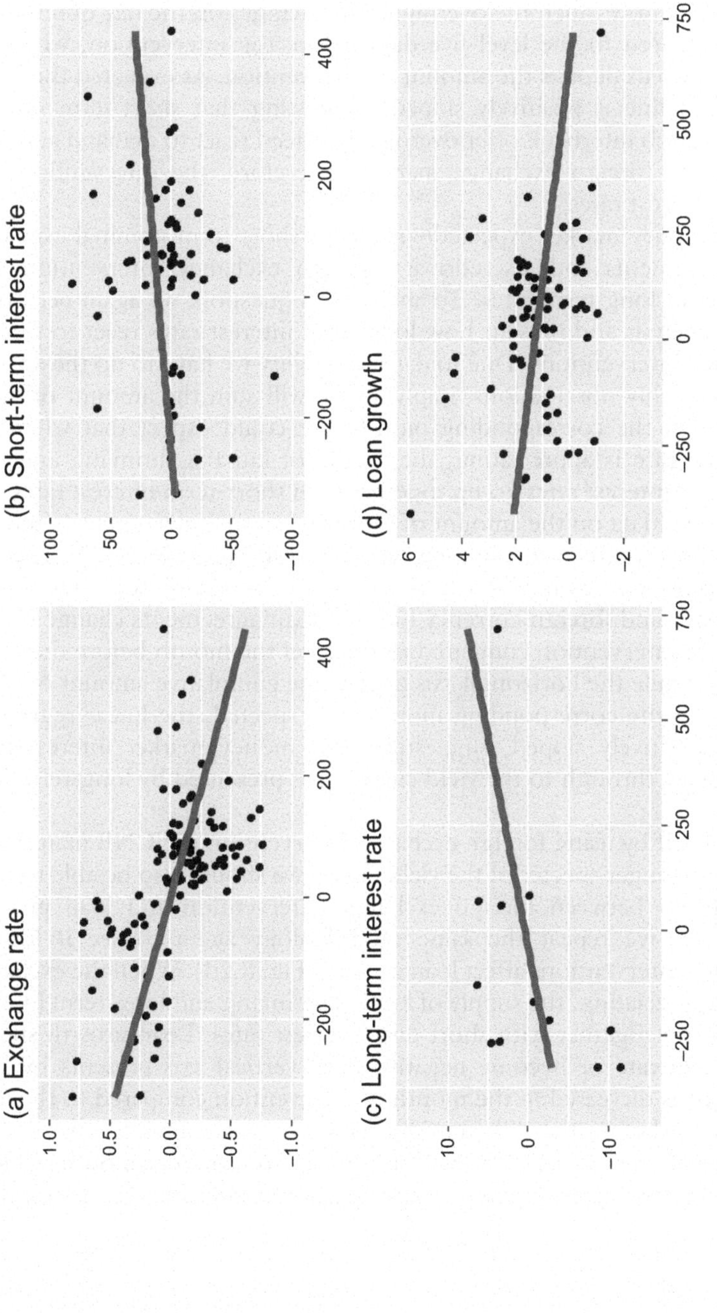

Fig. 8.2 Foreign exchange interventions (Sources: Croatian National Bank and Reuters)

intervention and the change in interest rates in Fig. 8.2b. The vertical axis presents by how much the overnight rate changes on the day of intervention compared to the level five days before the intervention, while the horizontal axis depicts the amount of intervention. As expected the linear regression line is positively sloped, suggesting that short-term interest rates (Zagreb interbank offer overnight) indeed react to demand and supply on the foreign exchange market. Therefore, the intervention also affects interest rates.

The money market expectedly reacts to short-term nominal exchange rate movements and discretionary foreign exchange intervention, but what about long-term rates? To answer this question, we again perform a similar analysis and present how long-term interest rates react to foreign exchange interventions. Due to data availability we have to do the analysis using monthly observations, implying we will sum the amount of interventions in the corresponding month. We could expect that when the exchange rate is appreciating, the supply of kuna is shrinking and that long-term interest rates go up together with short-term interest rates. We present the data on the amount of intervention in a given month and the month-on-month change in long-term interest rates in Fig. 8.2c. The vertical axis presents by how much the weighted average interest rates on new kuna loans and foreign currency indexed loan agreements change on the month of intervention compared to the level the month before the intervention, while the horizontal axis depicts the cumulative amount of intervention in the corresponding month. As expected, the linear regression line is positively sloped, suggesting that money market interest rates indeed pass through to the yield curve, here presented by long-term loan rates.

Finally, if by using foreign exchange intervention the CNB manages to affect the longer specter of the yield curve, we should also be able to see a relationship between foreign exchange intervention and loan growth. Therefore, we repeat the same methodology again to see if foreign exchange interventions affect loan growth (Fig. 8.2d). When the exchange rate is appreciating, the supply of kuna is shrinking and long-term interest rates go up together with short-term interest rates. Loan growth should then decelerate or become negative. The vertical axis presents by how much loans increased in the month of intervention compared to the level the month before the intervention, while the horizontal axis depicts the cumulative amount of intervention in the corresponding month. As suggested by the negative slope of the regression line, loan growth indeed decelerates when the foreign exchange intervention tries to curb appreciation.

These four empirical exercises have demonstrated the strength of simple foreign exchange intervention. When expectations are anchored and the central bank commits to the goal of a stable exchange rate, the instrument is efficient not only in managing this goal but also in achieving additional goals—money market interest rate stability that passes through to interest rates on loans for households and enterprises.

8.5 Monetary Policy and Currency Mismatch

Unlike some other European postsocialist economies that abandoned the exchange rate targeting regime quite early in the transition phase, the regime in Croatia has persisted to this day. At the moment it seems the regime is deeply rooted in the Croatian economy because episodes of hyperinflation in the 1980s and 1990s made citizens skeptical towards the domestic monetary anchor (Kraft 2003). The distrust pushed them to save in foreign currency, which propelled deposit euroization to very high levels, normally above 80% (Fig. 8.3). Having foreign currency on their liability side made banks match their currency positions on the assets side as well, leading to high credit euroization, normally around 75%. Croatia therefore has banks almost fully matched in currency, while most of households and enterprises earn in domestic currency but pay debts in foreign currency. In that respect, Croatia is to some degree different from some other postsocialist economies as credit euroization was not dominantly driven by carry trade, a case in which borrowers take on foreign currency loans due to lower borrowing rates. In Croatia, taking loans denominated in euro was imposed by the logic of ensuring matched currency position by banks.

This peg to the euro, although it constrains monetary policy in achieving macroeconomic goals, is crucial for financial stability. If the exchange rate had been used to improve the country's competitiveness by nominal depreciation, payments for loans denominated in foreign currency would have gone up, thus impairing debtors, mostly households. In the years before the GFC hit, the CNB took many prudential measures in order to fight credit euroization (Kraft and Jankov 2005). Those measures in the period covering 2003–2009 were extensively explained in the first part of this chapter. They had the dual role of preventing excessive borrowing and fighting euroization (IMF 2008). However, credit euroization decreased

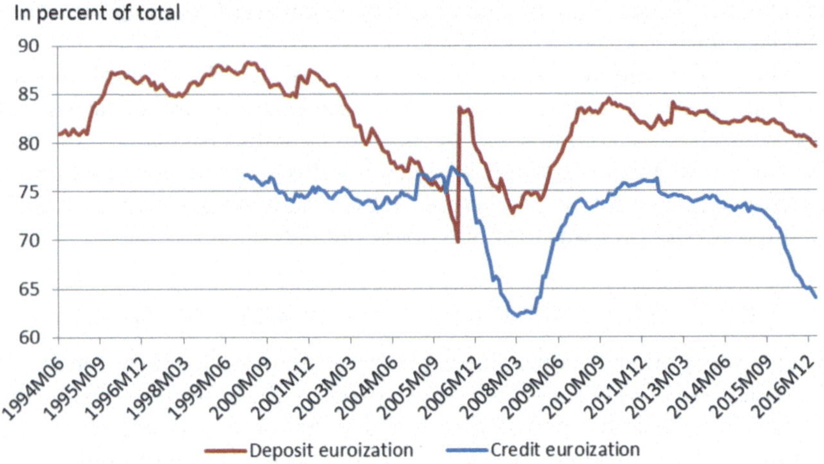

Fig. 8.3 Financial euroization in Croatia (Note: The break in deposit euroization in June 2006 is due to the change of methodology. In the case of credit euroization, loans indexed to the exchange rate were classified under kuna loans before June 2006 making euroization undervalued in that period. We have therefore imposed the currency structure from the second half of 2006 for the period up to June 2006) (Source: Croatian National Bank)

only slightly and the measures were successful as they kept the system stable during the financially turbulent 2008–2009 period (Fig. 8.3).

Despite all of the above-mentioned efforts, the Croatian economy had considerable balance sheet imbalances on the eve of the GFC (Tkalec and Verbič 2013; Tkalec et al. 2014). The financial sector significantly increased its borrowing from firms, households and from abroad up to 2009. It had a negative short-term position in foreign currency with the nonfinancial sector, and large net positive long-term position in foreign currency, as well as negative short- and long-term positions with nonresidents. Firms and households on the other hand had a large net positive position against the financial sector and borrowed massively from abroad. Their short-term position in foreign currency against the domestic financial sector was positive and negative for long-term positions. Households and firms held a large negative position against nonresidents.

Although the currency mismatch and with it the associated balance sheet vulnerabilities were calling for deeuroization and a more flexible monetary policy regime, unfortunately, joining the EU in 2013 only hindered central bank efforts to deeuroize. Before Croatia joined the EU, the most effective measure to fight euroization were higher risk weights for unhedged borrowers, but due to the new regulation they had to be replaced with less efficient capital buffers. With little choice of measures left to fight financial euroization and with prospects to adopt the euro, it seems that Croatia will have to bear with high euroization and the household-dominant currency mismatches. This will last at least until the euro adoption, when households will finally match the currency of their incomes with the currency of their loans.

8.6 Currency Mismatch and Political Economy of Swiss Franc Loans

Adopting the euro, however, is a remedy for only one set of mismatch, the HRK-EUR one; and one set of borrowers: the ones that borrow in euro. Although this mismatch is the dominant one, Swiss franc appreciation recently demonstrated around Emerging Europe that even a small group of borrowers can pose a threat, if not to the monetary and financial system, then certainly to the social and political one. During the 2000s, foreign-owned, mostly Austrian banks, extended large amounts of Swiss franc-denominated or loans indexed to Swiss francs to households in post-communist Europe. The attractiveness of these loans lay in very low interest rates, when compared to the ones in euro, and especially to domestic currency rates. In Croatia, the biggest share of these loans was extended to households buying houses, around 53,000 of them. When the GFC started, it made many investors worldwide move their assets into Switzerland as a safe haven, which in turn appreciated the value of the Swiss franc since 2009. The annuities for Swiss franc loan holders started to increase and soon households were drastically burdened by this unanticipated expense. Already in 2010, borrowers in Croatia formed Franak, an NGO that sued the banks for underreporting the potential currency risk at the moment when their clients were taking the loans. The court ruling was slow, as the final decision was made as late as 2017, but the government was faster in its solutions to help ease the burden.

In 2014, the government imposed an interest rate ceiling on Swiss franc loans. Although this measure provided comfort to borrowers, it was only temporary as the franc sharply appreciated in January 2015 when the

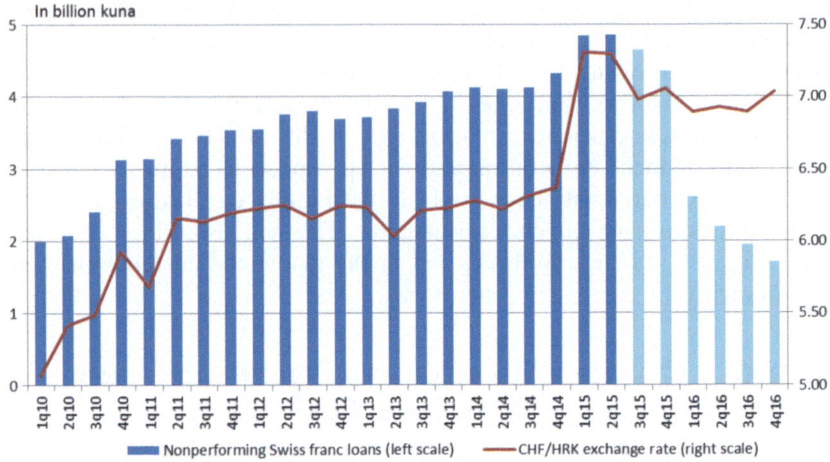

Fig. 8.4 Swiss franc nonperforming loans (Note: The light blue color depicts the period of permanent policy solution for Swiss franc loan debtors) (Source: Croatian National Bank)

Swiss National Bank abandoned the floor to the euro (Fig. 8.4). The Government initially froze the level of HRK-CHF exchange rate for household borrowers but with upcoming parliamentary elections in September 2015 it decided that a permanent solution was needed. In September 2015, the HRK-CHF exchange rate was about 55% above the rate in September 2008, which implies that losses so far have been huge and borne entirely by the borrowers. At the time, therefore, it seemed that the most sensible solution was that all the parties share a part of the burden: the borrowers, the banks, and possibly even the government. The latter, however, decided to shift the burden entirely to the banks, by passing a separate bill for Swiss franc loans under the argument that past bank lending practices had been unfair and that the borrowers needed to be compensated.

Banks were required to retroactively convert their clients' Swiss franc-denominated or indexed loans to loans indexed to the euro, in cases where clients requested such a conversion. All previous payments had to be recalculated as if borrowers took loans indexed to the euro and not to the franc. The positive difference in the amount already paid and the newly calculated previous obligations was, in most cases, used to decrease the leftover principal. The conversion resulted in big bank losses in 2015; but already in 2016, banks posted profits as reservations for nonperforming loans decreased precisely due to this permanent Swiss franc loan solution (Fig. 8.4). Due to high capital requirements, the Croatian banking system remained stable, households reduced their debt, and the central bank successfully mitigated interest rate risks by providing the euro liquidity necessary for the conversion. Although there are still risks associated with potential lawsuits by the banks against the government, bank profits in 2016 hint that the solution was balanced, although probably not completely fair.

One of the legacies of the Swiss franc loans is lower credit euroization that was not driven by any CNB measure, but simply by demonstration effects. Figure 8.3 shows that credit euroization decreased in the aftermath of the strongest Swiss franc appreciation, as the public faced massive protests by desperate borrowers that were on verge of bankruptcy. The incident brought exchange rate risk to consciousness, and many loan owners reprogrammed their existing euro to kuna loans, while new borrowers were asking for loans in domestic currency. Despite the tight exchange rate regime that by nature creates moral hazard in terms of exchange rate risk, the Swiss franc slightly contributed to a somewhat lower moral hazard for both nonfinancial sector borrowers and banks.

8.7 Conclusion

Monetary policy in Croatia in the aftermath of independence was determined by hyperinflation, economic downturn, and macroeconomic instability. As in many other post-communist economies, little choice was left, except to run an exchange rate-based monetary policy regime by fixing the nominal exchange rate towards the German mark and import low inflation from Western Europe. Unlike other post-communist countries, this exchange rate regime in Croatia has persisted to this day, mostly because the central bank managed the exchange rate tightly, keeping adequate foreign exchange reserves and profusely using macroprudential policies to guard exchange rate stability. Having a history of hyperinflation in the 1980s and early 1990s, residents had insisted on keeping their savings in the German mark and later in euro, which led to very high levels of deposit euroization. Having liabilities in foreign currency drove banks to match their balance sheet positions and decrease their net open foreign currency positions and the associated currency risks, resulting in very high credit euroization as well. Such circumstances were perfect for developing significant moral hazard problems and formed implicit incentives for both the financial and nonfinancial sectors to borrow in foreign currency. While the financial sector hedged its currency risk exposure by issuing foreign currency or foreign currency indexed loans, the nonfinancial sector, especially households, were left completely exposed to exchange rate risk. With such potentially catastrophic foreign currency debt overhang, euroization thus amplified the CNB's 'fear of floating', and its exchange rate regime remains one of the most resistant soft pegs in Europe.[10]

The Croatian monetary policy was largely set by the stabilization plan in 1993. In the light of a Mundell–Fleming open economy framework, Croatia did not choose a clear-cut solution for the irreconcilable trinity, but rather lives with an ongoing dilemma between a relatively stable exchange rate and an independent monetary policy (whereby capital mobility represents a default option within the Single Market). Hence, Croatia's exchange rate regime can be labeled as a 'dirty float' and has the role of discouraging speculation-driven exchange rate fluctuations (Bokan et al. 2010). It offers the best of both worlds since it gives a certain degree of stability and improves monetary policy scope in curbing two-way bets. Since 1993 the HRK-EUR exchange rate has fluctuated within a +/−6.5% interval, but the CNB has not committed to any target band (Kraft and Galac 2011).

Croatian monetary policy transformed and adapted throughout four different phases and is now in its fifth and possibly final phase. After transitioning from a socialist to a market economy and fighting hyperinflation via an exchange rate anchor in the early 1990s (Phase 1), Croatia entered a long period of gradual capital account liberalization and abundant capital inflows towards 2008 (Phase 2). The global financial crisis reverted the direction of capital flows and the Croatian economy faced sudden stops, threatening exchange rate stability. The CNB managed to stabilize the monetary anchor (Phase 3) and in the crisis aftermath it tried to obtain dual goals of both exchange rate stability and expansionary monetary policy as the economy struggled with a six-year-long recession (Phase 4). In another expansionary phase that started in 2015, Croatia seems determined to introduce the euro as its currency, finally eliminating exchange rate risks (Phase 5).

Croatia is hoping to join the euro area as soon as possible. The exchange rate mechanism prior to adopting the euro will most probably not present a nuisance to Croatian monetary policy and the economy, as the nominal HRK-EUR exchange rate is rather stable and evidence suggests that the exchange rate level is in equilibrium. Although being part of a monetary union would permanently solve risks associated with the high level of financial and real euroization in the economy, it also implies losing an independent monetary policy. The gains for this small open EU economy outnumber the losses though, and if it manages to keep its fiscal spending under control, Croatia could easily become a new euro area member in the near future.

Notes

1. Serbian commercial banks significantly increased their placements in order to cover current expenditures that had been financed by retrieving reserves deposited at the NBJ. Other banks soon followed suit. After independence, Croatia took over the obligation to repay foreign currency deposits to savers, lost through the NBJ's maneuver.
2. At the beginning of 2017, HRK-denominated monetary aggregate M1 was totaling more than 11 billion EUR, while CNB's FX reserves amounted to almost 16 billion EUR, implying coverage of more than 100%.
3. Croatian kuna (HRK) was introduced as an official currency in May 1994.
4. Legislation on central bank independence (CBI) was coded on 16 dimensions related to four components of CBI (appointment, policy formulation, etc.) and combined into a single weighted index.
5. In the 1994–2007 period Croatia received one of the largest gross capital inflows as a percentage of GDP among transition countries, despite the strategy of gradual capital account liberalization (Ötker-Robe et al. 2007).
6. As of 2015 (the latest data available), Croatia kept the same level of restrictiveness as Poland and Slovenia, while other CEE economies preferred a more liberalized approach.
7. CNB might have used loan-to-value and loan-to-income ratios to prevent households from taking too much debt but it regrettably abstained from it. However, this would not solve the issue of corporates borrowing abroad.
8. The only significant interest group actively lobbying for HRK depreciation is the Association of Croatian Exporters.
9. Among eight offered barriers to doing business, entrepreneurs identified financing as the fourth biggest barrier while exchange rate came as the least important. Of the sample (460 enterprises), 86% consisted of exporters (HGK 2016).
10. Croatia's external debt amounted to 91.4% of GDP in 2016. Other non-euro area economies such as Poland and the Czech Republic had significantly lower external debt and the advantage of very low levels of deposit and credit euroization. Besides, Croatia's ratio of 182.8% between external debt to total exports was the highest among postsocialist economies.

Unlike Poland and the Czech Republic, which could use the lever of sharp discount rate reduction to protect their economies against headwinds emanating from the GFC, the CNB has been more limited in cutting rates. Finally, CNB's role as of a lender-of-last resort (LORL) is restricted by the existing levels of FX reserves, since the bulk of commercial banks' liabilities are denominated in euro.

References

Baletić, Z., & Zdunić, S. (1999). Stanje hrvatskog gospodarstva i izbor razvojne strategije. In Z. Baletić (Ed.), *Hrvatsko gospodarstvo u tranziciji* (pp. 203–220). Zagreb: Institute of Economics.

Benazić, M., & Rami, J. (2016). Monetary Policy and Unemployment in Croatia. *Economic Research – Ekonomska istraživanja, 29*(1), 1038–1049.

Bokan, N., Grgurić, L., Krznar, I., & Lang, M. (2010). *Utjecaj financijske krize i reakcija monetarne politike u Hrvatskoj.* Zagreb: Hrvatska narodna banka.

Brkić, L., & Kotarski, K. (2009). Euroization, Monetary Union and the Credibility of Monetary Policy. *Annals of the Croatian Political Science Association, 5*(1), 443–460.

Brown, M., & Stix, H. (2014). The Euroization of Bank Deposits in Eastern Europe. *University of St. Gallen, School of Finance Research Paper No. 2014/12.* https://doi.org/10.2139/ssrn.2551729. Downloaded 20 July 2017.

Brunnermeier, M. K., & Sannikov, Y. (2016). The I Theory of Money. https://www.princeton.edu/~markus/research/papers/i_theory.pdf. Downloaded 24 July 2017.

Deskar Škrbić, M. (2017). Hrvatska i euro II: sažeta Cost-Benefit analiza. https://arhivanalitika.hr/blog/hrvatska-i-euro-ii-sazeta-cost-benefit-analiza/. Downloaded 30 July 2017.

Družić, I., Tica, J., & Arčabić, V. (2016). Ekonomski razvoj i gospodarske krize. In A. Obadić & J. Tica (Eds.), *Gospodarstvo Hrvatske* (pp. 1–40). Zagreb: Ekonomski fakultet Sveučilišta u Zagrebu.

Faulend, M., Šošić, V., & Žigman, A. (2000). Inflacija i neovisnost središnje banke – završena priča? *Financijska teorija i praksa: časopis za financijsku teoriju i praksu, 24*(1), 41–64.

Garriga, A. C. (2016). Central Bank Independence in the World A New Dataset. *International Interactions, 42*(5), 849–868.

Globan, T. (2017). O "pogrešnom" tečaju i zašto nam izvoz raste. https://arhivanalitika.hr/blog/o-pogresnom-tecaju-i-zasto-nam-izvoz-raste/. Downloaded 1 August 2017.

HGK. (2016). 'Očekivanja poslovnog sektora u 2017. godini, Istraživanje Eurochambres Economic Survey 2017'. http://www.hgk.hr/documents/

istrazivanje-eurochambres-economic-survey-20175866399064847.pdf. Downloaded 1 August 2017.

IMF. (2008). Croatia: Article IV Consultation. *IMF Country Report 8-158.*

Ivanov, M. (2014). Kontraciklička monetarna politika u Hrvatskoj. In G. Družić & I. Družić (Eds.), *Zbornik radova znanstvenog skupa Razvojni potencijali hrvatskog gospodarstva* (pp. 77–98). Zagreb: HAZU i EFZG.

Kraft, E. (2003). Monetary Policy Under Dollarisation: The Case of Croatia. *Comparative Economic Studies, 45*(3), 256–277.

Kraft, E., & Galac,T. (2011). Macroprudential Regulation of Credit Booms and Busts: The Case of Croatia. *The World Bank Policy Research Working Paper 5772.* http://documents.worldbank.org/curated/en/438101468232747295/Macroprudential-regulation-of-credit-booms-and-busts-the-case-of-Croatia. Downloaded 2 August 2017.

Kraft, E., & Jankov, L. (2005). Does Speed Kill? Lending Booms and Their Consequences in Croatia. *Journal of Banking & Finance, 29*(1), 105–121.

Lang, M., & Krznar, I. (2004). Transmission Mechanism of Monetary Policy in Croatia. *The 10th Dubrovnik Economic Conference.*

Ötker-Robe, İ., Polański, Z., Topf, B., & Vávra, D. (2007). Coping with Capital Inflows: Experiences of Selected European Countries. *IMF WP/07/190.* https://www.imf.org/en/Publications/WP/Issues/2016/12/31/Coping-with-Capital-Inflows-Experiences-of-Selected-European-Countries-21206. Downloaded 3 August 2017.

Radošević, D. (2011). Neizvjesnost i anticiklična monetarna politika. In D. Jakovčević, I. Lovrinović, & D. Radošević (Eds.), *Novac i ekonomski rast: Monetarna politika ekonomskog rasta i zaposlenosti* (pp. 25–39). Zagreb: Ekonomski fakultet Zagreb.

Šonje, V., & Vujčić, B. (2000). *Hrvatska u drugoj fazi tranzicije 1994.–1999.* Zagreb: Hrvatska narodna banka.

Tica, J. (2009). *Tranzicijska ekonomika tečaja i hrvatsko gospodarstvo.* Zagreb: Politička kultura.

Tkalec, M., & Verbič, M. (2013). A New Look into the Prevalence of Balance Sheet or Competitiveness Effect of Exchange Rate Depreciation in a Highly Euroised Economy. *Post-Communist Economies, 25*(2), 225–240.

Tkalec, M., & Vizek, M. (2009). The Impact of Macroeconomic Policies on Manufacturing Production in Croatia. *Privredna kretanja i ekonomska politika, 19*(121), 61–92.

Tkalec, M., Vizek, M., & Verbič, M. (2014). Balance Sheet Effects and Original Sinners' Risk Premiums. *Economic Systems, 38*(4), 597–613.

Vujčić, B. (2003). Monetary Policy and Management of Capital Flows in a Situation of High Euroisation – The Case of Croatia. *BIS Papers No. 17.* https://core.ac.uk/download/pdf/6274283.pdf. Downloaded 3 August 2017.

Vujčić, B., & Dumičić, M. (2016). Managing Systemic Risks in the Croatian Economy. *BIS Papers No. 86*. http://www.bis.org/publ/bppdf/bispap86l.pdf. Downloaded 3 August 2017.

Databases

The World Bank (2017a). Bank nonperforming loans to total gross loans (%). http://data.worldbank.org/indicator/FB.AST.NPER.ZS?locations=HR. Downloaded 5 August 2017.

The World Bank (2017b). Current account balance (% of GDP). http://data.worldbank.org/indicator/BN.CAB.XOKA.GD.ZS?locations=HR. Downloaded 4 August 2017.

CHAPTER 9

Fiscal Policy and European Semester in Croatia: Why Should We Focus on Public Debt?

Hrvoje Šimović and Milan Deskar-Škrbić

9.1 Introduction

The European Semester was launched in 2010 and thus Croatia, having joined the European Union in mid-2013, had to adjust its economic policy to the new EU economic governance framework even before accession (in 2013 Croatia participated in the European Semester informally). However, partly due to a prolonged recession and partly due to a passivity of fiscal policy-makers, Croatia failed to comply with fiscal rules and to deliver on the structural reforms agenda. This led to the activation of the Excessive Deficit Procedure (EDP) and the Macroeconomic Imbalances Procedure (MIP) almost immediately after the accession. At the end of 2015, economic growth finally picked up

H. Šimović (✉)
Faculty of Economics and Business, University of Zagreb, Zagreb, Croatia
e-mail: hsimovic@efzg.hr

M. Deskar-Škrbić
Erste Bank, Zagreb, Croatia
e-mail: mdskrbic@erstebank.com

Z. Petak, K. Kotarski (eds.), *Policy-Making at the European Periphery*, New Perspectives on South-East Europe,
https://doi.org/10.1007/978-3-319-73582-5_9

and in 2016 the fiscal position started to stabilize, which led to the abrogation of the EDP in mid-2017. However, Croatia remains in the preventive arm of the Stability and Growth Pact (SGP), subject to the debt rule. As for the MIP, a number of critical areas were reduced from seven in 2013 to three in 2016.

However, although the current fiscal picture looks more promising there is still a big challenge on the fiscal policy-makers' agenda, as Croatian public debt remains excessive. This can be seen from the following facts: (i) Croatia is one of the countries with the highest debt-to-GDP ratio among New Member State peers, which is reflected in the highest risk premium in the region; (ii) public debt is explicitly indicated as the largest imbalance under MIP framework and, as noted above, Croatia still does not satisfy the so-called debt rule under SGP; (iii) it represents the last (besides ERM 2 membership) formal obstacle, regarding convergence criteria, on the Croatian path towards monetary union; and (iv) it translates into one of the highest shares of interest expenditures in GDP (Croatia is third in the EU, after Portugal and Italy). Thus, in this chapter we will mostly focus on the determinants and sustainability of public debt in Croatia and emphasize the importance of its stabilization and reduction, in addition to the termination of EDP and MIP procedure and improved risk perception.

This chapter is structured as follows. After the short introduction in the first part, in the second part we will briefly discuss the political economy of public debt in Croatia. In the third part we analyze the Croatian position under the European Semester framework. In the fourth part we will analyze the sustainability of public debt trajectory, while in the fifth part we will examine the effects of excessive public debt level on the effectiveness of fiscal policy in Croatia. The chapter concludes with the main findings, discussion on the debt management strategy and policy recommendations.

9.2 Public Choice versus Public Finances: Political Economy of Public Debt in Croatia

The evolution of the public debt level in Croatia can be best explained through the prism of political economy. As always, excessive deficit is always a product of the imbalance between public expenditures and public revenues. We consider that the level and structure of public expenditures present greater fiscal risk than the revenue side, although common tax changes and selective quasi-reforms also contributed to fiscal (in)stability in the observed period. Expenditure structure of the Croatian public budget has not significantly changed during the last two decades. The main expenditure categories include social security (mostly pensions), health and compensations for employees in the public sector. The given structure implies a lack of elasticity of public expenses, especially during recessionary periods. Nevertheless, it has been subject to a certain change due to increasing interest expenses (more than 3.5% GDP in 2016), as well as decreasing capital expenses and public investments during and after a prolonged recession from 2008 to 2014 (Šimović et al. 2015).

Furthermore, demographic development implies huge fiscal risk in the future with regard to the public pension system. Several interest groups, such as political parties, public sector labor unions, SOEs employees, local administration employees, prematurely retired war veterans, as well as various NGOs dependent on state financing, exert the strongest pressure on fiscal sustainability. Almost all of them rally under the banner of preserving the welfare state to gain popular support for their particularistic claims. Besides bankrolling important social issues such as healthcare and education, the Croatian government is heavily involved in economic activity via state-owned enterprises (SOEs). Unfortunately, their poor competitiveness, considerable corruption and weak management contribute substantially to latent fiscal risks, mostly via government guarantees.

Furthermore, current developments in 2017 brought about a new form of government intervention with significant fiscal risks down the line. We refer to the special law called Lex Agrokor that put the biggest national private company Agrokor under government-appointed management. Its main goal has been to prevent a disorderly bankruptcy process due to systemic risk. Regardless of how successfully the restructuring will pan out, the process entails fiscal risks due to potential legal actions against the Croatian government. The contested issue refers to the arbitrary, uneven and politically motivated treatment of Agrokor's creditors.

On the other hand, there is no substantial space on the revenue side to alleviate fiscal deficits. Croatian tax system is consumption based, i.e. the majority of tax burden is placed on consumption. Private consumption has the largest share in Croatian GDP and this played a major role in widening fiscal deficits during the long recession of 2008–2014, given the dependence on VAT. This drop in tax revenues was partially compensated by procyclical measures, such as an increase of VAT from 22% to 25%, as well as a hike in excise duties. Since 2014, there have been several income tax reforms to reduce the burden on labor and stimulate consumption and labor market activity, but with no real short-term effect. When it comes to tax burden on capital, this kind of taxation remains one of the lowest in the EU (see more in Deskar-Škrbić and Šimović 2014).

During the recessionary period (2008–2014) Croatia had two governments that were fragmented, that is to say, a coalition of six or more parties. In that period there were four ministers of finance, and a central budget was amended more than once per year. Political instability, the imperative of buying social peace, and the absence of structural reforms were all aided or enabled by deficit financing. Additionally, the Croatian credit rating had been decreasing in the given period, followed by financial markets' loss of confidence in Croatian bonds. The expected outcome was the growth of interest rates and yields, with an attending 'snowball effect'. Finally, the aforementioned pathologies of public finance in Croatia led to textbook examples of political business cycles and political budget cycles. Generally, politicians systematically manipulate economic conditions and behave opportunistically in order to increase their chances of re-election (Vučković 2011; Mačkić 2014).

After this short presentation of key issues on both the revenues and expenditures side of the budget we will delve into the European Semester and Excessive Deficit Procedure (EDP) analysis, as they represent a new framework for conducting fiscal policy in Croatia. We argue that besides their potentially beneficial impact on economic growth due to the imposition of fiscal sustainability criteria, there is also a positive political dynamics at work. This framework can serve as a kind of political justification for unpopular fiscal measures and can contribute to structural reforms enforcement in the coming years.

9.3 Croatia Under the European Semester Policy Framework

The main goals of the European Semester and EU's economic governance framework are to ensure sound public finances (avoid excessive government debt), prevent excessive macroeconomic imbalances in the EU and support structural reforms, to create more jobs and growth and boost investment. This means that measures and instruments resulting from the coordination of economic policies of member states are fairly broad and they are aimed at different sectors and segments of their respective economies. However, the focus of this chapter is on public finance and fiscal policy-related reforms[1] so in the remainder of this section we will briefly highlight key remaining policy challenges for Croatia in this area, which are covered in key European Semester-related documents.

Croatia formally contributed to the European Semester policy cycle for the first time in April 2014 with two key documents, the National Reforms Programme (NRP) (Government of the Republic of Croatia 2017a) and Convergence Programme (CP) (Government of the Republic of Croatia 2017b). The main reform objectives and areas set out in these documents reflected key structural deficiencies of the Croatian economy: (i) public finance sustainability (deficit, debt, public enterprises, pensions, healthcare and social security systems); (ii) financial sector; (iii) labor market; and (iv) competitiveness. Such structure of the adopted key policy goals reflected and resulted from the main findings of an in-depth review, as well as conclusions and recommendations from the Economic and Financial Affairs Council of June 2013. A comparison of the Council's recommendations, NRPs and CPs from 2014 and 2017, shows that Croatia has made only modest progress on the structural reforms agenda so far and that key reform areas stayed relatively unchanged. The NRP 2017 defines following reform areas: (i) competitiveness, (ii) labor market, and (iii) public finance sustainability. When compared to 2014, current reforms framework defined in this way suggests that only reforms related to the financial sector were fully implemented, which moved this reform area from the reforms agenda, while others are still challenging. However, in that context it is important to notice that although fiscal sustainability is still highlighted as one of the key reform areas, the nature of planned instruments and measures changed.

In 2014–2016, according to Semester-related documents, the focus of fiscal policy-makers in Croatia, had to be aimed at significant consolidation efforts due to rising public debt, a deficit figure above Maastricht/ SGP 3% of GDP rule and active EDP. But during 2016, the fiscal situation improved notably (which will be shown in the next section). Consequently, in May 2017, the Commission recommended abrogation of EDP for Croatia (European Commission 2017); COM (2017) 529 final) due to the deficit correction, and as from 2017, the year following the correction of the excessive deficit, Croatia is subject to the preventive arm of the Stability and Growth Pact due to the debt rule.

Thus, Semester-related documents adopted in April 2017 by the Croatian Government are not focused on short-term corrective measures but on the fiscal institutional framework. The main institutional reforms recommended by the Council and officially planned by the Croatian government are summarized below:

Council Recommendations

- reinforce budgetary planning and the multiannual budgetary framework, including by strengthening the independence and mandate of the Fiscal Policy Commission
- reinforce the framework for public debt management, including by ensuring annual updates of the debt management strategy (the institutional set-up for public debt management, including communication with the markets, risk management and the update of the strategy at regular intervals, is deficient). There is also insufficient consideration of off-budget transactions with potential impact on public debt.

National Reform Programme and Convergence Programme designed by Croatian government

- new Fiscal Responsibility Act—stronger harmonization with Stability and Growth Pact; strengthening of the position and the autonomy of Fiscal Policy Commission; numerical rules on total balance, structural balance, government expenditures and public debt; obligation of the adoption of Council recommendations if the country is under EDP
- expected amendments to Budget Law—aimed at better mid-term planning; budget proposal will have to contain mid-term objectives for all fiscal variables and more detailed explanations of revenues and expenditures with the quantitative analysis of some programmes on the expenditure side; information on contingent liabilities; fiscal reporting by MoF in accordance with ESA 2010 methodology (instead of GFS 2011)
- organizational changes in State Treasury.

These reforms should play an important role in increasing the quality of strategic fiscal management in Croatia, with the focus on the mid-term and long-term sustainability of public finances and public debt.

In the next section we turn to the quantitative analysis of public finance sustainability to show that despite recent improvements in Croatia's fiscal position it is still important to implement recommended and adopted measures under European Semester mentioned above because current fiscal developments reflect more favorable (better than expected) economic environment and they are not a result of some strong fiscal effort and structural changes. In addition, as already mentioned, we will focus on public debt as a key fiscal indicator since public debt is a mirror of past 'fiscal sins'. It also sets to a great extent the ground for future fiscal policy stance.

9.4 Public Debt Sustainability in Croatia

According to Šimović (2017) there are many different approaches for the measurement of public debt sustainability. Usually sustainability of public debt is observed through a broader framework called fiscal or public finances sustainability. Such analysis includes three groups of indicators: fiscal vulnerability indicators, fiscal stability indicators and composite indicators.[2] For the purpose of this chapter, only several key indicators are taken into account. More precisely, we analyze key aggregate indicators of public debt, budget balance and interest payments as vulnerability indicators.[3] As for the stability indicators we will determine and analyze fiscal balance and interest rate needed to stabilize the public debt trajectory. This provides a better insight in the interdependence between current (budget balance) and past (interest rate expenses) fiscal performance on the one side, as well as economic growth on the other.

9.4.1 Public Debt and Fiscal Balance Dynamics

The need for the analysis of fiscal (un)sustainability in Croatia implies and reflects inadequate fiscal policy and public debt management in the past (Šimović et al. 2015). The aforementioned policies had proven to be particularly ineffective during the period of a prolonged recession in Croatia, in which public debt has increased more than twice. In 2008 public debt amounted to 39.6% of GDP and at the end of 2016 it stood at 84.2% of GDP, after peaking at 86.7% of GDP in 2015. Figure 9.1a presents public debt burden in Croatia and EU average in the 2001–2016 period. It clearly shows dynamics of Croatian public debt where Croatia broke the Maastricht benchmark and diverged significantly from CEE peers during the recession (only Slovenia and Cyprus experienced similar boom in the public debt figure but fiscal developments in these countries are mostly related to the banking crisis, as well as recovery and resolution of the banking system by the governments).

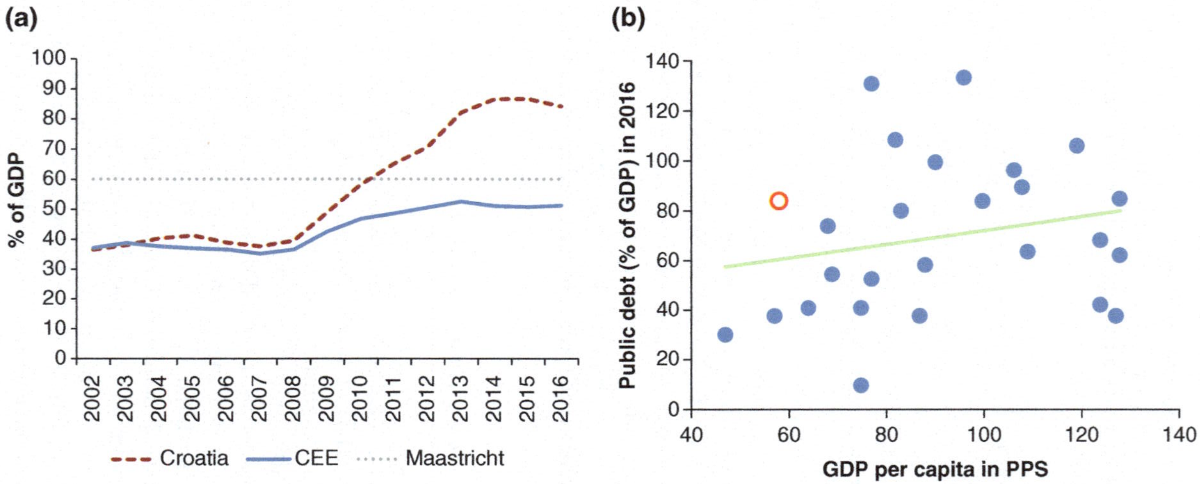

Fig. 9.1 (**a**) Public debt in Croatia and EU (% of GDP) and (**b**) Public debt (% of GDP) vs. level of development (GDP per capita in PPS) (Note: Public debt in CEE is weighted by the GDP share of each country in the region; PPS is expressed as a share of EU average) (Source: AMECO 2017; Eurostat)

To get an even clearer picture on the excessiveness of public debt, Fig. 9.1b presents Croatia's position regarding the public debt burden in terms of the level of development. Croatia's GDP per capita in PPS terms is at around a modest 60% of EU 28, while public debt, as is shown in Fig. 9.1, already exceeded the EU average. When we compare the level of development and public debt burden we can see that the current debt-to-GDP ratio is excessive, as shown on Fig. 9.1b. The empty red circle is positioned well above the regression line (simply put, the circle on the regression line would indicate that debt burden in some countries is adequate considering the level of development) (AMECO 2017).

However, the current situation is not a long-term phenomenon. In the period before the recession there was a decreasing trend in public debt to GDP ratio, while at the same time the amount of nominal debt was slightly increasing. In the pre-crisis period Croatia implemented a strategy of public borrowing on domestic markets, which resulted more in the growth of internal debt as compared to external public debt. Since 2009, due to the influence of the global economic and financial crisis, which generated decreased revenues and increased budget deficits, there has been a sudden increase in public debt and its share in GDP. The upward trajectory of public debt was influenced mostly by the growth of total general government deficits. Apart from the loss in tax revenues, the growth of budget deficit was a result of inadequate adjustment of public expenditures and rising interests on public debt (Fig. 9.2).

A primary balance shows the connection between current expenditures and revenues; the amount of budget deficit if interest expenses did not exist. The graph clearly shows that in the recessionary period the Croatian government did not adjust its primary balance. Moreover, due to rising principal and interest rates there has been a dramatic increase of interest expenses, which amounted to 3.3% of GDP by the end of 2016 (although global interest rates were falling since 2008/9, Croatian risk premium kept the cost of debt servicing at high levels).

Furthermore, budget deficit and public debt growth was largely caused by a change in interest rates, the so-called snowball effect. This effect arises from the interaction between the differential cost of refinancing debt and economic growth on the one hand, and the level of public debt on the other hand. Considering that in the time of recession the cost of (re)financing debt was rising, the level of public debt would have been unsustainable even if the government had not generated (primary) budget deficits. In other words, public debt would have increased due to rising

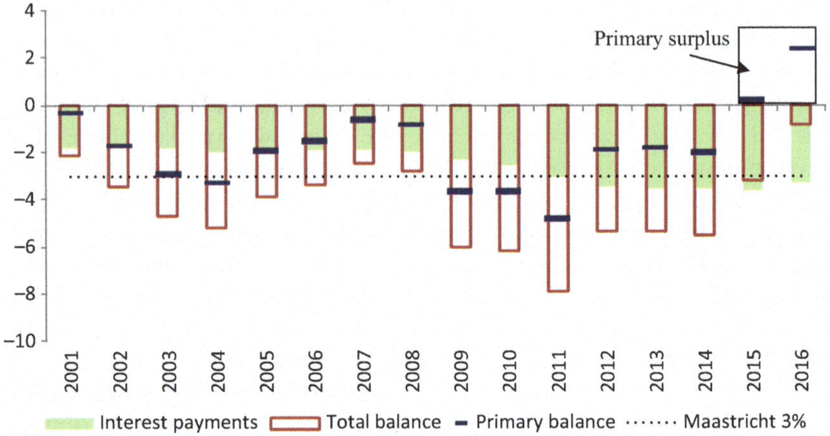

Fig. 9.2 Total balance, primary balance and interest payments (% of GDP) (Source: AMECO 2017)

interest rates even if the government had been able to carry out fiscal adjustment and decrease its budget deficit. However, stronger fiscal effort would have mitigated the snowball effect and could have improved investors' perception and lower the risk premium, which in turn could have led to more favorable re-financing conditions.

9.4.2 *Stability Indicators*

Stability indicators of public debt and fiscal balance present values needed to stabilize public debt at previous year's level. The main stability indicators are total balance (b_t^*), primary balance (b_t^{*p}) and interest rate (r_t^*) needed to stabilize public debt[4]:

$$b_t^* = -\frac{g_t^n}{\left(1+g_t^n\right)} d_{t-1} \tag{9.1}$$

$$b_t^{p*} = \frac{i_t^n - g_t^n}{\left(1+g_t^n\right)} d_{t-1} \tag{9.2}$$

$$r_t^* = g_t + \left(1+g_t\right)\frac{b_t^p}{d_{t-1}} \tag{9.3}$$

where g_t^n presents the nominal GDP growth rate, d_t is the public debt-to-GDP ratio, i_t^n is the nominal interest rate, g_t the real GDP growth rate and b_t^p is the primary balance.

Equations (9.4) and (9.5) present the calculation of total fiscal effort (FE_t) needed to stabilize both public debt and real interest rate gap (i_{gap}):

$$FE_t = b_t^* - b_t \tag{9.4}$$

$$i_{gap} = r_t^* - r_t \tag{9.5}$$

Table 9.1 gives an overview of stability indicators, namely total fiscal balance, primary balance and real interest rate needed to stabilize public debt, necessary fiscal effort and interest rate gap in Croatia from 2001 to 2016.

Data presented in Table 9.1 imply similar conclusions as the previous analysis, where the end of 2008/beginning of 2009 can be seen as a structural fiscal break point. In the first regime, from 2001 to 2008, both total and primary balances needed to stabilize the debt were rather stable and had negative values, while the bearable interest rate stood at around 4%. This means that in that period public debt trajectory would be stable even with continuous deficits and relatively high interest rates, due to relatively strong and robust real growth figures. After 2009, Croatia continuously needed fiscal (primary) surpluses to stabilize the debt level at the previous year's level. Because of numerous factors like political instability, a large but weak welfare state and unfavorable structure on the expenditure side of the budget (see Šimović et al. 2015), that goal was impossible to achieve. Instead, Croatia had excessive (total and primary) deficits that had largely contributed to the instability and unsustainability of the public debt, which changed throughout 2015 and 2016 when Croatia started to finally record primary surplus.

Further, Croatian credit ratings and real interest rate developments did not contribute to fiscal stability. The real interest rate needed to stabilize public debt level achieved negative values, which was also impossible goal to achieve. On the contrary, in the same period Croatian credit ratings dropped and real interest rates increased, so interest payments and a snowball effect additionally contributed to fiscal instability. However, the bearable real interest rate started to rise again and stood at around 3% in 2016, which is a bit lower than the effective interest rate of around 3.4%.

Table 9.1 Total balance, primary balance and real interest rate needed to stabilize the public debt, fiscal effort and interest rate gap

	Balance needed to stabilize the public debt (% of GDP)	Total fiscal effort (% of GDP)	Primary balance needed to stabilize the public debt (% of GDP)	Primary fiscal effort (% of GDP)	Real interest rate needed to stabilize the public debt (%)	Interest rate differential (%)
2001	−2.56	−0.48	−0.69	−0.37	3.43	0.63
2002	−2.98	0.50	−1.11	0.60	5.20	3.20
2003	−3.28	1.40	−1.41	1.48	5.47	3.87
2004	−2.81	2.39	−0.90	2.36	3.99	2.39
2005	−2.89	0.97	−0.82	1.08	4.11	2.11
2006	−3.40	−0.01	−1.72	−0.22	4.75	4.33
2007	−3.36	−0.92	−1.61	−1.03	5.13	4.34
2008	−2.75	0.01	−0.64	0.16	2.03	1.71
2009	2.00	7.99	5.25	8.93	−7.47	−12.38
2010	0.44	6.63	3.54	7.18	−1.77	−7.19
2011	−0.80	7.05	2.96	7.76	−0.36	−5.15
2012	0.42	5.73	4.44	6.32	−2.22	−6.69
2013	0.19	5.48	3.51	5.29	−1.09	−4.93
2014	0.29	5.79	3.63	5.64	−0.38	−4.42
2015	−1.53	1.95	1.49	1.12	1.60	−1.83
2016	−2.36	−1.56	0.59	−1.81	2.93	−0.67

Source: Authors' calculation
Shaded areas show "structural" breaks in fiscal sustainability analysis

Fiscal effort represents a difference between realized general government balance and the balance needed to stabilize public debt. In 2009, Croatia should have had a fiscal effort of 8% of GDP just to stabilize the public debt at the 2008 level. Such effort could only have been achieved by decreasing expenditures and/or increasing taxes. After 2009, owing to certain fiscal consolidation efforts, the trend declined a little. During the recessionary period (2009–2014) in Croatia, the average fiscal effort needed to stabilize the debt hovered at 6.45% of GDP. With economic recovery that kicked off in 2015 there is more fiscal space. In 2016, the necessary fiscal effort slipped below zero, indicating that the current deficit level is more than adequate to stabilize public debt. However, this favorable circumstance should not be seen as a motivation for increasing the deficit figure again but rather as an encouragement for continued fiscal discipline.

Finally, the real interest rate gap represents a difference between the real interest rate needed to stabilize the debt and realized real interest rate. Again, in 2009, we can observe the largest gap of 12.4 percentage points between the real interest rate realized (4.9%) and the one needed to stabilize public debt (−7.5%). As noticed above, the current gap is close to zero because interest rate needed to stabilize the debt and effective interest rate (interest expenses divided by public debt) are approximately at the same level.

9.5 Effects of Public Debt Level on Fiscal Policy Effectiveness

There are various determinants of the size of fiscal multipliers. Besides marginal propensity to consume and tax burden, which are the main determinants in the pure theoretical model of fiscal multipliers, empirical literature shows the importance of several other important determinants, which can be divided into structural and conjunctural groups (according to Batini et al. 2014).

Starting with the structural determinants:

(i) high degree of *trade openness* reduces the size of fiscal multiplier through the 'outflow effects' of imports
(ii) countries with more rigid labor markets have larger fiscal multipliers since rigid wages tend to amplify the response of output to demand shocks
(iii) countries that have flexible exchange rate regimes have lower fiscal multipliers because effects of fiscal policy on domestic economy are limited by the effects on international flows
(iv) countries with high levels of public debt have lower fiscal multipliers because additional fiscal expansion can lead to an increase in risk premium and decrease in private sector confidence, thus destimulating consumption and investment
(v) countries with higher tax burdens tend to have lower fiscal multipliers as the fiscal capacity of the country is limited and there is a stronger possibility of the prevalence of Ricardian households, and finally
(vi) large economies have large domestic markets so the multiplicative effects of fiscal policy are stronger.

As for the conjunctural determinants, fiscal policy is more effective in conjectures than in the expansionary phase of a business cycle. In this chapter we are focusing on structural determinant (iv), namely public debt.[5] Following the methodology presented in Deskar-Škrbić and Šimović (2017) and Šimović (2017), which is based on a structural VAR mode, we calculate the size of fiscal impulses in the baseline (closed economy) model and in the extended model with public debt. We expect that the impulse response in the extended model should show a weaker effect of government consumption on economic growth when compared to the baseline model.

Figure 9.3 presents the impulse response functions from the SVAR model. It can be seen that the effects of discretionary government spending shock in the closed model is positive and statistically significant in the first eight quarters after the shock. On the other hand, in the extended model with the debt-to-GDP indicators fiscal shocks have positive, but milder statistically significant effects on the economic growth in the second and third quarter. However, this effect turns to negative and statistically significant impact in the eighth quarter. To get a clearer view on the size of fiscal impact on the economic growth, presented results show that in the first year after

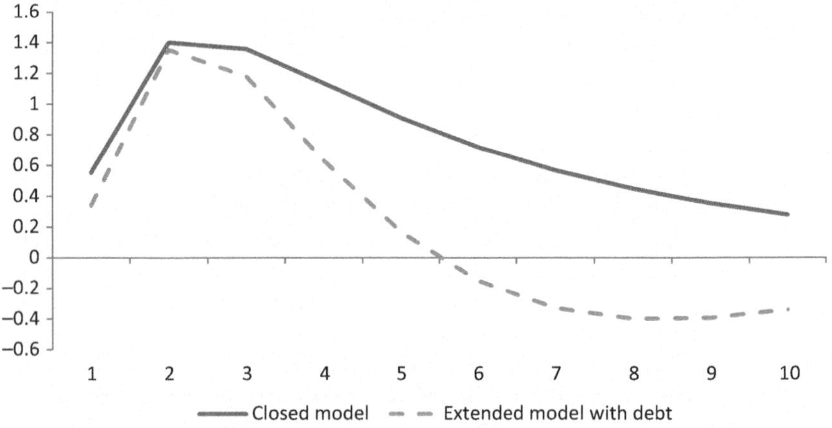

Fig. 9.3 Impulse responses (*confidence intervals are not shown to make the figure clearer; impulse response is statistically significant in the first seven quarters in the baseline model and first four quarters in the extended model; results with CI are available on request) (Source: Authors' calculations)

the shock, fiscal impact in the closed model is almost double the size of the fiscal impact in the extended model with public debt. Also, in the second year the first model indicates milder but positive impact, while the second model shows the negative impact. Based on the impulse response analysis, it seems that public debt posts limitations to the effectiveness of fiscal spending in Croatia. This is especially important when one takes into account the fact that fiscal policy is the key economic policy instrument due to various limitations of monetary policy channels (for details see Šimović et al. 2015).

9.6 Conclusion

Even though Croatia joined the European Union in mid-2013, it had to comply with the EU's economic governance framework even before the accession, as already in 2013 cycle Croatian policy-makers contributed to the European Semester informally. The first formal European Semester-related documents, the National Reforms Programme and the Convergence Programme, were adopted in April 2014 and they were mostly shaped and marked by the notable fiscal imbalances and active EDP. Growing public debt and fiscal instability started to progress by the end of 2008 due to the onset of prolonged recession, as well as passivity and the lack of effort on the fiscal policy front. By the end of 2016, the level of public debt reached 84.2% of GDP, more than double the share compared to the beginning of the 2000s and significantly above the Maastricht and SGP criteria of 60% of GDP. Our brief analysis of public debt sustainability in Croatia presented in this chapter has shown that public debt was mainly sustainable until the end of 2008, while in the recessionary period from 2009 to 2014 all indicators showed a high degree of unsustainability. Analysis of sustainability indicators has shown that total budget deficit, primary deficit and real interest rates needed for stabilization were far from the recorded levels. Furthermore, fiscal sustainability analysis indicated that in the same period public finance vulnerability was also pronounced, reflecting high liquidity risk connected with high interest expenses and financing needs. It can be concluded that the growth of public debt was influenced by negative economic trends and the lack of fiscal adjustment, but also by worsening in financing terms and the increase of interest rates in the period of recession. In 2015, sustainability indicators improved as the fiscal position and economic environment became more encouraging, while in 2016, Croatia made a strong fiscal adjustment, which led to a reduction of public deficit below 3% of GDP, stabilization of public debt trajectory and abrogation of EDP in 2017.

However, as we have emphasized, despite the more favorable fiscal position, public debt in Croatia is still excessive when compared to SGP and Fiscal Compact rules, the level of economic development and CEE peers. This is especially worrying as our empirical results confirmed the thesis that public debt level significantly affects and reduces the effectiveness of fiscal policy, the main economic policy instrument in Croatia. The extended SVAR model with public debt, compared to the closed economy model, clearly showed the reduction of impact and cumulative government spending multipliers.

Thus, policy makers should not only focus their efforts on further and stronger reduction of public debt only to comply with EU economic governance rules but also to mitigate the negative effects of debt burden on the effectiveness of fiscal policy. This requires more quality mid-term fiscal planning, a strategic approach to public debt management (in terms of long-term refinancing, hedging, and so on), implementation and improvement of public debt management strategy and the strengthening of the Fiscal Commission (independent fiscal body), in line with the European Semester-related recommendations of the European Council.

Acknowledgments This work has been supported by the Croatian Science Foundation under project "Public Finance Sustainability on the path to the Monetary Union – PuFiSuMU" (IP-2016-06-4609).

Notes

1. In this chapter we focus on a narrower definition of public finance, as well as on institutional framework, while other related reforms like healthcare, pension system, healthcare and state-owned enterprises are mostly covered in other sector-specific chapters by our respected colleagues.
2. Composite (complex) indicators are omitted from this analysis. Most common composite (complex) indicators are credit ratings, bond spreads and credit default swaps (that closely track the current financial markets' assessment of a given country).
3. Beside aggregate indicators like public debt level, or liquidity indicators like interest payments level, vulnerability indicators include the analysis of maturity and currency risk which goes beyond the scope of this text (due to extensiveness of the analysis and limited space).
4. Methodology is adjusted according to Hiebert and Rostagno (2000) and Mihaljek (2003).
5. Empirical papers regarding impact of public debt on fiscal policy effectiveness are rather scarce for Croatia. Only one paper, using SVAR, is found

where structural characteristics like trade openness and public debt level are used to analyze fiscal multipliers in Croatia along with Slovenia and Serbia (see Deskar-Škrbić and Šimović 2017). Regarding analysis of public debt sustainability, there are many papers that deal with certain types of public debt sustainability issues. The most common are static analyses of stability indicators (e.g. see Mihaljek 2003; Sopek 2010; Šimović and Batur 2017), or certain dynamic analyses of fiscal sustainability (Babić et al. 2003; Sopek 2011), and analyses that involve composite indicators (Mihaljek 2009; Cota and Žigman 2011; Bajo and Primorac 2013; Šimović and Batur 2017). Almost all papers alert to mostly unsustainable projections of public debt level and fiscal policy in general.

References

AMECO. (2017). Annual Macro-Economic Database (AMECO). http://ec.europa.eu/economy_finance/ameco/user/serie/SelectSerie.cfm. Downloaded 10 July 2017.

Babić, A., Krznar, I., Nestić, D., & Švaljek, S. (2003). Dinamička analiza održivosti javnog i vanjskog duga Hrvatske. *Privredna kretanja i ekonomska politika, 13*(97), 77–126.

Bajo, A., & Primorac, M. (2013). The Cost of Government Borrowing and Yields on Croatian Government Bonds. http://www.ijf.hr/upload/files/file/newsletter/83.pdf. Downloaded 12 July 2017.

Batini, N., Eyraud, L., Forni, L., & Weber, A. (2014). Fiscal Multipliers: Size, Determinants, and Use in Macroeconomic Projections, *IMF Technical Notes and Manuals*, 14/04. https://www.imf.org/external/pubs/ft/tnm/2014/tnm1404.pdf. Downloaded 10 July 2017.

Cota, B., & Žigman, A. (2011). The Impact of Fiscal Policy on Government Bond Spreads in Emerging Markets. *Financial Theory and Practice, 35*(4), 385–412.

Deskar-Škrbić, M., & Šimović, H. (2014). Porezna politika Milanovićeve vlade od 2012. do 2014. *Političke analize, 5*(20), 22–32.

Deskar-Škrbić, M., & Šimović, H. (2017). Effectiveness of Fiscal Spending in Croatia, Slovenia and Serbia: The Role of Trade Openness and Public Debt Level. *Post-Communist Economies, 29*, 336–358.

European Commission. (2017). Recommendation for a Council Recommendation on the 2017 National Reform Programme of Croatia and Delivering a Council Opinion on the 2017 Convergence Programme of Croatia, European Commission, COM(2017) 510. https://ec.europa.eu/info/sites/info/files/2017-european-semester-country-specific-recommendations-commission-recommendations-croatia.pdf. Downloaded 5 July 2017.

Government of the Republic of Croatia. (2017a). Nacionalni Program Reformi. https://vlada.gov.hr/UserDocsImages/Sjednice/2017/04%20travanj/33%20sjednica%20VRH/33%20-%201.pdf. Downloaded 5 July 2017.

Government of the Republic of Croatia. (2017b). Program konvergencije Republike Hrvatske za razdoblje 2017.–2020. http://www.mfin.hr/adminmax/docs/Program%20konvergencije%20Republike%20Hrvatske%20za%20razdoblje%202017.%20-%202020.pdf. Downloaded 5 July 2017.

Hiebert, P., & Rostagno, M. (2000). Close to Balance or in Surplus: A Methodology to Calculate Fiscal Benchmarks, *Fiscal Sustainability* (pp. 95–133). Banca d'Italia. https://www.bancaditalia.it/pubblicazioni/altri-atti-convegni/2000-fiscal-sustainability/095-134_hiebert_and_rostagno.pdf?language_id=1. Downloaded 10 July 2017.

Mačkić, V. (2014). Political Budget Cycles at the Municipal Level in Croatia. *Financial Theory and Practice, 38*(1), 1–35.

Mihaljek, D. (2003). Analiza održivosti javnog i vanjskog duga Hrvatske pomoću standardnih financijskih pokazatelja. *Privredna kretanja i ekonomska politika, 13*(97), 29–75.

Mihaljek, D. (2009). The Global Financial Crisis and Fiscal Policy in Central and Eastern Europe: The 2009 Croatian Budget Odyssey. *Financial Theory and Practice, 33*(3), 239–272.

Šimović, H. (2017). Impact of Public Debt (Un)Sustainability on Fiscal Policy Effectiveness in Croatia, *EFZG Working Paper Series*, No. 17-05.

Šimović, H., & Batur, A. (2017). Fiskalna održivost i održivost javnog duga u Hrvatskoj. In H. Blažić, M. Dimitrić, & M. Pečarić (Eds.), *Financije na prekretnici: Imamo li snage za iskorak?* Rijeka: Ekonomski fakultet, forthcoming.

Šimović, H., Ćorić, T., & Deskar-Škrbić, M. (2015). Mogućnosti i ograničenja fiskalne politike u Hrvatskoj. *Ekonomski pregled, 65*(6), 541–575.

Sopek, P. (2010). Budget Deficit and Public Debt in Croatia. http://www.ijf.hr/eng/newsletter/49.pdf. Downloaded 12 July 2017.

Sopek, P. (2011). Testing the Sustainability of the Croatian Public Debt with Dynamic Models. *Financial Theory and Practice, 35*(4), 413–442.

Vučković, V. (2011). Političko-poslovni ciklusi: postoje li u Hrvatskoj. *Privredna kretanja i ekonomska politika, 20*(125), 61–88.

CHAPTER 10

Banking Regulation in Croatia: Qualitative and Quantitative Assessment

Milan Deskar-Škrbić, Kristijan Kotarski, and Luka Brkić

10.1 Introduction

In terms of three key interrelated economic policy goals—price stability, financial stability and debt sustainability—Croatia formally merged price and financial stability under the auspices of the Croatian National Bank (CNB) in the early 2000s. However, these goals were already intertwined in the 1990s. Taking care of financial stability through the CNB's bank supervision and macroprudential regulation before the GFC enhanced the scope of implementable monetary policy after the crisis hit in 2008. Hence, Croatian banks were unable to 'corner' the CNB in a situation of moral hazard whereby they can rely either on stealth or overt recapitalization in the case of insolvency. On the contrary, they have

M. Deskar-Škrbić (✉)
Erste Bank, Zagreb, Croatia
e-mail: mdskrbic@erstebank.com

K. Kotarski • L. Brkić
Faculty of Political Science, University of Zagreb, Zagreb, Croatia
e-mail: kristijan.kotarski@fpzg.hr; luka.brkic@fpzg.hr

Z. Petak, K. Kotarski (eds.), *Policy-Making at the European Periphery*, New Perspectives on South-East Europe,
https://doi.org/10.1007/978-3-319-73582-5_10

remained robust and well-capitalized throughout the crisis and post-crisis period.[1]

Additionally, the CNB has successfully avoided obtrusive attempts at 'cornering' by the fiscal authority, which relates to an attempt at monetary financing of fiscal deficits. As a matter of fact, the previously mentioned form of fiscal dominance in a small and open economy such as Croatia is harder to materialize due to built-in structural characteristics, such as high deposit and loan euroization. However, the existence of partial fiscal dominance is still possible. Precisely, this can be proxied by Croatia's rise in public debt, which more than doubled from 39.6% of GDP in 2008 to 84.2% in 2016 due to crisis magnitude and inelasticity of expenditures (Šimović and Deskar-Škrbić 2018). This was possible even though the CNB abstained from unconventional or heterodox monetary policy measures to alleviate public debt (re)financing (Eurostat 2017).[2] Nevertheless, monetary and fiscal dominance have not openly collided during the recessionary period. To put it more plainly, keeping price stability along with an unwillingness to balance the budget was only possible due to painful deleveraging and a drop in prices. Presumably, this unwillingness to balance the budget will be neutralized in the following years by the European Semester and EDP framework.[3]

The above-mentioned arguments represent a clear testament that CNB retains only partial monetary dominance in its hands, since it indirectly facilitates fiscal policy by its regulation of commercial banks' behaviour, who in turn finance budget deficits. (Brunnermeier and Sannikov 2012). Moreover, the CNB finds itself between the two extremes of strict discipline and pronounced elasticity, and its monetary stance can be categorized as relatively accommodating within the broader confines of established monetary regime in Croatia. In this volume Kotarski and Tkalec (2018) claim that the CNB reacted to the crisis through reduced general reserve requirements, as well as through the removal of marginal and special reserve requirements. This improved liquidity of the banking sector and enabled regular servicing of the government's liabilities.

Furthermore, joint statements by the CNB's ex-governor Željko Rohatinski and former Prime Minister Jadranka Kosor that Croatia does not need some sort of arrangement with the IMF (unlike the experience of several CEE countries) underline previously stated arguments. Unfortunately, the result of this stance is the missed opportunity to embark on a strong and credible course of reform by starting to put an emphasis on countercyclical fiscal policy which would increase both monetary and fiscal policy efficiency in future crises. In spite of this weak spot, considering its overall track record, the CNB should be praised for establishing and ensuring the macroeconomic and financial stability framework. Nevertheless, the path towards this framework was preceded by the difficult transition phase in which Croatia had to shed a burdensome legacy with regard to banking regulation and supervision.

This chapter is structured as follows. In the first part we will delve into a short historical account of how the Croatian banking system evolved after the breakup of Yugoslavia until recently. In the second part we introduce the political economy element of banking regulation in Croatia through the prism of the 'Game of Bank Bargains'. Next, we provide the empirical assessment of the effects of regulatory measures introduced by the CNB on lending activity to the private sector. The chapter ends with the conclusion.

10.2 The Evolution of the Croatian Banking System from Independence until 2000

The Croatian banking system was effectively insolvent in 1989. Non-performing loans (NPLs) amounted to twice the size of banks' equity (Jankov 2000). The main reason for such a bad performance lies in the fact that banks in socialist Yugoslavia were owned by big state-owned enterprises. At the same time, those enterprises took out loans from the very same banks. Connected lending and moral hazard were prevalent but they served the main goal of cementing socialist political structure. Insolvent banks were frequently bailed out through the generous federal central banking system, and incentives for market-oriented behaviour by bank management were subdued (Šonje 1996).

In 1991, 13 out of 28 banks were in negative equity (Šonje and Vujčić 2000). The Croatian Government issued bonds to boost banks' equity (linear bank rehabilitation) but the ownership structure and incentives remained the same. The largest banks at that time, such as Privredna banka (90% owned by the state) had a politically mandated role to provide financing to the largest SOEs such as INA, necessary to fight a war. They were also indispensible in the creation of the Croatian version of crony capitalism through 'tunnelling'. In spite of the introduction of a market-oriented legal framework at the beginning of 1990s, old incentives persisted. This resulted in the resurgence of the NPL problem in 1996. Four out of six of the largest banks accounting for 46% of total bank assets were rendered insolvent (Privredna banka, Riječka banka, Splitska banka and Slavonska banka). The total cost of this bank recovery and resolution was assessed at 6.1% of GDP (Laeven and Valencia 2008). This time around the ownership structure and management gradually started to change. It was decided that those banks would be privatized.

However, before this process had commenced Croatia was engulfed in a systemic banking crisis in 1998. Its gross fiscal cost amounted to 6.9% of GDP, while NPLs peaked at 10.5% and real GDP contracted by −0.9% (idem). Generally, the issue arose due to rapid growth in the number of small and mid-sized banks without a clear separation of ownership and management. Adverse selection, moral hazard and connected lending were rampant (Ahec-Šonje 2017). Bad news first started to spread from Dubrovačka banka (fifth in size), a series of bank runs ensued. The episode ended with insolvency procedure for six banks and two banks were again bailed out by taxpayers. At that time the CNB had tied hands and could not control the appointment of banks' board members and check their formal qualifications. However, this changed with the passing of the Banking Act at the end of 1998. This phase of banking regulation in Croatia shows the sheer challenge of building a bulletproof regulatory framework in the context of war, weak democracy and crony capitalism.

The experience of a largely dysfunctional banking system inherited from the Socialist Federal Republic of Yugoslavia (SFRY), the attempt at muddling through with bank recapitalizations and recoveries during the Homeland War and the experience of a systemic banking crisis in 1998 finally created a climate conducive to full-scale privatization. The dilemma between business as usual (the existence of soft budgetary constraints, crony capitalism and clientelism) and financial deepening was solved in favour of the latter choice. In 1999 and 2000 four of the largest banks were privatized to foreigners, while the largest bank (Zagrebačka banka d.d.), which had already been privatized to a dispersed set of domestic owners, was bought by the Italian Unicredit (Kraft and Galac 2011).[4] Large foreign ownership of assets represents one of the central features of the Croatian banking system. This amounts to 90% of total assets (a level only surpassed by Estonia and Lithuania among CEE peers). Financial deepening and banking system stabilization in Croatia were propelled by foreign direct investment (FDI). Since that critical juncture in 2000, Croatia's financial system has remained bank-based, while the role of the stock exchange in funding has always been meagre (Farkas 2017).

10.3 The Croatian Banking System and the 'Game of Bank Bargains'

In setting the political economy framework for the analysis of the Croatian banking system we rely on the logic of the 'Game of Bank Bargains' (Calomiris and Haber 2014). The players in this game have a stake in the performance of the banking system. Their interaction produces specific coalition that determines the basic structure of the banking system (financial deepening and the level of competition), as well as the distribution of benefits among its members. Sometimes their interaction shapes institutions that improve market outcomes and sometimes the opposite prevails. In the Croatian context we identify several key players: the group in control of the government, bankers, debtors, depositors, tax payers and regulators. Hence, our goal is to give a brief overview of the extent to which the structure of the Croatian banking system, which reflects specific political balance of power, caters to players' priorities.

We start off with the government as the most important player. The main goal of any group in control of the Croatian Government is to ensure the continuous provision of credit that is flowing towards state or state-owned enterprises (SOEs). Figure 10.1 shows that relatively high bank credit to state and SOEs (as a percentage of GDP) represents an important feature of Croatian political economy. The aforementioned ratio in Croatia has been higher since 1994 as compared to the CEE-10 average, especially

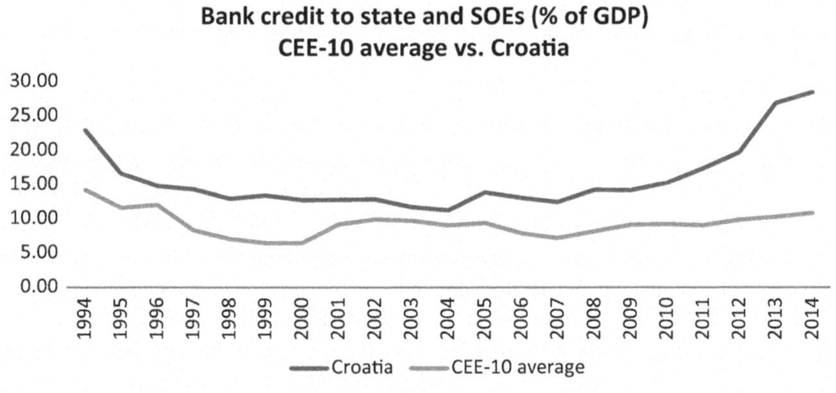

Fig. 10.1 Bank credit to state and SOEs (% GDP), CEE-10 average vs. Croatia (Source: Global Financial Development Database (GFDD))

after the crisis hit in 2008 and Croatian banks accommodated a large fall in government revenues (GFDD 2017). Unlike regular arm-twisting of banks during the Homeland War (1991–1995) to finance various state expenses, public sector financing by banks has since been voluntary.

However, banks have been cajoled into buying government securities by a favourable regulatory framework and lower risk perception. With regard to tax revenues from banking business, Croatia had the lowest spread between return-on-equity (RoE) before taxes and RoE after taxes in the period between 1996 and 2015, compared to other CEE-10 EU member states (GFDD 2017). This shows that collecting taxes on bank activities had a lower priority for the government, since a higher tax burden would compromise other important goals, such as credit growth and budget deficit financing.

The second entity with a major impact on the structure of the Croatian banking system is epitomized by the CNB. The CNB's regulatory role has been very prominent in demanding high mandatory capital adequacy ratio. In the period from 1998 until 2015 the Croatian banking system enjoyed the second highest average capital adequacy ratio when compared to the CEE-10 group (GFDD 2017). Furthermore, the CNB has managed to prevent the emergence of a banking crisis, indicated by GFDD's data on banking crises. This has to be contrasted with the experience of Slovenia, Hungary and Latvia since 2008. Even though the CNB could not have prevented one of the largest NPL ratios compared to CEE-10 group, in the period following 2008, its insistence on capital cushions definitely mitigated costly bank failures.[5]

The third group of players in the Croatian version of the 'Game of Bank Bargains' refers to bank shareholders. In this case, a single foreign owner regularly represents more than 90% of foreign-owned banks' shareholders (Unicredit, Intesa Sanpaolo, etc.). In the period from 1996 until 2015 the Croatian banking system churned out an average after tax RoE of 8.52%, which is lower than the average for other CEE-10 countries, except Slovenia, Lithuania and Latvia. Lower RoE has been mostly caused by one of the highest NPL ratios among CEE-10 group (GFDD 2017).[6] However, the only year marked by negative RoE is 2015, a year in which the Croatian Government passed a law that capped the HRK–CHF exchange rate for Swiss franc denominated loans.[7] Soon afterwards, the largest bank in

Croatia, Zagrebačka banka d.d., owned by Italian Unicredit, filed a lawsuit against the Republic of Croatia at the International Centre for Settlement of Investment Disputes (ICSID). It is to be seen how this issue will play out but this is the first case of an openly antagonistic relationship between a large part of the Croatian banking system and the Croatian Government since 2000. However, due to their mutual dependence the reasonable expectation is that banks hit by the law will be granted tax credits to compensate losses and the case will be settled without formal verdict.

The borrowers as the fourth group of players have been able to tap into the credit market due to significant financial deepening that occurred since 1996. Average domestic credit to private sector of 52% to GDP has been only surpassed by Estonia and Slovenia (GFDD 2017). Outstanding credit portfolio (kuna and foreign currency denominated) skyrocketed between 2003 and 2008. It was primarily focused on households and the non-financial corporate sector came second (see Fig. 10.2). It is noteworthy to add that besides domestic credit by banks, borrowers could also count on modest equity financing and direct borrowing abroad. On average, 20% of Croatian enterprises reported access to financing as a major constraint in the period from 2002 to 2013, which is a lower percentage than the one for Romania, Bulgaria, Czech Republic and Poland (GFDD 2017). However,

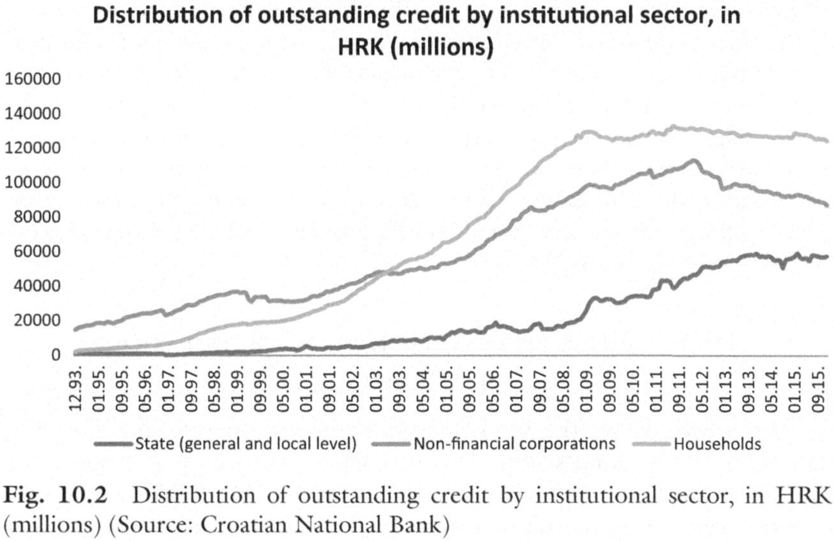

Fig. 10.2 Distribution of outstanding credit by institutional sector, in HRK (millions) (Source: Croatian National Bank)

Croatia's corporate sector debt remains second highest among CEE-10 group, only slightly behind Bulgaria (Martinis and Ljubaj 2017).

As can be inferred from the aforementioned data, the structure of the Croatian banking system generated a steady supply of credit throughout the observed period. However, what about the terms of financing for borrowers? Since 2012, comparable data on lending rates for Croatia and the CEE-10 have been published by ECB Statistical Data Warehouse (2017). Long-term credit to Croatian enterprises came with slightly higher interest rates than the 2012–2017 average for CEE-10. The average rate for Croatian enterprises was 5.6% while Czech Republic and Estonia had average rates equivalent to 3.9% and 4.4%. On the other hand, households in Croatia could count on one of the lowest rates on consumer loans compared to CEE-10 while mortgage loans have been more expensive and their rates averaged 5.2%.

Depositors as the fifth group of players have been lured to Croatian banks due to their perceived safety and underdeveloped capital market. In the period from 1996 until 2015 Croatia boasted the second largest bank deposit to GDP ratio (52%), only surpassed by the Czech Republic. According to the ECB Statistical Data Warehouse, Croatian savers enjoy higher interest rates on their long-term deposits than the CEE-10 average (3.2% vs. 2.3% on deposits with maturity of two or more years). Additionally, their deposits of up to 100,000 EUR have been guaranteed by the state since 2013. This combination of a large deposit base and perceived safety have contributed to the balanced credit to deposit ratio in the Croatian banking system (unlike the experience of Baltic economies in the boom years). Finally, taxpayers represent the largest group of players and their interests have been well protected since privatization took place in 1999 and 2000. Unlike the costly bailouts of the 1990s, the absence of large bank failures and associated bailout costs has put Croatian taxpayers in a favourable position.[8]

10.4 Effectiveness of Banking Regulation in Croatia

As mentioned above, the CNB played an important role in preserving stability in the banking sector. This was also recognized by a respectable magazine, *The Banker*, which awarded ex-governor Mr. Željko Rohatinski with the title of the Central Banker of the Year Global and Europe.

The reasoning for such decision can be found in a set of conventional and unconventional measures and instruments, which were introduced by the CNB from 2000 onwards. In the pre-crisis period, the CNB introduced various measures focused on the prevention of credit bubbles (see below), while after the disruption of the Great Recession in 2008/9, the CNB released abundant liquidity by notably reducing the regulatory burden.

In this section we will empirically test the effectiveness of the CNB regulatory instruments by analysing the effects of regulation on loans to the private sector, namely households and corporations.[9]

As regulatory framework in Croatia is complex and includes various instruments and rates, the first step of the analysis was to construct a single indicator of regulatory burden. Following Hannan (1989) and Šonje et al. (2005) we can define the cost of regulation as the marginal cost of financing additional unit loans with required reserve, deposit insurance and capital regulation, minus the marginal cost of financing in the case of no regulation:

$$\frac{i^d + c}{1 - r} + \left(\frac{p}{1 - t} - \frac{i^d + c}{1 - r} \right) k - i^d \qquad (10.1)$$

where:

i^d – passive interest rate
c – deposit insurance premium
r – reserve requirement rate
p – marginal return on equity after tax
t – profit tax rate
k – capital requirement

Notice that $k = 0$ until the additional unit of new lending that is financed through deposit base does not reduce the capital adequacy ratio below the regulatory minimum (or bank's own requested level). More precisely, there is no additional regulatory capital requirement if new lending does not push the capital adequacy ratio (CAR) below the regulatory minimum. Equation 10.1 can be expressed as:

$$\frac{i^d + c}{1 - r} - i^d \qquad (10.2)$$

However, in order to adjust this theoretical model to Croatian regulatory framework we have to expand the denominator by including marginal cost of minimum FX requirement *l*:

$$\frac{i^d + c}{1-(r+1)} - i^d \tag{10.3}$$

In addition, as liquid FX sources can be used to cover both, the FX part of required reserve and minimum FX liquidity requirement, we have to adjust Eq. 10.3 by introducing term *p*. If *p* is a share of FX part of the reserve requirement and (1 − *p*) is used for coverage of minimum FX liquidity requirement than we can write:

$$\frac{i^d + c}{1-l-pr} - i^d \tag{10.4}$$

Finally, as deposit base in Croatia includes various types of deposits (local currency, local currency indexed to FX and pure FX deposits), which bear different passive interest rates, we have to use weights, expressed as a share *s* of certain type of deposit in total deposit base ($\sum_{i=1}^{I} s_i = 1$):

$$\sum_{i=1}^{I} s_i \frac{i^d{}_i + c_i}{1-l_i-pr_i)} - \sum_{i=1}^{I} s_i i^d{}_i \tag{10.5}$$

Figure 10.3 shows indicators of regulatory burden (IRB), expressed in percentage points, annual growth of lending to private sector and periods of administrative constraints to credit growth (shaded area).

Regulatory burden increased intensively in the period from 2003 to 2006, mostly due to changes in reserve requirement calculation and introduction of new regulations, while in 2008 and 2009 one could observe a strong cut in regulatory burden. In the following paragraphs we will briefly explain key changes in the regulatory framework in these periods (based on the CNB's Annual Reports).

At the beginning of 2003, the reserve requirement rate stood at 19% and it was calculated on the basis of kuna and foreign exchange components. Of the calculated foreign exchange component, 24% was allocated in kuna and added to the calculated kuna reserve requirements. This percentage

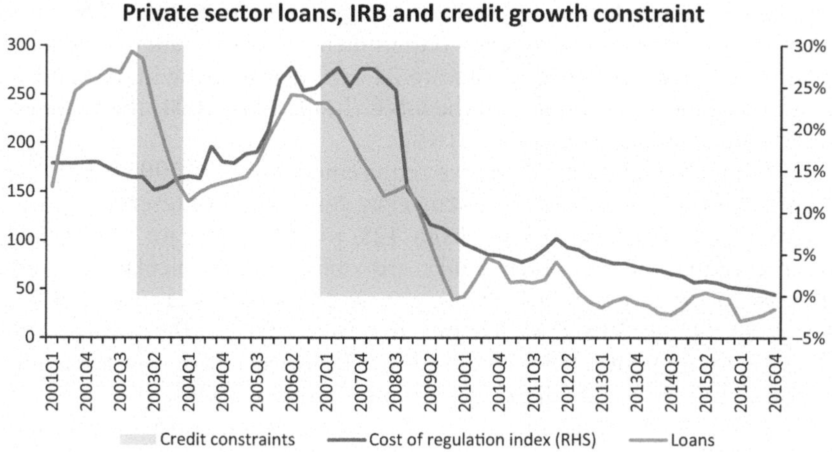

Fig. 10.3 Private sector loans, IRB and credit growth constraints (Source: Croatian National Bank; authors)

was increased in to 35% in September, to 40% in November and finally to 42% in December. In addition, the CNB introduced compulsory purchase of CNB bills for banks that showed loan growth above 16% (or 4% in a given quarter), in an amount equal to 200% of the exceeded growth.

In 2004, the most significant changes were made with respect to the reserve requirement instrument in order to limit bank foreign borrowings and discourage domestic placement growth based on external sources. Within these measures, the percentage for allocating the FX component of reserve requirements was increased to 100%, while the minimum percentage of calculated reserve requirements that is allocated to accounts with the CNB was increased from 40% to 60%. The key monetary policy instrument of the CNB was the newly introduced marginal reserve requirement. The quantitative loan restriction in the form of a compulsory purchase of CNB bills was abandoned, but it was initially replaced by raising capital requirements for rapidly growing banks. This measure compelled banks whose loans and off-balance sheet items grew by more than 20% to retain a portion of dividends, unless the bank's capital adequacy ratio exceeded a high level. If growth exceeded 30%, capital adequacy ratio had to be even higher to avoid mandatory dividend retention.

To discourage further growth in foreign borrowing, the CNB has introduced the marginal reserve requirement as a permanent measure. This means that banks had to allocate 24% of their increase in foreign liabilities to a special account with the CNB. In October 2004, the required reserve rate was cut from 19% to 18%.

The kuna component of reserve requirements rose in 2005 due to an increase in the calculated foreign currency component of reserve requirements that is allocated in kuna from 42% to 50%. The rate of marginal reserve requirements, which banks are obligated to calculate on any increase in their foreign borrowing, was raised on two occasions in 2005, first from 24% to 30% in March and then from 30% to 40% in June. The reserve requirement rate was reduced to 17% in December, but the application of this lower rate did not begin until January 2006.

In 2006, the CNB additionally tightened its existing instruments and introduced new ones for slowing down external debt growth and introduced a new measure for restricting bank placements growth, in effect as of 2007. It changed its instrument of marginal reserve requirements in order to expand their scope and also introduced special reserve requirements on banks' liabilities arising from issued securities whose purpose is the same as that of marginal reserve requirements. In February, the central bank introduced a special reserve requirement, to be allocated at a rate of 55% against bank liabilities arising from issued securities, which was aimed at preventing residents from indirectly borrowing abroad by selling the securities to non-residents in the secondary market. Towards the end of the year the central bank also introduced a new measure in the form of subscription of compulsory CNB bills, applicable as of 2007, to help restrict the growth of bank placements (restricting the growth of bank placements not subject to a purchase obligation in that year to 12%). In addition, the CNB decided to lower the additional capital requirement for rapidly growing banks from a 20% limit (introduced in 2004) to 15%, which made the dividend-retention measure much more relevant as there were only few banks that recorded 20% y/y growth in loans.

During 2007, there were no additional major changes in banking regulation but in 2008 the CNB started to react to the first effects of the financial crisis. In May, the minimum required amount of foreign currency claims was reduced from 32% to 28.5% of foreign currency liabilities, which provided banks with foreign currency funds for government financing. Also, the marginal reserve requirement was abolished in October so as to increase the foreign currency liquidity of banks. The reserve requirement rate was lowered from 17% to 14% in December, which freed a substantial amount of previously immobilised funds. On the other hand, the CNB made the dividend-retention measure stricter, as banks growing faster than 12% per annum had to maintain a higher than usual minimum capital adequacy ratio, proportionate to the share of non-core (potentially unstable) funding in their total funding structure.

In 2009, the CNB terminated the special reserve requirement on banks' liabilities arising from issued securities and revoked the obligation to purchase compulsory CNB bills. The minimum required amount of foreign currency claims was reduced to 20% of foreign currency liabilities.

The described frequency of changes in the banking regulation shows that the CNB played a very active role in the observed period. In order to empirically test the effectiveness of introduced measures we use two econometric techniques in this chapter.

Firstly, we use the Granger causality test for loans and indicators of regulatory burden to test whether the CNB's decisions related to changes of rates, calculation methods of reserve requirements and minimum required FX liquidity can improve prediction of credit activity. More precisely, if the Granger test confirms that IRB Granger-causes loan growth we can conclude that the CNB regulatory interventions played an important role for credit activity and that CNB interventions were not entirely post hoc. Table 10.1 presents the results of Granger test.[10]

The results show that we cannot accept the null hypothesis that indicators of regulatory burden do not Granger-cause loan activity (p-value of 3.5% is below the standard significance level of 5%). Such result is supportive for the thesis that the CNB affected the credit activity of banks through regulatory changes.

Table 10.1 Granger causality test[a]

Null hypothesis:	Obs	F-statistic	Prob.
LOANS do not granger cause IROC	56	0.46278	0.7626
IRB does not granger cause LOANS		**2.82275**	**0.0352**

Source: Authors

[a]Results are invariant to changes in lag numbers from 1 to 6

Secondly, we use a small-scale VAR model to test the effect of credit growth constraints but take into account other important factors, as well as the dynamic and endogenous nature of this analysis. The VAR model can be written as:

$$X_t = A_0 + \sum_{i=1}^{p} A_i X_{t-i} + u_t \quad (10.6)$$

As variables we use annual growth rate to private sector *LOANS*, GDP growth figure *GDP*, to capture the effects of demand side pressures, 1 m Zibor rate *ZIBOR* (short term money market rate) as a proxy for liquidity and supply side determinants and dummy variable *LIMIT* which takes the value of 1 during periods when credit growth limits were active. Therefore, X_t = [$LOANS_t$, GDP_t, $ZIBOR_t$, $LIMIT_t$] is a vector of endogenous variables. The exogenous variable included in the model is constant A_0. The number of time lags i is 2, according to AIC and HQ criteria. Also, a larger number of lags is not preferable because of the small sample. Stability and adequacy tests (they are available upon request) show that the specified VAR model is stable and that there are no problems of autocorrelation and heteroscedasticity. The results are presented in Fig. 10.4 in terms of impulse response functions (one standard deviation shock).

Impulse response functions show that the effect of shock in the Zibor rate, which is associated with liquidity problems on the money market, has a negative effect on lending activity (effect is statistically significant in the first three quarters after the shock). As for demand-side factors, captured by GDP growth rate, an increase in GDP has a positive and statistically significant effect on lending activity. Finally, the main variable of interest, credit growth constraint, has negative and statistically significant effect on lending activity, even when controlling for demand and supply shocks.

Our findings are in line with the conclusions of Galac (2010), who uses regression analysis to estimate the effects of credit growth reserve on credit to the non-government non-financial sector and concludes that the introduction of credit growth restrictions indeed succeeded in meeting its stated objective, on both occasions (2003 and 2007–2009). Also, our results correspond to the conclusions of Kraft and Galac (2011), who also use regression analysis and show that credit growth constraints had negative impact on lending activity, although the results are statistically significant only for loans to non-financial corporations.

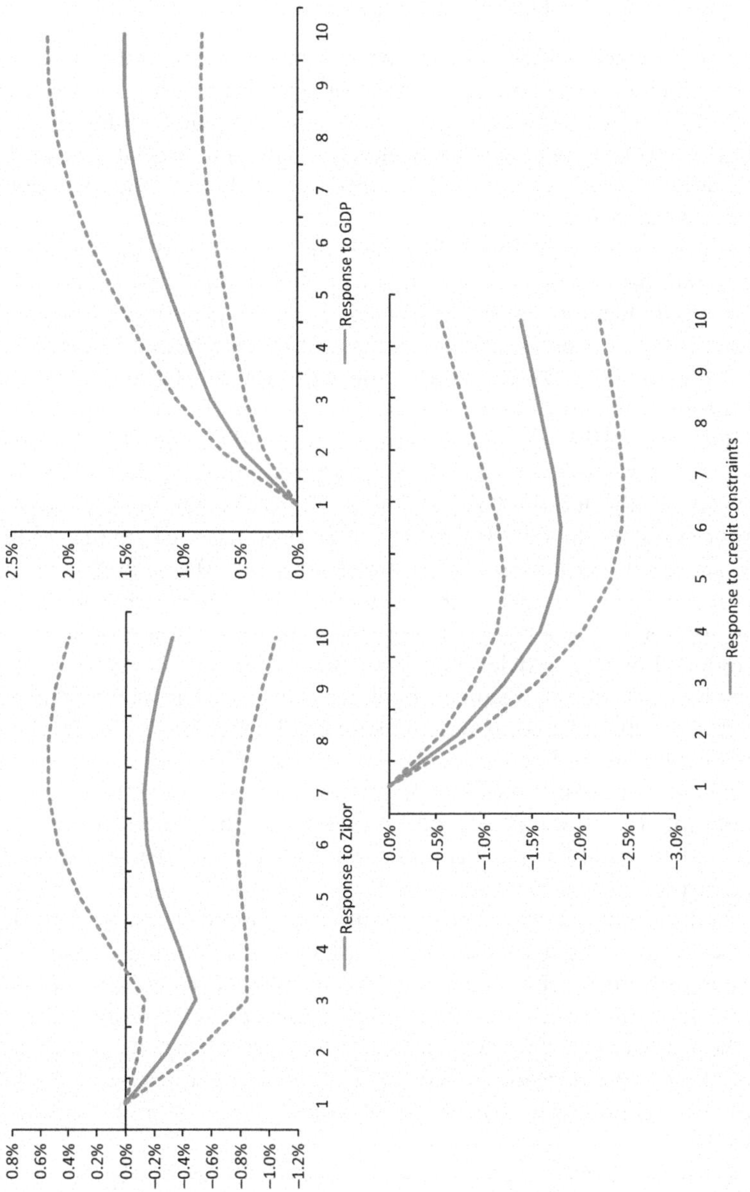

Fig. 10.4 Impulse response functions. (Source: Authors. Note: dotted lines represent 68% confidence interval)

10.5 Conclusion

Unlike the politicized nature of banks in the socialist period and war years, when banks had a crucial role in the creation and distribution of political rents, as well as upholding newly acquired sovereignty, the Croatian banking system nowadays incorporates relatively high standards of efficiency and transparency. Competition had an important role in enforcing good corporate governance.

After privatization in 1999/2000, the basic structure of the Croatian banking system has not been determined by political imperatives. The only remaining alternative for rent-seeking activities on the part of political elite and their clients has been tied to the domain of fiscal policy and operation of SOEs. This is visible in the continuing gap between Croatia and the CEE-10 group in terms of general government expenditures as a percentage of GDP. Until 1997 general government expenditure level in Croatia was lower or at par with the CEE-10 group. On the contrary, after 1998 the gap between Croatia and the CEE-10 amounted to a staggering 6-percentage points of GDP (Eurostat 2017). Only after 2008 has the banking credit portfolio allocated to the state/SOEs increased from 10% to 20% of their total credit portfolio (Hrvatska narodna banka 2017). Nevertheless, this is not to be interpreted as a politically controlled process but a spontaneous process induced by strong deleveraging pressure in the private sector.

Generally speaking, the 'Game of Bank Bargains' and the historical evolution of the Croatian banking system produced both a favourable level of financial deepening and managed to avoid costly banking crises since 2000. The current coalition of key players in the Croatian version of the game upholds the system's overall stability, despite some room for improvement, especially when it comes to banks being increasingy exposed to state entities.

Our results show that the CNB's regulatory framework proved to be effective as various regulatory measures affected the lending activity of banks, thus preventing the creation of the worst kind of credit bubbles before the crisis and cushioning the degree of stress on the lending market during the outbreak of the financial crisis and prolonged recession. In addition, the CNB's decisions since 2012 prevented the excessive credit exposure of commercial banks to Agrokor, the biggest national company.[11]

The room for further interest rate reductions for wider segments of society and the solution to the issue of NPLs is to be sought in the improvement of the Croatian legal system, structural reforms and lower risk premia attached to Croatia's credit ranking. To conclude, after a tumultuous 1990s, the Croatian banking system gradually developed into a strong and functional element of Croatian political economy, while Croatian National Bank upheld its image of credibility and contributed to the overall stability of the system.

Notes

1. This shows the absence of financial dominance whereby banks refuse higher capital adequacy standards. The other important factor refers to the CNB's limited LORL role.
2. In spite of an increase in public debt, the CNB's role of ensuring nominal exchange rate stability was not compromised since domestic savings increasingly absorbed it. Since 2008, the share of foreign public debt component has been steadily shrinking.
3. On the issue of debt sustainability see the chapter by Deskar Škrbić and Šimović in this volume.
4. Public debate with regard to bank privatizations has been contested ever since that turning point. The discontent with that decision is primarily framed by allegedly a very large and unacceptable fiscal cost, upon which formerly ailing banks were sold to foreign investors on the cheap. However, an independent study by Arhivanalitika shows that the total cost of bank recovery and resolution from 1995 to 2000 is limited to HRK 12.9 billion. This figure is often conflated with a much larger figure covering the public cost of paying for foreign currency-denominated deposits to savers in Croatian banks, the problem that was caused by the Yugoslav central bank (NBJ) withholding access to common SFRY FX reserves (HUB Analize 2015).
5. According to GFDD, Croatia's average NPL share out of gross loan portfolio was the third largest when matched with other CEE-10 countries. In the period from 2008 until 2015, Croatia's NPL average share amounted to more than 10%, surpassed only by Bulgaria and Lithuania.
6. High NPL ratios are a reflection of several factors such as a weak and slow legal system, weak aggregate demand, and the absence of prudent government intermediation between creditors and debtors.
7. See chapter by Kotarski and Tkalec in this volume.
8. Over the last 20 years, the State Agency for Deposit Insurance and Bank Resolution used the mandatory insurance premium paid in by banks and paid out depositors of several small-scale banks, which had been facing bankruptcy.

9. A series of loans to non-financial corporations was adjusted for the effects of sales; both series are adjusted for the changes in exchange rate, annual growth rate is defined as a weighted average of loans to households, and non-financial corporations (weights are defined as shares of each category in total loans to private sector).
10. Results are invariant to changes in lag numbers from 1 to 6.
11. See Chap. 1 by Kotarski and Petak in this volume.

References

Ahec-Šonje, A. (2017). Kad bikovi polome rogove: valutne krize u Hrvatskoj. https://arhivanalitika.hr/blog/kad-bikovi-polome-rogove-valutne-krize-u-hrvatskoj/. Downloaded 8 August 2017.

Brunnermeier, M. K., & Sannikov, Y. (2012). Redistributive Monetary Policy. http://scholar.princeton.edu/sites/default/files/04c%20Redistributive%20Monetary%20Policy.pdf. Downloaded 4 August 2017.

Calomiris, C. W., & Haber, S. H. (2014). *Fragile by Design: The Political Origins of Banking Crises and Scarce Credit.* Princeton/Oxford: Princeton University Press.

Farkas, B. (2017). Market Economies of the Western Balkans Compared to the Central and Eastern European Model of Capitalism. *Croatian Economic Survey, 19*(1), 5–36.

Galac, T. (2010). The Central Bank as Crisis-Manager in Croatia – A Counterfactual Analysis, *Croatian National Bank Working Papers,* W-57. http://old.hnb.hr/publikac/istrazivanja/w-027.htm. Downloaded 20 August 2017.

Hannan, T. H. (1989). The Impact of Bank Regulatory Requirements on Large Corporate Lending, *Federal Reserve Board Finance and Economics Discussion Series,* No. 63.

HUB Analize. (2015). Sanacije banaka u Hrvatskoj: petnaest godina poslije. http://www.hub.hr/sites/default/files/hub_analize_51_-_sanacije.pdf. Downloaded 9 September 2017.

Jankov, L. (2000). Problemi banaka: uzroci, načini rješavanja i posljedice. *Pregledi, br. 2,* Zagreb: Hrvatska narodna banka.

Kotarski, K., & Tkalec, M. (2018). Monetary Policy in a Highly Euroised Economy (this Volume).

Kraft, E., & Galac, T. (2011). Macroprudential Regulation of Credit Booms and Busts: The Case of Croatia, *The World Bank Policy Research Working Paper 5772.* http://documents.worldbank.org/curated/en/438101468232747295/Macroprudential-regulation-of-credit-booms-and-busts-the-case-of-Croatia. Downloaded 2 August 2017.

Laeven, L., & Valencia, F. (2008). Systemic Banking Crises: A New Database, *IMF Working Paper WP/08/224*. https://www.imf.org/external/pubs/ft/wp/2008/wp08224.pdf. Downloaded 10 September 2017.

Martinis, A., & Ljubaj, I. (2017). Corporate Debt Overhang in Croatia: Micro Assessment and Macro Implications, *Croatian National Bank W-51*. https://www.hnb.hr/documents/20182/783865/22-dec-martinis-ljubaj.pdf/c9ae14a1-dc60-483d-8288-c06c4d1248f0. Downloaded 20 September 2017.

Šimović, H., & Deskar Škrbić, M. (2018). Fiscal Policy and the European Semester in Croatia: Why Should We Focus on Public Debt? (this volume).

Šonje, V., Božić, J., & Ognjenović, Đ. (2005). Regulacijsko opterećenje banaka u sedam zemalja srednje Europe, Hrvatska udruga banaka.

Šonje, V., & Vujčić, B. (2000). *Hrvatska u drugoj fazi tranzicije 1994. —1999*, Zagreb: Hrvatska narodna banka.

Šonje, V. (1996). Banking System in Croatia: Evolution, Structure and Performance. *Privredna kretanja i ekonomska politika*, *6*(54), 45–63.

Databases

Croatian National Bank. (2017). Konsolidirana bilanca drugih monetarnih financijskih institucija. http://old.hnb.hr/statistika/h-statistika-statisticki-pregled.htm. Downloaded 22 August 2017.

ECB Statistical Data Warehouse. (2017). Financial markets and interest rates. http://sdw.ecb.europa.eu/browse.do?node=9691099. Downloaded 21 August 2017.

Eurostat. (2017). Government Finance and EDP Statistics. http://ec.europa.eu/eurostat/web/government-finance-statistics/data/database. Downloaded 18 August 2017.

Global Financial Development Database (GFDD). (2017). Global Financial Development, https://data.worldbank.org/data-catalog/global-financial-development. Downloaded 14 July 2017.

CHAPTER 11

The Competitiveness of the Croatian Economy: A Comparison of Private and Public Sector Enterprises

Velimir Šonje

11.1 Introduction

In 1990, it seemed that the Croatian economy had been well positioned for transition to a market economy. The Yugoslav system of self-management involved more enterprise autonomy, better micro management and higher freedom of market prices' formation compared to other socialist economies. In the late 1980s, GDP per capita assessments (Maddison Project), despite their lack of methodological reliability, pointed out that only Slovenia and the Czech Republic recorded higher income per capita than Croatia. Twenty-seven years later, Croatia is a laggard compared to transition peers. In particular, at the end of the Homeland War in 1995, Croatian GDP per capita according to the Eurostat's purchasing power standard stood at 44% of the EU-28 average: it was below that of Slovenia, the Czech Republic and Slovakia. The same indicator in 2016 stood at 60% (Eurostat 2017). Convergence was slow

V. Šonje (✉)
Arhivanalitika Consulting, Zagreb, Croatia
e-mail: vsonje@arhivanalitika.hr

Z. Petak, K. Kotarski (eds.), *Policy-Making at the European Periphery*, New Perspectives on South-East Europe,
https://doi.org/10.1007/978-3-319-73582-5_11

compared to peers: GDP per capita was below an additional five countries in the New Europe compared to 1995. Three Baltic states and Poland surpassed Croatia in the meantime, while Romania caught up with Croatia, recording 58% of EU-28 average in 2016.

Homeland War (1991–1995) and late EU entry (2013) represent exogenous factors that slowed down the relative pace of political and economic modernization in Croatia. However, they do not tell the whole story. A number of subjective weaknesses—bad governance, corruption and generally weak institutions and economic policies (partial reform equilibrium as described by Kotarski and Petak in this volume)—contributed to a relatively slow growth.

State-owned enterprises (SOEs) played an important role in this process. It is not easy to decompose the contribution of specific factors to a relatively slow economic growth in Croatia after the second half of the 1990s. Nevertheless, significant misallocation of factors of production in a number of studies has been found as a critical factor of slow growth. Some studies put emphasis on market distortions created by the large sector of SOEs.

The SOE sector is relatively large in Croatia (Vizek 2014). It is weakly managed, with significant politicization and lack of professional management, which makes it prone to corruption (Petrović and Šonje 2015). This situation differs from the standard set of transition problems SOEs were facing in the 1990s. In the initial stage of post-communist transition, state monopolies and the absence of control led to rampant asset stripping by privileged managers and loss-making under soft budget constraints. This amounted to spontaneous privatization (Aslund 2013). The Croatian case is different: political control that consolidated early in the transition process has been strong and, as of 2017, no one has the intention to privatize remaining SOEs on a larger scale.

The SOE sector was not necessarily a loss-maker in Croatia. Relative prices adjusted very early in the transition due to better initial conditions, more open markets and freer prices during the late stage of socialism. SOEs that were markedly inefficient (for example railways and shipyards) received subsidies from the government budget. With government subsidies constantly above 2% of GDP since the inception of the transition, Croatia has always been among top users of subsidies in Europe. Lack of competition and associated inefficiencies were reflected in the relatively high cost of SOEs' outputs that served as inputs to households and private enterprises, thereby eroding competitiveness and living standards. It led to large consumption of fiscal resources and malinvestment. Investment failures took the form of both overinvestment and associated excessive indebtedness (for example, debts incurred for construction of highway network) or underinvestment (for example, electrical grid, railways).

SOEs became firmly integrated within the political structure and the logic of the political cycle. Professional managers mainly come and go in line with political elections when both state and local governments change. SOEs are associated with a lack of professionalism and ministers' direct involvement in the control of a number of enterprises (far beyond their corporate governance capacities). This system supports the political aspirations of professional politicians and members of political parties to influence control, direct management or employment in SOEs. This strategy is indirectly supported by voters who prefer public sector employment (Kotarski 2017).

Consequently, the quality of competition for managerial positions in SOEs is weak. Managerial talents (scarce anyway) do not want to place their careers at risk in a politicized system where performance criteria are not transparently set. On top of that, managerial wages are set significantly below the private sector average, thereby deterring top managers who can earn more in private companies and attracting those who cannot occupy top positions in private enterprises.

The political elite perceive SOEs as economic instruments for the realization of narrow political and material aspirations, rather than for realization of some public policy goals (which are present, but their role is secondary in comparison to the prime purpose of political control over economic resources). A number of corruption cases involving privileged employment and financing of political parties via SOEs emerged (this is one of the charges against former Prime Minister Ivo Sanader (2003–2009)), affirming the general population's mistrust in public institutions. As substantial vested interests consolidated around SOEs, slowdown of privatization process in the twenty-first century came out as both a cause and a consequence of partial reform equilibrium (Kotarski and Petak 2018).

It is beyond the scope of this chapter to provide exact estimates of contributions of SOEs to a relatively slow economic growth in Croatia since 1995. The purpose is to provide some numbers on Croatian SOEs, relate problems of their performance to competitiveness of the entire economy, point at feedback loops between inefficient SOEs and weak institutions, and derive policy recommendations.

Section 11.2 relates measures of international competitiveness to the role of SOEs in Croatia. Section 11.3 provides an overview of research on market dynamics in Croatia, in order to identify the role of SOEs in the petrification of market processes. Section 11.4 provides fresh new evidence on comparative performance of SOEs within the top 1000 Croatian companies in 2016. Section 11.5 contains policy recommendations and Sect. 11.6 outlines the conclusions.

11.2 Measures of International Competitiveness

Kotarski and Petak (2018) showed that Croatia was a laggard among the CEE-8 in terms of institution building.[1] They described this situation as partial reform equilibrium, which explains Croatia's middle-income trap. Hence, their emphasis is on state capture by winners of the transition rather than opposition to reforms by losers in the process.

Failure to complete the market and institutional reforms in the first stage of transition is also reflected in the underdevelopment of narrowly defined economic institutions as measured by the IFC's and the World Bank's Ease of Doing Business (DB). DB measures the efficiency of institutions, which is critical for market dynamism, such as starting up a business, contract enforcement, protection of minority shareholders and market exit (resolving insolvency). DB 2017 places Croatia in 43rd place among 190 countries in the world, with Hungary in 41st place, Bulgaria 39th, Romania 36th, Slovak Republic 33rd, Slovenia 30th, Czech Republic 27th, Poland 24th, Lithuania 21st, Latvia 14th and Estonia 12th.

The World Economic Forum's Global Competitiveness Index (GCI) is wider in coverage compared to DB. It includes measures of technology and infrastructure development and a wider set of institutional characteristics. Croatia is ranked 74th among 138 countries. Hungary is 69th, Slovak Republic 65th, Romania 62nd, Slovenia 56th, Bulgaria 50th, Latvia 49th, Poland 36th, Lithuania 35th, Czech Republic 31st and Estonia 30th. All in all, Croatia is a laggard in the CEE peer group. Other relevant international ranking systems of competitiveness and institutional quality such as Transparency International Corruption Perception Index, Fraser Institute's Economic Freedom Index, Worldwide Governance Indicators and a number of others, also show Croatia's position behind the CEE peer group on average.

The most interesting assessment for the purpose of this chapter is the Organisation for Economic Co-operation and Development's (OECD's)

Product Market Regulation (PMR) index (OECD 2017). It is not up to date, because the last measurement that reflects the Croatian situation is related to 2013 (Croatia is not an OECD member but was included in the measurement). Nevertheless, PMR reflects structural issues that do not change annually; so, it will suit the purpose.

PMR is a weighted measure of barriers to trade and investment, barriers to entrepreneurship (reflecting complexity of regulation, administrative burdens and protection of market incumbents) and, most important of all, state control. State control reflects government involvement in business operations and public ownership in the enterprise sector. Public ownership reflects the scope of SOEs, public involvement in network sectors, direct control over enterprises and SOEs' governance. Excerpt from PMR results (Table 11.1) shows that Croatia significantly differs from the CEE average both in terms of the wide scope of SOEs and in terms of government involvement in the network sectors (maximum indicator value is 6, which represents the worst assessment).

The scope of SOEs is measured by the presence of at least one SOE in 30 key sectors. Government involvement with networks is measured proportionally to the percentage of shares held by the government in six key networks (rail, airlines, post, telecom, electricity and gas). One may conclude from the results presented above that Croatia experiences large government involvement in the corporate sector. It also translates into a large general government sector, as some SOEs are consolidated with the

Table 11.1 Excerpt from PMR results, 2013 (lower assessment = better, max = 6)

PMR element	*Croatia*	*CEE average*[a]
State control		
Scope of SOEs	4.7	3.3
Government involvement in network sectors	4.2	3.6
Direct control of business enterprises	0.9	1.2
Governance of SOEs	2.3	3.7
Other selected assessments		
Price controls	1.2	1.3
Barriers to entrepreneurship	2.0	1.7
Barriers to trade and investment	1.7	0.5

[a]Estonia, Latvia, Lithuania, Poland, Czech Republic, Slovakia, Hungary, Slovenia, Romania, Bulgaria

Source: OECD, PMR

general budget (Croatian Railways, Croatian Highways, etc.) because their market revenues do not cover 50% of their operational costs. Total general government revenue in Croatia represents 46.2% of GDP according to Eurostat's data for 2016. Croatia is ninth in the EU according to this indicator, next to the Scandinavian countries, and France, Austria and Greece.

In terms of direct control over enterprises, Croatia and other CEE countries recorded better (lower) values due to rare legal or constitutional constraints for disposal of shares. This largely reflects the adoption of EU standards. However, PMR measures formal rules on the books rather than actual functioning of SOEs' management and control systems. This is especially important for interpretation of the PMR indicator of governance. Croatia's assessment of 2.3 is better than the CEE average of 3.7, but both values are high (meaning bad governance). High values generally reflect weak governance related to direct ministerial control rather than involvement of specialized independent institutions, which keep policy makers at arm's length away from SOEs (like in Romania, Slovenia, Austria, Finland or Sweden). On the other hand, some formal rules qualify as good governance, such as the application of company law and availability of the same terms of financing as for private companies.

In summary, relatively weak institutions and lack of competitiveness in Croatia occurred in parallel to large government extension over the economy as measured by its involvement in a number of sectors where SOEs are present. One may see it as a consequence of unfinished privatization and equilibrium of partial reforms. However, it is impossible to know whether government extension over the economy via SOEs is a true cause or consequence of growth problems. That can only be inferred deductively from studies of actual market dynamics. If there were dynamic markets and a vibrant enterprise sector with efficient factors of production allocation, there would be no reason to see SOEs as a problem and vice versa.

11.3 Market Dynamics: Literature Review

Vizek (2014) measured the impact of SOEs by using annual financial statements. She summed up certain financial indicators for both majority- and minority-owned SOEs. Their total annual expenditures amounted to around 50% of GDP in 2012, which was higher than the consolidated general government budget. 50% should not be confused with SOEs' share in GDP, which is much lower. Nevertheless, total expenditures show the macroeconomic power, that is, SOEs' impact on economic transactions and the allocation of factors of production. Large purchases of inputs, both materials and services, as well as hiring policies, influence private sector behaviour too. Given weaknesses of procurement in the public sector and general public sector inefficiency, Vizek (2014) speculated about the existence of para-private sector—a large sector populated by formally private entrepreneurs who are not competitive enough to survive in free private markets, who rather look for rents in quasi-private dealings with the public sector. Shielding from the open and competitive markets and rent-seeking has been identified as a widespread behaviour in Croatia. Political economist Vuk Vuković's (2014) analysis of suspicious public procurement transactions prove this hypothesis to be true. On more formal grounds, Vizek (2014) showed lower productivity and higher average wage despite lower revenue per employee in SOEs.

Nestić et al. (2015) showed significant distortions created by SOEs in the labor market. Authors depicted positive wage differential adjusted for age, education and gender in favour of SOEs' employees; adjusted average wage in SOEs was significantly higher than in both private and narrow government sectors. The adjusted wage gap declined from 2000 to 2012, but remained significant anyway.

There are three negative impacts of this distortion. First, labour market segmentation. Wages above marginal product of labour divert workers from more efficient private sector jobs to SOEs, which operate shielded from the markets. Probably a lot of potentials and talents who could excel in private markets were wasted in the comfort zones of political hierarchies of SOEs. Those hierarchies do not award innovations and individual initiative but rather function as politicized bureaucracies. Second, there is a general mistrust of public institutions. People are generally aware of the way SOEs function, as media devote a lot of attention to this problem, especially since the beginning of the Great Recession. Although people prefer public sector employment, they condemn the political nepotism behind privileged jobs and earnings in SOEs, and look at incumbents' employment in SOEs as both undeserved privilege and envied shield from market volatility, especially after 150,000 people lost their jobs in the private sector during the Great Recession (which lasted in Croatia longer than elsewhere, from 2009 to 2014). This had an adverse impact on Croatian politics, creating a kind of permanent tension between the public and private sectors. Third, wage differential fuelled aggressive wage demands by trade unions in the rest of the government sector (administration, teachers, doctors and nurses, etc.). This slowed down the fiscal adjustment. Escalating public debt (which reached 87% of GDP in 2015, the highest level compared to CEE new member states) and cost of debt service (interest payments of close to 4% of GDP, which is among the highest in the EU) led to protracted recession which further aggravated problems after 2009.

There are three additional channels by which SOEs may have played a major role in creating lack of market dynamism in Croatia. Iootty et al. (2014) showed that Croatia had by far the lowest rates of market entries and exits compared to the CEE-8 during the Great Recession. This may be due to: (1) weak institutions and cumbersome regulation of market entry and exit, (2) capital market imperfections, and/or (3) market distortions created by SOEs. Of course, it is hard to separate the three channels as they interact in many different ways.

The International Monetary Fund (2015) directly addressed the role of SOEs in their Article IV Report for 2015. The first part was inspired by the European Commission's report:

> State-Owned Enterprises (SOEs) continue to play a large role in Croatia's economy. At end-2013, SOEs accounted for 18% of non-financial corporate (NFC) employment and administrated more than one third of non-financial companies' assets. The average SOE employs more than 10 times more workers than private enterprises and is highly unionized. Given Croatia's uncoordinated and decentralized wage bargaining system, this grants SOE unions much influence over labour conditions in the entire economy.

The IMF (2015: 20) continues by criticizing the governance system and concludes with a warning about the impact of SOEs on allocation of capital and labour:

> Comparable cross-country data on SOEs are hard to come by, but the EBRD transition indicators provide some insight. The depth and length of the slump in investment following the 2008/09 crisis correlates strongly with the degree of transition from a centralized to a market-based non-financial corporate sector. While far from conclusive, the evidence is consistent with SOEs hampering corporate adjustment and delaying the recovery.

Croatian governments were successful in having not a single agreement with the IMF since the early 2000s. So, the IMF could analyse the situation, but it had no leverage over policy decisions in Croatia.

However, the European Commission (EC) and Council of the EU have some leverage. Croatia is a member of the EU, subject to the European Semester policy development cycle. It involves in-depth analyses and recommendations that are monitored annually. Monitoring was in-depth during Croatia's Excessive Deficit Procedure (2014–2017) and is still going on under the Macroeconomic Imbalance Procedure. Croatia's 2017 Country Report issued by the EC identified Croatia's productivity gap and explained it by a cumbersome business environment that depresses productive investment and productivity growth. Interestingly enough, the EC (2017) finds productivity recovery after 2010 at or above peers. However, allocative efficiency measured by market shares of the most productive firms is weak, therefore offsetting substantial improvements in firm level productivity. The EC relates this finding to SOEs: "Such sub-optimal allocation of resources is typically associated with a weak functioning of markets, rigid regulation (often in specific sectors) and the widespread presence of large state-owned enterprises" (EC 2017: 43).

In the latest microeconomic research of firm performance, Valdec and Zrnc (2017) pointed at very heterogeneous firm behaviour with respect to productivity developments. The Croatian economy is split between a small share of highly productive and a large share of unproductive firms. The Great Recession led to the improvement of allocation of labour towards more productive enterprises, especially in the tradable sector, which helped positive changes in terms of aggregate labour productivity. This is in line with the EC's quotation above.

However, Valdec and Zrnc's (2017) research indicates problems with capital mobility across firms and industries. It may be related to exit and other regulatory and institutional insufficiencies, as well as to capital market imperfections. Valdec and Zrnc (2017) do not specifically address the role of SOEs, but their findings are important for framing further analysis and recommendations.

Finally, Martinis and Ljubaj (2017) addressed the role of SOEs in their analysis of corporate (over)indebtedness. They found high sensitivity of investment and recovery to debt levels among small and medium-sized enterprises (SMEs) and exporters. Foreign-owned enterprises and SOEs, perhaps for different reasons, did not exhibit this kind of investment sensitivity. Lack of market pressures probably explain absent sensitivity among

SOEs. Martinis and Ljubaj (2017) also point at weak resolution and restructuring processes, which hamper efficient capital allocations.

11.4 Public versus Private: What Do Financial Indicators Show?

Firms in any economy are very heterogeneous. Their productivity depends on a number of factors, such as industry characteristics and size. It is not easy to isolate the sole impact of ownership besides a number of other factors that affect firm performance.

In order to minimize the firm heterogeneity problem, a sample of the top 1000 Croatian companies was sorted according to their 2016 total revenue and segmented in order to provide a clearer picture of SOEs' role and performance. Table 11.2 shows four key findings based on the simple segmentation of the top 1000 companies (based on 949 non-financial companies among top 1000 Croatian enterprises—the 51 remaining are financial institutions, which are not interesting for this analysis). Four key findings are:

Table 11.2 Basic descriptive financial statistics—top 1000 Croatian companies in 2016

	Number of companies	*Share in total[b] revenue (%)*	*Revenue growth 2016/2015 (%)*	*Share in total[b] employment (%)*	*Employment growth 2016/2015 (%)*	*Share in total[b] equity (%)*
100% SOEs	66	13.7	−0.8	22.0	−1.6	50.0
<50% SOEs[a]	17	1.9	−3.8	12.2	−2.2	13.4
>50% SOEs[a]	63	12.1	−3.2	12.8	−0.4	1.8
Private	803	72.3	5.4	63.0	4.4	34.8
Financial institutions	51					

[a]Mixed private–public ownership; <50% means that government is minority shareholder

[b]Total for non-financial companies (not including financial institutions—financial sector is more privatized than non-financial companies because only one large bank and government-owned development bank involve state ownership

Source: FINA, authors' calculations

1. SOEs 100% owned by the government have significantly lower share in total revenues (13.7%) compared to their share in total employment (22%) and in particular, compared to their share in total equity (50%) of 949 largest non-financial enterprises.
2. During 2016, which was a year of recovery (GDP grew by 3.2%), only private non-financial enterprises managed to boost revenues (+5.4%), while all types of SOEs recorded decline in sum of revenues, representing a significant drag on growth.
3. Private non-financial companies (among top 1000) are much more efficient in utilization of capital, because with 35% of total equity they created 72% of total revenue (they also used labour more efficiently because revenue share is produced with significantly lower share in total employment).
4. Two other types of SOEs by ownership (companies with mixed ownership are divided in two groups—those with >50% of state share and those with <50% of state share) are also inefficient as measured by this simple method of share comparisons. However, the degree of inefficiency is much less pronounced than in the case of 100% SOEs.

The information in Table 11.2 should be interpreted having in mind that there are capital-intensive network utilities among SOEs (in particular, roads, highways, railway and electricity network). Network utilities are the main reason why SOEs have lower debt-equity ratios on average compared to private non-financial enterprises (debt-equity ratio for the overall sample is 0.90 and 0.63 for SOEs). Capital-intensive state-owned networks also bias the results. So, more sophisticated analysis is required in order to reach reliable results about potential differences in terms of efficiency between private companies and SOEs.

In-depth analysis was performed by mimicking the Cobb-Douglas production function on the cross-section of large firms for 2016. Dependent variable is revenue from sales (Y) and explanatory variables are number of workers (L), accounting value of equity (K) and dummy variable (D) for SOEs. Nominal variables of output and capital and one annual period in the cross-section sample limit strict interpretations within economic theory of production. However, the specification helps in estimating whether output (nominal sales revenue) can be explained by government ownership, given inputs of labour and capital. The expected sign with binary variable is negative: lower output is expected, given factor inputs, when the government owns the company.

A cross-section of firms' approach is also convenient for isolating the impact of large capital-intensive network utilities; in particular, electricity company HEP, Croatian Roads, Croatian Highways and Croatian Railways Infrastructure. These four network utilities comprise 39% of the equity's accounting value of non-financial companies included in the sample. It is very important to control for capital networks' effects, because they can produce biased results pointing at the inefficient use of capital when positive externalities are not included in the measure of output. For that reason, four large network utilities were excluded from the sample. Also, companies with less than 30 employees were eliminated from the sample. They may be the members of the business groups (for example holding companies) with high accounting revenues due to output produced elsewhere in the business group. It may distort results and produce biased negative parameters with labour input, as such companies usually employ small numbers of staff at companies' headquarters. After the elimination of utilities and holding companies with a small number of employees and of some enterprises with missing data points, the sample was reduced to a still satisfactory 789 medium and large non-financial enterprises out of top 1000.

Finally, regression results in Table 11.3 below were estimated based on ordinary least squares ($\ln(Y) = a*\ln(L) + b*\ln(K)$ for N = 789 medium and large non-financial firms). In a recent literature based on time series and/or panel data, two-stage estimation procedure is used in order to eliminate endogeneity bias (Levinsohn and Petrin 2003), but OLS is allowed in a simple cross section framework because the purpose is not to identify exact measure of productivity, but rather to check if ownership matters.

Table 11.3 Regression results

Explanatory variable	*Parameter value*	*t-test*
L:Number of employees, annual average	0.31	5.99[a]
K:Equity, reported accounting value	0.98	63.00[a]
Dummy = 1 for 100% SOEs	−1.11	−5.97[a]
Dummy = 1 for >50% SOEs	−0.94	−4.94[a]
Dummy = 1 for <50% SOEs	−0.96	−2.58[a]

[a]99% confidence level

The results in Table 11.3 show negative signs of parameters with binary variables:

1. 100% SOEs are generally inefficient (produce less than expected given inputs), even when electricity, railways, road and highway utilities are excluded from the sample.
2. The same conclusion applies to enterprises in mixed ownership, although size of negative parameters is marginally smaller than for 100% SOEs.

11.5 Policy Recommendations

The results presented so far do not distinguish between internal enterprise X-inefficiencies and cross-industry and economy-wide allocative inefficiencies. They also do not allow for the exact estimation of SOEs' impact on relatively slow economic growth in Croatia compared to CEE peers in this century. Exogenous factors—war and late EU entry— certainly contributed to Croatia's problems during the post-socialist transition. However, they do not provide a full explanation.

The relative size and role of SOEs is representative for a wider set of economic and social problems that can be identified as unfinished transition or partial reforms equilibrium (Kotarski and Petak 2018). This wider set of problems frames technical policy issues, which are discussed first.

Technical recommendations are relatively easy to grasp. Internal enterprise X-inefficiencies should be dealt with regard to the revival of privatization, fighting monopolies and monopolistic practices (pro-competition policy in general) and further market liberalization. Reforming business environment (better regulation initiative) is a bridge between solving the X-inefficiencies and allocative inefficiencies in order to boost competitiveness. There are many tools, such as Doing Business score and EU Services Directive implementation, which may help execution of such policies. Croatia was by far too late in recognizing these policy priorities. Only in 2013 the centre-left government set it high on the policy agenda, but did not do much in terms of the execution. Present centre-right government (since 2016) adopted a better regulation action plan and seems to be moving faster in this direction, but the big impact is still missing.

Allocative inefficiencies, in particular related to the allocation of capital which seems to be a more pressing problem for the time being, should be dealt with institutional reforms. Key institutional reform should be related to dealing with insolvency. Croatia ranks 54th in the world according to the Doing Business score with respect to resolving insolvencies. Latent problems in this area escalated after the Great Recession broke out in 2009. Martinis and Ljubaj (2017) found the strange absence of corporate deleveraging during the crisis. The centre-left government which came to the office in 2012 followed the logic of saving (over)indebted enterprises and Croatia gave up regular court controlled insolvency procedures of enterprises by enacting a special law which made state administration responsible for the resolution processes. Ministers, in particular the Minister of Finance, played a key role in the process which is usually dealt with creditor councils and courts. This law was amended five times until 2015. Then, procedures were finally brought back under the auspices of judiciary under EU pressure in 2015. Anyway, bankruptcy and restructuring processes are still largely controlled by debtors. Creditors' rights compared to sound insolvency principles are eroded, which creates lots of legal uncertainties and structural risks. At a deeper level, it probably slows down reallocation of factors of production by prolonging the lives of many enterprises with unsustainable business models (zombie firms), in line with interest of those who created debt.

The recent failure of the largest company in Southeast Europe, Croatia-based Agrokor, whose contribution to employment and GDP was close to 2% (Šonje 2017) also showed that the legal tools and capacities of the judiciary are insufficient to deal with a major company failure. The Croatian Government undertook a heavy risk by enacting a special law for dealing with the Agrokor resolution. This process is underway and it is too early to judge the outcome.

The situation is equally cumbersome with respect to consumers' insolvencies. Consumer bankruptcy was introduced as late as 2016, but less than 100 persons are using the protection under the new law. Late adoption and very narrow application of the consumer bankruptcy procedure is an indicator of immature institutions and debtors' opportunistic behaviour. It also contributes to rollover of debt problems and keeping many consumers out of credit markets. Around 330,000 citizens (close to 10% of adult population) have "blocked accounts". It means there are automatic restrictions on the use of their money under legal enforcement procedure due to unpaid debt. However, the law on enforcement provides generous debtors' protection. Previously 2/3 of the average wage was protected from enforcement and recent amendments of the law provide protection of up to 3/4 of the average wage. So, a number of small claims cannot be collected.

In general, debt restructuring and the resolution framework are weak and should be strengthened significantly. It should also involve finding appropriate tax treatment for debt restructuring operations. Recent amendments to tax regulations did not facilitate bad debt resolution and cleaning of bad debts from banks' books. This problem is related to a wider issue of capital markets development. While there are some objective obstacles to capital markets development—for example small size of the market—weak institutional mechanisms for creditor and investor protection prevent deeper capital markets development and integration. This is especially related to the riskiest types of equity funding. In general, there are both supply and demand obstacles for private companies in Croatia in raising new equity.

On a broader level, institution building should primarily involve reforms of public administration and judiciary in order to provide for reliable and fair institutional environment with equal access and predictable treatment without evasion, privileges and other corruptive practices. Transparent privatization and professional management of remaining SOEs via specialized agency or a holding company (or a fund) is a way to design a new system, which would keep politicians at arm's length from operational management of SOEs (Petrović and Šonje 2015). It does not involve full depoliticization, because SOEs that remain after the privatization effort, especially those producing positive externalities and network effects, need to follow strategic goals that are set politically. More precisely, they need to be controlled by political agents, as goals do not necessarily follow from profit maximization but rather from the accomplishment of some public interest. However, efficiency and protection of SOEs from political employment, crony contracts and other forms of asset stripping is a paramount public interest, which can be realized only by implementing firewalls between SOEs and a corrupted portion of political elite.

It is pretty much clear what the reforms should technically look like. However, the key issue is who has the political will and capacity to undertake institutional reforms described above. At a proximate level, underdeveloped institutions as well as inefficient SOEs arose as the consequences of lags in transition that can be explained by war, late EU entry and weak administrative capacities. However, at a more fundamental level, underdeveloped institutions are consequences of *political choices* that were taken in the last 25 years. These political choices are rooted in ideas and interests that shape these institutions. So, the key question is: how can political choices be altered to move Croatia towards the next stage of institutional modernization? SOEs can be modernized and made more efficient only within a wider reform agenda, aiming at development of efficient, impersonal and impartial institutions.

There are many peculiar features of the Croatian political system that are relevant for political framing of technical recommendations. Two are the most important: continuity of political elites and wide participation in party politics.

First, two dominant political parties (social democrats SDP, which inherited both economic and political assets and liabilities of former communist party and the Christian democrats HDZ, which arose as a movement for independence in 1989–1990) ruled in Croatia since the first democratic elections in 1990. This kind of bi-party political continuity is hard to find in any other post-communist country. It is an indicator of continuity of political elites and the lack of political innovations and competition.

Second, Croatia has the largest share of party members among the population in the EU, mainly thanks to widespread HDZ membership. What seems to be a significant democratic achievement (citizens' political participation) can be interpreted as exactly the opposite—the capture of public democratic institutions by numerous interest groups and political professionals who pursue their careers via widespread and influential political/public sector hierarchies that comprise central and local government levels as well as SOEs. Of course, a large number of party members implies strong political competition within the largest parties, but this internalized political competition is muted by party leadership and is not enough to produce political change in terms of the next step of modernization.

Two features of the political system illustrate the power of bad political equilibrium, which has practically frozen modernization process and slowed down institutional development. A large sector of SOEs is a critical element in this system, as SOEs, with their economic resources, provide a magnet for political elites (jobs, power, prestige and contracts for cronies). This self-perpetuating partial reform equilibrium is stable as long as political incentives do not change. So, how can they change?

1989–1990 is far away in the past. Political change cannot be motivated by ideas about market reforms that can provide betterment for the majority of the population. Disbelief in market solutions and reforms is widespread. Powerful interest groups that cannot survive open market competition fuelled anti-market sentiment, usually by warning against neoliberal evils. This sentiment was also fuelled by the Great Recession, which created wider suspicion towards capitalist institutions. So, there are only two ways for changing the partial reform equilibrium.

The first is by way of a big bang crisis, like in Greece. There are two arguments why this is unlikely. First, Croatia has its fiscal problems (public debt at 82.9% of GDP in 2016 was the highest among peers). However, the level of debt, stability of the banking system and policy control mechanisms under the European Semester, make full-blown crisis of the Greek type highly unlikely. Second, the case of Greece has shown that some societies have generally weak capacities for reforming institutions, including proper privatization of SOEs. Severe financial crises slow down the development of such societies without unleashing hidden capacities for reform, as there are none.

The second way is by evolutionary political change. Being a member of the EU creates new competitive pressures in the open single market as well as political pressures for reform. Open borders imply emigration as many people find jobs in other EU countries. So, competition, political pressure (including institutional competition and a mere urge for the imitation of more successful societies) and emigration, may create more fertile political environments for market reforms. However, political evolution, at least up to 2017, did not bring about strengthening of the pro-reform agenda. On the contrary, two anti-establishment movements (Most [Bridge] and Živi zid [Living Wall]) that entered the parliament after elections in 2015 and 2016, mostly advocate anti-reform agendas. Some of their general calls for the betterment of institutions, fairness and better control of two long-standing leading political parties HDZ and SDP, are the positive elements of their political programmes. However, in terms of economic policies, new political parties generally call for the protection of producers, consumers and debtors. Their emphasis is on the urge to protect state assets from foreigners and private investors. They also have a strong anti-banking appeal, which they borrowed from similar anti-capitalist movements in Southern Europe (Syriza, Podemos). They are either highly suspicious towards EU integrations (Most is silent about the issue) or openly oppose them (Živi zid).

The new political landscape is a part of a wider movement of newly rising belief in the state against markets prompted by reform fatigue, the Great Recession and consolidation of interests for status quo. The centre-right government, which has been in office since 2016, gave up on any significant privatization effort (centre-left government 2012–2015 tried and failed due to opposition by trade unions and other interest groups). The incumbent government early in the mandate promised to bring some previously sold assets under state control (for example oil company INA). They dismantled the previous specialized agency for the management of state assets under the auspices of a newly created Ministry for State Assets, based on the ideas of Christian social conservativism that highly values collectivism, common good and state ownership. This new political landscape is a mixture of interests and ideas of different kinds, new and old. It cannot be properly understood in terms of old concepts of left and right or state versus markets and the like. This is not 1989 any more, three decades have passed. Evolution of the political landscape and reforms remains highly unpredictable.

11.6 Conclusion

Several studies have shown that SOEs are much more inefficient than privately owned enterprises in Croatia. Results presented in this chapter confirmed those findings for a sample of large enterprises as well. The mere size of this sector, which still controls large segments of employment and, in particular, the bulk of equity of non-financial enterprises, points at the economy-wide impact of SOEs. These enterprises take part in the creation of allocative inefficiencies. Together with internal X-inefficiencies they are at the root of a relatively unsuccessful transition in Croatia and the lack of competitiveness of the Croatian economy.

Privatization, liberalization and protection against monopolistic practices belong to the first generation of post-communist reforms, which were not carried out successfully in Croatia. The political sector consolidated rapidly in the 1990s, incorporating the new balance of powers between old and new elites. Rent-seeking and crony practices became pervasive. Institutional development progressed very slowly, mainly thanks to the outside pressures from the EU.

Kotarski and Petak (2018) see it as a partial reform equilibrium that mimics the Southern European type of (crony) capitalism. Their hypothesis set out in this volume is that the transition winners captured the state in order to protect their rents and privileges by eliminating competition. Looking at the problem from the perspective of the large and inefficient sector of SOEs, which are firmly controlled via political hierarchy, the political and economic landscape seems to be somewhat richer. Partly it is a legacy of socialism, which has been reshaped into new forms of national collectivism (for example protection of state assets for the purpose of protection of common national assets). Partly it is a shield from the market for a number of politicians and their cronies who can do business inside and within SOEs, not in order to get rich, but merely in order to survive. In this sense, SOEs protected some of the potential losers of the transition.

The relatively recent EU entry created new pressures and opportunities. The market is open and competitive pressures get stronger every day. Political pressures are present because Croatia is now integrated in the European Semester policy cycle. Open borders and emigration created nationwide frustration due to prompted fears of demographic decline, lack of a qualified workforce and the escape of potential taxpayers abroad (which is a nightmare for professional politicians). These are the forces that can filter change towards better policies, among them policies that will revive privatization and generally improve SOEs' management, and increase economic efficiency and competitiveness. However, political evolution can go either way. There is no historical necessity for better economic policies to emerge.

Notes

1. CEE-8 comprises of Estonia, Latvia, Lithuania, Poland, Czech Republic, Slovakia, Hungary and Slovenia.

References

Aslund, A. (2013). *How Capitalism Was Built: The Transformation of Central and Eastern Europe, Russia, The Caucasus, and Central Asia* (2nd ed.). Cambridge: Cambridge University Press.

European Commission. (2017) Country Report Croatia 2017: Including an In-Depth Review on the Prevention and Correction of Macroeconomic Imbalances. https://ec.europa.eu/info/file/96682/download_en?token=k-4wwF_K. Downloaded 23 February 2017.

Eurostat. (2017). GDP Per Capita in PPS. http://ec.europa.eu/eurostat/tgm/table.do?tab=table&init=1&language=en&pcode=tec00114&plugin=1. Downloaded 27 August 2017.

International Monetary Fund European Department. (2015). Republic of Croatia: Staff Report for Article IV Consultations. *Country Report 15/163*.

Iootty, M., Correa, P., Radas, S., & Škrinjarić, B. (2014). Stylized Fact on Productivity Growth: Evidence from Firm-Level Data in Croatia. *Policy Research Working Paper No. 6990*, Washington, DC: The World Bank.

Kotarski, K. (2017). Hrvatska u raljama klijentelizma. Ekonomski lab. http://arhivanalitika.hr/blog/hrvatska-u-raljama-klijentelizma/. Downloaded 31 August 2017.

Kotarski, K., & Petak, Z. (2018). Croatia's Post-Communist Transition Experience: The Paradox of Initial Advantage Turning into a Middle-Income Trap, (this Volume).

Levinsohn, J., & Petrin, A. (2003). Estimating Production Functions Using Inputs to Control for Unobservables. *The Review of Economic Studies, 70*(2), 317–341.

Martinis, A., & Ljubaj, I. (2017). Corporate Debt Overhang in Croatia: Micro Assessment and Macro Implications. *CNB Working Papers W-51*, Zagreb: Croatian National Bank.

Nestić, D., Rubil, I., & Tomić, I. (2015). Analiza razlika u plaćama između javnog sektora, poduzeća u državnom vlasništvu i privatnog sektora u Hrvatskoj 2000.–2012. *Privredna kretanja i ekonomska politika, 24*(1), 7–50.

OECD. (2017). Indicators of Product Market Regulation Homepage. http://www.oecd.org/eco/growth/indicatorsofproductmarketregulationhomepage.htm. Downloaded 21 July 2017.

Petrović, S., & Šonje, V. (2015). Je li privatizacija državnih poduzeća nužan uvjet njihovog uspješnog poslovanja u Hrvatskoj. *Privredna kretanja i ekonomska politika, 138*(1), 37–87.

Šonje, V. (2017). Agrokor prvi dio: veličina i ekonomski učinak. Ekonomski lab. http://arhivanalitika.hr/blog/agrokor-prvi-dio-velicina-i-ekonomski-ucinak/. Downloaded 1 August 2017.

Valdec, M., & Zrnc, J. (2017). Microeconomic Aspects of Productivity Developments During the Great Recession in Croatia – The CompNet Productivity Module Research Results. *CNB Surveys S-22*, Zagreb: Croatian National Bank.

Vizek, M. (2014). Dualni značaj javnih poduzeća za ekonomsku aktivnost u RH. In *Zagreb Economic Forum*. Zagreb: Friedrich Ebert Stiftung.

Vuković, V. (2014). *Korupcija u javnim nabavama i posljedice na politički reizbor: primjer lokalne samouprave u Hrvatskoj*. Zagreb: Hrvatska udruga banaka.

PART III

Sectoral Public Policies

CHAPTER 12

The Croatian Pension System and Challenges of Pension Policy

Predrag Bejaković

12.1 Introduction

After independence in 1991, the Croatian pension system followed the Bismarckian continental model of public intergenerational solidarity, the so-called pay-as-you-go (PAYG) system. The Homeland War at the beginning of 1990s and the economic and political transition had a harmful impact on the Croatian pension system. The Croatian central budget had taken over responsibility for previous federal obligations, newly established merit pensions, increased number of retirees (early retirement was often used as a means to solve the social consequences of open unemployment), all of which caused increasing budget deficits and contributed to the growing public debt. Croatian policy-makers attempted in vain to refinance and reform the pension system, until a serious discussion on the restructuring of the system began in November 1995.

The Croatian pension system has experienced many reforms: one systemic reform (in the period between 1998 and 2002 resulted in the creation of the three-pillar pension system), and numerous parametric

P. Bejaković (✉)
Institute of Public Finance, Zagreb, Croatia
e-mail: predrag.bejakovic@ijf.hr

Z. Petak, K. Kotarski (eds.), *Policy-Making at the European Periphery*, New Perspectives on South-East Europe,
https://doi.org/10.1007/978-3-319-73582-5_12

reforms,[1] the last one encompassing all three pillars of the pension system (2013–2016). The existing pension system of unfunded pensions at the beginning of 2002 was replaced by a combined system of unfunded and funded pensions. The purpose of the chapter is to analyze the policy-making process and the reform of the Croatian pension system, with particular attention towards its sustainability and adequacy.[2]

The pension system is a popular issue and it is constantly debated by the public. Although there are many reasons for that, two of them can be particularly underlined. The first one is connected with the general public dissatisfaction with pension benefits that are generally low and in many cases do not offer protection against poverty.[3] The second one is related to the internal inconsistency of the system due to a series of partial changes, which has led to different positions for pensioners who have entered their pension in different years and/or from various positions (*regular* and *privileged* pension benefit). That general dissatisfaction with the pension system has also a gender dimension.

After the introductory remarks, the first section explains the main characteristic of the pension system in Croatia. That is followed by the presentation of key problems and their causes and by a short history of reforms in the pension system, which shows insufficient consistencies and scarce prudence in the approach adopted by various legislators. Those factors, as well as numerous and recurrent legislative changes combined with the pressure from various interest groups of privileged pensioners, endanger the long-term financial sustainability and adequacy of pension benefits. The final section contains concluding remarks and several recommendations for improvement.

12.2 Main Characteristics of the Pension System in Croatia: Insured Persons and Rights

According to the Pension Insurance Act (OG 157/13), insured persons in the mandatory pension insurance are all employees in public and private sectors, self-employed persons and farmers. Apart from these groups, according to the legal regulation, members of a farmer's household who perform agricultural activities as their only or principal occupation must also be mandatorily insured. The regulation also stipulates that members of the management boards of trading companies have to be insured, unless they are insured on another basis. Furthermore, priests, monks, nuns and other clerical officers shall be mandatorily insured during the service in a religious community, unless they are insured on another basis. The Act regulates the mandatory insurance of a parent who performs parental duties during a child's first year, provided that the person is not insured on another basis. In Croatia, there are three main types of pension: old-age retirement pension, survivor benefits or family pension and disability pension (Bejaković 2004).

A person who retires at the statutory age and has at least 15 years of an insurance period (*mirovinski staž*) obtains full old-age retirement pension (*starosna mirovina*). The amount of pension depends on received wages and related contributions during the complete working period (see below). A person who retires at most five years before the statutory age and has at least 35 years of service in 2014 (31 for women) can obtain early retirement pension (*prijevremena starosna mirovina*). The amount of this pension is also based on previous wages and related pension contributions, but a penalizing factor is applied. It depends on age and years of service; the maximum penalty is 20.4% for men who retire with 35 years of service at the age of 60.

Survivor benefits or a family pension (*obiteljska mirovina*) is received by a widower of the deceased insured person, if the person is above 50 years, or below 50, if he or she is unable to work or if taking care of children. A child of the passed-away insured person (PAIP) is a beneficiary if involved in secondary or tertiary education; the age limit is 26, unless a person is unable to work. The pension amount is obtained as the *base* multiplied by a factor, which depends on the number of survivors, and ranges from 0.7 for one survivor to 1.0 for four or more survivors. The base is equal to the PAIP's last pension (if the PAIP was a pensioner) or to the eventual PAIP's invalidity pension. Certain minimum years of service are required (Urban and Bezeredi 2016).

Persons with partial or full loss of working ability receive disability pension (*invalidska mirovina*). Certain minimum years of service are required, depending on age. A disability pension can be obtained if an insured person has occupational or general incapacity for work, in addition to a completed qualifying period. The former is considered to be total disability and the latter partial. A temporary disability pension has also been introduced in 2015 for persons with reduced working capacity who, even after having completed professional rehabilitation remained unemployed for at least five years, provided that their unemployment lasted until the age of 58. The amount of disability pension is calculated as in the case of retirement pensions; however, the years of service are augmented by a certain factor. The amount also depends on whether a person suffers from partial or full loss of working ability.

12.3 The Number of Pension Beneficiaries and Their Structure

The number of pension beneficiaries has grown continuously in Croatia, from about 0.656 million in 1990 to about 1.230 million (*regular* and *privileged*) pensioners currently. This means that their number almost doubled. In the new millennium, the number of pensioners in Croatia increased by 201,000 or almost by one fifth, from 1.03 million in 2000 to 1.23 million in 2016. By contrast, the number of insurees under the PAYG system fell from about 2 million in 1990 to 1.4 million in 2000, but it rose again to 1.6 million in 2008. During the economic crisis from 2009 to 2014, the number of employed and actively insured persons in Croatia dropped by more than 200,000, and it just recently started to increase (Fig. 12.1). Thus, at the end of 2016 there were 1.44 million actively insured persons, which means that the dependency ratio (the total number of actively insured persons in comparison to total number of beneficiaries) amounts to only 1.17. This ratio is very unfavorable, particularly having in mind that in 1990, there were around three insured persons per pensioner. Of total 1.14 million *regular* pensioners at the end of 2016, 783,000 (68.6%) were old-age pensioners, 228,000 (20.0%) were family pensioners, while there were 130,000 (11.4%) invalidity pensioners (various sources by Croatian Pension Insurance Institute, particularly Hrvatski zavod za mirovinsko osiguranje 2017).

Some other forms of so-called *privileged* pension are not related to the previous pension insurance period or received wages and paid contributions. The *privileged* pension beneficiaries include the National Liberation War participants; employees performing certain activities within the Internal Affairs and Justice Ministry; members of the Croatian Home Guard Army 1941–1945; former political prisoners; members of the former Yugoslav National Army; full members of the Croatian Academy of Science and Art; members of the Parliamentary Executive Council, Federal Executive Council and administratively retired public servants relating to the former Yugoslavia; members of *Sabor* (the Croatian Parliament), members of the Government, Constitutional Court judges and the Auditor General; federal cadres (former delegates

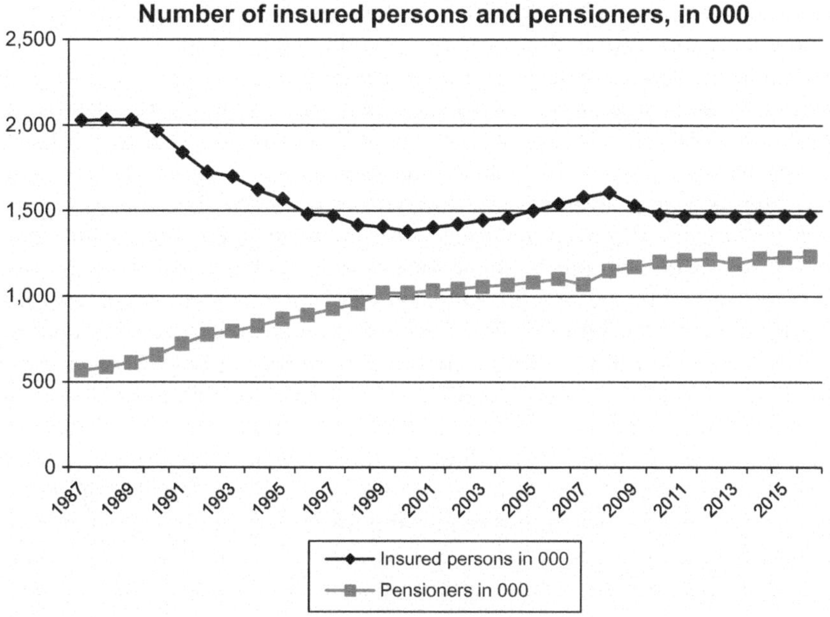

Fig. 12.1 Number of insured persons and pensioners, in 000s (Source: Croatian Pension Insurance Institute)

to the Federal Council and similar who resigned from their duty); miners from the Istrian coal mines 'Tupljak' in Labin, workers professionally exposed to asbestos; members of the Croatian Army; Croatian Homeland War veterans; and finally, members of the Croatian Defense Council (CDC). Altogether, there are 17 different groups of receivers of the privileged pension. The amount of this type of pension differs significantly from the regular pension amount, and generally, it is significantly higher (Bađun 2009).

12.4 Amount of Pension and Replacement Rate

Minimum and maximum pension rules apply for retirement and early retirement pensions, as well as for survivors' and disability pensions. The minimum pension is proportional to the years of service and depends on the type of pension. It does not depend on earnings but only on the insurance period. For a man with 40 years of service retired at the statutory age, it amounts to HRK 2362 (€ 320) as at January 2015. The maximum pension equals about three times the average old-age pension.

While the replacement rate (the percentage of the average pension in average salary) was above 60% in the first three years of the 1990s, it declined to 52% in 1994 and to around 46% in the period from 1995 to 1998. At the end of 1990, there was another drop in the replacement rate and its lowest level was in 2000 with only 37.6%. The share of average pension in the average wage has somewhat risen after 2000, but continues to be just a little above 40% of the average wage. Thus, as the average monthly income in January 2015 in Croatian legal entities amounted to HRK 5656 (€ 764), the replacement rate was around 42%. However, one should not forget that in spite of the stipulated legal retirement age of 60 for women and 65 for men, most people get retired early while still under 60 years of age and with less than 29 years of pension insurance (see below). According to the calculation by the Croatian Pension Insurance Fund, if insured persons reach the legally stipulated age and obtain the full period of pension insurance, the replacement rate would be around 61%, which is comparable with international pension rates. In the following section, attention is oriented towards the causes of problems.

12.5 Causes of Problems in the Croatian Pension System

Financial and benefit-related problems in the Croatian pension system during the 1990s were caused by demographic and systemic factors. *Demographic reasons* are population ageing caused by a fall in the fertility rate (which brings a low birth rate) and extended life expectancy. The fertility rate is the average number of children that would be born per woman if all women lived to the end of their childbearing years and conform to the age-specific fertility rates of a given year. The total fertility rate (TFR) shows the potential for population change in the country. This indicator is a more direct measure of the level of fertility than the crude birth rate, since it refers to births per woman. While the TFR in Croatia during the 1950s had been almost three, at the beginning of the new millennium it fell below 1.5, with the tendency for further decrease (Croatian Bureau of Statistics 2016). The rate of two children per woman is considered as the adequate replacement rate for a population, resulting in the relative stability in terms of the population size. In that way, the population of Croatia has been rapidly and constantly shrinking.

Additionally, the demographic picture of Croatia has noticeably changed due to the ageing population (which should not be confused with personal biological ageing). It represents the increase in the proportion of older persons (65+) in the total population from 7% in 1953 to 17.7% in 2011 (Central Bureau of Statistics 2012). It is caused by the extended life expectancy in the mentioned period, from 59.1 to 73.8 years for men and from 63.2 to 80.4 for women. As a result of better nutrition, ancillary services and improved health care, the average life expectancy in Croatia increased noticeably in the period 1953–2011, especially for women (by 17.2 years), but also respectively for men (14.7 years). Finally, one should not forget the consequences of the Homeland War, where many people (particularly the young) were killed and which caused a further increase in the number of pensioners (the disabled and victims of war, as well as survivor pension beneficiaries of persons killed in war). Some of the *systemic factors* before the pension reform were:

- Relatively low legal age conditions for full old-age pensions were set before the pension reform (60 years for men, and 55 for women; age conditions for early pension were 55 years of age for men, and 50 for women, and temporary reductions of 1.33% were applied per each year of earlier retirement).
- The amount of pension was often not enough related to paid contributions, so a person has been eligible for the pension rights regardless of his or her regular payment of the pension contribution.
- The possibility of old age retirement with 40 years of insurance (men) or 35 years of insurance (women) contributions regardless of age. Those factors contributed to a much lower actual average retirement age than stipulated legal age and consequently to early withdrawal from the labor market, which is still a serious problem today. For example, the average age of new old-age pension beneficiaries who were retired at the end of June 2015 was 62 years, 63 years for men and 60.5 years for women. For people receiving a disability pension that is considerably lower and is 53 years, or 53.7 years for men and 50.8 years for women. In that way, the average female age pensioner can expect to receive a pension for more than 19 years, and the average male age pensioners around 11.

- A loose definition of disability and incentives for many to retire early and to receive relatively high pensions.
- Pensioning people off in the early 1990s as a way of managing the welfare status of people who had lost their jobs because of the war or because of restructuring or closing in the economy that was in the process of transition.

Additionally, the number of pensioners in the period 1990–1998 more than doubled and continued to increase afterward, because new groups of beneficiaries appeared:

- Beneficiaries (refugees) in Croatia who acquired pension rights in other republics of the former Yugoslavia.
- Members of the former Yugoslav army.
- Those disabled during the Homeland War and the families of soldiers killed in the war, according to the legislation that has been introduced—while this was to some extent an unfortunate and inevitable consequence of the conflict, less than stringent assessment procedures almost certainly made the inflow of these groups higher than was warranted.
- Former political prisoners according to the accepted legislation.

During the first years of transition, the Croatian pension system inherited an excessively permissive eligibility criteria, which were further relaxed to build a social safety net. Very often, in the case of bankruptcy of many former successful firms, relatively young persons (in their 50s) were sent to retirement with the intention to avoid their unemployment. Furthermore, the system was repeatedly abused to grant favors to clients and was simultaneously squeezed to cut public spending. Approximately one quarter of the retired population is receiving a pension based on disability, so Bađun (2017) examines the reasons for such a situation. Around three-quarters of such persons received their pension according to the general Pension Insurance Act, followed by Croatian Homeland War veterans and by members of the Croatian Army and the Croatian Defense Council, whose pension rights are determined by special laws. The author believes that there are manifold causes for the large number of beneficiaries of disability pensions in Croatia. They are based on the poor structure of educational attainment and the fact that most of the people do not take care of their own health. Furthermore, conditions in health and safety at work are poor, and the Homeland War also had an impact. Finally, inappropriately considered legislative framework, as well as widespread corruption, have led to a large number of beneficiaries of disability pensions.

The pension system has faced the problem of collecting funds for pension benefits for a long time. The rapid expansion of pension-related expenditures has not been followed by an increase in contribution revenues, resulting in growing fiscal deficits financed by general revenues. As the share of contributions in pension revenues has diminished, transfers from the central budget have become increasingly important. The share covered by contributions fell from 96.6% to just above 50%. Thus, almost one half of the total revenues needed for the payment of pension expenditures come from the budget, causing pensions to become one of the most important generators of the Central and also the Consolidated National Budget deficits. Pensions absorbed 72.5% of total Central Government transfers, while the share of state budget in transfer payments has been increasing from 1.1% of Gross Domestic Product (GDP) in 1994 to 9% in 1999 and 8.6% in 2000, meaning that the earmarked funds simply could not cover expenditures (Anušić et al. 2003).

Succinctly, the average pension in Croatia is relatively small, but the system carries a huge number of pensioners, which means that outlays for the pension system have been very high. The total expenditures for pension and disability insurance during the 1990s and early 2000s were around 12% of GDP (for example, more than 13% in 1999) with the tendency to increase. All of the aforementioned factors contributed to the vulnerability of the long-term financial sustainability of the pension system, so there was an obvious need to reform the existing model of pension insurance.

12.6 A Short History of Reforms in the Croatian Pension System

The first reform of the pension system (the so-called small pension reform) in 1998 was oriented towards better control of pension-related expenditures. The Pension Act gradually increased (six months per year) the retirement age (for men to 65 and for women to 60 years of age) until 2008. The formula for calculating the pension amount was changed, so that, by 2008, the entire work life span was taken into calculation, and not only the best consecutive ten years with the highest earnings. This should also be a stimulus for paying pension contributions or at least not to evade their payment, because it could decrease the amount of future retirement income. In line with the provisions contained in the new Law on Pension Insurance (OG 102/98), the legal age for early retirement has been elevated from 50 to 55 for women and from 55 to 60 for men and the permanent decrement for early retirement has been increased. An early pension can be taken within five years before the required age for a full old age pension. By 2008, the age limit was increased to 60 with 35 years of employment for men, and 55 with 30 years of employment for women.

Early retirement pensions are subject to a permanent reduction of 0.34% for every month before the statutory retirement age (penalization was lately reduced). The definition of disability was changed and has become more rigorous. Procedure for the determination of disability was modified. So, the inflow of disabled pensioners was reduced in comparison to the previous period. Pensions are adjusted (indexed) 50% to salaries and 50% to the consumer price index (CPI). In 1999, three previous Institutes—for workers, self-employed and for private farmers—merged and the Croatian Pensions Insurance Institute was established. From 1999, the new Law on Pension Insurance introduced equal contributions rates for all insured persons.

The Croatian Government started designing the reform of the pension system with the aid of experts from the World Bank in the second half of 1995. The existing public PAYG system was replaced by a mixed system at the beginning of 2002, consisting of a public PAYG system (1st pillar) and a mandatory fully funded system (2nd pillar). The second pension reform, called 'the Great Reform', which was defined with the Mandatory and Voluntary Pension Funds Act (OG 49/99) and Pension Insurance Companies and Benefit Payment Based on Individual Fully-Funded Retirement Savings Act (OG, 106/99), is based on three pillars:

- The first pillar is a mandatory pay-as-you-go public pension system and all insured people should be included in the first pillar—employees, self-employed and farmers. Under this system, all insured persons pay 15% of their gross monthly income.
- The second pillar is a mandatory pension system, based on individual capitalized savings. When introduced in 2002 it was mandatory for all those aged under 40 to contribute 5% of their gross monthly income (or a quarter of their pension contributions) to privately

managed pension funds. Those between 40 and 50 could opt either to remain in the PAYG system or to move part of their contributions to the second pillar. The insured persons decide where they want to invest among the mandatory private pension funds.
- The third pillar is a voluntary pension insurance system based on individual capitalized savings for those who want even more insurance against the risks of old age, disability and death. The insurance operates according to the same principles as the second pillar with one exception—the insured person decides on the amount of the contribution he/she desires to make in the pension funds.

Current retirees and older insured persons remain fully in the first pillar. The joint pension contribution rate is 20% paid by employees. For some categories of insured persons (younger than 40, and for those between 40 and 50 if they opt for it), the contribution rate for the first pillar is 15% of gross wage, while 5% of gross wage is earmarked for the second pillar. Between 15 November 2001, when people started enrolling into the mandatory pension funds (2nd pillar) and the end of the June 2016 year, 1,815,363 pension insurance beneficiaries became members in the mandatory pension funds (HANFA 2017). Insured persons younger than 40 years of age that failed to select a mandatory pension fund within the legally prescribed period (three months from the beginning of the compulsory pension insurance) have been assigned in accordance with the prescribed algorithm. The membership in 8 open voluntary pension funds increased from 1345 persons in 2002 to 269,000 by the end of June 2017. Membership in 19 closed voluntary pension funds increased from 1112 in year 2004 to 29,732 insured persons by the end of June 2017 (HANFA 2017).

The Mandatory Pension Funds Act of 2014 introduced lifestyle funds with a life cycle approach, with an intention to lower the investment risk as an insured person approaches the retirement age. Each mandatory pension fund has to have three sub-funds of different investment risk exposure (A—aggressive, B—balanced, C—conservative). Participation in the sub-funds automatically changes with age. All three pillars of pension insurance should together enhance social security, support the diversification of risk and enable a higher overall amount of pensions. Thus, insurance risks for old age, sickness and death are divided into several levels and insurance institutions. This should be positive both for pensioners and for the overall economy because pension funds should increase domestic savings and investment. Moreover, this should stimulate the development of capital markets, economic growth and increase living standards, but also enable other positive results, such as mitigation of poverty.

Women and men of the same age, having the same amount of pension savings, are entitled to the same amount of pension from the second pillar of individual capitalized savings. However, the different age for entitlement to old-age and early old-age pension increases the risk for women retiring at a younger age to be entitled to a lower pension from both the first and the second pillar than men. Individual savings in the compulsory individual scheme are calculated with unisex actuarial tables. Additional contributions are paid by employers for employees in arduous and unhealthy occupations (listed in special legislation), from 1.25% to 4.51% of the payroll to provide for the extension of insurance periods where 12 months of a career is calculated as 14–18 months of the insurance period (European Commission 2014).

Persons who have not worked and paid contributions, and have not obtained pension rights due to family or survival status, do not receive a pension. Their exact number is unknown, but it is estimated around 12–13% of persons older than 64 years. One of the goals of the government has been for providing long-term security for older citizens without pensions by means of introducing the social pension. The realization of this measure was anticipated in the government's mandate by 2011, but was suspended due to the economic crisis. In the meantime, the elderly persons without sufficient resources for living are entitled to certain benefits within the social welfare system. The elderly mostly use various rights within the social assistance system.

With a goal to enhance the long-term sustainability of the pension system, various measures have been performed: (1) reduction of the amount of privileged pension rights and change in their indexation, (2) alterations in disability pensions, (3) pension increments for working longer, and (4) retirement age increases.

The amounts of the majority of the *privileged* pensions have been lowered twice by 10% (from July 2010 and from January 2014). Further, there is a new Pension Insurance Act from 2014, for these kinds of pension stipulate different adjustment (indexation) rules than for *regular* first pillar pensions. Those pensions are adjusted by government decision only if the growth of the real GDP in each of the three previous consecutive quarters was at least 2.0% compared to the same quarter of the previous calendar year and if the state budget deficit was under 3%.

Changes were introduced for disability pensions, with the intention to lower the expenditures for such benefits. During 2013, an ad hoc control examination system was introduced that reduced the total number of disability pensioners. Additionally, automatic recertification of disability pensions every three years is prescribed. In 2014, the new unified model for obtaining disability pensions was established so as to reduce fraud and the vocational rehabilitation system was improved. Disability definition, linked to the remaining work capacity, has been altered so that if a person is not able to work full-time after 'vocational rehabilitation', or at least 70% of full-time on an adjusted job, he/she will qualify for total disability pension.

The retirement age for the old-age pension has been gradually increasing for women from 60 to 65 by 2030. The process began in 2011 (with a yearly increase by three months) with 15 years of qualifying period. The same applies for early retirement, so it is increasing from 55 to 60 by 2030 with 35 years of qualifying period. Hence, retirement age for both sexes will be increased from 65 to 67 and the early retirement age from 60 to 62, only coming fully into effect as of 2038. In view of the population ageing projections, increases in life expectancy and erosion of the pension system's support ratio, Vukorepa (2012) deems that that such slow and small increase will only have a slight influence on the financial sustainability of the pension system.

In 2011, for persons who continue working after the legal retirement age, the augmentation of 0.15% per each month of later retirement was introduced. This measure should stimulate later retirement, but as it is limited for a maximum of five years, the total increment is 9%, which is a relatively small increase. Unfortunately, numerous measures have been accepted that more or less endanger the long-term financial sustainability of the system. These measures are among others: (1) decrease in early retirement decrements, and (2) two new types of early retirements without reduction in the pension amount. Vukorepa (2015) believes that all these countermeasures will probably lead to an increase in the number of pensioners above the level that could be supported, taking into account only demographic trends.

Reduction of benefits for early retirement was introduced in 1999 and until the end of 2007; it was 0.34% per month (thus, 4.08% per year of early retirement or 20.40% for maximum five year period of early retirement). This amount was close to an actuarially neutral correction of the pension benefit due to the longer period of payments (World Bank 2011).

However, during the election year 2007 it had been decreased to only 0.15% per month (thus to 1.8% per year; 9% for five years). Such a decreased level was applied from 2008 to 2010. Since 2011, a maximum reduction for early retirement depends not only on the months of early retirement but also on the years of insurance (mainly years of contributions), which discriminates against contributors who have served fewer years. From 2011 to 2013, it was from minimum 9% to maximum 20.4% for five years of early retirement. The new Pension Insurance Act of 2013 further reduced the early retirement decrement for persons with long years of contributions so that since January 2014 it is in the range from 6% (for insured persons with 40 years of insurance) to 20.4% (for persons with 35 or less years of insurance). All these changes have significantly influenced the increase in the take-up of early pensions.

Furthermore, two new types of early retirement pensions without decrement have been applied since 2014. The first type is an early retirement pension due to long-time insurance for persons after reaching 60 years of age and 41 qualifying years. The amount for this type of pension is determined without an application of early retirement decrement, although these groups use pension rights longer than regular old age pensioners do. Furthermore, they are entitled to be rewarded if they are working over the age of 60 (0.15% for each month, up to maximum 9%). The second type is *an early retirement pension due to bankruptcy*, which was introduced for persons fulfilling early retirement conditions and whose insurance status was terminated due to employer's bankruptcy, provided they have been on unemployment for at least two years continuously prior to retirement. Thus, due to these legislative changes in the last few years there is an evident rising trend in the number of beneficiaries of early retirement.

12.7 Conclusion and Recommendations for Improvement

From the presented analysis of the Croatian pension system, certain recommendations for policy-makers can be made. Firstly, there is a need for more consideration and preparation for the changes to the legislation, because possible errors can have long-term, costly and serious consequences. Once the error is made it is a difficult and demanding task to correct it. In the pension insurance system there is an obvious need for strengthening the link between paid contributions and the future amount of pension; or in other words, to ensure that the amount of the pension depends on the contributions made in the past. In addition, it is necessary to consider options for raising the age limits for retirement and to increase the penalization for early retirement.

Regarding the privileged pensions, apart from causing inequality and inequity in the system, the differences between privileged and non-privileged (regular) pension beneficiaries also increase the burden on the state budget. Thus, there is a need to change the system of privileged pensions and to equalize rights deriving from various sorts of disability. Therefore, policy-makers in Croatia should review the categories of privileged beneficiaries and control (also if possible to reduce) the total number of new recipients of these pensions. In addition, particularly under the conditions of labor force deficit and huge expenditures for the pension system, more emphasis is needed on rehabilitation programs and inclusion of all persons with available working capacity into the labor market.

There is a need for smart and careful regulation of pension funds' management with the goal of limiting the burden placed upon the budget in the category of pension expenditures. In Croatia, there are constant discussions on the possibility and the need to freeze payments and/or eliminate the mandatory pension savings; the so-called second pillar. This is a dangerous idea, which could have very adverse economic effects, primarily through seriously jeopardizing Croatia's financial stability. Moving in this direction would lead to the breakup of confidence in the savings system, which has developed successfully over a decade and a half. Furthermore, this would be a gross violation of legal certainty, which would undermine the already weak rule of law in Croatia. Creating trust in some form of a public policy is a long and demanding job that requires dedication and commitment of all the participants, especially the beneficiaries. On the other side, breaking that trust is very easy and a fast, almost instantaneous activity, with long-lasting negative implications.

Due to unfavorable demographic trends and major misallocations there is a need to reduce pension rights, envision further reform of the pension system and enhance labor market flexibility, as well as implement structural reforms in the economy. Due to the complexity of the system and long-term consequences of any changes to it, it is important that the pension system should not be subject to unrealistic promises by politicians. Reducing the existing pension rights certainly causes opposition by citizens, but it is the only way to preserve the long-term financial sustainability of the system. Citizens should not have unrealistic expectations of the public pension insurance and the government in general. The most important thing is that the working age population realizes that they themselves should save more for their old age. Thus, they cannot and must not blame someone else for insufficient savings during their active working age. Therefore, it is necessary to systematically develop and promote voluntary pension insurance.

Notes

1. Parametric reforms are aimed at maintaining the basic structure of the existing system while attempting, through changes in the various main parameters of the system, to reduce the budgetary cost of ageing and/or to increase the incentives to work for older workers. These basic parameters include, for example, prolongation of the legal retirement age, increase of the contribution rate and the lowering of replacement rate.
2. Adequacy of the pension system means providing people with income in old age that allows them a decent living standard and protects them from poverty.
3. Net prospective Theoretical Replacement Rates—TRR (the share of an average pension in an average salary) at average earnings for Croatia is 40.2%; while for Belgium it is 74.7%; for Bulgaria 50.9%; for France 59.8%; for Germany 67.6%; Hungary 81.9%; for Italy 70.2%. Countries with lower TRR than Croatia: Ireland 38.4%; Poland 37.7% and UK 35.9%. (Source: European Union 2015: 27, Table 2: Prospective TRRs for the different core cases (net, average earnings) and underlying standard pensionable ages—SPA).

References

Anušić, Z., O'Keefe, P., & Madžarevic-Šujster, S. (2003). Pension Reform in Croatia. http://documents.worldbank.org/curated/en/318831468770635745/pdf/multi0page.pdf. Downloaded 14 August 2017.

Bađun, M. (2009). Pension Beneficiaries Who Have Been Granted Pensions Under More Favorable Conditions. *Newsletter 44*, Zagreb: Institute of Public Finance.

Bađun, M. (2017). Determinants of Disability Pensions in Croatia: The Role of Institutions. *Public Sector Economics, 41*(1), 109–128.

Bejaković, P. (2004). The Collection of Pension Contributions in Croatia. In E. Fultz & T. Stanovnik (Eds.), *Collection of Pension Contributions: Trends, Issues, and Problems in Central and Eastern Europe* (pp. 59–104). Budapest: ILO Central and Eastern European Team.

Croatian Bureau of Statistics. (2016). Women and Men in Croatia 2011. www.dzs.hr/Hrv_Eng/menandwomen/men_and_women_2016.pdf. Downloaded 14 August 2017.

Croatian Financial Services Supervisory Agency (HANFA). (2017). Statistic Pension Funds. Zagreb: Croatian Financial Services Supervisory Agency. http://www.hanfa.hr/publications/statistics/#section2. Downloaded 22 August 2017.

European Commission. (2014). The 2015 Ageing Report Underlying Assumptions and Projection Methodologies. Brussels: European Commission. http://ec.europa.eu/economy_finance/publications. Downloaded 28 July 2017.

European Union. (2015). The 2015 Pension Adequacy Report: Current and Future Income Adequacy in Old Age in the EU. Volume I, Brussels: European Union. https://europa.eu/epc/sites/epc/files/docs/pages/para2002_en.pdf. Downloaded 30 September 2017.

Hrvatski zavod za mirovinsko osiguranje. (2017). Statističke informacije Hrvatskog zavoda za mirovinsko osiguranje. http://www.mirovinsko.hr/default.aspx?id=723. Downloaded 31 July 2017.

Urban, I., & Bezeredi, S. (2016). EUROMOD Country Report Croatia. Colchester: University of Essex. https://www.euromod.ac.uk/sites/default/files/country-reports/year7/Y7_CR_HR_Final.pdf. Downloaded 28 July 2017.

Vukorepa, I. (2012). *Mirovinski sustavi: kapitalno financiranje kao čimbenik socijalne sigurnosti*. Zagreb: Pravni fakultet u Zagrebu.

Vukorepa, I. (2015). Lost Between Sustainability and Adequacy: Critical Analysis of the Croatian Pension System's Parametric Reform. *Revija za socijalnu politiku, 22*(3), 279–308.

World Bank. (2011). Croatia: Policy Options for Further Pension System Reform, Croatia Policy Notes, Washington, DC: World Bank. http://siteresources.worldbank.org/INTCROATIA/Resources/Croatia_Policy_Notes-Pension.pdf. Downloaded 28 July 2017.

CHAPTER 13

Health Policy in Croatia: A Case of Free Falling

Dagmar Radin

The system does not actually function at all, it works with Brownian motion. Brownian motion is a random movement of small particles in one space. When there is no air blowing, then the particles are doing a strange trajectory and it's called Brownian motion. Our system has no clear conception because no one has created it.
Former Head of Hospital, 2016.

13.1 Introduction

During the dual transition of the early 1990s, as part of the economic stabilization package conditioned by international lending institutions, and not unlike what other transition countries underwent, Croatia postponed most of its health care restructuring reforms to the second wave of reforms that would follow the macroeconomic stabilization reforms. However, the second wave of reforms, which required a significant restructuring of the health care system, never came on the government's agenda with the same urgency. As a consequence, more than a quarter of a century

D. Radin (✉)
Faculty of Political Science, University of Zagreb, Zagreb, Croatia
e-mail: dagmar.radin@fpzg.hr

Z. Petak, K. Kotarski (eds.), *Policy-Making at the European Periphery*, New Perspectives on South-East Europe,
https://doi.org/10.1007/978-3-319-73582-5_13

after its independence, and nine government administrations later, Croatia's health care system still suffers from the same chronic structural problems. As the second most costly sector of the economy, following the pension system, health care represents a so-called Croatian trademark (universal care for all, all the time) that needs to be preserved. At the same time, the system cannot survive for much longer because of the chronic lack of funding, outdated organizational structures, and a crony system of incentives causing poor working conditions and corruption, all of which are driving the best medical staff away, while hurting the end user—the patient.

While the Croatian health care system is faced with many problems today, it is helpful to present its main problems (and achievements) within the framework of its performance, or end goals (health status, customer satisfaction, and risk protection), intermediate performance measures or goals (efficiency, quality, and access), and the knobs controlling them (focusing here on the financing and organization) (Roberts et al. 2003). This will enable us to understand what problems lay at each stage of the health care system process and how these stages are interconnected.

One of the main challenges is the understanding of the state of the health care system in Croatia because of the lack of accessibility of data, which often either does not exist (it is not collected) or the data is guarded within institutions (e.g. Ministry of Health) that hold exclusivity over its access and use. Thus, beyond the data which Croatia is required to report to international organizations (European Union, United Nations World Health Organization, World Bank, etc.), or the data gathered in studies by independent organizations (e.g. Health Consumer Powerhouse) and which is readily accessible, data which originates and is stored domestically is often beyond reach, or poorly organized and unreliable. This is exacerbated by the lack of transparency in reporting of information on performance and financing of the system, which prevents any kind of reliable analysis and evaluation of the system. In fact, some have labeled the health care system in Croatia as the most closed off system regarding data access, excluding the military and defense system (Vehovec 2014). This seems to be, in part, a leftover of the processes that characterized the previous political regime, but also an indicator of the current state of democratic consolidation in Croatia where data openness, responsiveness and responsibility of the state towards its citizens have significant work left to do.

Available data and analyses from international organizations show a mixed bag of success when looking at the health outcomes in Croatia.

While Croatia performs well in relationship to its past and to the neighboring countries, or those in the same economic cohort, measures of chronic illnesses point out to weakness in the system's ability to address new health challenges, those that require a comprehensive, multisector approach, such as cancer and cardiovascular illnesses. More specifically, between 1990 and 2010, Croatia has improved its life expectancy at birth by four years, and outperforms its regional country cohort, and at the same time it has slashed infant mortality by more than half (World Bank 2014). Even so, Fig. 13.1 shows that Croatia still falls below the EU average in expectancy measures.

While Croatia has been able to address most of its health issues related to communicable diseases and maternal and infant mortality successfully, it does not perform well in respect of chronic illnesses and cancer. Table 13.1 shows a 14-year comparison of Croatia on some leading illnesses such as diabetes, cardiovascular illnesses and cancer. Additionally, Croatia is facing changes in its population structure due to the negative population growth and, in recent years, large-scale emigration fueled by economic stagnation.

Many of the chronic illnesses are related to the high consumption of tobacco products in Croatia. Despite the introduction of a law controlling the sale and marketing of tobacco products in 2009, Croatia's compliance with the advertising ban received a score of 7 out of possible 10 by the World Health Organization (WHO) (2012). According to the most recent data available, over 36% of Croatian adults smoke (World Bank 2015) with 21% of 15-year-old boys admitting to smoking every day (HBSC 2014). Part of the problem for which the 2009 law is ineffective is that it has not been accompanied by public anti-smoking campaigns, especially those targeted towards smoking prevention as well as cessation that have been shown to have a positive long-term effect (Bajde and Vida 2008; McAfee et al. 2013, Duke et al. 2015). Alcohol consumption, although on a path of decline since 1990, still represents a serious health concern. There is evidence of increased binge drinking among youth, and the per capita consumption of alcohol is still higher than the EU average (WHO 2017).

While the health indicators are dismal, the insurance system offers a high level of protection from financial risk incurred in health care. Namely, health care costs are covered by obligatory and supplementary insurance in the public system, which now covers most of the population. While the percentage of household expenditures spent on health care costs are about 3.2%, this represents an increasing financial burden on the population.

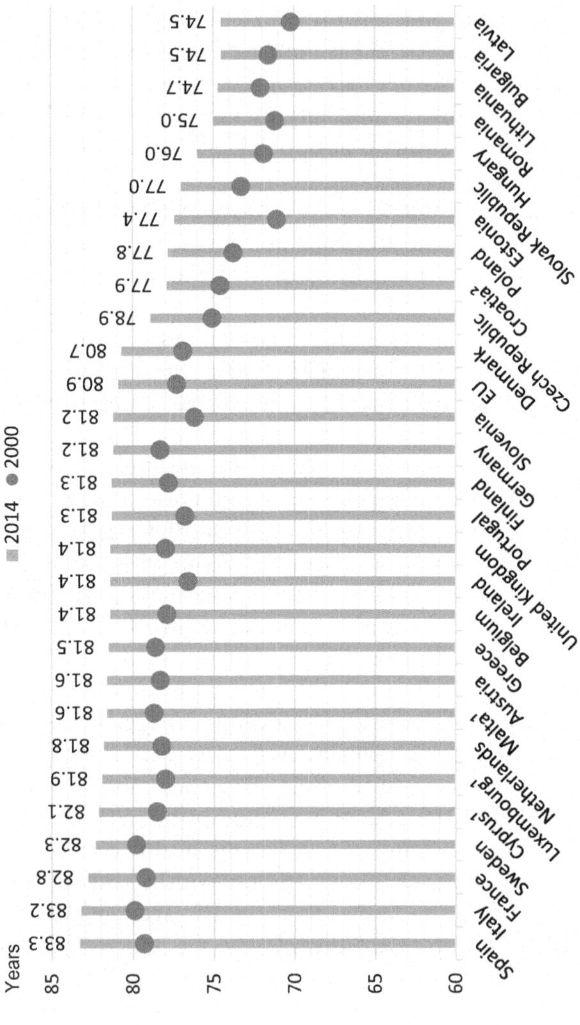

Fig. 13.1 Life expectancy in Europe (1. Three year average: 2002–2004, 2012–2014 and 2. For Croatia, the 2000 figure refers to 2001) (Source: Eurostat Database)

Table 13.1 Top 10 causes of death in Croatia

Illness	*% change in number of deaths*
Ischemic heart disease	17
Stroke	−12
Other heart disease	−48
Lung cancer	14
Colorectal cancer	39
Lower respiratory diseases	69
Diabetes	48
Falls	101
Breast cancer	27
Liver diseases	−28

Note: Growth rates are based on the absolute number of deaths

Source: Eurostat

Out-of-pocket payments for health care, whether it be additional supplementary insurance or visits to private practitioners to avoid long wait times, have increased and represent a substantial burden on low income households in particular (Mastilica and Kušec 2005; Broz and Švaljek 2014). When looking at patient satisfaction with the health care system there is a correlation between direct payments and level of satisfaction, where higher levels of dissatisfaction are correlated with higher out-of-pocket payments (Nestić and Rubil 2014), suggesting that to have a satisfactory level of care, one must spend more, in addition to what is being paid into the system through social insurance. While Croatia has an overall below average level of private funding of the health care system (15%) when compared to countries of Central and Eastern Europe, its out-of-pocket payments tend to be higher (17%) than the EU average (15%) (WHO 2016). Thus, while the system still provides protection from financial burden, there is a trend towards passing the cost of care on to the patient through the implementation of reforms over a 25-year period.

When looking at equity, access, and quality, despite its move towards the commodification of care and cost cutting trends over the decades, Croatia still upholds the principle of solidarity as one of the main pillars of its health care system. In that respect, access to care has not been affected, although wait times signal inefficiencies in the system and have an impact on equity, since those better off can use alternative private and timely diagnostic care, and thus effective care, compared to those from lower socio-economic classes. Part of this inefficiency is attributable to the fragmentation of the organization of the health care system where primary and secondary care do not work together effectively to provide integrated and timely care, resulting in redundancies of tests, unnecessary delays and suboptimal care.

13.2 The Dismantling of 'Care'

While the primary focus of this chapter is on the reforms in the financing and organization of the health care, it is important to note how these reforms fit into the larger picture of health care goals and aims. As a result of the health care system's inability to meet its patients' needs, the deaths are high from some illnesses, such as colon cancer, whereas prevention programs have been successful in mitigating deaths in other countries. While historically the health system in Croatia has been vested in and organized around hospital care, public health has also been a so-called trademark of the Croatian health care system around which the Andrija Štampar School of Public Health was founded as early as 1927.[1] While at that time considered a pioneer of public health due to the success in the prevention of communicable diseases through hygiene and sanitation programs, as well as vaccination programs, the role of public health in Croatia has not advanced much beyond its initial role. Thus, the holy grail of Andrija Štampar's public health principles of prevention, health education, and social determinants of health, among others, have remained mostly an ideological underpinning without implementation. Adding to this passivity of public health in Croatia is the arrival of the dual transition and with it, as we will see in the following sections, the storm of reforms which have moved the operational aspects of the system towards the market, but without considering the greater role that public health care has in addressing changing needs of the population. While public health officials have successfully addressed incidences of the spread of HIV/AIDS, for which Croatia had a very low rate of infection (HZJZ 2017), their ability to address issues of opioid substance abuse, high smoking rates and creeping obesity have not been successful.

The reforms that begun in the 1990s, which were mainly focused on cost containment, increased the distance between what should be integrated care and service provision, where the system has focused mainly on treating illness rather than integrating care around the patient.[2] The partial privatization of family practitioners further shifted the health care system away from primary care and prevention and towards more expensive hospital care by limiting their involvement with the patient once he is referred on to secondary care (Majnarić Trtica et al. 2009). Hence, instead of understanding how moving the 'control knobs' (Roberts et al. 2003) of financing, organization and management would affect the performance of the system, the health care reforms became firehose interventions used to put out burning health problems but without understanding its structural interconnectedness and systemic inefficiencies. The following section analyzes the effects of some of those reforms in the financing mechanism of the health care system.

13.3 Financing

There have been four waves of health financing reforms: 1990, 1993, 2002, and 2008. The goals of all the reforms have been to stabilize the rising health care costs, but their success to date is questionable (Švaljek 2014, Vončina et al. 2007, Mastilica and Babić-Bosanac 2002). The 1990 legislation's immediate attempt was to centralize the revenue and operational activities of the system to have better control over its financing and administration. The 1993 Health Care Act laid out the basic premises upon which the Croatian health care system is set up: inclusivity, accessibility and continuity. It also set up the Croatian Health Insurance Fund (CHIF) which, to this day, covers most of the health care expenses (about 85%) while the remaining 15% is covered through out-of-pocket payments and private health insurance (World Bank 2013), and is obligatory for all citizens. It is funded primarily through employer contributions and retiree contributions, while the state covers the costs for the unemployed and other vulnerable groups (children, war veterans, students, low-income retirees) from general tax revenues. However, although they are covered, presently the state is not fulfilling its financial obligation towards health coverage fully and on a regular basis. The result is that the CHIF is not receiving compensation for treating these individuals, but has the obligation to cover the services they use.

The goal of the 1993 reform, as is the case with the ones that would follow, was cost containment through the reduction of the type of free health services at the point of service, while at the same time laying the ground for the private health insurance system to cover additional services. Private health providers are not obligated to accept CHIF, and many do not. This was a significant departure from the egalitarian system where patients incurred virtually no additional costs at the point of service. While it achieved temporary cost containment, the system's health care cost kept rising so that by 2002, the World Bank estimates that Croatia spent USD 630 per person (low in comparison to other new member states) corresponding to 9.1% of the GDP (Vončina et al. 2006). The attempt to reduce costs on the supply side did not last for several reasons. In addition to an aging population, and the expectation of unlimited care, the Croatian health care system has other complicating factors that contribute to an inefficient health care system: outdated technologies, poor management of staff and resources, and inefficient infrastructure and its use (World Bank 2004). Another problem is that only roughly one in three able and working Croatians are contributing to the health insurance funds that are used to cover the costs for all. Thus, 1.5 million active workers cover a population of 4.4 million (now in decline due to emigration) (World Bank 2014). Thus, while the individual contributions amount to 15% of the individual gross income representing a significant portion of the income, they are not sufficient to cover the needs of the total population. Thus, part of the problem is that the attempts to contain costs are not accompanied by reforms necessary to eliminate the inefficiencies creating them.

After several 'bailouts' by the national government due to unpaid debt in the health system, the government passed and implemented another health insurance reform in 2002. It further limited the scope of coverage of compulsory health insurance, raising copayments, and introducing supplemental insurance for services no longer covered by basic insurance (specialist visits, hospital stay, etc.). However, it retained the safety nets for vulnerable groups. The reform did not contain costs or add a significant source of funding (through supplementary health insurance) because of the low insurance purchase rates, given the generous exemption policy to broad groups of patients. The escalating costs and rising inefficiencies were reflected in long queues (in part due to the financing scheme, which prevented primary care physicians from acting as 'gatekeepers'), which, coupled with the decentralized public procurement in the medical devices market, led to the 2008 reform. This last reform limited the exemptions to supplementary insurance, enacted more strict controls of paid sick benefits, planned to centralize the public procurement system (still not implemented), and introduced e-medicine to integrate all levels of care and prescription medications. The reform also increased significantly its revenue from supplementary insurance by 230% in just one year (Švaljek 2014). However, at the same time, the expenditures due to the supplementary insurance rose more than its revenues. Some argue this was caused by the increased moral hazard created by the purchase of an additional insurance policy, which covered everything including copayments, making cost containment measures impotent (Vukina and Nestić 2008).

While for a period of two years the CHIF was part of the general fund, in January of 2015 the Health Ministry decided to separate health care revenues from the central budget in order to gain better control over them. This has had little positive impact on cost containment because the government failed to address the significant causes of health care system deficits, including the soft budgeting principle of the Croatian Health Insurance Fund, which obligates the Ministry of Finance to cover the deficits; and the problematic and non-transparent funding scheme of hospitals, as explained in the next section (Vehovec et al. 2014). Furthermore, the Ministry of Finance has repeatedly failed to fulfill its obligation to cover services provided to vulnerable groups exempt from the mandatory health insurance payment as well as the out-of-pocket health care costs.

In summary, the reforms conducted over the past 25 years have mostly been focused on cost containment, but without regard to the inefficiencies that have caused financial problems and without the consideration that the funding structure may no longer be adequate, given the changes in the population structure and high unemployment rates. Part of the inefficiency is related to the organization of health care that has always relied heavily on secondary, hospital care and whose reforms over the past decades have moved the bulk of care even further into hospital care, escalating costs further, as is explained in the next section.

13.4 Organization

The organization of the Croatian health care system has changed since its transition, albeit it still suffers from old maladies. The state established a social insurance scheme that centralized all the funding, both in its initial phase with obligatory insurance as well as with supplementary insurance. However, there has been a slow trend in decentralizing the provision of care in Croatia over the past 25 years. This is in part due to the acknowledgment that Croatia is quite diverse both in terms of geography as well as health needs.

While the provision of care is still in large part under the management of the government (national and local), some portions of the system have transformed to allow the entry of private practice, which has brought contradictions in primary care. The first to privatize was dental medicine and pharmacies, followed by the primary care doctors. However, there are two tiers of private practitioners: those who established separate, independently financed practices and who are mostly contracted with the CHIF, and primary care physicians who work within the existing county system of health center. The latter ones were, until 1997, the main organizing units of primary care within the health center system (Katić et al. 2009) and operated according to the A. Štampar model inherited from the previous system, which placed the health centers at the center of the organization of the health care system. They were offered to become private holders of concessions (from being public state employees) within the health center and are almost exclusively contracted by CHIF. This has, over time, limited the scope and function of health centers and has fragmented the health care system into a series of unconnected units, primarily focused on curative services rather than health promotion (Rašić-Bakarić 2014).

The private sector also has clinics, policlinics and small private practices that are operating parallel to the publicly funded health system and is mostly used by those who want a more expedient process of care, but who must pay for it out of pocket, similar to private dental medicine. This creates a two-tier system of those who can pay for more expedient treatments, and those who are left waiting in lines in the public system.

Large health institutions (hospitals) are, for the most part, owned by the national government, counties, and the city of Zagreb. Health centers and general hospitals are owned and managed by the county government, while higher tier hospitals (clinical hospitals, university hospitals, and specialized hospitals) are owned by the national government. Emergency medical care is organized and managed separately from other segments of the health care system.

One of the problems with the organization of care in the public health care system is that their function and operations have not kept up with the changing needs. Namely, while chronic and terminal illnesses are now the main problem, which could be addressed at the public health and primary care level, hospitals (the largest generators of health costs) are still the center of care. It is only with the 2008 reform that the status and function of the health centers were redefined to include prevention and health promotion, in addition to its traditionally curative focus. Secondly, there is a discrepancy between ownership and responsibility, where county hospitals are managed by the regional governments but are not responsible for their funding, which comes directly, and is negotiated with CHIF, based on previous year's budgets (universal budget). Thus, there is ownership without responsibility where counties hold no responsibility for the (in) solvency of their hospitals, often blaming inadequate budgets for their financial troubles. As some note, in the private sector continually insolvent hospitals would, at some point, have to declare bankruptcy, but this is a politically and socially unacceptable option in a country where care is assured 'to all, and any time' (Vehovec et al. 2014). Thus, when hospitals become insolvent, the national government bails them out and takes control over them to rein in the cost and eliminate inefficiencies in the future. However, the scenario repeats itself; so far, 15 times in the past 25 years. Another attempt to redesign the role of the hospital occurred in 2014 with a new hospital reform whose implementation plan was funded by a World Bank project the same year, but is now struggling to get implemented. According to the latest implementation status report, the reforms are encountering substantial risks to implementation success, particularly in the political climate segment (World Bank 2017). Namely, due to entrenched interests in the system, any attempt to make significant changes in the system encounters counter pressures by some actors. In the case of hospital reforms, county governments have been some of the biggest opponents of the functional integration of hospitals because in some instances this would mean the closure of hospital units or departments (Radin and H.H 2016).

13.5 Stakeholders: How Special Interests Captured Health Care

The role of stakeholders is an aspect of the health care system and policy-making that is crucial to our ability to understand the dynamics of policy-making and its present effects, but that has not been sufficiently studied in the Croatian context. In Croatia, the formally strong, but operationally weak Ministry of Health is captured by special societal interests within the health care system that dominate the policy-making arena and influence the course of reforms in this system.

The Ministry of Health (MOH) and the Ministry of Finance are the most powerful, constitutionally vested actors affecting the health care system. There are other 'advisory' bodies within the national government that have formal access to the central government (the National Health Senate, and the Parliamentary Committee for Health and Social Policy), and their role is primarily to discuss issues and to advise the government on health policy problems and solutions. Other formal actors include the

Croatian Health Insurance Fund (CHIF), as the primary health insurance body, and the Institute of Public Health. In addition to collecting revenues for insurance and purchasing services from providers, the CHIF also defines the scope of services covered by the insurance, defines standards at which services have to be provided, and advises the MOH. It is a quasi-autonomous public entity, controlled by the government, which names the members of its steering committee. While the MOH is a formal and most powerful actor in the system, directing the system, there are different pressures coming from informal actors that make it relatively weak and non-autonomous. Among the non-governmental organizations, the most powerful are the Croatian Medical Chamber, the Croatian Medical Association, and the Croatian Association of Hospital Doctors.

There are several actors not formally vested with powers within the health care system but have informal power, and still others are actors with great interest but little power in the system. The *power vs. interest grid* (Fig. 13.2) (Eden and Ackerman 1998) illustrates the position of actors in the health care system within four categories based on their political interest (Campbell and Marshall 2002) in the issue at hand and their power to affect the issue's future. Because the grid only allows for four squares it

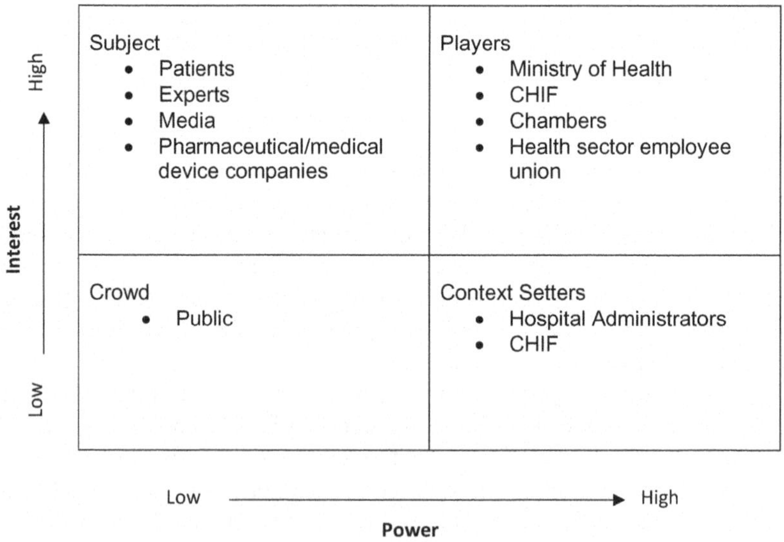

Fig. 13.2 Power vs. interest grid—health financing

overlooks the nuances in the degrees of power and interest, but it is a useful tool to begin the analysis.

The position of patients in Croatia is troublesome. There are several patient associations in Croatia, but they are powerless. Most of them are concerned with specific issues (rare diseases, disabilities, etc.) and out of the two main associations, one is almost defunct (it has no existing financial reports, and no members). The associations lack professional leadership and active membership numbers, and are directly or indirectly headed by physicians, which is problematic because of conflict of interest in representing patients' rights independently. One head of a health association interpreted this as a reflection of the fact that: "professional health associations are still not ready to give patients the right to make decisions, and the fact that patients are too passive and think that they cannot change anything …" (Radin and I.B 2017). Among other informal actors, physicians and in particular, hospital physicians, dominate the health care system, mainly through their professional organizations, associations, and chambers. Medical doctors are the second most represented professional group in the current Croatian Parliament with 16 physicians (11%, exceeded only by economists), a tradition that has continued over the years (Hrvatski Sabor 2017).

They nearly always, as an informal rule, hold all the formal positions in the system: they are ministers (all except one were hospital physicians), deputy ministers, assistants, heads of the Croatian Health Insurance Fund, heads of the Croatian Public Health Institute, heads of all levels of hospitals (something many of the interviewees considered problematic), heads of health committees in the Parliament, and so on. The single most powerful professional association is the Croatian Association of Medical Doctors (HUBOL). One former health minister illustrates the process which led to the dominance of this group in that the association was created in reaction to the work in shifts, and to the perceived passivity of the physicians' unions, which led them to solidify power by appointing their leader to the Head of the Medical Chamber (HLK) and by financing the Chamber, which was the target of an investigation. At the time of the interview and today, the Minister, the Deputy, and three assistants were all hospital doctors highly ranked in the HUBOL.

The professional medical chambers in the health care system include those of physicians, dentists, pharmacists, biochemists, and nurses. The chambers issue licenses to medical health professionals that fall under their jurisdiction. They also represent the interests of their professions in health care reforms, license private hospitals, and so on. When looking at their budget for the HLK as well as the Association of Employers in Health Care (UPUZ) in comparison to other informal actors for which such data was available, it is evident that their budgets are significantly larger (Table 13.2). While HUBOL does not have a large budget, their power comes from their ability to position their own members in key government offices as well as other groups with public authority (such as the Croatian Medical Chamber).

There is some form of cooperation between informal actors. The UPUZ, which brings together mostly heads of hospitals and health centers, and the medical chamber both reported having excellent relationship with one another. However, this relationship has been volatile as very often media outlets report that the two groups are in legal battles and there have been several examples of open public attacks coming from each side. When discussing this relationship, one former deputy health minister says that the two associations have 'mafia-like' properties in that since they could not agree on who would dominate, they decided to split the turf, the chamber representing (mostly) hospital doctors, and the UPUZ representing their employers. The relationship between the CHIF and MOH continues, but it amounts to bureaucratic relations and there is no real effort in cooperating to address problems strategically. The relationship between the media and MOH is limited because the only form of communication is through public relations representatives, while getting close to the minister is almost impossible; although there had been halfhearted efforts from a former minister to change that. Most of the communication is delivered through prescreened questions and administrative, written responses from the MOH. On the other hand, the relationship of the media groups with the NGOs and unions has been more open and coop-

Table 13.2 Budgets of nonprofit organizations in health care

Name of organization	*Total budget (2015)*
Croatian Medical Chamber (HLK)	\$ 3,700,000.00
Croatian Association of Medical Doctors (HUBOL)	\$15,000.00
Association of Employers in Health Care (UPUZ)	\$1,000,000.00
Coalition of Health Associations (KUZ)	\$9600.00
Coordination of Croatian Family practice (KOHOM)	\$33,400.00
Croatian Patients Association	\$0
Croatian Association for the Promotion of Patient Rights (HUPPP)	\$13,000.00

Source: Croatian Ministry of Finance

erative. Top down communication with the MOH is extended to the counties, who are owners of hospitals. The MOH communicates decision to the association of counties once decisions are made and there is an expectation of implementation. Thus, it appears that most of the actors outside of the government are open and view communication with others as positive and desirable, while at the same time they, with the exception of the medical associations and the pharmaceutical lobby, achieve little to no cooperation with the MOH. If the communication has varied in the past, it has been exclusively at the will of the minister in charge of the system.

On the one hand, this lack of communication between formal and informal actors and strategic placement of dominant actors at the head of formal institutions (sectoral capture) is only one of the reasons for the lack of strategic planning and continuity in health care reforms in Croatia. The other problems lay in how they view the problems and the solutions in healthcare. Some of the problems in the financial sector that the actors see is unsustainable financing, para-fiscal charges, not following the law, political distribution of money, social transfers, expensive and unavailable medications, and more. More specifically, actors see three reasons for which the system is financed in an unsustainable way: the state treasury not paying its obligation to the CHIF for vulnerable groups; the low employment rate which makes the contribution insufficient; and the excessive spending pushed by special interests, not the patients. The budget for health care used to be, until recently, part of the state treasury, which a former deputy minister argues was a better condition because it provided for multiple levels of spending oversight, but a former minister claims it allowed him manage the costs more independently. This multitude of views of problems and how to approach them, as well as the tradition of nepotism and clientelism creates an environment where health policy is a product of competition where the strongest actor wins, as opposed to cooperation founded on communication. As one former head of a hospital said, "In Croatia, in politics as well as in great things like healthcare, decisions are made at all levels. Everyone thinks they have the right to a decision, and now the only question is who is politically stronger, who is close to someone who will promote him, so that his idea is adopted whether it is a smart, or not so smart one" (2016).

13.6 Conclusion

The health care policy changes in Croatia over the past 25 years have been a compilation of ad hoc reforms that have secured financing by centralizing it into a social insurance fund, but has not done much to improve the administration, organization or personnel management of the system. Health indicators and data on patient satisfaction in Croatia point to the weaknesses in the performance of the health care system. The uncoordinated and selective reforms point out the overall lack of understanding of the scope of the health system problems by key actors. Unfortunately, the policy-making process in Croatia's health system has been hijacked by the most powerful special interests, resulting in suboptimal policy results.

Notes

1. Dr. Andrija Štampar was a distinguished Croatian scholar who is credited for pioneering the development of the field of social medicine in Croatia and beyond. In addition to being a scholar and practitioner, as well as the founder of the School of Public Health, he was also actively involved in global health activities. It is noteworthy to mention that he was one of the leading members and the first President of the Assembly of the World Health Organization with various international expert consulting engagements including China, the US, etc.
2. Integrated care, often used as a synonym of comprehensive care and disease management or complete care, in the terminology of the systems theory, brings together inputs, delivery, management and organization of care in order to improve access, quality, user satisfaction and efficiency of the same (Gröne and Garcia-Barbero 2001). Furthermore, Kodner and Spreeuwenberg (2002) create a patient-centered definition of integrated care to mean 'Integration is a coherent set of methods and models on the funding, administrative, organisational, service delivery and clinical levels designed to create connectivity, alignment and collaboration within and between the cure and care sectors.'

References

Bajde, D., & Vida, I. (2008). The Impact of Ad Characteristics on Adolescents' Attitudes Towards Antismoking Ads. *Managing Global Transitions, 6*(1), 75–93.

Broz, T., & Švaljek, S. (2014). Financing of Health Care in Croatia: From Reform to Reform. In M. Vehovec (Ed.), *O zdravstvu iz ekonomske perspektive* (pp. 51–75). Zagreb: Ekonomski institut.

Campbell, H., & Marshall, R. (2002). Utilitarianism's Bad Breath? A Re-evaluation of the Public Interest Justification for Planning. *Planning Theory, 1*(2), 163–187.

Duke, J. C., Davis, K. C., Alexander, R. L., MacMonegle, A. J., Fraze, J. L., Rodes, R. M., & Beistle, D. M. (2015). Impact of a US Antismoking National Media Campaign on Beliefs, Cognitions and Quit Intentions. *Health Education Research, 30*(3), 466–483.

Eden, C., & Ackerman, F. (1998). *Making Strategy: The Journey of Strategic Management*. London: Sage.

Gröne, O., & Garcia-Barbero, M. (2001). Integrated Care. *International Journal of Integrated Care, 1*(2). https://doi.org/10.5334/ijic.28.

HBSC. (2014). Health Behaviour in School-Aged Children – HBSC Croatia. http://www.hbsc.org/membership/countries/croatia.html. Downloaded 5 December 2014.

Hrvatski Sabor. (2017). http://www.sabor.hr/zastupnici. Downloaded 7 September 2017.

HZJZ. (2017). Hrvatski zavod za javno zdravstvo. https://www.hzjz.hr/sluzba-epidemiologija-zarazne-bolesti/epidemiologija-hiv-infekcije-i-aids-a-u-hrvatskoj/. Downloaded 8 September 2017.

Katić, M., Rumboldt, M., Materljan, E., & Gmajnić, R. (2009). Analiza stanja u obiteljskoj medicini u Hrvatskoj i nužnost promjena. *Medix, 15*(80/81), 51–56.

Kodner, D., & Spreeuwenberg, C. (2002). Integrated Care: Meaning, Logic, Applications and Implications – A Discussion Paper. *International Journal of Integrated Care, 2*, 1–6.

Majnarić Trtica, L., Strnad, M., Gmajnić, R., Ebling, B., Ebling, Z., Marković, I., & Šamija, M. (2009). Efforts in Fighting Against Cancer in Croatia Have to be Focused on the Primary Health Care. *Collegium Antropologicum, 33*(3), 709–724.

Mastilica, M., & Babić-Bosanac, S. (2002). Citizens' Views on Health Insurance in Croatia. *Croatian Medical Journal, 43*(4), 417–424.

Mastilica, M., & Kušec, S. (2005). Croatian Healthcare System in Transition, from the Perspective of Users. *British Medical Journal, 331*(7510), 223–226.

McAfee, T., Davis, K. C., Alexander, R. L., Pechacek, T. F., & Bunnell, R. (2013). Effect of the First Federally Funded US Antismoking National Media Campaign. *The Lancet, 382*(9909), 2003–2011.

Nestić, D., & Rubil, I. (2014). Privatni izdaci za zdravstvo u Hrvatskoj. In M. Vehovec (Ed.), *O zdravstvu iz ekonomske perspektive* (pp. 79–108). Zagreb: Ekonomski institut.

Radin, D., & H.H. (2016). Interview. Actors Involved in Croatian Health Policy Formulation. NEWFELPRO (Marie Curie, FP7) Research Project, 2015–2017.

Radin, D., & I.B. (2017). Interview. Actors Involved in Croatian Health Policy Formulation. NEWFELPRO (Marie Curie, FP7) Research Project, 2015–2017.

Rašić-Bakarić, I. (2014). Primarna zdravstvena zaštita između učinkovitosi i dostupnosti. In M. Vehovec (Ed.), *O zdravstvu iz ekonomske perspektive* (pp. 143–165). Zagreb: Ekonomski institut.

Roberts, M., Hsiao, W., Berman, P., & Reich, M. (2003). *Getting Health Reform Right: A Guide to Improving Performance and Equity*. Oxford: Oxford University Press.

Švaljek, S. (2014). The Recent Health Reform in Croatia: True Reforms or Just a Fundraising Exercise? *Health Policy, 115*(1), 36–43.

The World Bank. (2014). Croatia Program-for-Results: Improving Quality and Efficiency of Health Services. https://openknowledge.worldbank.org/handle/10986/20077. Downloaded 15 August 2017.

The World Bank. (2017). Health System Quality and Efficiency Improvement. Implementation Status and Results Report. http://documents.worldbank.org/curated/en/975841492432651926/pdf/ISR-Disclosable-P144871-04-17-2017-1492432636286.pdf. Downloaded 15 August 2017.

Vehovec, M. (2014). Foreword. In M. Vehovec (Ed.), *O zdravstvu iz ekonomske perspektive* (pp. 15–23). Zagreb: Ekonomski institut.

Vehovec, M., Rašić Bakarić, I., & Slijepčević, S. (2014). Challenges of Hospital Restructuring. In M. Vehovec (Ed.), *O zdravstvu iz ekonomske perspektive* (pp. 167–200). Zagreb: Ekonomski institut.

Vončina, L., Jemiai, N., Merkur, S., Golna, C., Maeda, A., Chao, S., & Džakula, A. (2006). Croatia: Health System Review. *Health Systems in Transition, 8*(7), 1–108.

Vončina, L., Džakula, A., & Mastilica, M. (2007). Health Care Funding Reforms in Croatia: A Case of Mistaken Priorities. *Health Policy, 80*(1), 144–157.

Vukina, T., & Nestić, D. (2008). Asymmetric Information in Health Insurance: Some Preliminary Evidence from the Croatian State-Administered Supplemental Plan. *Privredna kretanja i ekonomska politika, 18*(115), 24–47.

WHO. (2017). Alcohol as a Public Health Issue in Croatia: Situation Analysis and Challenges. http://www.euro.who.int/__data/assets/pdf_file/0014/340052/Final-report-Croatia.pdf. Downloaded 7 September 2017.

Databases

WHO. (2012). Global Health Observatory. http://www.who.int/gho/publications/world_health_statistics/2012/en/. Downloaded 13 August 2017.

WHO. (2016). Global Health Expenditure Database. http://apps.who.int/nha/database. Downloaded 20 August 2017.

World Bank. (2004). World Bank Development Indicators. http://databank.worldbank.org/data/reports.aspx?source=world-development-indicators&preview=on. Downloaded 30 August 2017.

World Bank. (2013). World Bank Development Indicators. http://databank.worldbank.org/data/reports.aspx?source=2&country=HRV. Downloaded 25 March 2017.

World Bank. (2015). World Bank Development Indicators. http://databank.worldbank.org/data/reports.aspx?source=2&country=HRV. Downloaded 17 August 2017.

CHAPTER 14

Education Policy in Croatia

Tihomir Žiljak and Nikola Baketa

14.1 Change of Education Policy in Transition

Croatian education policy was constituted after 1990, under circumstances where an independent state was being created, and during the breakup of Yugoslavia. After 1990 political circumstances were characterized by the process of abandoning socialist heritage. After 2000, the new cycle of education policy began, which had been marked by the process of Europeanization. This chapter analyses two cycles of change of education policy in Croatia, with the emphasis placed on the processes that occurred after 2000. In our analysis we use Howlett's elements, which are deemed important for the success of the policies: programme defining, policy processes and the political circumstances within which the education policy is created (Howlett 2012). Education policy changes in Croatia are similar to the education policy changes of most European post-socialist states. These changes were initiated by a political transition and resumed by severing ties with the old system. This process was followed by an initiation and a construction of a new system, as well as by bringing forth a new

T. Žiljak (✉)
Faculty of Political Science, University of Zagreb, Zagreb, Croatia

N. Baketa
Institute for Social Research, Zagreb, Croatia

Z. Petak, K. Kotarski (eds.), *Policy-Making at the European Periphery*, New Perspectives on South-East Europe,
https://doi.org/10.1007/978-3-319-73582-5_14

legislative framework. The changed elements were incorporated and institutionalized, new procedures were being routinized and new structures were being consolidated (Cerych 1997). During the transition, we can identify several important channels of influence by transnational actors such as the EU, UNESCO and the World Bank (Silova 2009).

When compared to, for example, the Czech Republic, Hungary or Estonia, Croatia's specificity remains in the fact that changes to education policy began in a war environment, which itself entailed difficulties for education policy (Koren and Baranović 2009). In that period, Croatia was marked by the constrained sovereignty, since the state institutions were being established only in one part of the state territory. The prerequisites for a unified education policy were created only when the state institutions began functioning on the territory of the entire state (peaceful reintegration of Eastern Slavonia, Baranja and Western Syrmia in 1998).

The first cycle of education policy in Croatia started in 1990 and was marked by the political, ideological and institutional deconstruction of the socialist education system. The second cycle began in 2000 and has been marked by the process of Europeanization. For the research of these two cycles, we rely on the analysis of general goals, actors and instruments. The basic course of action includes general goals that are established at the macro-level by the key governmental actors in the field of education policy (Howlett 2011). Classical typology of actors (state and non-state actors and various forms of partnerships and networks) is used in the analysis of actors (Birkland 2010; Howlett et al. 2003). On the other hand, we also use classical taxonomy of education policy instruments developed by McDonnell and Elmore (1987), supplemented by the market regulation (Mok 2005: 297), discursive dissemination (Jakobi 2009) and the nodality (usage of information and persuasion) from Hood's typology (Hood 1983). Instruments are divided into informing and persuasion, public authorities (including the market regulation), financing and systematic organizational changes. The relationship of instruments and their results will be analysed in the final section.

14.2 Severing Ties with the Old System in the 1990s

Key changes to education policy began with severing ties with the old system and establishing new goals and the new policy direction. The first President of Croatia, Franjo Tuđman, pointed out in 1990 in the Croatian

Parliament: "The old regime leaves spiritual and material emptiness in many areas, particularly in terms of schools and education. We both need to return to our general European education traditions and a thorough turn towards the future informatics era." (Tuđman 1990). This speech emphasized the goal of change: severing ties with the socialist regime, retrospective Europeanization and modernization of education. Under the idea of modernization, elements of retraditionalization of education were introduced into Croatia (Pastuović 1996). The return to the European roots and joining Europe is conducted through reaffirming the traditional national values. The Europeanization itself is introduced as a return to the European roots of Croatia, and Grubiša names this process the retrospective Europeanization (Grubiša 2006). The first cycle does not entail particular strategic documents that would determine the development of education and, after the radical political actions, changes to education policy were implemented incrementally. During the first years of independence, a series of changes was introduced. The most common instruments that were used were authorities.

The state used authorities in order to change the administrative staff in the school system and make a series of changes in management, as well as interventions to the system with the aim of severing ties with the socialist heritage (Klapan et al. 2001). This included subjects with emphasis on nurturing national identity (Croatian Language and Literature, History, Geography, Music), introduction of religious education, purification of Croatian language from loanwords, abolishment of pioneer organization in schools, and abolishment of Marxism and Theory and Practice of Self-governing Socialism (Koren and Baranović 2009: 96). Catalogues of knowledge, instructions and new programmes were used to change content that did not fit into the post-socialist system. Other than severing all ties to the old system, some elements of modernization were introduced, like the 1994 Information Technology plan and programme that have not been altered to the present day. Legislative changes occurred regarding the elementary, high school and higher education (HE), but most of the regulations were being conducted via bylaw acts. Key authorities were those of central government. At that time, the system was regulated by the central government through the competent ministry, determination of plans and programmes, employee salaries and supervision, while the local self-government provided certain support for renovation of buildings, part of the equipment, and so on (OECD 2003).

Organizational changes in the field of education were also common. Since 1994, education has been delegated to an independent ministry, and prior to that point, it was under the authority of the Ministry of Education, Culture and Sports. Indicative were the institutional changes with regard to the Institute of Education of the Republic of Croatia. Experts from the institute developed the curricula, conducted pedagogical supervision, compiled state analyses, conducted action, applied researches and provided professional assistance to teachers and professors. The Institute was abolished in 1994 by the decision of the minister at the time. A smaller number of employees were transferred to the Ministry of Education and Sports (MES) while the rest were either dismissed or retired. The unpopular occupationally oriented high school education was changed and traditional gymnasiums and vocational education and training schools were returned. Elements of Europeanization were also visible in the trades and crafts education that introduced a dual system with applied experience and the support of the Bavarian Chamber of Trades and Crafts (Miliša 2000).

For the most part, education was financed by the state; however, private education was introduced in the field of adult education and in the field of tertiary education, as well as in elementary and high schools, but to a smaller degree (Krbec 1999). In the market of educational services, an increasing part of the services was financed by the attendees themselves (Klapan et al. 2001), which particularly intensified after the Higher Education Act of 1996 was brought in. Babić et al. (2006: 30) concluded that "a very sharp 'market' game had begun between the faculties for 'self-financed full-time students' and 'full-time financed students'." In the 1990s, the Open Society Foundation (OSF) donated significant financial means for the civil society development, the media and various education programmes. However, it was not considered politically acceptable to state institutions, and financed organizations were presented as political enemies (Bežovan 2002: 81). In spite of that, the donated financial means of the OSF were, at the time, several times greater than the means of the EU (Bežovan 2002).

Nodality was used as a part of the broader political campaigns for establishing independence, strengthening the national consciousness and severing ties with the socialist heritage. The overall political climate influenced the education policy as well.

State actors dominated in education policy, especially those related to the governing party HDZ. In this fashion, these actors are given the possibility of arbitrary decision-making, while the decisions often depended on the current attitude of the key actor. Experts were allowed to participate in the initiation and discussion of policy recommendations, but their propositions depended on the HDZ's political filter. NGOs were divided into politically eligible and non-eligible, while the elite in power were motivated by the particular aversion towards organizations that were financed by the international donors (Bežovan 2002).

The key goals of severing ties with the old system, introducing national values and retrospective Europeanization were achieved. However, the authors of the White Paper on Croatian Education from 2001 claim that, during the 1990s in Croatia, "elementary and obligatory education is both structurally and content-wise incompatible with education systems in developed European states" (Pastuović et al. 2001: 11). This primarily refers to the duration of elementary education and the absence of a curricular reform. Antun Mijatović briefly described the negative sides of these changes, that the "broad area of belittling of already achieved advances in Croatian schools, belittling of the work of educational workers on almost every level of the system, disintegration of all resources of professional and scientific work in pedagogical and school practice, these are merely some of the obvious consequences where, under the pretenses of de-ideologization and confrontation with the Bolshevism, a vulgar primitivization of the idea of national education is being conducted. On top of that comes normativism, as well as unnatural and inefficient centralization" (Mijatović 1996: 1).

14.3 Changes Within the Europeanization Cycle

At the beginning of negotiations in 2001 for entry into the EU, a new policy cycle began and the Europeanization process[1] encompassed the educational system on a deeper level. It began by placing education on the agenda, connecting education changes with the process of negotiations. Furthermore, goals were harmonized with the goals of EU policies. It was followed by Europeanization of decision-making, implementation and institutional design.

The discourse of the Lisbon Process was transferred to the national strategies without particular questioning. Lifelong learning for increased employability of citizens and economy competitiveness within the society of knowledge was prioritized (Žiljak 2005). After 2010, Lisbon goals were transformed into the Europe 2020 programme, followed by a more distinct adaptation of national goals to the aforementioned goals in the

Guidelines for the Strategy of Education, Science and Technology (MSES 2012).

Invoking the notion of Europe as an argument or a legitimation was significant within these changes. A distinctive example of this was also the first draft of the Primary and Secondary Education Act in 2008 that emphasized structural, normative and content adaptation to the EU. Also, the Education Sector Development Plan 2005–2010 justified its goals by harmonizing with the European and global trends, while the implementation was based on financing by a loan from the World Bank and accessible EU funds (MSES 2005). The choice of policy instruments is also determined by the relationship with the EU. In this cycle, the tendencies to use authorities for drafting strategic bases of change are clearly visible. In the ensuing years, the Education Sector Development Plan 2005–2010 (MSES 2005), the Development Strategy of the Vocational Education System in the Republic of Croatia 2008–2013, and the unified Strategy of Education, Science and Technology in 2014, were passed (Vlada Republike Hrvatske 2014). The first significant part of the implementation of this Strategy was supposed to be the curricular reform. The essential role in this reform was given to experts and educational practitioners (teachers). However, influential actors (political parties, the Croatian Academy of Sciences—CASA, some interested experts) prevented its implementation. In the very controversy regarding the curricular reform, key public visibility belonged to associations that advocated modern curriculum (the GOOD Initiative—initiative for systematic and quality introduction of civic education in schools) and associations that advocated traditional values (*U ime obitelji*). In this manner, political discordances prevented its implementation.

Strategic decisions and legitimate assumptions were brought in for all educational levels. This referred to joining the Bologna Process (2001 in Prague), the Primary and Secondary Education Act (2008), the Act on State Matura (2008), the Act on Quality Assurance in Science and Higher Education and the Act on Vocational Education (2009), and the Adult Education Act (2007). Starting points of the Croatian Qualifications Framework (CQF) were brought in during 2008. The Croatian National Educational Standard (CNES) was introduced into elementary schools from 2006. Nearly two decades after they were brought into law, the National Pedagogy Standard for Primary Education (2008 and 2010) and National Pedagogy Standard for Secondary Education (2008 and 2010) were introduced and they are to be implemented gradually by the year 2022.

The Croatian education system still remains centralized to a significant degree, in spite of some measures of decentralization. In this cycle, the central state also brought all key decisions referring to the curriculum, employee salaries, textbooks, and supervision (Vlada Republike Hrvatske 2014: 45). In addition to the authorities, the state also uses organizational changes. In this period, institutional changes are used to alter the structure of organizations that participate in the preparation and implementation of education policy. In 2002, the independent Institute of Education of the Republic of Croatia was renewed. During this period, most of today's educational agencies were established and they became one of the key actors in conducting the education policies. They fit into the process of agencification and were formed as a direct outcome of pre-admission projects (CARDS – Community Assistance for Reconstruction, Development and Stabilization programmes) for institutional strengthening with the classical arguments, such as an increase of the system's efficacy. Key agencies were founded: Agency for Vocational Education and Training (AVET) in 2005, Agency for Adult Education (AAE) in 2006 and Agency for Mobility and EU Programmes in 2007. The process of de-agencification began approximately 10 years later. In the context of education, this was introduced by the merging of the AVET and AAE. One of the key generators of change was supposed to be the introduction of the CQF. It was considered a key instrument of the education policy (Žiljak 2007a).

In this entire period, nodality was relatively poorly represented. There were campaigns for enhancing the lifelong learning (Lifelong Learning Week), local campaigns for enrolment into high schools or university fairs. However, the very changes in education policy were far more influenced by the transferred European ideas, changes in financing or structural changes, as compared to the effects of these campaigns or education analyses. Information and data that revealed the state of education system had a relatively poor influence on the policy change. Programme for International Student Assessment (PISA) testing was conducted in Croatia in 2006, 2009, 2012 and 2015. However, published results did not provoke a discussion regarding the necessary education changes within the professional or general public. Data from the Eurobarometer, Eurostat or any other data related to educational attainment also did not provoke a systematic discussion or policy change, with just a few exceptions (Pastuović 2014).

The financial influence of the EU was becoming stronger in this period. It included a series of projects for structural changes (Žiljak 2007b).

CARDS programmes were the key financial instrument of the EU influence on the education policies in Southeast Europe and were, from 2003 to 2009, also significant for all institutional and programmatic changes in the vocational education and training, qualifications, adult education and partially HE (CARDS 2001–2004). When it came to changes in HE since 2001, the Tempus programme (Trans European Mobility Scheme for University Studies) had a significant contribution to the harmonization of HE, quality assurance, internationalization and the legislation changes. Financial means of the IPA, the European Social Fund and the Lifelong Learning Programme (later the Erasmus+) became essential. According to the Eurostat (2017) data, it is clear that the public allocation of national funds for education as a percentage of GDP was mostly below the EU average for approximately 1%. According to the available data, allocation of funds was between 3.71% in 2002 and 4.7% in 2015.

Other than the state actors, key actors in this cycle were the institutions that proposed strategic changes to the education system. This primarily included the CASA that initiated the processes of change with the Declaration of Knowledge (2004) and the National Competitiveness Council, which prioritizes education as an instrument for creating a competitive economy (NCC 2003: 8–23). By emphasizing employability, the inclusion of the Ministry of Economy, Labor and Entrepreneurship became more evident. The Chamber of Trades and Crafts also had an important influence in the changes of vocational education and training. An important role was played by the foreign consultants (key experts) as well, which transferred the educational models and provided meaning for the changes that had been occurring. Their participation in education policy was most commonly associated with the pre-admission programmes (CARDS) or with the introduction of CQF. Other than the influence of the EU actors, there was also a significant influence of the part of epistemic communities that transferred some of the key development educational strategies. Experts that participated in the projects of the Council of Europe and UNESCO were transferring knowledge of certain key education contexts (lifelong learning, civil education, qualification framework) to the state actors responsible for education policy (Žiljak 2007a). In addition, global actors such as the Organisation for Economic Co-operation and Development (OECD) were important in introducing PISA tests.

Key state actors increasingly acted according to the model of horizontal coordination, which implied that, in addition to the Ministry of Science, Education and Sports, an important role was also given to agencies, the Ministry of Labor and Pension System and the Ministry of Regional

Development and EU Funds. This confirmed the instrumental function of education: employability and balanced regional development with the support of EU funds. Other actors started taking more active roles—pupils, students and teachers. Regarding the actors that displayed dissatisfaction with the HE, particular emphasis was placed on the social dimensions of change (availability of education tuition fees, commercialization of education). Discussions regarding the changes in the Higher Education Act caused a conflict between a part of the academic community and the Ministry (Horvat and Štiks 2010). Such circumstances postponed changes in the Higher Education Act on multiple occasions.

14.4 Comparison of Goals, Actors and Instruments from 1990 to 2000 and After 2000

14.4.1 Goals

In the first cycle (until 2000), key goals referred to the reinstalment of values pertaining to bringing national identity into education, severing ties with the socialist system and the technical modernization of schools. In the second cycle (after 2000), key goals referred to achieving the society of knowledge with qualified workers that are both employable and competitive.

14.4.2 Instruments

(a) Informing and persuasion do not have significance in Croatia as they do in the EU. Research is rare and irregular, data is scarce, research networks are weak, public impact of research is small. The most important forms include campaigns for the enrolment into high schools and campaigns prior to the enrolment into HE. The first cycle entails key political campaigns that refer to the defence of state independence and severing ties with socialism. The second cycle emphasizes key values of the discursive dissemination of the EU goals that are becoming legitimate basis of changes and basic content of Croatian strategies.

(b) Both cycles state that the main instrument are authorities and are marked by the normative optimism. Ivo Josipović uses this term to describe belief (in his words "illusion") that changes in the law, regulations and acts will solve all social problems (Josipović 2002), which is why both cycles, and particularly the second, emphasize laws and regulations. In both cycles, the state is the key regulator that brings or approves educational programmes, and accredits institutions that provides certificates. After 2000, a portion of those roles has been taken over by the agencies. Laws also regulate the education market. In addition to educational laws, other laws that influence the market are also deemed important, such as the laws that regulate taxes (programmes of formal and non-formal education do not entail the same taxes). During the first cycle, the state brings decisions by adapting to the current political circumstances and educational needs (incrementally and ad hoc). The second cycle entails strategies (after 2000, 2005 and 2014) that present a basis for regulating education.

(c) Regular education is financed from the state budget, for the most part, in both cycles, while allocation of funds for education are small. Fiscal decentralization is only partially implemented. Privatization of education and the increasing number of programmes on the market is causing the portion of programmes funded by the actual attendees to grow (especially after 2000). The second cycle presents a growing portion of programmes that are being financed by the Croatian Employment Service (CES). Development of capacities in the first cycle was financed both by the state and the OSF. The financial means from the EU (Lifelong learning programme, Erasmus+, CARDS, ESF) are crucial in the second cycle.

(d) Organizational changes in the first cycle primarily refer to the severing of ties with the old system (from the reintroduction of gymnasiums to abolishment of the Institute of Education). The second cycle emphasizes important influence of changes within the process of Europeanization. Numerous educational agencies are introduced; important changes are expected from the development of the CQF.

14.4.3 Actors

From 1990 to 2000, key actors are the state actors, along with great influence of the party in power. After 2000, the state actors remain important, but do not simply include the Government and the competent ministry, but also agencies whose role is becoming increasingly important. Also important are initiatives and financing by the EU, as well as initiatives of the CASA. Non-governmental organizations, students, pupils and professors are becoming organized and influential actors that can both encourage or prevent changes.

14.5 Education Policy Outcomes

Most of the established goals were achieved during the first cycle (1990–2000). Ties with the former systems were severed (change of administrative personnel, change of the socialist content within the programmes, changes in the ministries and institutions). National values had become an important part of educational programmes (which is particularly visible in the History syllabus—Najbar-Agičić and Agičić 2007); actors that did not fit into this dominant discourse were marginalized. Modernization was observed through the introduction of informatics education programmes. At the end of this cycle, the state could take on the obligation for the overall education programme in the area of the entire state. After the state had been founded, education policy was supposed to provide highly educated and competitive workers that would guarantee development.

In accordance with the established goals in the second cycle of the education policy it is possible to refer to the goal of employment. Namely, according to the available data by CES (2017) in the period from 2004 to 2015, it is possible to notice certain trends in the recorded unemployment rate according to the level of education. The overall rate drops during the first four years, but this trend is followed by the continuous increase of the registered unemployment rate from 2008 to 2013. From 2013 to 2015, a mild drop was noted, as well as the return to the rate that had been recorded in 2005. The drop in the unemployment rate of the population with lower levels of education coincides with the economic recovery, Croatia's entry into the EU and, according to the data by the Croatian Bureau of Statistics (CBS 2017), an increase in emigration since 2013. On the other hand, the growth in the unemployment rate regarding people with completed degrees at HE level was suddenly growing during the five-year period after the Bologna Process was introduced. Therefore, according to data by the CBS (2010, 2015), the number of graduated students had increased from 17,391 in 2004 to 32,243 in 2010, and to 36,488 in 2011. This is why the goal of increasing the number of people with HE is only partially achieved since the goal was also to meet the needs of the job market. However, it is clear that a great number of people with HE still remain unemployed (in 2004 there were 20,500 registered unemployed people with HE degree, 29,997 in 2011 and 40,492 in 2014, CES 2017).

Results of the PISA testing can also be observed as one of the indicators of achieving goals in the second cycle. Four tests have been conducted in Croatia up to the present day. During the observed period, available PISA data demonstrated that significant progress had not been noted amongst the students in Croatia, not even within a single evaluated segment (natural science, mathematical and reading literacy). The results remain statistically significant below the OECD average (OECD 2017). Allocations of financial means for education were minimally increased during the observed period and were not harmonized with the established goals, which was also reflected in the lack of progress according to the PISA testing.

Furthermore, even though it could be concluded that there had been an increase in the quality of education according to the ratio of students and teachers concerning the full-time equivalent, it is still necessary to be careful. Namely, in elementary schools, the establishment of a more beneficial ratio was noted in the school year 2015/2016, as compared to the school year 2005/2006. Within the framework of elementary schools, the ratio was 14.45 in 2005/2006, while in 2015/2016, the ratio was 11.25 (CBS 2006, 2016a). A similar trend occurred in high schools. At the beginning of the school year of 2005/2006, the ratio was 11.91, while in 2015/2016, the ratio was 9.27 (CBS 2007a, 2016b). However, such change is primarily the result of a decline in the number of students. In the previously mentioned period, the number of students in elementary schools dropped from 387,952 to 320,017, while in high schools, the number dropped from 198,661 to 170,661. A slight increase in the number of teachers in the full-time equivalent was also noted in this period, but it entails 1605 teachers in elementary and 2454 in high schools. HE also experienced the decrease of this ratio (from 14.4 in 2006/2007 to 13.27 in 2015/2016), but in the context of an increase in the number of students by 21,537 (CBS 2007b, 2016c).

A few more indicators that reveal the failure at achieving set goals and ideas associated with the knowledge society include the innovation index, which is published by Bloomberg (2017). In 2016, Croatia had been ranked in 38th place, and 41st in 2017. According to the same index, but in comparison to the EU states, it had been ranked 24th in 2017.

Also, according to the World Robotics Report for 2016, Croatia achieved results that are below average. In 2010, it had 4 robots per 10,000 employees, and in 2015 this number increased to 19. On the other hand, the average for Europe generally was 50 in 2010, and 85 in 2015 (Jerbić 2016: 24). It should be emphasized that the Information Technology programme from 1994 is still in effect to this day, while the introduction of robotics does not emerge from the system of public institutions but is encouraged by private initiative, which suggests that it is uncertain how thorough and comprehensive it can actually be.

Finally, if the IMD Competitiveness Ranking is taken into consideration, it is evident that in the period 2006–2017, Croatia's ranking deteriorated. In 2008, Croatia was at 49th place and in 2017 at 59th place, the same as in 2006 (IMD 2017). A more detailed report (Schwab 2016) reveals that, in spite of large allocations per student in education (11th place) and student–teacher ratio (10th place in primary and 11th place in secondary education), it does not achieve the envisaged results. This is particularly evident in the education and skills pillar,[2] where Croatia was ranked 53rd. This reveals that the current investment in education does not bring forth the results associated with the competitiveness of the workforce in the job market, as well as necessary skills. Also, as mentioned before, the public expenditure on education as a percentage of GDP remains 1% lower than the EU average (see Table 14.1). However, it is important to point out that according to OECD (2016) the financial means are not sufficient for better performance at PISA.[3] In this regard, the inefficiency of the Croatian education system after 2000 is discussed in Sopek (2011) and Aristovnik (2012). Both of these authors show that the efficacy at different levels of the education system in Croatia remains low and that there is significant space for improvement. Sopek (2011) referred

Table 14.1 Public expenditure on education—(%) GDP

	2002	*2003*	*2004*	*2005*	*2006*	*2007*	*2008*	*2009*	*2010*	*2011*
EU (27 countries)	5[e]	5.04[e]	4.95[e]	4.92[e]	4.91[e]	4.93[e]	5.04[e]	5.38[e]	5.41[e]	5.25[e]
CEE-10*	5.04	4.92	4.79	4.72	4.81**	4.56	4.83**	5.04	4.84	4.66
Croatia	3.71[d]	3.93[d]	3.87	3.98[d]	4.04[d]	4.02[d]	4.32[d]	4.42[d]	4.31[d]	4.21[d]

e – estimated; d – definition differs; *definition differs for some countries; **No data for Romania

Source: Eurostat (2017)

to the issues associated with a great portion of students in public institutions, which entailed more resources that the state itself needed to allocate; modest teaching norms of teaching staff; the lack of meritocratic criteria for teacher promotion; and a subsidy system that does not exclusively focus on excellence and socially deprived pupils/students.

14.6 Conclusions

After 1990, since the establishment of independent Croatia, two cycles of education policy can be identified. The first cycle encompasses the period from 1990 to 2000, and the second cycle begins after 2000. These cycles substantially differ regarding goals and actors, but the difference in instruments is insignificant. Binding decisions and organizational changes in the system dominate both cycles. Public financing is minimally increased, yet the biggest changes refer to the European financing of capacity strengthening. Nodality is being minimally used—in the first cycle, it is mostly associated with broader political/national campaigns, while in the second cycle, campaigns with narrower focus are rare in education.

Differences regarding actors are also significant. During the first cycle, the key role belonged to a single party and its leader (in the semi-presidential system), which then uses state organs in achieving the determined goal. There are not enough influential actors that might initiate a discussion or jeopardize the implementation. Diversification of actors has taken place in education policy during the second cycle through the inclusion of non-state actors and the existence of clear resistance to implementation of individual goals. Other than national, the European actors, primarily the EU, are very influential.

All key goals of education policy in the first cycle were achieved. Success in achieving those goals during the first cycle does not necessarily entail a more positive influence on the final outcome of the education policy. What is important is the difference in the nature of goals that influenced the success of their implementation. In the first cycle, outcomes are associated with severing ties with the former notion of education, and reaffirming of traditional values, and this could be achieved with instruments such as binding decisions, changes in organizational structure and the level of financial investment. The goals in the second cycle demand more concrete results associated with employability and the knowledge society. In this process, it was not enough to use just the binding decisions and organizational instruments. The aims of this cycle demanded bigger financial investments, based on the research and nodality.

However, the mere increase in financial resources does not guarantee improvement in outcomes. Unfortunately, the underperformance did not become a political question or a policy campaign issue. Some other research and assessment such as The Programme for the International Assessment of Adult Competencies are not even considered. This indicates the neglect of nodality as an instrument necessary to combine with financial instruments in order to improve overall efficiency. Unfortunately, the change in instruments was largely absent and Croatia remains an underperformer relative to other EU states with regard to educational attainments.

Notes

1. Europeanization refers to: "Processes of (a) construction (b) diffusion and (c) institutionalisation of formal and informal rules, procedures, policy paradigms, styles, 'ways of doing things' and shared beliefs and norms which are first defined and consolidated in the making of EU decisions and then incorporated in the logic of domestic discourse, identities, political structures and public policies"(Radaelli 2003: 30).
2. It measures "both the quantity and quality of skills and the training that today's worker possess, as well as the level of education and skills of tomorrow's workforce, with particular emphasis on the use of ICTs in school and the style of teaching" (Sala-i-Martin et al. 2016: 57).
3. According to OECD (2016: 265) "Money is necessary to secure high and equitable performance in school, but it is not sufficient. Only one of the ten PISA-participating countries with the highest cumulative public expenditure per student up to age 15 – Singapore – is among the seven countries/economies where less than 20% of students are low achievers in any of the three domains. [...]What matters are how resources are allocated and the qualitative differences in education policies, cultural norms and professional practices that underlie the performance differences between and within countries."

References

Aristovnik, A. (2012). Relative Efficiency of Secondary Education: A Comparative Analysis of Slovenia and Croatia. *Knowledge and Learning: Global Empowerment; Proceedings of the Management, Knowledge and Learning International Conference Celje 2012*, 213–224.

Babić, Z., Matković, T., & Šošić, V. (2006). Structural Changes in Tertiary Education and Impacts on the Labor Market. *Privredna kretanja i ekonomska politika, 16*(108), 26–65.

Bežovan, G. (2002). Struktura civilnog društva u Hrvatskoj. *Politička misao: časopis za politologiju, 39*(1), 63–87.

Birkland, T. A. (2010). *An Introduction to the Policy Process: Theories, Concepts and Models of Public Policy Making*. London: Routledge.

Bloomberg. (2017). Bloomberg Innovation Index. https://www.bloomberg.com/news/articles/2017-01-17/sweden-gains-south-korea-reigns-as-world-s-most-innovative-economies. Downloaded 25 June 2017.

CASA. (2004). *Deklaracija o znanju – Hrvatska temeljena na znanju i primjeni znanja*. Zagreb: HAZU.

Cerych, L. (1997). Educational Reforms in Central and Eastern Europe: Processes and Outcomes. *European Journal of Education, 32*(1), 75–97.

CES. (2017). Croatian Employment Service – Unemployment Statistics. http://statistika.hzz.hr/. Downloaded 25 June 2017.

Croatian Bureau of Statistics. (2006). Basic Schools – End of 2004/2005 School Year and Beginning of 2005/2006 School Year. https://www.dzs.hr/hrv/publication/2006/8-1-2_1h2006.htm. Downloaded 10 July 2017.

Croatian Bureau of Statistics. (2007a). Upper Secondary Schools – End of 2004/2005 School Year and Beginning of 2005/2006 School Year. https://www.dzs.hr/hrv/publication/2007/8-1-3_1h2007.htm. Downloaded 10 July 2017.

Croatian Bureau of Statistics. (2007b). Academic Staff, 2006/2007 Academic Year. https://www.dzs.hr/Hrv/publication/2007/8-1-1_1h2007.htm. Downloaded 10 July 2017.

Croatian Bureau of Statistics. (2010). Higher Education 2008. https://www.dzs.hr/Hrv/publication/2009/SI-1387.pdf. Downloaded 10 July 2017.

Croatian Bureau of Statistics. (2015). Higher Education 2014. https://www.dzs.hr/Hrv_Eng/publication/2015/SI-1545.pdf. Downloaded 10 July 2017.

Croatian Bureau of Statistics. (2016a). Basic Schools – End of 2014/2015 School Year and Beginning of 2015/2016 School Year. https://www.dzs.hr/Hrv_Eng/publication/2016/08-01-02_01_2016.htm. Downloaded 10 July 2017.

Croatian Bureau of Statistics. (2016b). Upper Secondary Schools – End of 2014/2015 School Year and Beginning of 2015/2016 School Year. https://www.dzs.hr/Hrv_Eng/publication/2016/08-01-03_01_2016.htm. Downloaded 10 July 2017.

Croatian Bureau of Statistics. (2016c). Higher Education 2015. https://www.dzs.hr/Hrv_Eng/publication/2016/SI-1570.pdf. Downloaded 10 July 2017.

Croatian Bureau of Statistics. (2017). Migration of Population of the Republic of Croatia 2016. https://www.dzs.hr/Hrv_Eng/publication/2017/07-01-02_01_2017.htm. Downloaded 10 July 2017.

Eurostat. (2017). Public Expenditure on Education – Percent of GDP. http://ec.europa.eu/eurostat/tgm/table.do?tab=table&init=1&language=en&pcode=tsdsc510&plugin=1. Downloaded 17 June 2017.

Grubiša, D. (2006). Europeizacija politike: izgradnja kategorijalnog aparata europskih studija. *Anali Hrvatskog politološkog društva, 2005*(2), 129–145.

Hood, C. (1983). *The Tools of Government*. London: Macmillan.

Horvat, S., & Štiks, I. (2010). *Pravo na pobunu: uvod u anatomiju građanskog otpora*. Zaprešić: Fraktura.

Howlett, M. (2011). *Designing Public Policies: Principles and Instruments*. New York: Routledge.

Howlett, M. (2012). The Lessons of Failure: Learning and Blame Avoidance in Public Policy Making. *International Political Science Review, 33*(5), 539–555.

Howlett, M., Ramesh, M., & Perl, A. (2003). *Studying Public Policy: Policy Cycles and Policy Subsystems* (Vol. 3). Oxford: Oxford University Press.

IMD. (2017). IMD Competitiveness Ranking. http://www.imd.org. Downloaded 25 June 2017.

Jakobi, A. (2009). *International Organizations and Lifelong Learning: From Global Agendas to Policy Diffusion*. London: Palgrave Macmillan.

Jerbić, B. (2016). Robotika – Izazov novom društvu. Presentation at Faculty of Mechanical Engineering and Naval Architecture. http://www.cross.fsb.hr/docs/pdfs/pdf_drugi_dio/09_prof_jerbic.pdf. Downloaded 19 June 2017.

Josipović, I. (2002). Reforma sustava visokog obrazovanja i znanosti: tranzicija iz nepoznatog u nepoznato. *Zbornik Pravnog fakulteta u Zagrebu., 52*(2), 443–464.

Klapan, A., Pongrac, S., & Lavrnja, I. (2001). *Andragoške teme*. Rijeka: Own Publishing.

Koren, S., & Baranović, B. (2009). What Kind of History Education Do We Have After Eighteen Years of Democracy in Croatia? Transition, Intervention and History Education Politics (1990–2008). In A. Dimou (Ed.), *"Transition" and the Politics of History Education in Southeastern Europe* (pp. 91–140). Göttingen: V&R Unipress.

Krbec, D. (1999). Private Schools and Educational Policy in Croatia. *Revija za socijalnu politiku, 6*(3), 269–278.

McDonnell, L. M., & Elmore, R. F. (1987). Getting the Job Done: Alternative Policy Instruments. *Educational Evaluation and Policy Analysis, 9*(2), 133–152.

Mijatović, A. (1996). Uz temu-europski izazovi i razvoj obrazovanja u Hrvatskoj. *Društvena istraživanja, 5*(1 (21)), 1–2.

Miliša, Z. (2000). *Izvješće o hrvatskom školstvu*. Zagreb: Zavod za unapređivanje školstva, Ministarstvo prosvjete i športa.

Mok, K. H. (2005). Globalization and Governance: Educational Policy Instruments and Regulatory. *International Review of Education, 51*(4), 289–311.

MSES. (2005). *Plan razvoja sustava odgoja i obrazovanja 2005. – 2010*. Zagreb: Ministarstvo znanosti, obrazovanja i športa Republike Hrvatske.

MSES. (2012). *Smjernice za strategiju odgoja obrazovanja znanosti i tehnologije*. Zagreb: Povjerenstvo za izradu smjernica za strategiju odgoja, obrazovanja, znanosti i tehnologije.

Najbar-Agičić, M., & Agičić, D. (2007). The Use and Misuse of History Teaching in 1990s Croatia. In S. P. Ramet & D. Matić (Eds.), *Democratic Transition in Croatia. Value Transformation, Education and Media* (pp. 193–224). Texas: A&M University Press.

NCC. (2003). *55 preporuka za povećanje konkurentnosti Hrvatske*. Zagreb: Nacionalno vijeće za konkurentnost.

OECD. (2003). *Reviews of National Policies for Education: South Eastern Europe 2003 Volume 1: Albania, Bosnia-Herzegovina, Bulgaria, Croatia, Kosovo*. http://www.oecd-ilibrary.org/education/reviews-of-national-policies-for-education-south-eastern-europe-2003_9789264100725-en. Downloaded 6 June 2017.

OECD. (2016). *PISA 2015 Results – Excellence and Equity in Education Volume I*. Paris: OECD Publishing.

OECD. (2017). OECD PISA Results. http://www.oecd.org/pisa/. Downloaded 25 June 2017.

Pastuović, N. (1996). Upravljanje i reformiranje obrazovnih sustava: osvrt na reforme u postkomunističkim zemljama. *Društvena istraživanja, 5*(21), 39–58.

Pastuović, et al. (2001) *Strategija razvitka Republike Hrvatske – Hrvatska u 21. stoljeću. Bijeli document o hrvatskom obrazovanju*. Zagreb: Ured za strategiju razvitka Republike Hrvatske

Pastuović, N. (2014) Kvaliteta predtercijarnog obrazovanja u Hrvatskoj s posebnim osvrtom na strukturu obveznog obrazovanja kao čimbenika njegove kvalitete, *Sociologija i prostor, 51*(2013) *197*(3), 449–470.

Radaelli, C. M. (2003). The Europeanization of Public Policy. In K. Featherstone & C. M. Radaelli (Eds.), *The Politics of Europeanization* (pp. 27–56). New York: Oxford University Press.

Sala-i-Martin, X., et al. (2016). Modernizing the Measurement of Drivers of Prosperity in Light of the Fourth Industrial Revolution: The Updated Global Competitiveness Index. In K. Schwab (Ed.), *The Global Competitiveness Report 2016–2017* (pp. 51–77). Geneva: World Economic Forum.

Schwab, K. (2016). *The Global Competitiveness Report 2016–2017*. Geneva: World Economic Forum.

Silova, I. (2009). Varieties of Educational Transformation: The Post-socialist States of Central/Southeastern Europe and the Former Soviet Union. In R. Cowen & A. M. Kazamias (Eds.), *International Handbook of Comparative Education Part One* (pp. 295–320). Dordrecht: Springer.

Sopek, P. (2011). Efficiency of Public Expenditure on Education in Croatia. *Newsletter: An Occasional Publication of the Institute of Public Finance*. http://

www.ijf.hr/upload/files/file/ENG/newsletter/61.pdf. Downloaded 18 May 2017.

Tuđman, F. (1990). Govor u Saboru 30. svibnja 1990. http://www.sabor.hr/Default.aspx?art=1765&sec=444. Downloaded 5 May 2012.

Vlada Republike Hrvatske. (2014). Strategija obrazovanja, znanosti i tehnologije. http://narodne-novine.nn.hr/clanci/sluzbeni/2014_10_124_2364.html. Downloaded 6 May 2017.

Žiljak, T. (2005). Politike cjeloživotnog učenja u Europskoj uniji i Hrvatskoj. *Anali Hrvatskog politološkog društva, 1*(1), 225–243.

Žiljak, T. (2007a). Europski okvir za nacionalne obrazovne politike. *Anali Hrvatskog politološkog društva, 3*(1), 261–281.

Žiljak, T. (2007b). Izazovi i koristi CARDS projekta za strukovno obrazovanje odraslih (europeizacija na djelu). *Andragoški glasnik, 11*(1), 15–22.

CHAPTER 15

Cohesion Policy in Croatia: What Have We Accomplished so Far?

Jakša Puljiz, Sanja Maleković, and Ivana Keser

15.1 Introduction

Accession to the EU enabled Croatia to start using Structural and Cohesion Funds, as well as funds related to rural development, maritime and fisheries, which are commonly called European Structural and Investment Funds (ESIF) in the multiannual financial framework (MFF) 2014–2020. Since Croatia's GDP per capita, expressed in purchasing power standard, is around 40% less than the EU-27 average, access to the ESIF is an immense opportunity for Croatia to speed up its economic growth and reduce the gap with the rest of the EU. With a very scarce domestic level of funding for public investments, ESIF are perceived as the 'golden opportunity' to boost growth and improve the standard of living. Even though Croatia had a fairly satisfactory experience in using pre-accession funds, this is not an indication that the problem of absorption capacity has been solved. Quite the opposite: Croatian authorities will have to continue with investing resources into building the absorption capacity, removing key bottlenecks for investments and ensuring that available allocations from ESIF are used in the most efficient and effective way.

J. Puljiz (✉) • S. Maleković • I. Keser
Institute for Development and International Relations, Zagreb, Croatia
e-mail: jpuljiz@irmo.hr; msanja@irmo.hr; ivana@irmo.hr

Z. Petak, K. Kotarski (eds.), *Policy-Making at the European Periphery*, New Perspectives on South-East Europe,
https://doi.org/10.1007/978-3-319-73582-5_15

It would be a mistake to equate cohesion policy only with increased investment opportunities. For the EU's New Member States (NMS), as well as other states with lower governance capacity, the cohesion policy provides a range of additional policy benefits, which later translate into palpable benefits for citizens, businesses and other key beneficiaries of policy-related interventions. The most important of these 'intangible benefits' is the multiannual planning process, the application of the partnership principle, monitoring and evaluation techniques and opportunities for policy learning (Bachtler and Gorzalek 2007; Mairate 2006). The cohesion policy has also influenced decision-makers in member states in shifting national policy interventions away from the traditional focus on infrastructure and business aid to focus on human resources, innovation, community development and horizontal themes (Bachtler and Mendez 2007). These distinctive features of the cohesion policy have been particularly relevant for the NMS whose regional policies were quite undeveloped. The cohesion policy has been seen as an opportunity to learn how these policies could be improved and how more balanced regional development could be achieved. In addition, funding opportunities provided by the EU's cohesion policy represent a strong motivation for the national policy actors to transform and adapt their national policy environment to that of the EU's cohesion policy (Adams et al. 2011).

This chapter begins by exploring the issue of the absorption capacity in Croatia, with particular focus on the reasons behind the slow progress in developing administrative capacity for the management of EU funds. It also reflects on the approach to management of EU funds in the post-accession period. In the fourth section the main obstacles affecting the absorption of EU funds are presented. This section is followed by an overview of the importance of investments from EU funds for socio-economic development, emphasizing areas where EU support should substantially change the current policy approach. It deals with the interplay between the EU's cohesion policy and domestic regional policy environment, with reflections on the wider governance issues in Croatia. In the last section we conclude and point out the key challenges for absorption capacity in the future.

15.2 Accession to the EU and the 'Absorption Shock'

The issue of the administrative capacity has been at the forefront of Croatia's efforts to manage EU funds since the beginning of the process and the opening up of the first EU programmes for Croatia, from CARDS up to PHARE, SAPARD and later IPA programmes. Insufficient institutional capacity has been highlighted as one of the major constraints for more successful absorption of EU funds in Croatia in the various reports of the European Commission (European Commission 2010, 2015). By recognizing the need to support the building up of Croatia's administrative capacity, the European Commission (EC) has allocated a significant portion of pre-accession funds for improving institutions in the field of EU funds' management before Croatia's accession. However, despite the significant resources that have been invested into strengthening administrative capacity, results were limited and Croatian administration continued to struggle with the issue of capacity in the first years of membership.

The problems with institutional capacity have been particularly emphasized in the preparation and management of complex infrastructural projects (European Court of Auditors 2011). Continuous delays in the process of preparation and implementation of projects were common. This has again been linked to the persistent problem of understaffed institutions, but also with the lack of stronger political support to institution building. The establishment of the Ministry of Regional Development and EU funds (MRDEUF) in 2012 gave a political boost to the process of building up institutional capacity and putting the topic of EU funds much higher on the Government's political agenda. Nevertheless, problems with the lack of institutional capacity have continued since 2012. Along with the increase of human and other resources, as well as the political support, the level of policy challenges also increased.

Particularly demanding challenges stem from the timing of the accession, which implied a significant additional administrative burden. By joining the EU on 1st July 2013, the Croatian administration faced the necessity of simultaneously managing activities related to the transition from Instrument for Pre-accession Assistance (IPA) to Structural and Cohesion Funds, absorption of first post-accession EU funds covering the last six months of 2013, as well as the preparation of the new programming, legislative and management framework for the management of ESIF covering the period 2014–2020. All of this put significant pressure on the administrative staff, which, along with the significant increase in the level of funding and sectoral coverage in the post-accession period, represented an 'absorption shock' for all stakeholders.

Furthermore, the MFF brought a range of new features for 2014–2020, which also contributed to the complexity of the cohesion policy. These include, among other: 'thematic concentration', which drives the investments from ESIF into thematic objectives closely connected to the Europe 2020 objectives; the so called 'performance framework', stipulating that part of the funding will be made available only in the case of fulfilment of target values of selected indicators; and the introduction of the so called 'ex-ante conditionalities', which required member states to secure necessary pre-conditions mainly in terms of strategic policy framework before the funding starts. New territorial development instruments with a specific set of rules, the Integrated Territorial Investments (ITI) were also launched. All of these new instruments and requirements meant that key national institutions dealing with coordination and management of EU funds had to increase their institutional capacity to effectively deal with the challenges before them. This also meant that the success in the absorption of ESIF into the new MFF had become more dependent on the capacity of the sectoral bodies to improve their policies.

15.3 Approach to Management of ESIF in the MFF 2014–2020

Policy response to the abovementioned challenges has started with the designation of the appropriate institutional framework for the 2014–2020 period. An important lesson from the pre-accession period has been the need to reduce the number of bodies in charge of managing the implementation of programming documents. Namely, keeping a rather high number of managing authorities from the period 2007–2013, in combination with their weak administrative capacity, could become a major problem for the administrative efficiency in the period 2014–2020, especially due to the strong increase in the size of funding. Having that in mind, the government decided that a better option would be to build up coordination and management capacity in a smaller number of institutions. As a result of this approach, the number of managing authorities has been reduced from five to three, while the number of programming documents has been reduced from seven to five.[1]

However, there was also a negative side effect in taking this approach, in the form of additional administrative effort that had to be invested into carrying out this significant change of institutional framework.[2] An additional effort was needed not only in 2013, but also during the whole period of implementation of the financial perspective in 2007–2013, which finished at the end of 2016, meaning that Croatia had been running simultaneously different institutional settings throughout the period.[3] The new institutional post-accession framework deprived regional units of any role in the management of EU funds, as was the case in the pre-accession period. Even though there has been a clear evidence on the growing institutional capacity in the form of the established network of development agencies in charge of the preparation and implementation of EU-funded projects and some authors called for the involvement of regional bodies in implementation (IRMO 2011; Bache and Tomšić 2010; Đulabić and Manojlović 2011), arguments for the more simplified institutional structure with stronger administrative capacity have prevailed. Croatia followed the practice of new member states, which have, with the exception of Poland, opted for a centralized approach in the management of EU funds in the first years after accession (Bachtler et al. 2014). This means that regional actors have been engaged mainly in activities related to the preparation of project proposals and their implementation, while programming, the selection of projects and their monitoring have been managed by the central level institutions. The only exception to this approach was applied in the case of seven major cities, which have been authorized to perform the project selection within the framework of the already mentioned ITI instrument. However, it should be noted that this delegation was the result of the stipulations from ESIF regulations, which prescribe that cities included in the ITI approach have to take part in the management process, at least to the level of the selection of projects.

The first test for the capacity of the new institutional structure—timely preparation of the programming documents for the period 2014–2020—has been successfully carried out and by the end of 2014 Croatia managed to receive the approval of the European Commission for three major documents (Partnership Agreement, Operational Programme Competitiveness and Cohesion and Operational Programme Efficient Human Resources), which covered in total 8.4 billion out of 10.7 billion euro of total ESIF.[4] However, this has been only the first step on the road to successful absorption of EU funds.

15.4 The Main Obstacles Affecting the Absorption of EU Funds

The latest data on member states' performance in drawing EU funds from the 2007–2013 period show that the absorption rate, measured as the ratio between funds allocated and actually spent, has reached 81% for

Croatia, which is the lowest rate among the member states. Next to Croatia is Romania, in which the absorption rate achieved 90%, while the EU average is 94.45% (see Fig. 15.1). These results show that, despite the effort undertaken and progress achieved, the issue of absorption capacity still remains a major problem for Croatia, especially having in mind the size of ESI funding for the period 2014–2020.

The first results on the contracting and absorption in the 2014–2020 period confirm that Croatia's performance is still far below the average. Based on the data from the European Commission, on 31st of July 2017 Croatia has been placed on the 24th place according to the contracting rate (22.3%) which is significantly below the EU average (36.5%).[5] A similar situation occurs with payments, where Croatia is placed on the 23rd place with 2.7% of the total allocation spent on projects so far, while the EU average is 5.0%.

A more detailed overview of reasons for the persistence of significant problems with the absorption of EU funds reveals the full complexity and challenges of the underlying situation. On the one hand, the increased recruitment in the management system is followed by high staff turnover (European Commission 2016) whereby, in most cases, an experienced staff member leaves a post and a less experienced person is employed,

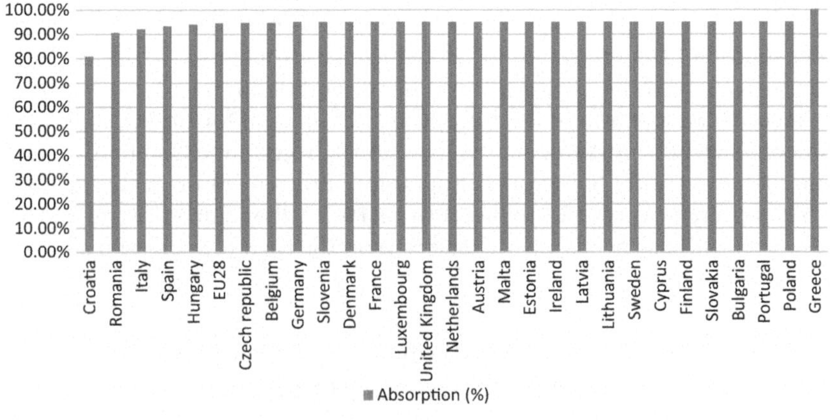

Fig. 15.1 Total percentage of available funds paid out by the Commission as a part of 2007–2013 EU's financial perspective (Source: European Commission, https://cohesiondata.ec.europa.eu)

meaning that retention policy is still an issue. Furthermore, the problem also lies within some of the major beneficiaries of EU funding, such as public companies and agencies like port authorities, Croatian Railways, Croatian Roads, local and regional utilities, and so forth, where the capacity to prepare, tender and operate complex infrastructural projects according to the procedures required by the ESIF is still lacking. Their organizational transformation and adaptation to the new and stricter regime of preparation and management of projects is progressing too slowly, thereby delaying the implementation of projects. This issue is partly related to the fragmented territorial organization of the country, which results in, for example, an extremely large number of utility companies at the local and regional level, but with a low capacity to manage larger infrastructural projects. In some areas, such as broadband development, waste and water treatment facilities, RDI infrastructure and others, there is a poor previous track record of similar investments, meaning that the technical and other expertise within central or local administration (and in some cases also in the construction sector) is lacking in comparison to the needs.

Other obstacles include well-known issues related to the investment climate in general, such as problems of slow resolution of property ownership issues, lengthy expropriation procedures, mismatches between the cadastre, land registry and the actual situation, differing administrative treatment of the same issues across different public administration bodies, and so on (European Commission 2017). Solving these problems will be neither simple nor quick, thus requiring patient and persistent work on their removal. An important advantage that should be exploited by Croatian policy-makers is that the EU funds, for example, allow funding of the activities that should enable removal of at least some of these obstacles through technical assistance projects.

15.5 Importance of Investments from EU Funds for Socio-Economic Development

Cohesion policy plays a very important role in development and public investments of NMS. Significant inflow of transfers from the EU to NMS has had considerable positive impact on their economic growth. Estimates show that investments from cohesion policy programmes have raised GDP in those countries on an annual basis in the range of 0.8% for Slovenia up to 2.1% in Latvia (European Commission 2014: 232). Investments from EU sources were crucial in helping the less developed member states to mitigate the fall in public investments due to the financial and economic crisis. According to the Commission's data, in the period 2011–2013, European Regional Development Fund (ERDF), European Social Fund (ESF), and Cohesion Fund allocations together with national co-financing ranged from 30% (Slovenia) to almost 85% (Slovakia) of total public investments (European Commission 2014: 156).

In the period 2014–2020 the total allocation for Croatia from ESIF amounts to 10.7 billion euro, which is over 3% of GDP on an annual basis or about 10 times as much as for the period 2007–2013. Such a significant allocation means that figures on the share of EU funding in total public investments for Croatia could also reach a very high share in the next couple of years, probably closer to Slovakia than Slovenia, under the assumption of the existence of the necessary absorption capacity. However, besides the direct financial effect of investments, accession to the EU implies for Croatia the possibility to significantly change the structure of the public investments and, consequently, to increase their effectiveness in boosting the country's long-term competitiveness. This becomes clear once the sectoral distribution of the ESIF is examined.

The need to clearly connect investments from the ESIF with selected thematic objectives is set by the regulation on ESIF. Application of the rule has created a new investment environment for Croatia compared to the one before accession. Policy areas like research, development and innovation (RDI), entrepreneurship, waste treatment, digital society, urban development, energy efficiency, railway network and others have faced a dramatic increase in funding opportunities in comparison with the level of funding from domestic sources. On the other hand, some investments in areas that have been highly preferred for years by national funding, such as road infrastructure and small-scale social and communal infrastructure, have received much less attention.

As shown in Fig. 15.2, most of the funding has been allocated to the area of environmental protection, which covers mainly big infrastructure projects in water and waste treatment facilities. This is no surprise given the significant obligations that Croatia still needs to fulfil with regard to the relevant EU directives in the water and the waste sector, which require significant investments. The second most important area is the support for the competitiveness of small and medium-sized enterprises (SMEs) where Croatia invested in relative terms even more than the EU average. With

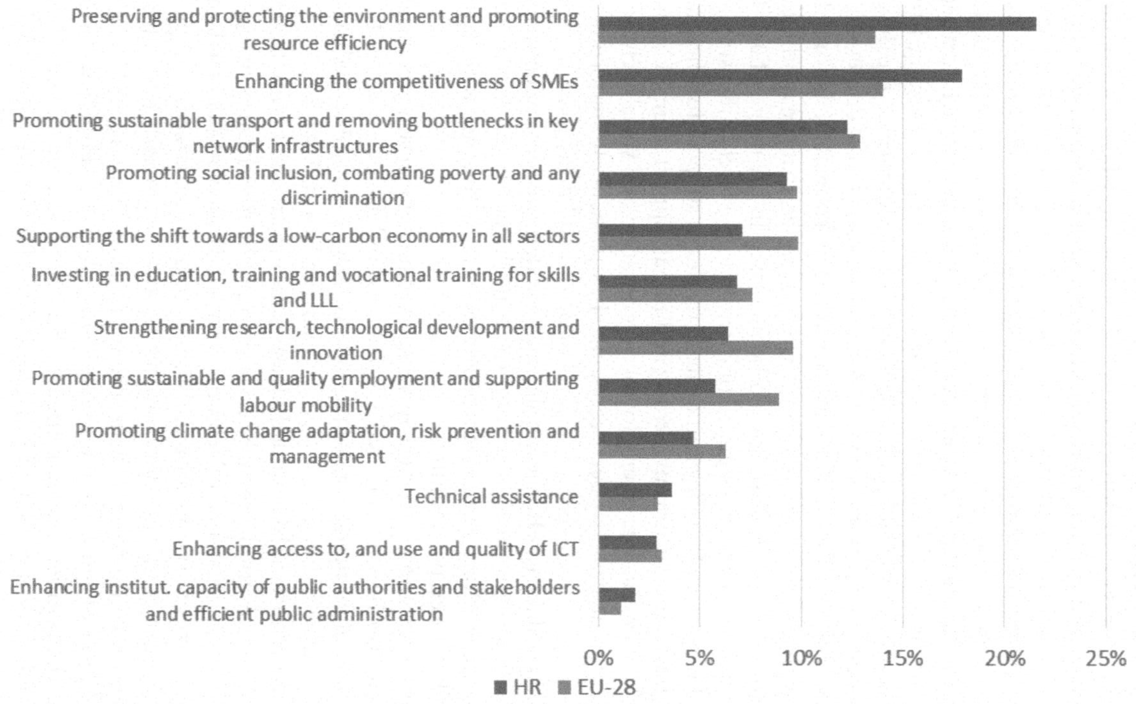

Fig. 15.2 Distribution of ESI funds 2014–2020 per thematic objectives (Source: European Commission, https://cohesiondata.ec.europa.eu)

the average annual allocation of 140 million euro just from ESIF, the support for entrepreneurship has been considerably increased in comparison to the national level of funding before the accession, when it amounted approximately to 25–30 million euro.[6] In the case of transport infrastructure, the most important change lies in the new structure of investments, as the railways are becoming the key priority, particularly the railway network that lies on the main EU corridors. One of the most striking changes in the level of financing has been occurring in the case of RDI, where significant funds are allocated for various types of support, ranging from investments into public and private RDI facilities to support for the development of new products and services. A simple comparison of domestically funded expenditures for similar activities in supporting RDI before the accession with available funding from EU funds shows that the funding of RDI activities on a yearly basis should be increased in the range of 10–15 times.[7] Another area where a significant increase in the level of investments is expected is energy efficiency and other activities in support for the transition to a low-carbon economy. Strong additional support from EU funds is also available in the area of employment, education and social inclusion. ICT development has also been recognized as particularly important in order to improve the currently low level of broadband development, especially in the rural areas. On the whole, it seems that the sectoral composition of EU funding is much more aligned with the needs and factors that enhance Croatia's long-term competitiveness than is the case with solely domestically funded programmes.

Another expectation is that the increased volume of investments should be followed also by the increased efficiency of public investments. Low efficiency of public-funded investments has been a well observed weak point of Croatia's public sector (see for example World Bank 2016). The growing importance of EU-funded investments in Croatia also implies the spill-over effect of good practices related to public investments management, such as the existence of relevant strategic framework; detailed and well-defined procedures on submission, selection and contracting of projects proposals; the independent project proposal appraisal; and strong monitoring and control mechanisms, particularly with regard to the implementation of public procurement. However, one should not overemphasize the positive effect of the conditionality mechanisms from the cohesion policy, as they will still be constrained by the previously elaborated obstacles for investments.

15.6 The Interplay Between the EU's Cohesion Policy and Croatia's Regional Policy Environment

Domestic public policies in Croatia, as was the case in other Central and Eastern Europe (CEE) countries, were strongly influenced by the EU enlargement and the process of conditionality. The impact of the accession process in the case of Croatia as the latest country joining the EU has been even stronger, particularly due to more extensive application of political criteria, as a result of the lessons learned from the 2004 and 2007 enlargements (Bojinovic Fenko and Urlic 2015). Croatia's regional policy has been one of those policy areas where the impact of accession has been substantial in the sense of strong policy-building effect. This effect can be undoubtedly connected to the low level of domestic regional policy development at the beginning of the process of accession, as has been noted in other CEE countries (Hughes et al. 2004).

For the process of shaping the new regional policy the role of the pre-accession instruments has been crucial as they provided on the one hand the incentive for the policy-building process and on the other hand the technical assistance necessary to carry out various policy-building projects. Consequently, all key documents related to regional policy in the pre-accession period—The National Strategy of Regional Development, the first Law on Regional Development, methodologies on the development level assessment of local and regional units, and so on—have been prepared as an outcome of the technical assistance projects funded from the pre-accession instruments (Zakon o regionalnom razvoju RH 2009; Zakon o regionalnom razvoju RH 2015).

Even though pre-accession instruments played a significant role in strengthening the capacity of domestic regional policy, the policy itself did not receive particular attention in the accession process. This has been similar to the case of other NMS, where the technical and institutional aspects, rather than strategic problems, were the primary interest during the accession process covering Chapter 22 on Regional Policy (Palne Kovacs 2016: 306). However, this will be a major challenge for overall Croatian public policy development in the forthcoming period since it seems that the Croatian approach to governance is, among other things, connected with the failure in achieving all types of coordination. The system of coordination is still based on ad hoc assessments of proposed policies and not on standard policy analysis tools (Petak 2009).

A further segment in which the preparations for cohesion policy were a major driver of change relates to the introduction of strategic planning as a concept. This has been a major novelty in the regional policy field but it also represented a novelty in other related policy areas. (Maleković and Puljiz 2009; Đulabić and Manojlović 2011:1063; Liha Matejiček 2014: 182).

The introduction of strategic planning related not only to the clear definition of methodology for the preparation of strategic documents at the national and regional level, but also to programme monitoring and evaluation. It was within the framework of regional policy that the first evaluations were implemented in Croatia, with the obligatory evaluations for county development strategies imposed and the evaluations of the National Regional Development Strategy implemented. It remains to be seen, however, to what extent ex-post evaluations will trigger improvements and a change in the current regional policy. Experience with regional policy strategic planning has been one of the contributing factors, together with programming process for the ESIF and preparation of National Reform Programmes, for the work on building the national strategic planning framework. MRDEUF, as the key coordinating body for strategic planning, has, in 2017, prepared a draft of the Law on the System for Strategic Planning, which aims at enabling a more coherent and better coordinated approach to national strategic planning (Bajo and Puljiz 2017).

The process of regional policy building also continues after the accession. New development themes, issues and concepts promoted by the cohesion policy, such as the already mentioned integrated territorial investments, but also functional urban regions and peri-urban development, are raising awareness and knowledge related to regional and local development. This refers not only to the regional policy-makers, but also to sectoral policy actors as well. Another important benefit from the cohesion policy is that these new concepts have been followed with substantial funding available through ESIF, which will enable their proper testing in reality. The lack of stable sources of funding has too often been a serious problem for the introduction of new concepts of regional policy in Croatia. Still, it is too early to judge as to the success of the application of these new approaches in practice, as their implementation is in an early phase.

Besides the positive impact at the central level, pre-accession instruments and changes to the national regional policy framework, the impact of cohesion policy concepts in supporting the local and regional empowerment was also not negligible. While many regional and local actors in

Croatia initially perceived preparations for participation in cohesion policy from the standpoint of new and abundant funding possibilities, the actual value of the policy transformation was perceived at much later stage (Maleković et al. 2011). This is, however, gradually changing, partly as a result of continuous and extensive awareness raising, training and all forms of capacity building, financed by pre-accession and ESIF, but also as the result of application of the partnership principle and higher involvement of regional and local actors in the discussion on shaping the national regional policy and absorption of ESIF (Keser et al. 2015).

The process of establishment of the county development agencies in the period before the accession is another example of the influence of policy concepts related to the cohesion policy. This process brought new actors on the scene with the primary task of supporting the process of preparation and implementation of development projects, but also of improving the coordination and strategic planning capacities at the regional level. Their role was particularly observed in raising the capacity of other actors in their counties, as well as providing all the necessary support to actors and practitioners engaged in project preparation and implementation (Đulabić and Manojlović 2011). The initial boost to the higher legitimacy of counties and county development agencies in the national context came through the Act on Regional Development of the Republic of Croatia from 2009, which officially entitled county agencies as the regional coordinating bodies. Also, through the new Act on Regional Development, from 2015 this role has been further strengthened and elaborated in more detail. In that respect, it may be concluded that the pre-accession and ESIF created a synergy between increased funding and policy-learning opportunities. This provided a good ground for the regional institutional-building process.

15.7 Concluding Remarks

The complexity of cohesion policy stems not only from the highly normative implementation procedures, resulting in a significant administrative burden for all participating sides, but also from its multi-sectoral and multi-level governance nature. The ambition to put sectoral policies into a common and coherent policy framework is not an easy task in any country and particularly not in countries like Croatia with a dominant sectoral approach in policy-making and lack of tradition and expertise in policy coordination. A similar situation can be seen in the culture of building partnerships between the central, regional and local level in policy design and implementation, which is a very demanding exercise for countries like Croatia with a long-standing tradition of a centralized approach in policy-making. In such circumstances, the increasing quality of governance in various policy fields related to the absorption of EU funds seems as a necessary ingredient of building Croatia's absorption capacity. Another more specific and related aspect is the level of knowledge and understanding that is built into the sectoral policies and regional policy and which needs to be continuously deepened to achieve desired effects from policy interventions.

Following previous observations on the interplay between the EU's cohesion policy and domestic (regional) policy, there is no doubt today that the influence of cohesion policy on governance was unequivocally strong. The very introduction of cohesion policy principles was distinctively persuasive for the promotion of institutionalization of a new role for both central government-level policy-makers, as well as for local and regional stakeholders and actors. New evidence points to their continuously rising sense of ownership, responsibility and accountability in regard to the implementation of regional policy measures and initiatives. When observing the achieved improvements in public planning and policy management, strategic planning merits to be singled out, serving as a unique tool for regional, as well as all public policies. Likewise, the raised awareness and knowledge as to the far-reaching constraints and threats caused by ineffective horizontal cooperation—the siloes between ministries dealing with related policies, the consequences of inadequate or no policy evaluation and the growing knowledge on integrated sustainable (urban) development approaches, among others—all confirm the relevance of the paradigm shift. Compared to the old hierarchical, legalistic and centralized, yet ineffective planning, a new paradigm tends to be more inclusive and accountable, encompassing modes of coordination (Antonopoulos and Bachtler 2014).

Regardless of the achievements, there are additional pressing needs for further improvements to regional and overall public policy management by way of introducing innovative and integrated, as well as more inclusive and transparent, approaches and modes of governance (Keser et al. 2015). Such governance changes will facilitate result orientation, as well as the reaching of relevant development impacts and sustainability of the finalized projects' results. Along with the already mentioned issues, sound management and policy implementation will ask for the setting of much longer term development objectives (climate change, education, research and development), which go beyond the existing MFF that encompasses period 2014–2020. Morover, along with the new complex global environmental covering economic, social and political issues and changing needs, Croatia's regional as well as other public policies will also need to be far more flexible in their implementation, in order to be able to respond to those issues in an effective and timely manner.

There is a very scarce empirical evidence as to actual achievements of EU funding in Croatia so far, particularly in the field of better public policy management, and in this regard the scholars in this field also have to meet the challenge to develop more empirically oriented research (Petak 2006). However, on the whole, it can be assessed that the preparations for cohesion policy and the management of EU funds gave an important push to the better design of regional policy. Having in mind the enormous financial impact, rules and regulations that follow their implementation in the new period, as well as the wide cross-sectoral nature of EU funds and recent circumstances in the cohesion policy in the period 2014–2020, it may be expected that cohesion policy will bring significant additional value not only to the regional policy, but to the overall public policy management in Croatia. The final extent of the impact of ESI funds on Croatia's socio-economic development will, however, depend on the ability of domestic policy makers to address the key obstacles which are currently confronting EU funds implementation, including successful policy coordination.

Notes

1. The number of managing authorities also includes authorities responsible for rural development and maritime and fisheries OPs. Furthermore, this number of documents also includes umbrella documents National Strategic Reference Framework in the period 2007–2013 and Partnership agreement in the period 2014–2020.
2. Just for illustration, the new institutional structure also required that new rules and procedures on the business processes related to the management of EU funds had to be prepared and put into written form. This set of documents is known as the common national rules, and its version from May 2017 had more than 120 separate documents.
3. Some activities such as so-called closure of the operational programmes (final clearing) will be finished even later, in 2018.

4. Two other programming documents, Rural Development Programme and Operational Programme for Maritime and Fisheries, were adopted in 2015.
5. According to data from https://cohesiondata.ec.europa.eu/overview accessed on 25th September 2017.
6. This figure is based on the figures from the reports on budget execution of the Ministry of Entrepreneurship and Crafts in 2012 and 2013 and does not take into account subventions for the Croatian Bank for Reconstruction and Development, which also supports SMEs through various financial schemes.
7. This assessment is based on the comparison of data from the Ministry of Finance on budget execution for 2012 and 2013 for the Ministry of Science, Education and Sport and Ministry of Entrepreneurship and Crafts, and data on the available funding from ESIF for the thematic objective covering RDI activities.

References

Adams, N., Cotella, G., & Nunes, R. (Eds.). (2011). *Territorial Development, Cohesion and Spatial Planning: Knowledge and Policy Development in an Enlarged EU, Regions and Cities.* London: Routledge.

Antonopoulos, E., & Bachtler, J. (2014). The Role of EU Pre-accession Assistance in the Establishment of National Coordination Structures for EU Funding: The Case of Croatia. *Journal of Contemporary European Research, 10*(2), 184–202.

Bache, I., & Tomšić, D. (2010). Europeanization and Nascent Multi-level Governance in Croatia. *Southeast European and Black Sea Studies, 10*(1), 71–83.

Bachtler, J., & Gorzelak, G. (2007). Reforming EU Cohesion Policy: A Reappraisal of the Performance of the Structural Funds. *Policy Studies, 28*(4), 309–326.

Bachtler, J., & Mendez, C. (2007). Who Governs EU Cohesion Policy? Deconstructing the Reforms of the Structural Funds. *Journal of Common Market Studies, 45*(3), 535–564.

Bachtler, J., Mendez, C., & Oraže, H. (2014). From Conditionality to Europeanization in Central and Eastern Europe: Administrative Performance and Capacity in Cohesion Policy. *European Planning Studies, 22*(4), 735–757.

Bajo, A., & Puljiz, J. (2017). Institucionalna potpora za strateško planiranje i gospodarski razvoj Republike Hrvatske. *Aktualni osvrti, 93*, 1–4.

Bojinović Fenko, A., & Urlić, A. (2015). Political Criteria vs. Political Conditionality: Comparative Analysis of Slovenian and Croatian European Union Accession Processes. *Croatian International Relations Review, 21*(72), 107–137.

Đulabić, V., & Manojlović, R. (2011). Administrative Aspects of Regional and Cohesion Policy in Croatia: In Search of a Better Coordination of Parallel Processes. *Croatian and Comparative Public Administration, 11*(4), 1041–1074.

European Commission. (2010). Croatia 2010 Progress Report. https://ec.europa.eu/neighbourhood-enlargement/sites/near/files/pdf/key_documents/2010/package/hr_rapport_2010_en.pdf. Downloaded 21 September 2017.

European Commission. (2014). *Investment for Jobs and Growth. Promoting Development and Good Governance in EU Regions and Cities. Sixth Report on Economic, Social and Territorial Cohesion*. Luxembourg: Publication Office of the European Union.

European Commission. (2015). Macroeconomic Imbalances. Country Report – Croatia 2015. *European Economy. Occasional Papers*, 218. Brussels: European Commission.

European Commission. (2016). Country Report – Croatia 2016. *Occasional Papers*. https://ec.europa.eu/info/publications/2016-european-semester-country-report-croatia_en. Downloaded 3 September 2017.

European Commission. (2017). Country Report – Croatia 2017. *Occasional Papers*. https://ec.europa.eu/info/files/2017-european-semester-country-report-croatia_hr. Downloaded 2 September 2017.

European Court of Auditors. (2011). Has EU Assistance Improved Croatia's Capacity to Manage Post-Accession Funding? *Special Report*, 14/2011. Luxembourg: Publications Office of the European Union.

Hughes, J., Sasse, G., & Gordon, C. (2004). *Europeanization and Regionalization in the EU's Enlargement to Central and Eastern Europe: The Myth of Conditionality*. Basingstoke: Palgrave Macmillan.

IRMO - Institut za razvoj i međunarodne odnose. (2011). Analiza kapaciteta za korištenje EU fondova na županijskoj razini. http://www.irmo.hr/hr/publikacije/analiza-regionalnih-kapaciteta-za-koristenje-eu-fondova-na-zupanijskoj-razini/. Downloaded 15 September 2017.

Keser, I, Maleković, S., & Puljiz, J. (2015). New Challenges for Urban Governance – Can We Learn from Each Other? 11th International Conference "Challenges of Europe". Split: University of Split.

Liha Matejiček, A. (2014). Institucionalna adaptacija Europskoj regionalnoj politici u Hrvatskoj. Thesis, (PhD). University of Zagreb.

Mairate, A. (2006). The "Added Value" of European Cohesion Policy. *Regional Studies, 40*(2), 167–177.

Maleković, S., & Puljiz, J. (2009). Challenges of a New Approach to Development on the Local and Regional Level in Croatia. In *New Croatian Local and Regional Self-Government*. Zagreb: Croatian Academy of Science and Arts.

Maleković, S., Puljiz, J., & Bartlett, W. (2011). Decentralisation and Regional Policy in Croatia: the Impact of EU Accession and the Prospect of Territorial

Reorganisation. In *LSEE Papers on Decentralisation and Regional Policy in South Eastern Europe, 5*. London: The London School of Economics and Political Science.

Palne Kovacs, I. (2016). Cohesion Policy in Central and Eastern Europe: The Challenge of Learning. In S. Piattoni & L. Polverari (Eds.), *Handbook on Cohesion Policy in the EU* (pp. 302–324). Cheltenham: Edward Elgar Publishing.

Petak, Z. (2006). Europeanization and Policy-Making in the National Context: The Work of Policy in Croatia. *Politička misao, 43*(5), 61–75.

Petak, Z. (2009). Oblikovanje javnih politika u Hrvatskoj i problem policy-koordinacije. *Anali Hrvatskog politološkog društva*, 5, 263–273.

World Bank. (2016). *Croatia Policy Notes 2016: Restoring Macroeconomic Stability, Competitiveness and Inclusion*. Washington, DC: World Bank Group.

Zakon o regionalnom razvoju Republike Hrvatske. (2009). Narodne novine, 153/09. https://narodne-novine.nn.hr/clanci/sluzbeni/2009_12_153_3746.html. Downloaded 7 September 2017.

Zakon o regionalnom razvoju Republike Hrvatske. (2015). Narodne novine, 147/14. https://narodne-novine.nn.hr/clanci/sluzbeni/2014_12_147_2751.html. Downloaded 7 September 2017.

CHAPTER 16

Features of Croatian Public Policies

Ana Petek

16.1 Introduction

Policy research is focused on policy change or on policy variation (John 1998: 12–20). Policy change studies that try to explain (in)stabilities within a single sector, usually throughout long periods of time, dominate the policy research (Birkland 2001: 135; Colebatch 2004: 80). This volume shows a lot of excellent work in this perspective. Research on policy variation strives to extract similarities and differences among the same policies in different countries or among different policies in one country, as the discipline of comparative public policies is formed around cross-national and cross-sectoral comparisons (Heidenheimer 1986; Hofferbert and Cingranelli 1996; Lodge 2007; Petak 2002; Schmitt 2013; Wilder 2017). Cross-sectoral comparison is the least developed part of policy research and almost non-existent in Croatia, even though this kind of research could produce rich insights into the functioning of the political system and constitutes a prerequisite for evidence-based policy-making coordination. This is really a huge gap in the research that needs to be addressed.

A. Petek (✉)
Faculty of Political Science, University of Zagreb, Zagreb, Croatia
e-mail: ana.petek@fpzg.hr

Z. Petak, K. Kotarski (eds.), *Policy-Making at the European Periphery*, New Perspectives on South-East Europe,
https://doi.org/10.1007/978-3-319-73582-5_16

The basis for cross-sectoral comparative policy research are policy classifications, taxonomies and typologies of public policies. As public policies are so numerous, multidimensional and diverse, solid comprehensive policy classifications are quite rare, and some scholars claim not even possible (Smith 2002). Still, this chapter will explore this approach as it makes a unique perspective to capture some general trends and characteristics of policy-making. Being one of the first works of this kind focused on Croatia, the purpose of the chapter is exploratory—to give some initial description of main similarities and differences between Croatian public policies. This research will be guided by a descriptive research question: What are the basic features of Croatian public policies?

This chapter is additionally inspired by theoretical thinking on policy accounts and policy design that state some basic features of all public policies, as only broad and loose theoretical frameworks in policy research are coherent within the exploratory purpose of the chapter. This framework is used as a basis for coding policy studies of 11 Croatian public policies with qualitative content analysis. Following the introduction, the first two parts of the chapter cover the theoretical framework and methodological approach. The central part consists of a detailed description of all the features of Croatian public policies that emerged from the analysis. The chapter then concludes with the discussion and final remarks on how Croatian public policies vary, by stressing some similarities and differences among Croatian sectors that this comparative analysis revealed.

16.2 Theoretical Framework: Policy Taxonomy, Policy Accounts and Policy Design

To gather original data for the proclaimed research question is a gigantic endeavor, in terms of time, financial support and researchers required, and is far beyond the reach of one book chapter. To still provide an answer to the proposed research question (and maybe prepare some foundations for the future research projects in this direction) this chapter analyzes existing case studies of Croatian public policies. Research papers on different sectors in Croatia were gathered to provide data and empirical material for the analysis. Sampling of policies, and policy studies that describe them, was guided by the policy taxonomy elaborated in the *Handbook of Public Policy in Europe: Britain, France and Germany* (Compston 2004). The aforementioned book is quite unique as it tries to develop a comprehensive list of all national public policies embodied into governmental ministries. The *Handbook* classifies sectors into six policy areas: defense and foreign affairs, law and order, economic policies, sectoral policies, social policies, and other policies. Both 'foreign policy and defense' and 'law and order' deal with the core state functions that secure survival of the country, its integrity and independence. Economic policies consist of macroeconomic policies that affect the integral working of the economy. Sectoral policies are somewhat connected to economic policies, but policies within this area affect some specific economic sector and not the economy as a whole. Social policies deal with social problems within society, and are often dedicated to some specific social groups. Other policies are a residual category with sectors that do not neatly fit into previously mentioned policy areas (Compston 2004).

Even though Compston's *Handbook* develops a quite unique comprehensive taxonomy of national public policies, it involves only cross-national policy comparison and doesn't analyze sectors with equal elements that enable cross-sectoral comparison. Therefore, to determine basic features of policy sectors, definitions of public policies themselves must be a starting point. Among numerous ways of defining and understanding the concept of public policy, quite useful is the systematization into three accounts: policy as authorized choice, as outcome of structured actors' interaction, and as social construction of public problems, as set out by Hal Colebatch (2004; 2006a, b). Policy as authorized choice is the first account that classically defines policy as 'whatever governments choose to do or not to do' (Dye 1987: 2). This account sees policies as choices and decisions of legitimate public representatives that are executed by the state apparatus. From this viewpoint, basic policy elements are goals and objectives that are set for each sector and instruments by which they should be achieved.

The second account that defines policies as the outcome of structured interaction among various governmental and non-governmental actors obviously stress actors as one of the main features of policy-making. The agency of actors, the power that they possess, their policy paradigms and values, and types of relationships they are involved with, strongly determine each policy sector. Finally, the third account develops an understanding of policy as a social construction of public problems. Discourses and linguistic features of argumentation on what public problems are and how they are prioritized are set to be a quite important aspect of each policy. Especially important is the social construction of policy target groups, as this conveys how the state perceives citizens and what they can expect from state action (Colebatch 2004, 2006a, b; Howlett 2011; Petek and Petković 2014; Schneider and Ingram 1993). The different sets of policy elements described above create diverse policy designs that deliver different outcomes. Policy design is usually developed on several levels, and literature postulates differently on what basic features each policy design has. Policy aims, goals and objectives, as well as different policy means and instruments are the central ones, but designs are also containing problems, targets, implementation structures, and so on (Birkland 2001; Howlett 2011; Howlett and Lejano 2012; Schneider and Ingram 1993).

16.3 Methodological Approach: Case Selection, QCA and Coding Scheme

This chapter is based on cross-sectoral comparison of 11 Croatian public policies by qualitative content analysis of policy studies. The sample contains one to three sectors from each of six major policy areas, depending on the size of specific area and the availability of detailed studies of each sector. Studies were chosen to cover changes in each sector in last three decades since Croatian independence, so they had to be published recently. For most sectors, two studies were chosen to achieve comprehensiveness. The sample contains: 1. foreign policy (Jović 2011; Turek 2001); 2. migration (Gregurović and Mlinarić 2012; Tatalović and Jakešević 2016); 3. employment (Bejaković 2015; Matković 2008); 4. fiscal policy (Benazić 2006; Šimović et al. 2014); 5. regional policy (Liha Matejiček 2015; Maleković et al. 2011); 6. agriculture (Franić and Ljubaj 2015; Jurišić 2014); 7. transportation (Božičević et al. 2008; Vedriš 2015); 8. environment (Tišma and Funduk 2015; Nekić and Krajnović 2015); 9. education (Žiljak and Molnar 2015); 10. health (Zrinščak 2007); and 11. culture (Katunarić 2010; Primorac et al. 2015).

It should be stressed that there is a small number of studies that comprehensively analyze most of the sectors. Different Croatian policies are predominantly researched either partially, only in some segments or on some specific measures, indicators or effects. Also, political scientists are still rarely present in the analysis of most public policies within the sample, so the policy-making process is often completely outside of the focus of research endeavors. This will significantly limit the scope of insights of this chapter. Furthermore, this was already evident with problems arising from coding scheme development. Nevertheless, as the purpose of this chapter is exploratory and as it is in effect the beginning of cross-sectoral comparisons of Croatian public policies, the end result still represents a contribution to policy research in Croatia.

Selected material was coded and analyzed according to the propositions of qualitative content analysis (QCA) (Schreier 2012). QCA is primarily focused on describing major dimensions of some material, so it is highly coherent with the stated exploratory purpose of the chapter and selected descriptive research question. The whole material for 11 policy sectors in the sample contains 20 studies with 432 pages in total. Some studies were not coded completely, but only selected sections that directly describe the sector and deal with data. Sections such as theoretical and methodological framework or paragraphs that, for example, bring data on other countries to compare Croatia were not included into coding as they do not refer to Croatian public policies. Each study was divided into coding and non-coding parts during initial detailed reading. Each paragraph was set as a coding unit. Formal criterion for determining coding units was chosen to simplify the segmentation process, as in this fashion it is not necessary to make a segmentation as a separate phase in coding. Also, selected studies presenting well-structured texts are quite fit for this kind of formal segmentation. Some exceptions were made for longer paragraphs, which were cut down into several coding units. Paragraphs were cut when they contained more than five codes.

The coding scheme was developed based on a hybrid strategy. Some codes were deduced from policy theory and previous research. Examples of those are basic elements of policy design, goals and instruments described in the previous section. This mostly refers to the first level codes or main categories of coding scheme. Most of the second level codes, subcategories, were inductively derived in a preparatory detailed reading of the whole material. The final coding scheme contains six first level codes: goals, instruments, actors, discourses, problems, and target groups. The coding scheme is further developed into 37 subcategories: nine substantive goals, four types of instruments, three groups of actors, five distinctive discourses, six subcategories of problems, and ten different target populations (see Table 16.1).

Subcategories within instruments and actors were derived deductively. To classify instruments, that are so diverse in policy practice, the NATO scheme was used and all instruments were divided by the main resource on which their efficacy is based on: authority, nodality, organization and treasure (Hood and Margetts 2007). Actors, which also vary to a great extent

Table 16.1 Coding scheme

1. Goals	2. Instruments	3. Actors
1.1. Development and competitiveness 1.2. Diversity 1.3. Equality 1.4. National identity and cohesion 1.5. Quality of life 1.6. Security 1.7. Social inclusion 1.8. Stability 1.9. Sustainability	2.1. Authority 2.2. Nodality 2.3. Organization 2.4. Treasure	3.1. International 3.2. Non-state 3.3. State
4. Discourses	5. Problems	6. Target groups
4.1. European 4.2. Globalization 4.3. Ideological and partisan 4.4. Public goods 4.5. Self-perception	5.1. Economic 5.2. External pressures 5.3. Overlapping 5.4. Social 5.5. Structural 5.6. Technical and physical	6.1. Business sector 6.2. Farmers and rural inhabitants 6.3. General population/citizens 6.4. Poor 6.5. Regions and local communities 6.6. Vulnerable groups 6.7. War veterans 6.8. Women 6.9. Workers 6.10. Youth

in practice, were divided into three broad theoretical categories: national actors as state/governmental/official actors and non-state or non-official actors, with the extra subcategory for international actors. All other first level codes had to be developed into sub-codes by a data-driven strategy, as there are no classifications of those features present anywhere in the literature.

Goals were elaborated by substantive aims and objectives present in the selected studies (e.g. development, quality of life or stability). Equal procedure was applied into the category of discourses to develop some substantive examples of discourses used in Croatian public policies (e.g. European, globalization or ideological). Discourses were scarcely present in the selected studies so the subcategories in this code are also underdeveloped. For the category of problems, six subcategories were extracted inductively from studies, some substantive (e.g. economic or social), and some not (e.g. overlapping or external pressures). This is the result of the way Croatian policy studies deal with the issue of policy problems. Target groups are the widest category, as material showed high variety within this feature.

Coding rules were defined by the QCA propositions (Schreier 2012). Coding was done only on the subcategory level. So coding units were coded into development, treasure or external pressures, and not into goals, instruments or problems. Each coding unit could be coded several times into subcategories of different main codes. For example, it could be coded simultaneously into subcategories 2.3, 4.5 and 6.2. The restriction was, by QCA rules, set on coding within the category. One coding unit was never coded twice within one main code, so one coding unit was never simultaneously coded into, for example, 3.1 international, 3.2 non-state and 3.3 state actors.

16.4 The Description of the Features of Croatian Public Policies

Qualitative content analysis of selected policy studies showed that Croatian public policies in the sample have 37 basic features, grouped into six major clusters. In this section for each feature frequency of appearance per policy sector is presented. Those initial numerical findings are then further elaborated and examined by specific content of particular features at subcategory level and by the prevalence of the feature among sectors. The overview of the features of Croatian public policies will start with the description of their goals.

Goals have the following rank by their total frequency of appearance in all selected studies: development and competitiveness (77), equality (26), social inclusion (25), sustainability (21), security (13), national identity and cohesion (11), stability (10), quality of life (8), and diversity (3). By spreading into several sectors, development and competitiveness again have the highest score with presence in nine sectors. Then, the quality of life and sustainability appear in six sectors, social inclusion in five, security and national identity in four, and stability and equality in just three. The least spread goal is diversity that is present in only two sectors. It is undoubtedly that development and competitiveness is the most important goal of Croatian public policies, present is almost all selected sectors, as only studies of culture and health policy do not contain this goal. This code also includes all references on growth as a policy goal.

Equality, social inclusion and sustainability follow by their frequency of appearance in selected studies. Equality is present in health, education and culture policy, as this code includes solidarity and accessibility. Still, for equality, the numerical result is quite exaggerated because one study of cultural policy has a focus on the access to culture and consumes almost all appearance of equality as a goal of Croatian public policies. Social inclusion as a policy goal is present within quite diverse sectors—culture, employment, foreign policy, migration and regional policy. It also includes integration. Interestingly, social policies such as health and education do not contain any reference to social inclusion as a goal. Sustainability also seems as an important goal of Croatian public policies, especially because it is present in agriculture, culture, environment, fiscal and regional policy and transport. This sub-category gathers all direct mentions of sustainability in the coded material, but also includes self-sufficiency, sustainable development and sustainable growth.

Five policy goals with much lower frequency of appearance and prevalence among sectors are security, national identity and cohesion, stability, quality of life and diversity. Security, broadly understood as national security containing territorial integrity and independence, but also as social security, is mentioned among goals of employment, foreign, health and transport policy. Issues of preserving national identity and cohesion are addressed by foreign policy and migration, education and culture. Stability, understood in a broad sense, is described dominantly as a goal of fiscal policy, but sometimes occurs also in discussions on education and culture. Quality of life, including standard of living, has quite a low frequency of appearance, but is present in agriculture, culture, employment, foreign policy, health and migration, which shows that its overall importance is probably higher. The same could not be said for diversity as a goal that is mentioned only three times in two sectors as biodiversity and cultural diversity.

The second most important element of each policy design is instruments. All selected studies do not employ detailed analyses of policy instruments, but mention them in a quite general manner. The coding tried to capture this imprecise discussion of instruments with sub-codes that appeared with following frequencies: treasure (181), authority (168), nodality (38) and organization (24). This shows two groups of instruments by their importance in Croatian public policies: authority and treasure on one side, and organization and nodality on the other. Authority and treasure dominate also by prevalence in all selected sectors (except the studies of foreign policy that do not discuss instruments). Nodality is present in eight and organization in six sectors.

This first impression of the results for instruments is a bit misleading and digging into concrete coding units is necessary to critically examine these findings. The sub-category treasure mostly contains general notions on spending on specific activities within sectors. None of the selected studies systematically explores particular financial instruments as subsidies, direct support, loans, user charges, and so on. The sub-code 'authority' is present in all sectors not because they all heavily rely on regulation as a policy tool, but because each study mentions key laws and strategies as foundations of the sector. In Croatia, lawmaking is a 'first step' in constituting any policy sector, and only some of them rely of producing regulations, ordinances, decisions, rules of procedures, conclusions, and so forth, as a dominant policy tool. So, the numerical results for these two sub-categories are exaggerated. Nodality is present in: informing, rising awareness, training and education, reporting and evaluation, prevention and promotion, and so on, within agriculture, culture, education, employment, environment, health, migration and regional policy. The least present is a set of organizational instruments that appear in selected studies of culture, employment, health, migration and transport.

Actors are also very roughly analyzed within studies of Croatian public policies, so they could be coded only into broad types. As expected, national state actors dominate in Croatian policy-making and their studies (146), and are followed by international actors (90), and then by non-state actors (37). State and international actors are present in all researched sectors, and non-state actors are missing from the studies of agriculture, environment and fiscal policy. State actors mostly refer to ministries, but also to agencies, local government and parliament. The most important international actor is the EU. Within the group of non-state actors mostly NGOs are mentioned as participants in policy-making, but sometimes also political parties and sporadically firms, religious groups and media.

Discourses are also an important policy element that is significantly under-researched in the studies of Croatian public policies. From a total of more than 1000 codes assigned to all coding units within the material, only 40 of them are related to discourses. Several sub-codes developed for representing types of Croatian policy discourses have following presence in the selected material: European (15) in three sectors, globalization (11) in four sectors, ideological and partisan (9) in two sectors, self-perception (4) in three sectors and public goods (1) in only one sector. Overall, this is too small a pile of material to be useful for some detailed policy comparison.

Policy problems are in a way motivating forces for creating different public policies. For Croatian policies those 'motives' are present in the selected material by following order: economic (56), external pressures (48), structural (28), social (25), overlapping (16) and technical and physical (16). These problems are shared among sectors as they are spilling over across different public policies in Croatia. External pressures, social problems and problems that are overlapping are features of eight sectors. Economic problems are stressed as motivating forces in seven sectors, structural problems in six, and technical and physical problems in four of them.

Therefore, economic problems, especially economic crisis, seem to be the most important type of problems in Croatian policy-making that stimulates policy change in economic sectors (as fiscal and regional policy), in sectoral policies (as agriculture and transport), but also in other sectors, such as health, migration and culture. External pressures, which refer to anything outside the national borders affecting domestic policy-making, including globalization pressures and war and its consequences, also heavily influences Croatian public policies. Those problems were not present only in environmental, fiscal and employment policy. Structural problems include malfunctioning of a given subsystem, for example within the structure of a supply and demand or within the structure of public revenues and spending. Corruption is also coded within structural problems. Structural problems are stressed in studies of agriculture, employment, fiscal, health, regional and transport policy.

Social problems that primarily refer to inequalities, among individuals, social groups or regions, are tackled within quite diverse sectors: culture, education, employment, fiscal, foreign, health, migration and regional policy. Studies of eight different sectors (culture, employment, environment, fiscal, foreign, health, migration and regional policy) stress multi-dimensional problems that are overlapping with some other problems. Examples are interconnections among foreign and domestic problems, issues of migrant and national minorities, fiscal and monetary issues, or of environmental issues with transport, energy, agriculture and tourism. Technical and physical problems capture specific issues, such as railways electrification, pollution of animal habitats, architectural barriers or different fatal diseases. Those are not significantly present in coded material, but some could be found in culture, health, transport and environment policy.

Even though studies of Croatian public policies are not devoted in detail to the analysis of target groups, they mention quite numerous beneficiaries of policy-making. This is the level of their presence in the selected material: workers (64), regions and local communities (40), youth (18), business sector (16), general population/citizens (16), vulnerable groups (15), farmers and rural inhabitants (11), poor (5), war veterans (5), women (3). Those target groups are just occasionally pointed out in the studies. A slightly higher presence of workers and regions is a result of the bias inherent in the case selection—it is a direct consequence of selecting employment and regional policy to the sample. A bit more revealing is the 'cross-listing' of some target groups among diverse policy sectors. Workers and youth are stressed as a target group for five sectors; business sector, regions and local communities and vulnerable groups in four; general population/citizens in three; farmers and rural inhabitants, poor and war veterans in two; and finally, women in only one sector.

The case selection bias that is connected to the workers as a target group is somehow diminished by the representation of this target group in five sectors, which are, besides employment, also agriculture, fiscal, health and migration policy. A broader prevalence of youth as policy beneficiaries (children included) is a positive surprise. They are stressed in studies of agriculture, culture, education, employment and health policy. This shows a small amount of evidence of the mainstreaming of youth issues in Croatian policy-making. This should be compared to women as a target group, as they are expected to be equally 'spread-around' diverse policy sectors. Women are still only found in the study of employment policy, so it seems that they are far less important as state action beneficiaries in Croatia. This should be investigated further in a more systematic manner.

Regions and local communities as targets of policy-making appear in culture, fiscal and health, besides the regional policy. In the culture and health sectors, local government has specified responsibilities and local communities are stipulated within the studies as the prime users of cultural and health services. Fiscal policy studies are partially devoted to determining revenues and expenditures of local government for the benefit of local inhabitants. Further decentralization that is so often prescribed as necessary in Croatia should enhance prevalence of regions and local communities as target groups of a broader list of sectors. The business sector is expected to be present in the studies of primarily economic and sectoral policies, and it was found within fiscal, agriculture, employment, and environment policy.

Vulnerable groups is a broader code, which captures not only direct mentioning of vulnerable groups, but also groups not covered by other codes, such as people with disabilities, pensioners and marginalized groups. Coding units that mention several groups, including youth, women, pensioners and people with disabilities, were also coded here. Having this in mind, it could be said that vulnerable groups are present only in culture, employment, fiscal and health policy. War veterans are undoubtedly an important target group of Croatian policy-making. Even without the veteran policy in the sample, they appear as a target group in employment and regional policy studies. Farmers and rural inhabitants appear, besides in the agriculture policy, as beneficiaries of specific programs in health care. The poorest part of the population has 'low visibility' as policy beneficiary, and is present only in employment and health policy. The general population or citizens as a target group are an indicator of the inherent public interest within policy-making. Still, they are slightly present in selected studies; this is, only in culture, migration and health policy.

16.5 The Analysis and the Discussion: How Policy Areas in Croatia Vary

Our analysis continues by comparing sets of policies to detect some basic similarities and differences among their features. The attempt is to see how much Croatian sectors vary in comparison to the taxonomy of European public policies that are classified into six policy areas. For that purpose, Table 16.2 was produced to highlight dominant codes in sampled Croatian public policies. For each main category, from goals to target groups, most represented subcategories were extracted. All second-level codes that have more than five appearances within the sampled studies of Croatian public policies were selected. The following text will try to capture most important similarities and differences among Croatian policy sectors that will be interpreted by the framework of European policy areas.

If goals are in the focus, there could be found some distinctive similarities and differences among Croatian policy areas. Development and competitiveness is a goal that both economic and sectoral policies share. This is coherent with the basic logic of the classification that stresses both areas as dealing with economy, economic policies with the economy as a whole and sectoral policies with specific economic sectors. Still, stability is emphasized as a second important goal in economic policies, and sustainability in

Table 16.2 Dominant features in sampled Croatian public policies

	Defense and foreign affairs	*Law and order*	*Economic policies*	*Social policies*	*Sectoral policies*	*Other policies*
Goals	Security	Social inclusion	Development and competitiveness Stability	*Equality*	Development and competitiveness Sustainability	Equality National identity and cohesion
Instruments	NA	Authority	Treasure Authority Nodality	Treasure Authority Organization Nodality	Authority Treasure	Authority Treasure
Actors	International	Nonstate* State*	State International	State International	State International	Nonstate State International
Discourses	*European** *Ideological and partisan**	*European** *Self-perception**	*Globalization*	European	NA	*Globalization*
Problems	*External pressures*	External pressures Economic	Economic Structural Social	Social	Economic External Pressures Technical and physical	External Pressures
Target groups	NA	Workers	Workers Regions and local communities Business sector* Vulnerable groups* Youth	General population/citizens Youth	Farmers and rural inhabitants	*Regions and local communities*

Notes: All features that had five or less than five appearances were used only when this was the highest score within the area. Those are marked with italic letters. Two features in the same box marked with * have equal results sectoral, which is primarily due to the environmental policy in the sample. Defense and foreign affairs are committed to security as a dominant goal, even though defense policy was not in the sample. This is also coherent with the initial definition of the policy area. The policy area of law and order was expected to have more similar goals to foreign affairs and defense, for example security, which is completely absent, or maybe national identity. Nevertheless, social inclusion dominates in this area, understood as integration within migration policy, and this policy area in general deals with issues of citizenship. On the other hand, social inclusion is completely absent from social policies, at least according to the studies selected for this chapter. Social policies are devoted to equality as a core goal, which is not surprising for the area dedicated to solidarity. Residual category of other policies shares equality as the main goal with social policies, but this results from the study of access to culture within the sample for this area.

Instruments were already marked in the description section as a part of the analysis that is not precise and detailed enough, which weakens the comparative potential. But even this rough analysis shows some interesting similarities and differences among policy areas. All sectors primarily rely on lawmaking and all studies deal with the issue of public spending in the sector. Differences again occur within the application of less prominent types of instruments—nodality and organization. It seems that economic and social policies are the most complex ones, as they employ also tools from those two groups of instruments. Still, only social policies significantly rely on organizational instruments, as this is where huge public sectors exist. The category of actors is also underdeveloped and that limits comparison. Nevertheless, this category still reveals several important details of Croatian policy-making. Namely, in all policy areas state actors dominate, which is expected. It is a bit less expected that international actors are more present then non-state actors in all policy areas. It dominantly refers to the EU within the sub-code of international actors, which explains this prevalence. Only area of law and order differs by more involvement of non-state actors as compared to international ones.

Discourses are the least useful category for the comparison of Croatian public policies from the policy studies coding. Again, Europeanization and globalization, namely, non-domestic aspects of policy-making dominate in almost all policy areas. Ideological/partisan discourse is not significantly represented, not even in social policies that are usually determined as a basis of partisan alignment. The category of problems continues to show that non-domestic impetus for Croatian policy-making dominates due to external pressures in four policy areas out of six, social and economic policies being the exception. Additionally, similarity among economic and sectoral policies occur as both areas primarily deal with economic problems. Results for target populations are not so revealing, as it seems that the selection of cases and analytical style of coded studies have produced quite incomprehensive results. For example, the area of law and order stresses only workers as target groups, and economic policies have the highest number of relevant target groups, including vulnerable groups, which is all due to employment policy in the sample. Only social policies posit all citizens as the main target group, which is coherent with the findings in the literature that social policies produce broadly distributed benefits.

16.6 Final Remarks

Qualitative content analysis of policy studies of 11 Croatian public policies presented in this chapter has several limitations. Most important are the ones pertaining to case selection, coded policy studies selections and their incomprehensive analytical style, especially on instruments, actors, and discourses. Nevertheless, corresponding to the stated exploratory purpose of the chapter, the analysis revealed some relevant insights. Croatian public policies do not differ significantly by their main features from the European public policies. The basic characteristics of each policy area is quite coherent with the expectations within the theoretical framework. Sectoral and economic policies have most similarities in Croatia, as it is proclaimed within taxonomy of European public policies. Overall, the main feature of all Croatian public policies in all policy areas represents a very strong influence of factors and actors outside the country on domestic policy-making. This remark is especially valid for actors involved, problems that policies deal with, and established discourses. Economic and sectoral policy areas seem to be the most alike one to another. On the other hand, social and economic policy areas seem to be more complex, with the biggest number of features present. This shows that further pursuit of cross-sectoral comparisons presents a fruitful research path that should be used more broadly, especially with the help of new original data that would enhance precision and comparability.

References

Bejaković, P. (2015). Croatian Employment Policy in the EU Context. In D. Lajh & Z. Petak (Eds.), *EU Public Policies Seen From a National Perspective: Slovenia and Croatia in the European Union* (pp. 254–266). Ljubljana: Faculty of Social Sciences.

Benazić, M. (2006). Fiskalna politika i gospodarska aktivnost u Republici Hrvatskoj: model kointegracije. *Ekonomski pregled, 57*(12), 882–918.

Birkland, T. A. (2001). *An Introduction to the Policy Process. Theories, Concepts, and Models of Public Policy Making*. Armonk/New York: M. E. Sharpe.

Božičević, J., Steiner, S., & Smrečki, B. (2008). Evaluation of the Croatian Transport System. In B. Hernavs & P. Meše (Eds.), *Proceeding of the 16th International Symposium on Electronics in Traffic (ISEP)* (pp. 1–10). Ljubljana: Electrotechnical Association of Slovenia.

Colebatch, H. K. (2004). *Policy*. Zagreb: Faculty of Political Science.

Colebatch, H. K. (2006a). Policy, Models, and the Construction of Governing. In H. K. Colebatch (Ed.), *The Work of Policy. An International Survey* (pp. 3–19). Lanham: Lexington Books.

Colebatch, H. K. (2006b). What Work Makes Policy. *Policy Sciences, 39*(3), 309–321.

Compston, H. (Ed.). (2004). *Handbook of Public Policy in Europe. Britain, France and Germany*. Houndmills: Palgrave.

Dye, T. R. (1987). *Understanding Public Policy*. Englewood Cliffs: New Jersey: Prentice Hall.

Franić, R., & Ljubaj, T. (2015). Common Agriculture Policy: The Case of Croatia. In D. Lajh & Z. Petak (Eds.), *EU Public Policies Seen From a National Perspective: Slovenia and Croatia in the European Union* (pp. 141–152). Ljubljana: Faculty of Social Sciences.

Gregurović, S., & Mlinarić, D. (2012). The Challenges of Migration Policies in Croatia: Migration History, Trends and Prospects. *AEMI Journal, 10*, 99–113.

Heidenheimer, A. J. (1986). Comparative Public Policy Studies Examined: An Odyssey in Four Parts. *International Social Science Journal, 38*(2), 159–177.

Hofferbert, R. I., & Cingranelli, D. L. (1996). Public Policy and Administration: Comparative Policy Analysis. In R. E. Goodin & H. Klingemann (Eds.), *A New Handbook of Political Science* (pp. 593–609). Oxford: Oxford University Press.

Hood, C., & Margetts, H. (2007). *The Tools of Government in the Digital Age* (pp. 1–20). London: Palgrave.

Howlett, M. (2011). *Designing Public Policy. Principles and Instruments*. New York: Routledge.

Howlett, M., & Lejano, R. P. (2012). Tales From the Crypt: The Rise and Fall (and Rebirth?) of Policy Design. *Administration & Society, 45*(3), 357–381.

John, P. (1998). *Analysing Public Policy*. London: Pinter.

Jović, D. (2011). Hrvatska vanjska politika pred izazovima članstva u Europskoj uniji. *Politička misao, 48*(2), 7–36.

Jurišić, Ž. (2014). Hrvatska poljoprivreda u Zajedničkoj poljoprivrednoj politici Europske Unije. Sadašnjost i sutrašnjica. *Civitas Crisiensis, 1*, 207–221.

Katunarić, V. (2010). Hrvatska kulturna politika i izazovi globalizacije. In N. Budak & V. Katunarić (Eds.), *Hrvatski nacionalni identitet u globalizirajućem svijetu* (pp. 105–116). Zagreb: Pravni fakultet Zagreb i Centar za demokraciju i pravo "Miko Tripalo".

Liha Matejiček, A. (2015). The Europeanisation of Regional Policy in Croatia: From Institutional Absorption to Transformation. In D. Lajh & Z. Petak (Eds.), *EU Public Policies Seen From a National Perspective: Slovenia and Croatia in the European Union* (pp. 167–179). Ljubljana: Faculty of Social Sciences.

Lodge, M. (2007). Comparative Public Policy. In F. Fischer, G. M. Miller, & M. S. Sidney (Eds.), *Handbook of Public Policy Analysis: Theory, Politics, and Methods* (pp. 273–288). London: Taylor and Francis CRC Press.

Maleković, S., Puljiz, J., & Bartlett, W. (2011). Decentralization and Regional Policy in Croatia: The Impact of EU Accession and the Prospect of the Territorial Reorganization, *LSEE Papers on Decentralization and Regional Policy.* http://www.lse.ac.uk/europeanInstitute/research/LSEE/Research/SEE_Programme/images/Research_Paper_5.pdf. Downloaded 10 June 2017.

Matković, T. (2008). Politika zapošljavanja i nezaposlenost. In V. Puljiz, G. Bežovan, T. Matković, Z. Šućur, & S. Zrinščak (Eds.), *Socijalna politika Hrvatske* (pp. 163–217). Zagreb: Faculty of Law.

Nekić, B., & Krajnović, A. (2015). Politika zaštite okoliša u RH nakon pristupanja Europskoj uniji. *Tranzicija, 16*(34), 39–58.

Petak, Z. (2002). Komparativne javne politike: mogu li se uspoređivati rezultati djelovanja vlada? *Politička misao, 34*(1), 51–62.

Petek, A., & Petković, P. (Eds.). (2014). *Pojmovnik javnih politika.* Zagreb: Faculty of Political Science.

Primorac, J., Obuljen Koržinek, N., & Uzelac, A. (2015). Access to Culture in Croatian Cultural Policy: Moving Towards Explicit Policies. *International Journal of Cultural Policies, 23*(5), 562–580.

Schmitt, S. (2013). Comparative Approaches to the Study of Public Policy-Making. In E. Araral, S. Fritzen, M. Howlett, M. Ramesh, & X. Wu (Eds.), *Routledge Handbook of Public Policy* (pp. 29–43). London/New York: Routledge.

Schneider, A., & Ingram, H. (1993). Social Construction of Target Populations: Implications for Politics and Policy. *The American Political Science Review, 87*(2), 334–347.

Schreier, M. (2012). *Qualitative Content Analysis in Practice.* London: Sage.

Šimović, H., Ćorić, T., & Deskar-Škrbić, M. (2014). Mogućnosti i ograničenja fiskalne politike u Hrvatskoj. *Ekonomski pregled, 65*(6), 541–575.

Smith, K. B. (2002). Typologies, Taxonomies, and the Benefits of Policy Classification. *Policy Studies Journal, 30*(3), 379–395.

Tatalović, S., & Jakešević, R. (2016). Novopristigli migranti i nacionalne manjine u Hrvatskoj. http://library.fes.de/pdf-files/bueros/kroatien/13058.pdf. Downloaded 10 June 2017.

Tišma, S., & Funduk, M. (2015). Croatian Environmental Policies in the EU Context. In D. Lajh & Z. Petak (Eds.), *EU Public Policies Seen From a National Perspective: Slovenia and Croatia in the European Union* (pp. 225–239). Ljubljana: Faculty of Social Sciences.

Turek, F. (2001). Prioriteti vanjske politike Republike Hrvatske. *Politička misao, 38*(2), 185–196.

Vedriš, M. (2015). Croatian Transport Policy in the EU Context. In D. Lajh & Z. Petak (Eds.), *EU Public Policies Seen From a National Perspective: Slovenia and Croatia in the European Union* (pp. 279–297). Ljubljana: Faculty of Social Sciences.

Wilder, M. (2017). Comparative Public Policy: Origins, Themes, New Directions. *Policy Studies Journal, 45*(S1), S47–S66.

Žiljak, T., & Molnar, T. (2015). Croatian Education Policy in the EU Context. In D. Lajh & Z. Petak (Eds.), *EU Public Policies Seen From a National Perspective: Slovenia and Croatia in the European Union* (pp. 279–297). Ljubljana: Faculty of Social Sciences.

Zrinščak, S. (2007). Zdravstvena politika Hrvatske. U vrtlogu reformi i suvremenih društvenih izazova. *Revija za socijanu politiku, 14*(2), 193–220.

CHAPTER 17

Quo Vadis Croatia? The Interplay of Institutions, Interests and Ideas

Zdravko Petak and Kristijan Kotarski

17.1 Introduction

While the issue of policy-making in Croatia has been receiving considerable attention from social science researchers for a long time now—particularly political scientists, economists, sociologists and administrative scientists—no integral study has been made yet that would present the policy-making process in Croatia in a coherent way. Of course, there have been various presentations of economic, social or sectoral policies, but the language used in these studies is mostly the language of standard policy studies, usually without systematized reviews of the roles of individual policy actors, policy goals and policy instruments. In addition, very rare are the works addressing the specific policy-cycle phases of the policy-making process in Croatia, such as agenda-setting, formulation, implementation or evaluation of policies.

In effect, of the four policy research areas developed by political scientists (Sabatier 1991: 144)—'substantive area research', 'evaluation and impact studies', 'policy process' and 'policy design'—only the first and

Z. Petak (✉) • K. Kotarski
Faculty of Political Science, University of Zagreb, Zagreb, Croatia
e-mail: zdravko.petak@fpzg.hr; kristijan.kotarski@fpzg.hr

Z. Petak, K. Kotarski (eds.), *Policy-Making at the European Periphery*, New Perspectives on South-East Europe,
https://doi.org/10.1007/978-3-319-73582-5_17

third of these areas has been developed in Croatia. Substantive policy area research is primarily developed among sociologists, economists, and some other social scientists. The first policy process studies have appeared lately, mostly among political scientists after 2000. The other two policy research areas—evaluation, and implementation and policy design studies—are still in their initial phase of development. This is why we decided to edit a book that would offer a coherent institutional context and main characteristics of the policy-making and policy implementation processes in Croatia, combining the political scientists and economists' research on the fundamental issues of the policy process and crucial economic policies implemented in the country.

The book therefore offers a unique blend of Croatia's political economy framework and public policy analysis, covering Croatia's economic and political transformation in the last 30 years. It spans the period between the disintegration of Yugoslavia and Croatia's independence and the present day (2017). The book takes into account the key phases of Croatia's economic and political transformation: the Homeland War and the competitive authoritarianism of the 1990s, the democratization and opening up in the context of the EU membership negotiations, as well as the full four years of EU membership and its impact on Croatia's policy-making and political economy context.

17.2 Key Findings Related to Policy-Making Context in Croatia

The first part, entitled 'Policy Making Process in the EU's Newest Member State', provides an in-depth analysis of the Croatian policy-making context and the impact of Europeanization upon the national institutional framework. In Chap. 1 the editors of this volume consider the crucial puzzle of Croatia's post-communist transition; namely, the extent of economic and institutional divergence with new EU member states bound by common historical legacy and imperatives of institutional transformation. They precisely indicate critical junctures in Croatia's economic development trajectory, which have led to severe economic divergence with other post-communist countries (CEE-10). First, political choices made after gaining independence, such as partial reform equilibrium, the establishment of vast clientelistic networks and captured state; belong to the major culprits for economic divergence with CEE-10 since 1999. In that regard,

Croatia developed a type of capitalism, which is more similar to the ideal type of South European capitalism, as opposed to capitalisms in other Central and Eastern European countries. Second, after the GFC hit in 2008, the nature of captured state in Croatia, deprived of essential steering capacity, collided with major external shock. Hence, the institutional and development constraints of such a system Kotarski and Petak describe by the concept of captured state and partial reform equilibrium.

In Chap. 2 Zdravko Petak first describes the fundamental features of the policy context in Croatia after separation from Yugoslavia and proclamation of independence. The chapter points to the emergence of various kinds of clientelistic arrangements, which developed during the authoritarian system of governance during the 1990s. Such a system of government has led to a pronounced centralization in decision-making and has thwarted adequate participation of various public policy actors outside the government structures, which have not became the part of the clientelistic arrangements. Such development has led to major deficits in policy formulation and implementation, which is a major constraint on the effective development of public policies in Croatia.

The process of Europeanization of the Croatian political system is described by Hrvoje Špehar and Ivan Pepić in Chap. 3. It shows that the impact of Croatia's Europeanization was primarily achieved through hard conditionality, a process which ended with Croatia's full EU membership on 1st July 2013. They explore how the process of Europeanization in Croatia was strongly marked by the resistance of Croatian authorities to the concept of Europeanization, contained within the regional agenda of the Western Balkans. In addition, the authors point out in detail all the conditions that Croatia had to fulfil during the Europeanization process, such as full co-operation with the ICTY, substantial changes in policy towards Bosnia and Herzegovina and resolving border disputes with Slovenia. This path to full EU membership had an unfavourable effect on democratic development in Croatia, as evidenced by EUI's democracy index score.

In Chap. 4 Daniela Širinić considers, on the basis of substantial empirical analysis containing over 40,000 agenda items, the agenda-setting process of Croatian governments from the beginning of 1990 to 2015. One of her most important findings is reflected by the statement that a lack of initial programme differences between party options directly transfers into agenda setting. She found that Croatian political parties forming government can hardly be distinguished based on their distinctive policy positions, and therefore their policy-issues attention is not dominantly guided by party preferences but mostly by the reaction to outside events.

In Chap. 5 Igor Vidačak and Kristijan Kotarski examine the influence of interest groups on policy-making in Croatia. They showed that Croatian system of organized interest has significantly evolved since Croatia's independence. The chapter brings basic insights into the main factors that determine interest groups' influence and choice of lobbying strategies in the EU pre-accession period and in the period after EU accession. In this regard, they dedicated a special attention to different forms of organization and articulation of interests that have become entrenched in policy-making processes in Croatia. In that sense they put a great emphasis on the still widespread clientelistic arrangements that encompass some of the most powerful distributional coalitions (interest groups), like SOEs, war veterans' associations and disability benefit users in the domain of social policy, as well as local and regional self-government. Their goal has been to show how those distributional coalitions led to a captured state and impaired evidence-based policy-making.

The case of Croatian corruption is taken up by Vuk Vuković in Chap. 6. He presents a detailed overview of the political economy of corruption, clientelism, and vote-buying in Croatian municipalities, by examining how corruption helps mayors to stay in power, by building their coalitions of interests with quasi-entrepreneurs and various clients. He clearly shows that these coalitions reduce any accountability of the mayors towards the voters and the taxpayers, meaning that mayors can easily get away with manipulating local public finances and by engaging in direct vote-buying with money from the central government. In an effort to explain why voters do not penalize such behavior by local politicians, Vuković provides a threefold argument. The first argument relates to the information problem, stating that voters are simply unaware that their mayor is corrupt and consider that such standards are widespread by biased media. The second explanation relates to the culture (mentality) issue where voters cynically accept that politicians are corrupt, but they tend to justify their corruption as long as some resources are returned to the voters. And the final argument relates to the importance of clientelistic networks, which do exist at local government level, indicating that the interests embedded in these networks are preferable to any disruptive politician primarily because they offer protection from risk and uncertainty to a large group of voters.

17.3 Major Insights from Studying the Evolution of Croatia's Political Economy

The second part, entitled 'Croatia's Political Economy', scrutinizes the political economy context with an opening chapter on Croatia's long-term macroeconomic underperformance, especially in comparison to other transition economies. In the following three chapters this analysis is compounded by an elaborate analysis of the key tenets of macroeconomic policy: monetary policy, fiscal policy and macroprudential regulation. And finally, this section also presents a detailed analysis of the impact of the aforementioned macroeconomic policies on Croatia's economic competitiveness.

In Chap. 7 Anita Čeh Časni, Petra Palić and Maruška Vizek analyse long-term trends in Croatian GDP growth. They showed that Croatia is the worst performer among new EU members in terms of β-convergence. In their analysis they applied stochastic income convergence tests with breaks, which suggest that Croatia is not able to catch up with old EU members, but could still diminish the difference between Croatian and new EU member states income levels in the long run. They found that Croatian GDP and GVA growth was driven by services-led growth fuelled by investments in non-tradable sector, as well as government consumption, which strongly contributed to the observed income divergence. On the other hand, new EU member states grew faster primarily due to personal consumption, international trade and manufacturing growth. Their research also confirmed that deindustrialization and technological downgrading of the tradable sector additionally contributed to slower GDP growth in Croatia, as compared to other EU post-communist countries.

The case of monetary policy and the role of the Croatian National Bank is developed in Chap. 8, written by Marina Tkalec and Kristijan Kotarski, in which they reviewed the evolution of Croatian monetary policy since independence up to the present day. Croatian monetary policy was largely set by the stabilization plan in 1993. Ever since then, Croatia's economy has remained heavily euroized, which precludes the option of using an activist exchange-rate policy for the purpose of macroeconomic adjustment. Despite many competing claims on the appropriate role of the Croatian National Bank (monetary policy 'doves' vs. 'hawks'), the evidence goes more in favour of monetary policy 'hawks'. They claim that Croatian political economy primarily suffers from both fiscal and structural flaws, and that the change of monetary regime (euroization) is not a practical and viable solution for boosting economic growth and ensuring monetary stability. Finally, Croatia is hoping to join the euro area as soon as possible, and Kotarski and Tkalec conclude that the gains for Croatian economy would outnumber the losses.

In Chap. 9 Hrvoje Šimović and Milan Deskar Škrbić consider the mid-term fiscal developments in Croatia through the lens of the European Semester-related policy framework. However, prior to embarking on this particular analysis they provide a fiscal policy context in Croatia, which contributed to both spiralling public debt and mounting tax pressures. Their analysis confirmed the statement that public debt level significantly affects and reduces the effectiveness of fiscal policy, the main economic policy instrument in Croatia. They conclude that fiscal policy-makers in Croatia should not only aim their efforts on further and stronger reduction of public debt primarily to comply with EU economic governance rules but also to cope with the negative effects of debt burden on the effectiveness of fiscal policy. They believe that such fiscal strategies require a more quality mid-term fiscal planning and substantial improvement in public debt management strategy.

Chapter 10, written by Milan Deskar Škrbić, Kristijan Kotarski and Luka Brkić brings forward the issue of banking sector regulation. They present the arguments that the Croatian banking system nowadays incorporates relatively high standards of efficiency and transparency, without the obstacle of soft-budget constraints that so heavily burdened the banking sector at the time of socialist political order, as well as during the first decade of Croatia's independence. The results of their analysis show that the Croatian National Bank's regulatory framework proved to be effective as various regulatory measures affected lending activity of banks, thus preventing the creation of the worst kind of credit bubbles before the GFC, as well as cushioning the degree of stress on the lending market during the outbreak of the financial crisis and prolonged recession. They also point out that in the 'Game of Banking Bargains' the Croatian banking system no longer plays a major role in creating and distributing rents among various well-connected factions, as was the case during the first years of Croatia's transition and socialist period. The baton for sustaining clientelistic networks has been passed to the hands of fiscal policy-makers.

In Chap. 11 Velimir Šonje presents an in-depth analysis of the competitiveness of the Croatian economy. He warns at the beginning of his contribution that a number of comparative international indicators point at the substantial weakness of the Croatian economy in terms of international competitiveness. In his analysis, Šonje devoted particular attention to general weakness of governance in state-owned enterprises (SOEs). He reviews the main results of international comparisons and presents the results of a number of studies of market dynamics (entry and exit) and company productivity. In the empirical part of his contribution he analysed the financial statements of the top 1000 Croatian companies segmented according to ownership structure. Comparison of a number of financial and supplementary indicators helped him to identify statistically significant differences between different ownership clusters, including 100% and majority government-owned (SOE), mixed (minority government-owned) and private companies. His findings do not bode well for sticking to the status quo with regard to SOEs' governance model.

17.4 The Transformation of Sectoral Policies in Croatia

The third part, entitled 'Sectoral Public Policies', deals with four sectoral public policies and includes an additional chapter that offers a comprehensive taxonomy of Croatian public policies. We have chosen these policies on the basis of two basic criteria. The first criterion refers to the share of these policies in the national budget. Put together, the public expenditures for pension, health care and education policies account for more than 50% of Croatia's national budget. The second criterion takes into account the degree of Europeanization of several public policies. In that regard, cohesion/regional policy as its most important part, qualified as the one of the most influential EU policies in terms of their share in the EU budget and the degree of harmonization of national laws.

In Chap. 12 Predrag Bejaković considers the fundamental features of all pension system reforms in Croatia since the establishment of independence in the early 1990s. He shows that Croatia inherited a 'premature' socialist pay-as-you-go pension system, which has undergone several reforms. One systemic reform (from 1998 to 2002) resulted in the establishment of the three-pillar pension system, and was followed by several parametric reforms. Bejaković points out a number of challenges faced by the Croatian pension system, indicating that due to unfavourable demographic trends there is a need to reduce the pension rights, envision further reform of the pension system, and enhance labor market flexibility, as well as implement structural reforms in the economy. He is aware of the fact that any reduction of pension rights causes great political resistance, but he holds that this is the only way to preserve the long-term financial sustainability of the system.

In Chap. 13 Dagmar Radin considers the basic features of the Croatian health system and policy-making process in that policy field. Through examples of health financing and health system organization she describes how the policies or lack thereof in this second costliest sector of the economy have brought about a gradual, but steady decline in the quality and efficiency of medical care, medical staff high turnover, as well as other unwanted consequences. In an effort to find a valid explanation for such development of the health system she discerns basic features of funding and organizational structure of the Croatian health system, as well as related problems such as lack of vision and strategy, corruption, and weak institutions, among others. The chapter also analyses the role of the various stakeholders involved in creating health policies both through their formal or informal relationship and channels of influence.

In Chap. 14 Tihomir Žiljak and Nikola Baketa consider the process of Europeanization of the education policy in Croatia. They clearly notice two periods in the development of education policy in Croatia. The first period covers the time frame from 1990 to 2000, and the second cycle starts after 2000. They show that these periods substantially differ regarding goals and actors, but not so much in instruments applied for developing education policy.

Chapter 15, written by Jakša Puljiz, Sanja Maleković and Ivana Keser, is devoted to the development of cohesion policy in Croatia. They explored the actual achievements in raising absorption capacity of EU funds in Croatia so far and the influence of Europeanization on policy developments in areas covered by the EU cohesion policy. They particularly emphasized the importance of the changes that came about in the policy processes in connection with planning and implementation of domestic public policies strongly related to EU funding. The particular feature of their contribution deals with a challenges for raising policy capacity in the domestic sector dealing with the management of EU funds.

This part ends with a taxonomy of Croatian public policies provided in Chap. 16 by Ana Petek. By using qualitative content analysis she has explored in detail 11 Croatian policies, considering the differences related to their goals, involved actors, instruments and discourses. Observed public policies were divided into economic, social and sectoral policies. She found that the main feature of all Croatian public policies is a relatively strong influence of factors and actors from outside the country on domestic policy-making. This particularly applies to the actors involved, problems that policies deal with and established discourses.

17.5 Croatia as a Mature Natural or Captured State

After this brief presentation of key findings by our contributors we have to embark upon the analysis of institutions, interests and ideas in Croatia. The interaction of all three ingredients of policy transformation offers a good framework for estimating the potential to overcome the status quo. We will first address institutions and then move over to interests and ideas in the final instance.

The fact that the character of national political and economic institutions marks a difference between successful and unsuccessful states has become a common place in recent years (North et al. 2009; Acemoglu and Robinson 2012). Their contribution to reducing uncertainty and facilitating cooperation cannot be overestimated. Therefore, after applying the typology outlined by North et al. (2009) Croatia can be characterized as a mature natural state.[1] The analysis conducted in Chap. 1 provides the bulk of the empirical data for this claim. Our WGI index average percentile score, a composite governance index, portrays Croatia as a country with one of the lowest levels of institutional development in the EU, in the period 1995–2015. In 2016, Croatia was ahead of Romania, Bulgaria and Greece, while years of Orban's rule deteriorated the quality of Hungarian institutions to the level that they are currently at par with those of Croatia (WGI 2017).

Our findings are also fully consistent with the Legatum Prosperity Index (LGI) for 2016 in three important sub-indexes, which are good proxies for the quality of political and economic institutions (LGI 2016). In the governance sub-index Croatia ranks 24th among the EU-28.[2] In the sub-index economic quality Croatia takes 25th place (better than Romania, Bulgaria and Greece).[3] Finally, the most pressing concern remains the score in the business quality sub-index, where Croatia represents the worst performer among the EU-28.[4] All of this translates into 24th place with regard to the prosperity index among the EU-28, while according to GDP per capita (PPP) Croatia remains only ahead of Bulgaria and is at par with Romania (idem). However, the long-term view offers an even better perspective on how Croatia carved its place at the European periphery. In the period since 1991, Croatia's GDP per capita (in 2015 US dollars, PPP) rose by a meagre 40%, while the CEE-10 sample posted a 103.3% change (HumanProgress 2017). In terms of life expectancy and infant survival (good indicators of prosperity) the CEE-10 also marks a larger improvement than Croatia. These findings time and again point to weak and disappointing institutional development.

17.6 Vested Interests and Impaired Institutional Development in Croatia

Impaired institutional development is tightly connected with powerful interests. In Chaps. 1 and 5 we showed that after claiming independence, the Croatian dominant coalition decided to hold on to power by relying on fiscal illusion and vote-buying, which led to captured state. Our proxy for clientelistic politics that aggregates the sum of subsidies, compensation of state employees and state's intermediate consumption (value of goods and services used as inputs for the process of production) remains far above the CEE-10 average. In 2001, those expenditure categories had a 20.8% share in Croatia's GDP, while the same percentage for the CEE-10 amounted to 17.91. In 2015, this differential increased from 2.89% to 4.43% (21.2% for Croatia and 16.77% for the CEE-10).

Unfortunately, the period since the GFC in 2008 has seen little change in the strength and number of key Croatian distributional coalitions. Some reduction in the number of SOE employees has been offset by new employment in the ranks of local government (Franić 2012; DZS 2008, 2011). The powerful class of politicians of all stripes and at all levels of government remains the core of the dominant coalition and their strength can be proxied by expenditures on 'legislative and executive organs, financial and fiscal affairs and external affairs'. They possess strong incentive to keep 'business as usual' since they are allocated 4.9% of GDP for their expenses. At the same time, the CEE-10 average amounts to 2.8% (Eurostat 2017). So, wherein lies the potential solution for transforming Croatia as a captured state? In our view, it lies in the realm of ideas, since they render interests more fluid and less determining (Rodrik 2014).

17.7 Dominant Ideas as Growth and Development Constraints in Croatia

To invoke just interests as an explanatory variable for Croatia's economic malperformance and impaired institutional development would lead to oversimplification. Institutions are not 'black boxes' that are set exogenously and interests are not set in stone. In new political economy models they become part of strategic choices by important stakeholders in the course of their agency (Blyth 2002). Furthermore, institutions are not exclusively set by material interests. Ideas also matter to a large extent and they are in a relation of mutual dependence with their institutional environment and corresponding interest groups. In that regard, Rodrik offers an interesting analogy to the production possibility frontier and introduces the notion of the political transformation frontier (Rodrik 2014). Similar to technological innovations that reduce growth constraints imposed by the lack of resources, institutional innovations propelled by various ideas eliminate growth constraints, which arise from the unfavourable structure of political power. In that regard, we claim that impaired institutional development in Croatia has been only in part a reflection of 'vested interests'. The other and potentially more fruitful part of the explanation lies in the realm of ideas.

Those ideas can be easily identified in the EBRD LITS data and provide a coherent explanation of how they constitute a 'political transformation frontier' (EBRD 2017a, b, c). LITS data are collected through the representative sample of respondents and they do not aim to differentiate between ideas espoused by key-decision makers and ordinary citizens. However, given the democratic nature of political system, it is reasonable to assume that ideas on appropriate forms of political and economic agency, which resonate well among ordinary citizens, are also prevalent among key-decision makers (elites). This is primarily ensured through the mechanism of demand and supply in the political market, irrespective of some serious flaws in the functioning of democracy in Croatia.

Croatian respondents' perception of key factors of success in life reveals a lot about the degree of opportunistic behaviour, anti-market attitudes and the erosion of social capital. Respondents were expected to choose among several factors such as effort and hard work, intelligence and skills, political connections and breaking the law. For the purpose of our research we calculated the difference between respondents choosing combined modalities 'effort and hard work' and 'intelligence and skills', versus those respondents who opted for the combination of 'political connections' and 'breaking the law'. Apart from the score for Bulgaria in 2016, according to Fig. 17.1, Croatia claims a much smaller difference than the rest of the sample, which confirms that opportunistic behaviour remains one of the surest ways of attaining economic security. The largest percentage of respondents among the CEE-10 group plus Croatia, 41%, deemed that political connections represent a key factor of success in life, while only 15% opted for intelligence and skills (idem).

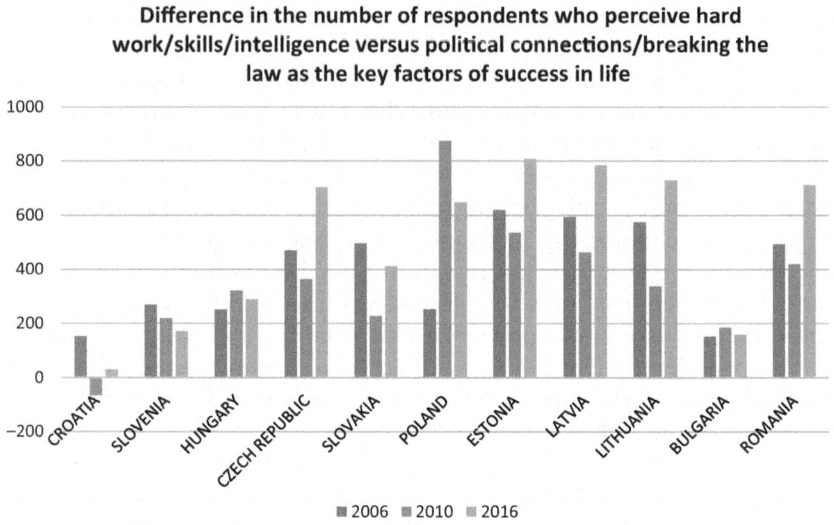

Fig. 17.1 Opportunistic behaviour (Source: EBRD Life in Transition Survey)

Furthermore, in 2016, only 27.54% of Croatian citizens unequivocally claimed that market economy is totally preferable to other alternatives (idem). This represented the lowest percentage when compared to the CEE-10 group score both in 2006 and 2010. Despite the fact that support for the market economy fell from 34.48% in 2006 to 27.54 in 2016, this support fell even more in Slovakia and Latvia (idem). Moreover, anti-market attitudes are still widely spread, regardless of recent improvements. In 2010, 62.13% of respondents identified competition as a force for good, the lowest percentage among the CEE-10 plus Croatia (idem).[5] In terms of promoting private ownership versus state ownership, 44.43% of respondents opted for private ownership in 2010, also much lower than the average for the CEE-10 (idem).[6] According to the analysed data we can claim that a large swath of Croatian citizens still perceives economy as a zero-sum game, which motivates competition for a limited pool of resources, as opposed to the view that reciprocity and cooperation lead to prosperity. One additional finding fits into the argument outlined above. Croatia has the biggest percentage of population formally included in political parties, when compared to the CEE-10 group. In spite of a drop from 8.83% in 2006 to 6.25% in 2016, this is double the average number for the CEE-10 (idem). Unfortunately, this percentage is not a genuine reflection of concern for the public good, but is more in line with the argument on continued importance of clientelism and distributional coalitions (see Chap. 5 by Vidačak and Kotarski).

Furthermore, Croatia exemplifies a case of serious depletion of social capital. Social capital that is proxied as a social trust is an indispensable ingredient to economic development, which manifests itself in several ways (Gould and Hijzen 2017).[7] Figure 17.2 displays our index of social trust for the sample of the CEE-10 and Croatia. The social trust index is calculated by including five subcategories, which we deem as essential for the smooth functioning of market economy.[8] When observing the whole decade between 2006 and 2016 one can identify that in 2006 Croatia had the second lowest level of social trust, only ahead of Bulgaria. In 2010, Croatia was the worst performer and in 2016 it finally staged a recovery.

Therefore, over several years in the past decade Croatia remained chained to the bottom of our social trust index. If one adds another important issue, trust to foreign investors, things get even more obvious as to why Croatia missed the train of economic convergence with the EU average in terms on GDP per capita (PPP).[9] To conclude, Croatia's entrapment in the 'zero-sum game' and 'low-trust' equilibrium serves as a

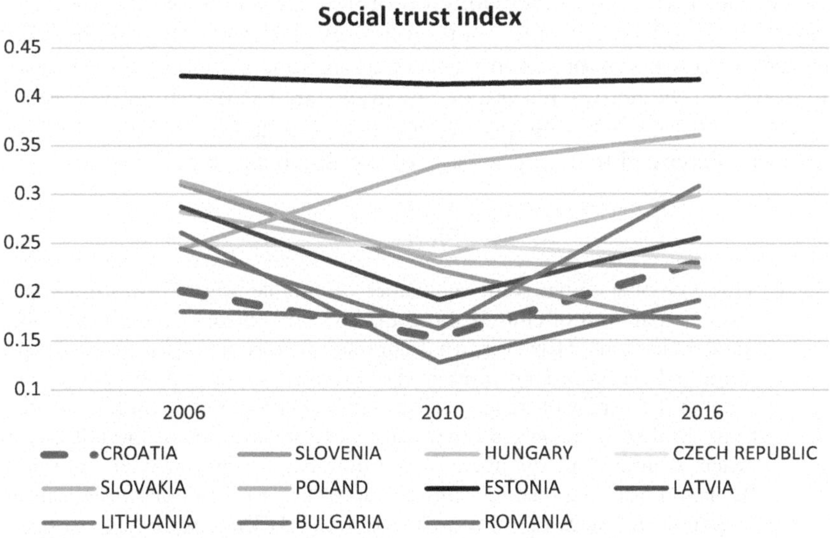

Fig. 17.2 Social trust index (Source: EBRD Life in Transition Survey)

fundamental constraint in transforming partitocracy and crony capitalism structures into an open-access order with depersonalized institutions.

17.8 Concluding Remarks

According to Blyth (2008), the experience of crisis represents a state of flux whereby actors' expectations are not met due to increasing institutional gridlock. In that context, a vacuum opens up for new policy entrepreneurs and fresh ideas. The depth of economic shock in the 2008–2014 period and an increasing trend of emigration represent a double whammy, conducive to the change of dominant ideas. In that regard, pro-market ideas have started slowly diffusing in the Croatian public sphere (EBRD 2017a b). Hence, for overcoming institutional gridlock and vested interests, it is more important to change dominant ideas than to merely insist on the change of existing power structure. The crisis experience of 2017 concerning the biggest national company Agrokor is a case in point.[10] In the parlance of Alesina et al. (2006), that crisis was either not systemic and deep enough to elicit institutional change or this avenue of policy change is less fruitful, as compared to the change of a government's composition, spearheaded by new policy entrepreneurs with fresh ideas. Therefore, the embracement and implementation of new ideas by those in power, as well as the reconceptualization of their interest, is the first step on the long journey of transformation. Only then we can hope for Croatia's transformation from the mature natural or captured state to flourishing depersonalized institutions, whereby privileges are superseded by rights and those rights are extended to actors outside of the dominant coalition.

Notes

1. This type of state has some semblance of durable private institutions, the formal separation of church and state, civilian control of the military and regular elections. However, what contrasts mature natural states (subtype of limited-access order) to other states termed as states with open-access order is the extent of depersonalization of political and economic institutions. Unlike open-access orders, access to institutions in limited-access orders is limited to members of the dominant coalition. Acemoglu and Robinson offer a similar account and according to their conceptualization Croatia could be categorized as a state which lacks a high degree of open economic and political institutions.

2. The sub-index covers effective governance, democracy and participation and the rule of law. Croatia is positioned ahead of Hungary, Slovakia, Romania and Bulgaria.
3. The economic quality index covers economic opportunity, foundations for growth, macroeconomic indicators, economic openness and financial sector efficiency.
4. LPI considers labour market flexibility, barriers to innovation, business infrastructure and entrepreneurial environment as indicators of business quality.
5. Respondents could air their preference by choosing one score on the scale from 1 (competition is good) to 10 (competition is harmful). For the purpose of defining a pro-competition attitude, we add only those respondents who opted for the scores between 1 and 5.
6. The same procedure as outlined above applies to our definition of respondents in favour of promoting private ownership.
7. First, social trust lowers transaction costs in law and contract enforcement. Second, it enhances cooperation and reduces collective action problem in the domain of procuring public goods. Furthermore, it also increases the credibility of public policy and boosts reform capacity. Third, social trust positively affects financial development.
8. Those are: trust in the government, the parliament, courts, banks and the financial system and trust in other people. In the first step we attribute the weight of 0.2 to each of our five subcategories. In the second step we multiply the weight for each subcategory with the percentage of respondents who choose modalities 'some trust' and 'complete trust'. In the third step all products are added and we arrive at the total score, which is on the scale from 0 to 1.
9. In 2006, only 10% of Croatian respondents displayed some or complete trust to foreign investors, a percentage lower than in any other country from the CEE-10 group. Things only improved in 2016 when Croatia lagged behind Lithuania, Poland and the Czech Republic with 20% of respondents trusting foreign investors.
10. In that regard it is important to point to Lex Agrokor, which was passed by the Government for preventing the collapse of companies with systemic significance in April 2017 (Buckley 2017). According to many experts this represents a haphazard effort, which might serve to sacrifice Agrokor for the survival of crony capitalist structures (Bićanić 2017). The potential for concerted political pressure by 30,000 employees of Agrokor and by employees of companies supplying Agrokor, as well as corresponding economic damage, was portrayed by the HDZ-led government as something akin to system meltdown. This came in spite of the fact that Agrokor employs slightly less than 2% of the Croatian workforce and makes up only

1.8% of Croatia's GDP (upon dividing Agrokor's gross value-added by Croatia's GDP) (Šonje 2017). The old adage goes that for things to stay as they are, things will have to change. The case of Agrokor has already been covered in detail in Chap. 1.

References

Acemoglu, D., & Robinson, J. (2012). *Why Nations Fail: The Origins of Power, Prosperity, and Poverty*. New York: Crown Business.

Alesina, A., Ardagna, S., & Trebbi, F. (2006). Who Adjust and When?: The Political Economy of Reforms. *IMF Staff Papers, 53*(Special issue), 1–29.

Bićanić, I. (2017). Agrokor čeka spora i bolna smrt!Na poslovni slom kompanije Vlada odgovara državnim kapitalizmom Potpuno krivo! *Jutarnji list*. http://www.jutarnji.hr/globus/Globus-politika/agrokor-ceka-spora-i-bolna-smrt-na-poslovni-slom-kompanije-vlada-odgovara-drzavnim-kapitalizmom-potpuno-krivo/5939809/. Downloaded 22 April 2017.

Blyth, M. (2002). Institutions and Ideas. In D. Marsh & G. Stoker (Eds.), *Theory and Methods* (pp. 292–311). London: Macmillan.

Blyth, M. (2008). The Secret Life of Institutions: On the Role of Ideas in Evolving Economic Systems. *Revue de la Régulation, Capitalisme, Institutions, Pouvoirs*, No. 3/4. https://regulation.revues.org/6043. Downloaded 3 October 2017.

Buckley, N. (2017). Crisis at Croatia's Agrokor Poses Threat Beyond Creditors, *The Financial Times*. https://www.ft.com/content/ad8ecc4e-1edd-11e7-a454-ab04428977f9. Downloaded 13 April 2017.

DZS (Državni zavod za statistiku). (2008). Persons in Paid Employment, by Activities. Priopćenje. https://www.dzs.hr/hrv/publication/2008/9-2-1_12h2008.htm. Downloaded 2 October 2017.

DZS (Državni zavod za statistiku). (2011). Persons in Paid Employment, by Activities. Priopćenje. https://www.dzs.hr/Hrv_Eng/publication/2011/09-02-01_12_2011.htm. Downloaded 2 October 2017.

EBRD. (2017a). Life in Transition Survey III: A Decade of Measuring Transition. http://www.ebrd.com/cs/Satellite?c=Content&cid=1395236498263&d=Mobile&pagename=EBRD%2FContent%2FContentLayout. Downloaded 24 June 2017.

EBRD. (2017b). Life in Transition Survey II: After the Crisis. http://www.ebrd.com/cs/Satellite?c=Content&cid=1395236498263&d=Mobile&pagename=EBRD%2FContent%2FContentLayout. Downloaded 24 June 2017.

EBRD. (2017c). Life in Transition Survey I: A Survey of People's Experiences and Attitudes. http://www.ebrd.com/cs/Satellite?c=Content&cid=1395236498263&d=Mobile&pagename=EBRD%2FContent%2FContentLayout. Downloaded 24 June 2017.

Eurostat. (2017). Government Finance Statistics (EDP and ESA 2010). http://ec.europa.eu/eurostat/web/government-finance-statistics/data/database. Downloaded 25 September 2017.

Franić, J. (2012). Zapošljavanje na lokalnoj razini u Republici Hrvatskoj tijekom gospodarske krize. *Institut za javne financije*, http://www.ijf.hr/upload/files/file/newsletter/71.pdf. Downloaded 2 October 2017.

Gould, E. D., & Hijzen, A. (2017). In Equality, We Trust. *Finance & Development, 54*(1), 37–39.

HumanProgress. (2017). Your Life in Numbers: A Project of HumanProgress. http://yourlifeinnumbers.org/. Downloaded 2 October 2017.

LGI. (2016). The Legatum Prosperity Index. http://www.prosperity.com/rankings. Downloaded 2 October 2017.

North, D. C., Wallis, J. J., & Weingast, B. R. (2009). *Violence and Social Orders.* Cambridge: Cambridge University Press.

Rodrik, D. (2014). When Ideas Trump Interests: Preferences, Worldviews, and Policy Innovations. *Journal of Economic Perspectives, 28*(1), 189–208.

Sabatier, P. A. (1991). Political Science and Public Policy. *PS: Political Science and Politics, 24*(2), 144–147.

Šonje, V. (2017). Agrokor prvi dio: veličina i ekonomski učinak. https://arhivanalitika.hr/blog/agrokor-prvi-dio-velicina-i-ekonomski-ucinak/. Downloaded 22 April 2017.

WGI (Worldwide Governance Indicators). (2017). Interactive Data Access. http://info.worldbank.org/governance/wgi/#home. Downloaded 24 September 2017.

Index[1]

[1] Note: Page numbers followed by 'n' refer to notes.

Z. Petak, K. Kotarski (eds.), *Policy-Making at the European Periphery*, New Perspectives on South-East Europe,
https://doi.org/10.1007/978-3-319-73582-5

The manufacturer's authorised representative in the EU is Springer Nature Customer Service Centre GmbH, Europaplatz 3, 69115 Heidelberg, Germany. If you have any concerns regarding our products, please contact ProductSafety@springernature.com

Printed and bound by CPI Group (UK) Ltd, Croydon, CR0 4YY
05/10/2026
02228138-0004